Absolute Madness

Absolute Madness

A TRUE STORY OF A SERIAL KILLER, RACE, AND A CITY DIVIDED

CATHERINE PELONERO

Skyhorse Publishing

Skyhorse Publishing books may be purchased in bulk at special discounts for sales promotion, corporate gifts, fund-raising, or educational purposes. Special editions can also be created to specifications. For details, contact the Special Sales Department, Skyhorse Publishing, 307 West 36th Street, 11th Floor, New York, NY 10018 or info@skyhorsepublishing.com.

Skyhorse® and Skyhorse Publishing® are registered trademarks of Skyhorse Publishing, Inc.®, a Delaware corporation.

Visit our website at www.skyhorsepublishing.com.

10 9 8 7 6 5 4 3 2 1

Library of Congress Cataloging-in-Publication Data is available on file.

Jacket design by Rain Saukas
Jacket photograph by Robert S. Bukaty

Print ISBN: 978-1-5107-1983-5
Ebook ISBN: 978-1-5107-1984-2

Printed in the United States of America

For my Father

Salvatore J. Pelonero

Buffalo, New York, Police Department, 1968–2002
United States Marine Corps, 1962–1967

Here's health to you and to our Corps
Which we are proud to serve;
In many a strife we've fought for life
And never lost our nerve.
If the Army and the Navy
Ever look on Heaven's scenes,
They will find the streets are guarded
By United States Marines.

CONTENTS

NOTE TO THE READER

The portrayal of people and events in this true story was at all times done as accurately as possible, drawn from primary sources and a wide variety of records and supplemental source material that was corroborated and cross-referenced to whatever extent possible. Dialogue is taken either directly from written records, in which case original spelling and punctuation have been left intact, or is constructed from recollections of persons who were present when conversations took place. A list of sources and references is included at the end of the book.

In some instances, pseudonyms have been used or names omitted to preserve privacy.

PART ONE
THE .22 CALIBER KILLER

Racism is man's gravest threat to man—the maximum of hatred for a minimum of reason.

—Abraham Joshua Heschel

Chapter 1
MONDAY, SEPTEMBER 22, 1980

THE GUNSHOTS WERE so loud, one of the witnesses said later, and so fast, the four cracking pops coming rapidly one after the other, it sounded as if someone were setting off firecrackers on her front lawn. Kids around here sometimes did that, especially around the Fourth of July. But July had come and gone. It was now late September and the nighttime summer shenanigans had ceased, returning the neighborhood to its normal after-dark quiet.

Looking out the window she could see nothing but her own startled reflection, due to the lights inside and the darkness beyond. She took a few quick steps, opened the door, and stepped out on the porch, the light from her home spilling onto the small front lawn. The yard was silent, undisturbed, empty except for the faded lawn ornaments and a fresh Go BUFFALO BILLS! sign staked in the grass. She saw no pops or flashes of firecrackers, no group of rowdy kids. At first she saw no one at all, until her eyes were drawn to light and movement in the distance.

The light came from the tall overhead lamps in the parking lot of the Tops grocery store directly across the street from her house, brighter and casting a wider beam than the aging streetlights that lined the block. The movement came from a single person, a slight figure who suddenly darted through an opening in the fence that separated the parking lot from her street, Floss Avenue. The man—she had the impression it was a male—wore a dark hooded jacket. As he emerged from the fence, he ran across

3

Floss Avenue in her direction. Veering to his left, he pulled the hood tighter around his head as he ran up Floss toward East Delavan Avenue, disappearing past darkened houses.

It all happened very quickly.

The witness, whose name was Barbara Wozniak, and who didn't realize at the time that she was in fact a witness to something of importance, remained at her door for a moment longer, staring in the direction where the man had run. Nothing happened. There was no one around; all was quiet again. Directly south of her home sat Genesee Street, a main thoroughfare that ran all the way from downtown Buffalo through the east side of the city and out to the suburbs. Even Genesee Street seemed unusually still. Then again, it was 10:00 p.m. or close to it on a Monday night, a school night, and it had been raining on and off for hours. Hardly the kind of weather for strolling or sitting on the porch. The peaceful stillness that had now returned was more typical than the odd popping sounds and the figure running off into the dark.

Barbara assumed he was some kid who had set off firecrackers in the parking lot and she didn't give it much thought, particularly with the silence that followed. The rising crime rate around the neighborhood had made residents a bit more alert, but this seemed inconsequential. She went back inside, closing her front door against the drizzle and the dark, and returned to watching *Monday Night Football* with her brother.

By the time the sirens shrieked and the news vans arrived, Barbara Wozniak had all but forgotten about the firecrackers, and she didn't make a connection between the figure in the hoodie and the sudden commotion in the Tops parking lot.

———

Despite what Barbara Wozniak would eventually tell them about the loudness of the gunshots, police were not finding anyone at the scene who had heard them at all.

The entrance to the Tops grocery store was less than fifty feet from where the Buick Century sedan was parked. Lieutenant William Misztal and patrolman Warren Lewis pulled into the parking lot in car L12E at 9:50 p.m., no more than two or three minutes after hearing the call from dispatch. Lieutenant Misztal and Officer Lewis were assigned to precinct 12. The shooting had occurred within the boundaries of the neighboring sixteenth precinct, but Misztal and Lewis had responded because of both the serious nature of the call and the location in particular. This Tops market regularly employed off-duty police officers as security guards. Misztal's first thought was that this must be an officer-involved shooting; either a police officer had shot someone or been shot himself.

Alvin Pustulka was waiting in the parking lot and waved the blue and white police cruiser over to where the Buick Century was parked, by the fence that divided the lot from residential Floss Avenue. Pustulka was a police officer out of a precinct in South Buffalo but worked security at this Tops on the east side of the city as a second-front job. As Pustulka explained to Lieutenant Misztal, he had not been involved in the shooting, nor had he witnessed it. A young man had run into the store and told him that someone had been shot outside.

Despite having been just inside the store entrance, Al Pustulka had not heard any gunshots or anything else out of the ordinary before the young man had rushed in to tell him of the shooting. He had seen this same young man exit the store only a minute before and had therefore been a little suspicious, wondering at first if this was some sort of a ruse to get him outside. Pustulka had followed the young man to the green Buick Century where he observed the victim, another young male, sitting in the driver's seat. Seeing that the young man in the Buick had indeed been shot, Pustulka had rushed into the store and told the manager to call 911 before returning to the lot to stand watch over the victim, who was unresponsive.

Peering inside the Buick, Lieutenant Misztal noted that the young man had been shot at least once in the left side of his face. The blood had thickened already, but the victim, eyes open wide and pupils dilated, was still trying to breathe.

Misztal radioed for an ambulance and a tow truck, and told dispatch to notify Homicide and the Evidence Unit.

———

Detective John Regan arrived within minutes of the call and noted right away that the Buick looked brand new, a 1980 or possibly even one of the first 1981 models, fresh off an assembly line in Detroit. Even in the dark, the exterior looked sleek, unblemished, and the interior was pristine, except for the fresh heavy bloodstains that soaked the upper portion of the driver's seat and headrest.

The driver's window was open, as it must have been when the shooting occurred. There was no broken glass anywhere. There were, however, some shell casings: one on the ground, one on the driver's side floor, and one on the rear seat of the Buick. To Detective Regan they looked like shells from a .22 caliber firearm of some kind. No weapon was present. It seemed that the shell casings were all that had been left behind from the shooting, aside from the bloody Buick Century and of course the victim, an unconscious black male with multiple gunshot wounds to the head.

This was not the scenario John Regan had expected. Regan and his partner, Detective Melvin Lobbett, had just settled down in front of the TV set at the thirteenth precinct, eating a late dinner of submarine sandwiches and watching *Monday Night Football*, when the call came of a man shot in the Tops parking lot at 2094 Genesee Street.

Details from the radio call had been sparse. Male in vehicle with gunshot wound to the head. No mention of an arrest. Regan had figured it was a suicide. The organized gang violence that exploded on urban streets in the 1980s and '90s had not yet come. In 1980, it made sense to assume a lone male found shot in a car likely meant a suicide, more so now perhaps than ever before, given Buffalo's dire and ever worsening economic crisis. Another depressed guy, out of work and out of hope. It wasn't uncommon for suicides to happen this way, lives taken in parked cars or motel rooms to spare family members from finding the body.

After arriving at the scene, however, Regan immediately realized that this was not a despondent soul who had decided to end it all. Someone else had made that decision. Multiple bullets had struck him in the face and head. Fired at close range. Intended to kill.

Whoever the shooter was and whatever had led up to the murder, the fact he hadn't bothered to pick up his shell casings was a plus for investigators. The task now for detectives John Regan and Melvin Lobbett was to find out exactly what had happened. From the start, getting any useful information proved a challenge.

The people closest to it all, the ones inside the Tops market—and eventually, in desperation, police would track down every soul who had been there that night—had heard nothing at all. Despite the proximity, not a single employee or patron had been aware of what was happening outside, least of all Larry Robinson, the young man who had alerted Officer Pustulka. Robinson now sat shaking in the drizzly night air, speaking as calmly as he could with police.

"I don't know what happened," Larry said, looking at the official faces standing above him. John Regan noted how Robinson rubbed his forehead, as if he were trying to rub out what he had seen in the Buick. Who could blame him? To Detective Regan's veteran eye, there was no evasiveness here, no disingenuous performance; Larry Robinson was genuinely shaken to the core.

"I don't know what happened. He was fine. We were talking. I went inside the store . . ." Larry paused. He seemed to be trying to make sense of it himself. "I don't know what happened," he repeated. "I didn't even know anything was wrong until I saw the blood . . ."

An hour earlier, Larry Robinson had been on his way here, the Tops market on Genesee Street. Larry was twenty-four years old. He lived nearby. He had been walking near the intersection of Genesee and Fillmore when he saw Glenn drive by in the Buick. Larry had waved and Glenn had pulled over and offered him a ride. Glenn agreed to take him to Tops, where Larry planned to withdraw some money at the store's service counter.

Glenn, the young man whose heart paramedics were now furiously trying to restart, was only an acquaintance, Larry told police. Just a guy from the neighborhood. How old is he? Larry didn't know. Where was he coming from? Larry didn't know that either. Like he kept telling them, Glenn was just someone he knew from the block, one of those guys who's always just around. They didn't travel in the same circles nor did they have the same friends, but you get to know people's names and faces when they live in your neighborhood. Where Glenn lived was about the only solid detail Larry could offer. He gave them an address and added that he thought Glenn lived with his parents. An officer was dispatched to the home.

Glenn Dunn did indeed live with his parents. Glenn was only fourteen years old. He had just begun his freshman year at nearby Kensington High School.

Larry Robinson meanwhile explained to Detective Regan and colleagues that he had only accepted the ride from Glenn because of the car. It was really sharp looking, roomy and plush, and it had that unmistakable new-car smell, a scent Larry didn't come across very often. He didn't know many people who had new cars, much less a $10,000 Buick.

That was easy enough for police to believe. Expensive new cars were generally not found in driveways over here on Buffalo's east side. Crumbling houses and overcrowded flats, yes. Poverty, unemployment, and deprivation, sure. The east side had plenty of all that.

It hadn't always been this way, of course. In fact, it had been anything *but* this way. Within living memory of many of its dwindling residents, Buffalo had been the picture of urban American prosperity, known for its robust industry, splendid architecture, and forward-thinking innovations. Buffalo had entered the twentieth century as the eighth largest city in the United States with a short but impressive legacy. Proximity to Canada—coupled with widespread antislavery sentiment among the populace—had allowed the city to play a notable role in the Underground Railroad, aiding the escape of fugitive slaves in defiance of federal law. (An article in the *New York Times* on September 8, 1855, criticized Buffalonians for their open and stubborn refusal to cooperate with the Fugitive Slave Act.) Presidents Grover Cleveland and Millard Fillmore had both lived in Buffalo, as had authors Mark Twain and F. Scott Fitzgerald.

The city's key waterways had made it a prime location for industrial development, generating employment for many and great wealth for some. Frederick Law Olmsted had developed the city's picturesque park system while major buildings and illustrious mansions had been designed by the foremost architects of the time, with no expense or luxury spared. Early in the century, Buffalo had the most widespread use of electrical lighting in the nation, courtesy of hydroelectric power from Niagara Falls, and at one point boasted more paved roads than New York City.

The opening of the St. Lawrence Seaway in 1959 rendered Buffalo's industrial waterways obsolete, landing the first major blow in what proved to be an intense downward economic spiral. Industries closed or downsized in rapid succession over the next two decades, disfiguring the Queen City of the Great Lakes into a pitiful picture of the American rust belt. Perhaps even more remarkable than the change itself had been how fast things had gone to hell.

John Regan had grown up in the city's First Ward, a solidly Irish working-class neighborhood south of downtown. Regan was thirty-eight years old and had been a detective since 1971. He had entered the Buffalo Police Academy in 1962, mainly because he needed a job and had no interest in college or a trade. Now he thanked God he'd chosen a profession in which he didn't have to worry about his employer shutting down or moving out of state. Many of his boyhood friends had not been so lucky. As a result, there were fewer and fewer of them around.

The 1970s had been the worst. The city had lost almost a quarter of its population in that ten-year span, mostly middle-class people leaving for opportunities in other states or fleeing to suburbs to escape the decay and rising crime in the city, not to mention the oppressive dark mood. There were actually billboards that read, WILL THE LAST PERSON TO LEAVE BUFFALO PLEASE TURN OFF THE LIGHTS?

In truth, the decline could be traced not to the evaporation of a single industry but to a variety of shifting technologies and calamitous policy decisions, the combination of which had effectively stripped Western New York of both its economy and charm. Olmsted parks had been carved through with expressways. Neighborhoods of single-family homes had been bulldozed to make way for high-rise public housing projects. Skyrocketing taxes—the highest in the nation—were the icing on the lousy cake. Buffalo thus began the 1980s with a population of 357,870, a good portion of whom were living below the poverty line and a great many of whom were living with constant uncertainty and fear.

The east side, where Detective John Regan and his colleagues now found themselves working not a suicide but a crime scene, had perhaps been hit harder by the downturn than anywhere else. The changes here had been especially dramatic, both economically and demographically.

The east side had one of the highest crime rates in the city, although this particular area, the easternmost point near the city line, was not among the most stricken. It was, however, undergoing a major racial transition.

Up until a dozen years ago, the neighborhood had been largely populated by families with working-class Italian roots, surrounded by larger sections of residents with German and Polish ancestry. Though never a high-end part of town, it had been comfortable and safe, at least for residents who looked and lived like their neighbors, which was pretty much everybody. Things were changing, though.

As the city's African American population grew—and as civil rights legislation had legally broken the boundaries of where they were permitted to live—black families had gradually begun moving from "their own" section of the lower east side (the area where blacks had traditionally lived since the 1800s) into adjoining communities. Throughout the 1970s, more and more black families had moved into homes vacated by whites.

There still were, of course, white residents to be found here, many of them from older generations who stubbornly resisted the efforts of their children or grandchildren to relocate them to suburbs like Amherst or Kenmore. They proudly declared that they had lived here for decades, refusing to move while at the same time lamenting the demise of the neighborhood, wistfully recalling how "it used to be so nice over here . . ."

The victim in this shooting fit the profile of both the typical resident and typical victim of crime on the east side. Glenn Dunn was black, as was his traveling companion, Larry Robinson.

According to Larry there had been nothing remarkable about the ride he and Glenn had taken that night in the Buick. Not until Glenn revealed to him that the car was stolen.

They had been riding around for a while, just enjoying a leisurely cruise, when Glenn hit him with this news. He hadn't given Larry any details about the car theft, and Larry hadn't asked for any. He didn't want to know. It was after learning this that Larry asked Glenn to stop at the store, as he had intended to do all along. He was already in the hot car now. Might as well get the errand done and then have Glenn drop him off at home.

They pulled up in front of the store and Larry hopped out. Glenn promised to wait for him.

No more than ten or fifteen minutes had passed before Larry exited the store. He didn't see Glenn or the Buick at first, but looking around he spotted the car parked by the fence. Larry called Glenn's name as he walked toward the car. Glenn did not respond. Larry approached the driver's side, where Glenn was sitting behind the wheel. He called to him again, louder this time, but Glenn only moaned.

Glenn was sitting very still, staring straight ahead at the windshield. Larry reached in, nudged his shoulder. Glenn's head tipped to the right and Larry saw what looked like blood. He also noticed a hole in the side of Glenn's head.

Larry ran back to the store and alerted the police officer.

That was all he knew.

Stolen car. *Bingo,* thought John Regan.

There were a few auto-theft rings operating on the east side. Glenn Dunn must have been involved. And gotten on somebody's bad side.

But still, something didn't fit. Regan had never known the car-theft rings to exact this kind of revenge, an execution-style hit. And if they were going to deal with an errant member that way, it didn't seem likely they'd kill him in one of the cars, if for no other reason than it ruined the inventory.

Had Glenn Dunn been an informant, killed for working with the cops on the side? A quick call to the robbery division could answer that, and did. No one in robbery had ever heard of Glenn Dunn. It looked like the Buick Century was his first stolen car. And quite likely his last, considering the severity of the bullet wounds.

As detectives were listening to Larry Robinson give his account of his last ride with Glenn Dunn, a woman named Madona Gorney sat in her idling car. Her groceries were in the trunk; she was ready to drive home. But she hesitated, staring at the flashing lights through her rain-streaked front windshield. She wanted to talk to the police. The store manager had fluffed off her inquiries and told her not to bother the officers. Still, something made her feel that she should. She didn't know exactly what was going on but thought maybe she should tell them about the black man she saw standing under the lamppost when she had pulled into Tops. She didn't see him now. And that car that the police were gathered around; it hadn't been there when she pulled in. Madona also recalled the odd man who had been sitting outside the store entrance when she went in, the young white guy wearing glasses and a blue jacket, with a paper bag by his feet and such a dazed look on his face. He had not looked well to her, not at all.

———

The ambulance carrying Glenn Dunn had already departed for the hospital and John Regan was preparing to follow when Lieutenant Misztal brought a young man over to speak with him. He was a slender white kid with a mop of dark brown hair. He said his name was Kenny Paulson. He was seventeen years old and lived a few houses down on Floss. He said he had been in the parking lot, coming out of the store, you know, when he saw a man walk up to that car, the one the police now had cordoned off, and shoot the driver.

Kenny Paulson described it for him. The guy who got shot, the black guy, was standing next to his car smoking a cigarette when Kenny first saw him. He tossed the cigarette and got in the driver's seat. About a minute later another guy, a white guy, walked up and shot him through the open window, then ran away.

He hadn't heard any arguing. He hadn't heard either of them say anything, in fact. The white guy just walked up, shot the guy in the car, and left. Kenny had been close enough to see the fireballs bursting from the barrel of the gun.

After the shooter took off there was no one else around—except for the guy in the car, of course, who didn't move or make any sound that he could hear. Scared, Kenny immediately ran home. Shortly after, though, he thought he'd better come back and tell the police what he had seen.

Detective Regan thanked him for coming back. He could understand why the kid's first instinct was to run home. It must have been a pretty shocking sight, especially for a teenager.

Regan had him tell the story again. Kenny Paulson had no idea what kind of a gun it was, but he described the shots as four quick, loud blasts.

Once again, he described the yellow flash of fire from the barrel, the way the shooter had walked up to the car, and the direction that he ran.

When it came to describing the shooter himself though, beyond saying he was a white guy, Kenny could not be at all specific. He was quite vague, in fact, not even willing to commit to whether the man was short or tall, thin or heavyset. He couldn't remember what the guy was wearing. He wasn't sure what color his hair may have been. He just didn't have any descriptive details for them at all. He even seemed sketchy on whether the shooter was indeed white.

At the time, Regan had no reason to believe Kenny was lying.

Chapter 2
TUESDAY, SEPTEMBER 23, 1980

LINDA SNYDER DECIDED to go to Burger King for lunch. It was a beautiful afternoon, bright and sunny after last night's rain, and stepping out from her office at the New York State Thruway Authority to grab a bite and enjoy the nice weather for a bit sounded like a good idea. As she was forced to recall this particular lunch break over and over again in the years to come, she would always think, *it was so nice out that day,* as if she could never reconcile the contrast between the pleasant setting and the ghastly scene that played out.

At noon, Linda and her coworker Gene Risius left the Thruway Authority building at 1870 Walden Avenue in Cheektowaga, a suburb of Buffalo. From there they made the two-minute drive to Burger King at 2940 Union Road. Burger King sat next to a restaurant called Polish Villa. Directly across the street was a shopping center called the Como Mall. The combination of nice weather and a selection of places to eat meant the area was fairly busy during the lunch hour.

Traveling in a Thruway Authority car, Linda and Gene pulled into the lot at Burger King and parked next to a small, two-tone brown car. Sitting in the driver's seat of the brown car was a person Linda later described as a neat, good-looking black man with a short Afro haircut, wearing big, tinted, rimmed glasses. As front-page news stories would later proclaim, the man was sitting quietly in his car, alone, eating his lunch.

14

Linda and Gene spent about twenty minutes inside Burger King before returning to the parking lot. Crossing the lot toward their vehicle, they stopped momentarily as a car drove past them. It was right after the car passed that they heard two quick bangs. Linda turned to Gene and asked, "Were they gunshots?"

No, Gene thought, it sounded like firecrackers.

As they took one or two more steps toward their vehicle, Linda looked up and saw a man darting away from the brown car parked next to theirs. The man ran very fast up into a grassy area that divided the parking lots of Burger King and the Polish Villa. He continued running past the front of the Polish Villa—so close to the building that if someone had opened the door, he would have run into it, Linda thought—and disappeared around the corner. Linda noticed that he wore a hat and had a brown paper bag tucked under one arm.

———————

Dominic Punturiero had also come to Burger King for lunch that day. He got a take-out order and sat in his car to eat. He was parked a couple spaces away from the small brown car. Dominic was almost finished eating his lunch when he noticed a person walking on the grassy area between Burger King and the Polish Villa. He glanced up for a second or two at the person, a man wearing a fishing-type hat, carrying a paper bag. When the man in the fishing hat looked back at him, Dominic turned away. The man walked from the grassy area into the parking lot, passing the rear of Dominic's car. About thirty seconds later, Dominic heard two noises that sounded to him like a car running over a manhole cover. Looking up and to his left, Dominic saw the man in the fishing hat running away from the brown car, darting back up into the grassy area and out of sight.

About a minute later, having now finished his lunch, Dominic drove out of his parking space. Making his way toward the exit, he looked over at the brown car and saw a black man slumped over in the driver's seat, the man's head almost hanging out the window. Dominic slowly pulled out of the parking lot onto Union Road, then stopped on the shoulder. He stayed there a couple of seconds, looking in his rearview mirror at the man slumped in the brown car.

———

Linda Snyder and Gene Risius took the few last steps toward their vehicle. Linda was about to climb into the passenger's side, but stopped short when she saw that the man in the car parked next to them was leaning sharply to his left, with his head on the sill of the open driver's side window. Linda saw him twitch. Smoke was rising from his head.

Linda recoiled, taking a few stumbling steps backward, away from the twitching, smoking body.

———

Dominic Punturiero drove back into the Burger King parking lot, stopped his car, and got out. He looked at the brown car and saw that the man inside was still in the same slumped posture. Dominic saw a man and a woman standing in the parking lot. He couldn't hear what they were saying, but he got the impression that they knew something was wrong. The man started pulling the woman away, urging, "Let's go! Let's go!"

Linda hurried around to the driver's side of the Thruway Authority car and got in, scrambling over Gene to the passenger's seat. She tried to avoid looking at the black man in the car next to them but she couldn't help it; there he was, and she could not look away, much as she wanted to. Gene told her to calm down as he started the car and backed out. They left the Burger King parking lot and drove back to work.

Dominic decided he didn't want to be here either. He got back into his own car and pulled away. As he passed the brown car, he noted again that the man inside had not moved. Dominic tapped his horn. The man didn't move.

Dominic drove onto Union Road but instead of heading back to work, he parked across the street at the Como Mall. He thought about calling the police.

He drove once again to Burger King, went inside, and told the employees that there was a man in the parking lot who might need help. A female employee at Burger King told him that they would check it out. Dominic left and went back to work.

———

Russell Sciabarrasi had just pulled into his driveway on Vern Lane in Cheektowaga. As he would later tell police, it was sometime between 12:30 and 1:00 p.m. when he stepped out of his car and noticed a strange man across the street. The man was walking quickly and appeared to be very nervous, looking all around him. He seemed out of breath and his walk was a little wobbly, as if he had just been running. The man carried a brown paper bag rolled up under his right arm. He dropped the bag and swooped down to snatch it up. Grasping the bag, the man looked around again and spotted Russell. The man started running.

He ran across a lawn and to the corner of Vern Lane and Fair Oaks, where he opened the passenger door of a red station wagon and tossed the paper bag inside, then got in on the driver's side and pulled away, tires screeching. He looked back at Russell a final time before speeding off.

Both the man's behavior and his appearance struck Russell as odd. He wore a fishing hat and a faded jacket. His pants seemed a bit too short. The clothing had been the thing that first caught Russell's attention because his whole outfit seemed out of place. He looked like he was dressed to go hunting.

Linda and Gene had arrived back at the Thruway Authority building shortly before 12:30. Linda had rushed into the ladies' lunchroom to tell her coworkers about the horrifying sight at Burger King. Dominic returned to his job shortly after 12:30 and he was also talking to his coworkers about the disturbing scene. One of the employees who worked with Dominic was a volunteer fireman with a portable radio that picked up emergency calls. Dominic asked if he had heard anything about Burger King. The man said yes, there had been a call concerning Burger King on Union Road.

Dominic called the police. It was 12:45 p.m.

At about the same time and a few miles west, Al Williams of the Buffalo Homicide Squad was observing the autopsy of Glenn Dunn. Williams had been a police officer for twelve years, the only black cadet in his graduating class of February 1968. Currently, he was an acting detective assigned to homicide, one of the only black detectives on the force. In the stark tomb of the Erie County Medical Examiner's Office, Williams recorded the extensive damage that had been done to the boy.

Glenn had four wounds caused by three bullets. One bullet had struck him in the lower left eyelid, another in the left cheek. These two wounds were surrounded by powder burns five inches in diameter. A third bullet had splintered on impact, causing a wound on his left ear and entering the left temple.

Williams noted that the stomach contents revealed bloody fluid and no evidence of food.

Two deformed bullets and fragments of a third were removed from his head. The bullets and fragments were put in glass jars and labeled. Detective Williams took the evidence and death certificate back to the Homicide Squad office along with a vial of Glenn's blood.

The murder of a child was always a disturbing case to work, even for seasoned officers who prided themselves on their professional equilibrium. Al Williams left the morgue determined as always to see the case through to whatever justice could be attained for the young victim, blissfully unaware of the impending firestorm and sleepless nights to come.

―――――

Detective Robert Grabowski and Officer Matthew Parsons were at the east-side home of Madona Gorney taking a report on what she had seen the night before outside Tops. Madona had discovered while watching the 11:00 p.m. news that the incident in the parking lot had been a shooting and that the teenaged victim had been pronounced dead on arrival at Erie County Medical Center. She had contacted the Buffalo police that morning.

Madona was twenty-eight years old, married, the mother of two small children. She worked as a psychiatric nursing assistant. She had been on her way home from a night class at Bennett High School the night before and stopped at Tops sometime between 9:35 to 9:40 p.m. As she pulled into the parking lot, she noticed a lone black male standing under a lamppost by the Floss Avenue fence. She paid attention to this man, Madona explained, because she was cautious; there was no one else around and she had almost $80.00 in her purse. She got out of her car, but instead of heading toward the entrance, she walked in the opposite direction toward Genesee Street in order to put some distance between herself and the man before circling around and entering the store.

She hadn't spent much time in Tops, probably less than ten minutes, before walking out the same door through which she had come. On the way to her car she passed by three men—the store manager, the security guard, and a young black man—walking hastily in the opposite direction, back toward Tops. She overheard the young black man ask the officer, "Was he shot, or what?"

Madona got into her car, backed out of her parking space, and drove slowly toward the exit. The black man who had been standing under the lamppost was no longer there. Instead, a car was parked in that spot.

Police cars with lights flashing were entering the lot. Madona pulled over and stopped her car. She sat there for a minute or two. An ambulance drove up.

Madona got out of her car and walked back to the store. She thought she should talk to the police and tell them what she saw, which wasn't much, but still. She approached the store manager instead, who didn't have much to say to her other than that things were under control. Madona felt uneasy about leaving before speaking with the officers, but she returned to her car.

A police car drove out of the parking lot, and she followed it up Floss Avenue. When it reached the corner of Floss and Lang Streets, she honked her horn to get the officers' attention. The police car kept going, turning on Lang Street, and Madona drove behind. She honked her horn again, then once more another block down, but the police car did not stop. She gave up and drove the short distance to her home.

Detective Grabowski and Officer Parsons took a description of the man Madona saw leaning against the lamppost: black male, twenty to thirty years old, six feet tall, close-cut hair. He wore a dark, bulky nylon-type jacket with a light-colored shirt underneath and dark pants. He had both hands in his jacket pockets.

After the officers left her home, Madona realized she had forgotten to tell them about the young white man outside the store, sitting on the railroad ties with that dopey stare and the brown paper bag at his feet. She thought maybe she should've mentioned him, since he may have seen more than she did.

———

At police headquarters, John Regan and Melvin Lobbett were interviewing Kenny Paulson, the teenage witness to the Dunn shooting. He and his father had come downtown so Kenny could make a formal statement. Police were meanwhile canvassing the neighborhood where the murder occurred in search of other possible witnesses. It wasn't long into the interview with Kenny Paulson that Regan and Lobbett started praying they'd find some. The Paulson kid was not exactly your dream witness. Even though he had actually seen the shooting take place, he seemed near worthless when it came to any sort of useful description of the gunman. All he had offered so far was that the killer was a male, five feet nine, of medium build, wearing a blue hooded sweatshirt.

Last night he said the shooter was white. Now he said he didn't know the man's skin color.

It wasn't unheard of for a witness to a shooting to have little recollection of the perpetrator. Witnesses are often transfixed by the gun itself rather than the person firing it. Still, something about Paulson's vague description didn't sit quite right. Lieutenant Bill Misztal, the first officer on the scene, had felt the same way. Regan didn't know it at the time, but Misztal had noted in his report that Kenny Paulson seemed reluctant to identify the assailant as white.

Regan and Lobbett had just concluded the interview when they received news about the shooting at Burger King in Cheektowaga. There were strong similarities to the Dunn murder in Buffalo just hours before. The crime scenes were only five miles apart.

———

The victim in the Cheektowaga attack was identified as Harold Green, age thirty-two, who lived at 211 LaSalle Street in Buffalo. He had been rushed to St. Joseph Intercommunity Hospital, arriving at 12:55 p.m. in a comatose condition. He had been shot twice in the left temporal region of his head.

Harold Green's mother and stepbrother arrived at the hospital and spoke with Detective Dombrowski of the Cheektowaga PD. Harold's mother, Reginie Green, said that her son was a very quiet individual whose whole life centered around his work and his education. Harold worked as an assistant engineer at Moog Industries and attended night classes at the State University of New York at Buffalo, pursuing his master's degree in engineering. He had served in the air force, returning home to Buffalo with an honorable discharge. He lived alone in the lower flat of the home he owned in Buffalo and rented the upper flat. Neither Mrs. Green nor Harold's stepbrother could name any of Harold's friends. He dated women occasionally, but otherwise his life was consumed by his work and his studies. Harold even used his limited spare time productively, spending every Saturday working around his home or his mother's.

As doctors performed an emergency craniotomy on Harold Green to remove necrotic brain tissue and bullet fragments, Cheektowaga police processed the crime scene. In addition to the bloodstains in Green's 1980 Honda, they found a bullet fragment on the rear deck of the passenger side and a .22 caliber shell casing on the driver's side.

As night fell on Tuesday, police in Buffalo and Cheektowaga were comparing the similarities in their two cases—the style of the attacks, the locations, the .22 shell casings. The only major difference was the victims, who seemed to have no connection to each other and were entirely different in age, background, and lifestyle. The only things Glenn Dunn and Harold Green seemed to have in common were their race and gender.

———

At 11:30 p.m., two black men were walking on Buffalo's east side. Emanuel Thomas, age thirty-one, and Franchoine "Frenchy" Cook, age twenty-six, were friends. They had spent an ordinary Tuesday evening playing cards with Emanuel's wife, Dorothy, and some friends at the home of a neighbor. Emanuel, Dorothy, and Frenchy had arrived back at the Thomases' home at 70 Zenner Street around 10:30 p.m.

As the 11:00 news was ending, Emanuel told his wife that he was going to walk to his mother's home, just a few houses down on Zenner. He said he'd be right back so she should leave the door open. Frenchy left with him.

Reaching the nearby corner of Zenner and East Ferry Streets, Emanuel and Frenchy spotted a friend, Butch Palmer. The three men stood at the corner talking for a moment before Butch turned and went to his home, two houses down on East Ferry. Emanuel and Frenchy followed. Emanuel stepped up to the door of Butch's home and spoke with someone inside.

As Frenchy stood waiting at the bottom of the front porch steps, a white man walked up and asked him a question. As Frenchy Cook would later tell police, the white man asked if he knew where Diane or Dorothy lived—it was one of the two, either Diane or Dorothy, but Frenchy could not remember which—and Frenchy replied that he didn't know. The white man walked away.

Emanuel returned to the sidewalk and said to Frenchy, "Let's go, man."

The two of them had only walked as far as the corner of Zenner and East Ferry when they heard a male voice behind them say, "Hey!"

They turned around. It was the same white man who had spoken to Frenchy just a minute earlier. The white man pointed a gun and fired.

Emanuel cried out. Frenchy ran. The white man fired again and again.

The sound of gunshots brought several neighbors to their windows. Some of them saw a white man get into a blue car and drive away down East Ferry.

Emanuel Thomas lay motionless on Zenner Street. A crowd gathered. A neighbor ran to the Thomas home and told Dorothy to come down to the corner quick, Emanuel was hurt.

"How could he be hurt?" Dorothy asked. "He just walked out."

The friend replied that Emanuel had been shot, and that if Dorothy didn't believe him, she should step out onto her porch and look at all the people gathered at the corner. Dorothy did so. Seeing the crowd, she ran down to the corner of Zenner and East Ferry to see for herself.

It was 11:35 p.m. Her husband had only been gone for five minutes.

The first patrol car arrived within two minutes, quickly followed by more. Calls were made for an ambulance and detectives. Responding officers knew instantly that the victim was dead. Some of the same officers had responded to the shooting of Glenn Dunn the night before, which had happened less than a mile away.

Before the ambulance took Emanuel Thomas to Erie County Medical Center, officers noted a gunshot wound on the left side of his head. They also found .22 caliber shell casings.

Chapter 3
WEDNESDAY, SEPTEMBER 24, 1980

JOSEPH MCCOY HAD no reason to fear walking the streets. He made a habit of walking every day, setting out from his home on Pierce Avenue in Niagara Falls for a leisurely stroll. McCoy had been unemployed for the past two years, but he was not one to sit at home. Always an active man, fit and muscular, McCoy had been a boxer in his younger days. He was now forty-three years old, a lifelong bachelor, living a quiet life and staying close to his siblings and elderly parents.

Twenty miles north of Buffalo, Niagara Falls had a constant flow of tourists visiting the majestic waterfall. Aside from the tourism trade, confined mainly to the actual Falls and a smattering of attractions along the banks of the Niagara River, the city itself was more like a sleepy town, and perhaps even drearier these days than the rest of the region. Niagara Falls shared all of Buffalo's economic problems but with the added infamy of Love Canal, a neighborhood at the eastern edge of the city that had been in national headlines a lot during the past two years because of the scandal over massive toxic chemicals in the ground and drinking water, and the scores of poisoned residents who had to be relocated.

At 9:00 a.m., Joe McCoy was walking alone on a section of Cleveland Avenue many blocks away from the river and the tourists. A motorist who was stopped at a red light noticed McCoy approach the intersection of Cleveland and Eleventh Street. A white man came up behind McCoy and grabbed him around the neck, pulling his head downward. One witness mistook this at first for two friends clowning around, jumping at each other like guys sometimes do, until the white man held a brown paper bag to the black man's head and fired two shots. Joe McCoy fell to the ground, and the white man fled down Cleveland Avenue.

A Niagara Falls police officer on patrol spotted McCoy lying in the street and pulled over. Two people were standing over the victim. They told the officer that the man had just been shot by another man who ran away. The officer had missed the shooting by less than a minute.

There were no shell casings on the ground, only the body of Joseph McCoy, blood oozing from contact gunshot wounds in his left temple. He was transported to a Niagara Falls hospital where he was pronounced dead on arrival at 9:18 a.m.

———

Emanuel Thomas had been pronounced dead on arrival at the Erie County Medical Center the night before. At his autopsy in the morning, the pathologist had removed a bullet from his head. Police had recovered three spent .22 caliber long rifle shell casings at the scene. Only one bullet had struck Emanuel, but it had been fired at close range and cut a path through his brain, killing him instantly.

The only other abnormalities on his body were track marks on both of his arms, apparently from intravenous drug use. The marks on his right arm looked fresh. Thomas had been arrested in 1974 on a minor drug charge for marijuana possession but had no record since.

Buffalo police had found several witnesses to the shooting and had spent the wee hours of Wednesday morning questioning them. Emanuel's distraught wife, Dorothy, did her best to answer their questions while at the same time comforting her two young daughters, who were confused and inconsolable over the loss of their father. Dorothy had no idea who would want to harm her husband. Emanuel was a good family man, she told them. They had been married for a decade and had lived on Zenner Street for years. Emanuel was a painter by trade but had been laid off. He was actively looking for work and otherwise spent his time at home with her and their children. Emanuel had used hard drugs a number of years ago, but in 1976 he went on a methadone program and kicked the habit. She had in fact questioned Emanuel last week about the marks on his arm, but he told her they had come from a fight he had with someone and denied he was using drugs.

The only problem they had had recently was a dispute with a neighbor, a black male, who had fired a shot over Dorothy's head with a shotgun last summer. They had a pending legal action against this neighbor, and the incident had produced some arguments between them and him. They had gotten a bit behind on their rent last year and still owed their landlords $125 in back rent, which they had agreed to pay off a little each month. These were the only difficulties they had. Dorothy could not think of anyone who would have wanted Emanuel dead.

Neither could Frenchy Cook, who had come to police headquarters that morning to give a formal statement to Detective Paul Delano. Frenchy described Emanuel as a homebody, no girlfriends or women on the side, a guy who never got into trouble and never went anywhere outside his own neighborhood. Asked if Emanuel used or was involved in selling drugs, Frenchy replied that if he was, Frenchy didn't know about it.

Frenchy repeated the chain of events. Nothing unusual had happened that night until a minute or so before the shooting. "I was standing on the bottom stairs and Emanuel was talking to someone at the door," Frenchy explained. "Then this guy comes up to me and says, 'Hey, you know where Diane or Dorothy lives?'" It was either Diane or Dorothy, but Frenchy wasn't sure which. "I told him no, I don't know where she lives, so he walked away. Emanuel came out and we started to walk across the street. This same guy comes up behind us. He said, 'Hey,' and we both turned around. He shot the first time and I heard Emanuel holler. I ran behind some cars and then I ran out across Zenner Street toward East Ferry. I ducked behind a car and I heard two more shots."

"Was the guy who you talked to white or black?" Delano asked.

"White."

"Can you describe him for me?"

"He was about five-foot-nine, clean shaven, about nineteen years old. He was wearing a blue snorkel jacket without the hood, a short one. He also had a Navy watch cap, I think it was black. He also had on blue jeans."

"Have you ever seen this white man before?"

"No."

"After the other two shots, what did you do?"

"After I saw all the people coming out of their houses," Frenchy said, "I got out from behind the car and that's when I saw Emanuel lying on the ground."

Detective Delano asked if Emanuel said anything when he was lying in the street and if Frenchy saw the gun that the white man fired. Frenchy answered no to both questions. As far as the gun, all he saw was the flame coming out of the barrel. The gunman had been standing only ten feet behind them.

"This white guy, was he alone both times you saw him?" Delano asked.

"Yes," Frenchy answered. The guy had not given a last name of the Diane or Dorothy he claimed to be looking for, and Frenchy said he didn't see anybody else around when the shooting took place.

"Has there been any trouble in the area with any white people recently?" Delano asked.

"No," Frenchy answered.

"Did the white guy act like he was trying to hold you up?"

"No, he never asked for nothing. He just said 'Hey' and started shooting."

"Would you be able to recognize this person if you saw him again?" the detective asked.

"Yes, I definitely would."

———————

A teenage girl had also been brought downtown to give a statement. She told Detective Delano that she and her eleven-year-old sister were standing near the intersection of Zenner and Ferry when a light-blue car with two men inside stopped at the corner. One of the men got out. She described him as a white man wearing a dark hat, jeans, and a short jacket. He looked eighteen or nineteen years old, about five feet eight, with a thin build and short hair. She had turned away to speak to a friend and didn't look back toward the corner until she heard three or four shots and saw someone running. She ran over and saw Emanuel lying in the street. She didn't know what became of the blue car or the white man, and she couldn't describe the other man she had seen sitting in the car.

A young man told police he had been in the living room of his home on Zenner when he heard at least four shots. He went out on his porch and saw a white male wearing a dark hunting cap and short jacket get into the driver's side of a dark-blue car and drive north on Zenner at a normal speed. Another witness claimed the blue car had sped off down Ferry Street.

Despite the discrepancies, which were not unusual when it came to eyewitness accounts, Buffalo police knew they were looking for one or possibly two men, at least one of whom was a young white male of average height and build, who took off in a car that was some shade of blue.

It wasn't much to go on, but it was more than they had for the Glenn Dunn homicide. With the similarities and proximity of the two attacks— and the fact they had occurred barely more than twenty-four hours apart—the possibility of a connection had to be considered, though until ballistics tests were done it remained only a possibility. The shooting of Harold Green the day before in Cheektowaga stayed very much on the radar of Buffalo detectives, with its eerie resemblance to the killing of the Dunn boy, though it still seemed unlikely that the same assailant had targeted two victims, much less three, with such disparate profiles.

Harold Green remained in critical condition at the hospital. He had so far not regained consciousness. X-rays revealed two small-caliber bullet marks, one on top of his head, the other on the left side of his head. Surgery had yielded one bullet and fragments. A second bullet remained in his brain.

A check of Harold Green's background and lifestyle revealed exactly what his family members had claimed. Harold was a devoted professional man with no questionable associates or activities, no skeletons in his orderly closets. His mother and sister had given permission for a search of his residence, which turned up nothing of note but a small amount of marijuana and a registered .22 caliber semiautomatic pistol, for which Harold had a permit. Witness Linda Snyder, after returning to work and gathering her wits, had given a statement to Cheektowaga police. A composite sketch of the suspect had immediately been put together based on the descriptions given by the three witnesses at the Burger King and was released that afternoon. The suspect sought was a white male, thirty to thirty-five years old, five feet ten, with a pale complexion and a chubby face, wearing khaki pants and a porkpie hat. Witnesses had described the hat as either a fishing-type or porkpie. Whatever the exact style, they all agreed it was light in color and had a brim.

On the Glenn Dunn investigation, John Regan and Melvin Lobbett had determined that the stolen car, in all likelihood, had nothing to do with Glenn's murder. The auto theft seemed to be linked to adolescent stupidity rather than a crime ring. On the day of his death, Glenn and two young accomplices had apparently stolen three 1981 Buicks from a dealership in Cheektowaga. The other two cars had been recovered Tuesday morning. No other witnesses to Glenn's murder had turned up and the only thing to be found at the home of the Dunn family was grief. Glenn had been one of eight children living in a cramped home on Fougeron Street with their parents and grandmother. Glenn was a fairly quiet teenager who liked sports, his family said. He played basketball outside with the other kids. He had hopes of making the high school football team. As far as they knew, the stolen Buick was the only lawbreaking he'd ever done. Glenn's background, so to speak, wasn't much different than that of any other boy who'd only lived for fourteen years.

This is where matters stood early on September 24. Three gun assaults that required further investigation and ballistics analysis. Enough similarities to take note, but not enough to cause panic.

But now there was the murder in Niagara Falls. Details from the McCoy shooting were still sparse, but the suspect description was a white male, midtwenties, five feet eight to ten, with a slender build, neck-length dirty-blond hair, who shot his victim in the left side of the head at close range and fled.

Four ambush-style shootings within thirty-six hours. Four black male victims. And maybe one white assailant.

If news of the fatal shooting of Joseph McCoy struck the region like a bolt of lightning on this otherwise sunny Wednesday, the lightning rod that most keenly absorbed its impact was Buffalo Police Headquarters.

The homicide bureau took up several rooms on the third floor at 74 Franklin Street. Homicide was typically a bustling division but in the past hours, as information filtered in from law enforcement in Cheektowaga and Niagara Falls, the normal buzz and exchange had intensified. No one wanted to jump to what might well turn out to be a wild conclusion, least of all professionals who are trained to weed out red herrings and value hard evidence over assumptions. The similarities here, however, though not yet conclusively linked, could not be overlooked.

Of course, the police were not the only ones with a keen interest in whether the attacks were connected. The local media had been inquiring on an hourly basis. With the fourth shooting in the Falls came a new urgency for answers and comments from investigators, of which there were now many, spread over three separate municipalities in Western New York.

In addition to John Regan, Melvin Lobbett, Al Williams, and Paul Delano, there were now numerous other detectives and patrol officers working on the Dunn and Thomas murders in Buffalo, canvassing neighborhoods, taking statements, and gathering evidence. All of the collected information was destined for room 328, the private office of a man whose job it was to oversee an investigation when one human being killed another in the City of Buffalo.

Leo Donovan had been chief of homicide for close to two decades, a police officer for almost four. Donovan had a reputation as a consummate lawman, a cop's cop, and a native son of the city's Irish First Ward, who had joined the force as a patrolman after serving in the navy during World War II. Donovan had worked several different details prior to his ascension to head of the homicide division in 1964. In his early days as a young patrolman, one of his first partners was James Cunningham, the current police commissioner. Donovan had at one time been commander of the motorcycle squad. Once he reached homicide, however, Leo Donovan had truly hit his stride. This was work he was born to do, with his analytical mind and penchant for deciphering the logic in situations where there appeared to be none.

Chief Donovan had already spent the better part of this Wednesday morning in conversation with both his own detectives and his counterparts in Cheektowaga and, of late, Niagara Falls. At noon, Donovan removed several recent additions from the evidence safe in his office. The evidence-gathering unit had delivered a total of twelve packets on the Dunn homicide and seven on Thomas. Cheektowaga police had brought over their ballistics evidence from the Green shooting. Donovan had all of it delivered to the Central Police Services lab on the fourth floor to the custody of ballistician Michael Dujanovich. The directive was clear: ballistics tests should be done without delay. A scientific link should be established or ruled out as soon as possible.

Donovan planned a meeting for the following day in his office with top brass from all three jurisdictions. Evidence from Joseph McCoy's shooting could only be obtained through his autopsy once the bullets that had killed him could be extracted from his head. Niagara Falls would provide it to the lab for comparison as soon as it became available.

That day's late edition of the *Buffalo Evening News* ran a story with the headline "Two More 'Executed'; Police Look for Link."

Before the day was done, there was no longer any doubt. The police lab determined that bullets retrieved from the bodies of Glenn Dunn, Emanuel Thomas, and Harold Green had all been fired from the same .22 caliber weapon.

Chapter 4
THURSDAY, SEPTEMBER 25, 1980

"YOU MIGHT SAY it looks like the cousin of the Son of Sam is on the loose," an unnamed investigator was quoted in the *Courier-Express*, one of Buffalo's two major newspapers. The same article stated that police were investigating the "strong possibility" that a single assailant was responsible for all four attacks but noted that ballistics tests from the Niagara Falls slaying were still pending. Chief Leo Donovan had declined to elaborate on the lab results, but a source had informed the *Courier* that tests indicated the same gun had been used in both of the Buffalo shootings and the one in Cheektowaga.

"Son of Sam" was a reference to serial killer David Berkowitz, whose highly publicized ambush attacks across New York City had ended three years earlier with his arrest on August 10, 1977. Berkowitz had christened himself "Son of Sam" in taunting notes he began leaving at the scenes of his crimes—prior to that, he had been known as the .44 Caliber Killer because of the .44 caliber Charter Arms Bulldog he had used in his street shootings of random victims. Thanks to an endless flow of screaming tabloid headlines that had been reprinted as far away as the Soviet Union, the moniker Son of Sam had become known throughout the world as a synonym for demented serial killer.

In all likelihood, few residents of Western New York were ready to contemplate the idea that there could actually be a serial killer on the loose here. That kind of thing happened in much larger and more exotic places like San Francisco and, of course, New York City; not in Buffalo. Though it was the second largest city in the state, Buffalo ran a distant second to the so called Big Apple, with its multimillion citizens living on top of one another in their own chaotic filth and lawlessness, as some Buffalonians might have put it. In terms of crime, culture, and social mores, the distance between Buffalo and its tawdry behemoth cousin downstate was much greater than the 450 geographic miles that separated the two. Even with their notorious Son of Sam killer now long off the streets, New York City's crime index had increased at a rate greater than 50 percent of the national average in the first six months of 1980 alone. Officials were predicting that 1980 would be a record year for crime in that city, a prediction that eventually proved true. While Buffalo certainly had its own problems with rising crime, most residents were more concerned about the hobbled economy than anything else. Serial murder in the City of Good Neighbors, as Buffalo was called, seemed about as far off the radar as another population boom.

Though an article in the *Buffalo Evening News*, the city's other major newspaper, likewise stated that the same gun had been used to shoot three of the victims—and included the composite sketch of a white suspect circulated by Cheektowaga police for the Harold Green assault—both papers mentioned the uncertainty about whether a single shooter was responsible. The *Courier-Express* noted confusion about the assailant's race. Witnesses to the Thomas and McCoy homicides claimed the gunman was white. For Harold Green, one had described a white suspect, upon which the composite was based, while others said they were unsure and that the man who fled the scene may have been black. Of the Glenn Dunn murder: "Witnesses said at first the gunman was white but then said they were uncertain as to his color."

Both papers reported that Harold Green remained in critical condition, on life support, and unable to give police any information. A Cheektowaga police lieutenant expressed dismay that the composite sketch hadn't produced any witnesses: "The shooting happened at the noon hour and the place had to be packed. Somebody should have seen something." Officers would continue canvassing the area businesses and restaurants. The public was meanwhile encouraged to look at the composite drawing and contact police with any information on the suspect, further described as "a white male, 30-35 years old, five-foot-ten, 165 pounds, with a very pale complexion and a chubby face with small dark eyes." He had been wearing a porkpie hat, dark-blue work shirt, khaki pants, and white sneakers.

The *Courier* gave some background on each of the victims. According to the article, high school student Glenn Dunn, killed in a stolen car, had been accused of sexually attacking a girl in August, but no criminal charge had been filed at the insistence of the victim. Emanuel Thomas's drug arrest of six years before was mentioned, as was Harold Green's career as a rising engineer at Moog. Joseph McCoy was reported to have had run-ins with the law in Niagara Falls years earlier stemming from drinking and disorderly conduct, but according to Police Captain Raymond Kumm, McCoy had been "straight for the last several years."

A separate article featured photos of all four victims and comments from their loved ones and acquaintances. Glenn Dunn's relatives said that another family member, not Glenn, was responsible for the sexual attack on the girl. Harold Green's family spoke of his modest hobbies—photography, playing the saxophone, and building stereo components—and how they viewed Harold as their guardian angel. "He was truly brilliant," said his sister. "He was not a pompous person and he just took what was given him in stride. I think that's the thing that troubles us. If he was the kind of guy who was looking for trouble, maybe we could understand it. But he was serious, hardworking, kept to himself, nothing but his family. He shunned trouble."

Emanuel Thomas's life as a family man was highlighted, his former neighbors describing him as "always respectable" and telling of the backyard barbecues he had with his wife and daughters. Emanuel had recently joined the choir at a local church. His mother, Clara Thomas, spoke tearfully of his efforts to find work. "So many times he'd come over here to use the phone, call people up for a job, ask 'em, beg 'em," she was quoted. "Why would anyone in the world kill him? Why? I will never know." Emanuel would be buried Saturday, on what would have been his thirty-second birthday.

Joseph McCoy had no enemies and his killing was senseless, his family said. He had last worked as a custodian for a community center, about two years earlier. He left behind three brothers, two sisters, and his parents. Joseph had helped care for his elderly father, who was paralyzed from a series of strokes. Speaking of his late brother's murder, Robert McCoy said, "He was just minding his own business, taking a walk like he does every day. Joe didn't have anything that anyone would want." He stressed that his brother had no enemies. He was convinced the shooting had been random since Joe "had virtually no white friends."

No one who knew the victims could think of a motive.

The police could not offer a motive either, beyond the obvious. "This guy, if it is the same guy, seems to be indiscriminately shooting black males," one officer commented.

Chief Leo Donovan took a more reserved approach in his remarks, stating that the investigation was ongoing, but acknowledged that there were so many similarities "that we cannot afford to not explore the possibility that the same person is responsible."

According to the *Courier-Express*, several investigators noted that the movie *Death Wish* had been on TV the previous weekend and they wondered if the film had maybe spurred a psychotic killer into action. *Death Wish* told the fictional story of everyman Paul Kersey, played by Charles Bronson, who takes to the streets as a gun-toting vigilante following the vicious murder of his wife and rape of his daughter during a home invasion. Though highly controversial and roundly criticized for its perceived glorification of vigilantism, the film had struck a chord with audiences upon its release in 1974 and became a box office smash.

The *Buffalo Evening News* and local TV station WKBW offered a joint reward of $1,000 for information leading to the arrest and conviction of the suspect or suspects. The reward would cover the fatal shooting in Niagara Falls as well if police established a link with the Buffalo and Cheektowaga attacks. "I'd like to say there's no connection between this homicide and the three other shootings," a Niagara Falls police captain was quoted, "but I can't say that."

Though scientific comparisons had yet to be done on the bullets that killed Joseph McCoy, word had spread quickly throughout law enforcement that they were .22 caliber slugs. As cautious as police may have been about jumping to conclusions of a serial killer in their midst, the specter of Son of Sam still loomed, differences between New York City and Buffalo notwithstanding. It *could* happen here, unthinkable as it might seem. After his capture, David Berkowitz had written a letter to the *New York Post* giving his improbable explanation that a demon-possessed dog had urged him to kill, ending the letter with a cryptic warning that was perhaps not so improbable: "There are other Sons out there, God help the world."

Chief Donovan and his fellow lawmen hoped to God they didn't have a Sam or a Paul Kersey out there. They definitely didn't want to raise the possibility with the media, particularly when such a presumption would have been premature and especially since it could spark widespread fear and panic like the Son of Sam case had in New York City. Cooler heads had to prevail here. Western New York needed a panic like they needed another crippling blizzard or factory closing.

At the same time, Donovan realized that a downplay of the situation or an overly zealous withholding of information could provoke the same result. A news photographer had been allowed to snap a picture of the meeting held that morning in Donovan's office. The photo appeared prominently in the *Buffalo Evening News* under the title "Grim Agenda" and showed Leo Donovan in conference with Lieutenants Henry Zablotny and Fred Netzel from Cheektowaga, and from Niagara Falls, Lieutenant John Zaccarella and Captain Raymond Kumm. Better to give the public a visual assurance that top law enforcement agencies in Western New York were giving the crimes immediate and serious attention.

Following the PR photo, the photographer and any lingering reporters were cordially shown the door. The actual meeting proceeded in private. Not that the assembled commanders knew much more than what had already been relayed or leaked to the newspapers. They agreed to work jointly on the cases and share information. Additional officers would be assigned to homicide. Canvassing of neighborhoods and re-questioning of witnesses would be given high priority. Nevertheless, they were all aware of the challenge they faced if this did turn out to be the work of a rogue with a warped agenda. The most difficult homicides to solve are those where killer and victim are absolute strangers and have contact for only a matter of seconds.

Unlike the first three shootings, no shell casings had been found at the Niagara Falls crime scene. Witnesses claimed that the gunman had held a paper bag to Joseph McCoy's head and fired with the gun still in the bag. This explained the absence of casings; they had ejected into the paper bag. To police, it also indicated that the killer might be following media accounts of his crimes—and learning from his mistakes. He obviously had the savvy to stop leaving his shell casings behind.

He was also brazen, obviously undeterred by the presence of witnesses. Two of the attacks had occurred in broad daylight, at times and places where there were bound to be plenty of people around. Aside from the hats and hoodie sweatshirt he apparently wore during the Dunn murder, there were no indications he had tried to disguise or otherwise conceal his face.

On the question of what their suspect looked like, in light of the conflicting eyewitness descriptions, the most reasonable deduction appeared to be a young or youngish white male, who was neither particularly tall nor particularly short. Not particularly anything, in fact, as far as any distinguishing characteristics that might set him apart from the hundreds of thousands of other white males under thirty-five in Western New York.

Frenchy Cook, Emanuel Thomas's walking companion, appeared to be the only person thus far with whom the shooter had communicated in any way prior to striking. Officers in Buffalo's precinct 12 were on a quest for a woman named Diane or Dorothy whom the suspect had said he was looking for immediately before shooting Thomas. So far this had been a dead end. There were indeed some Dianes and Dorothys living in the area; more than a few, and of course Emanuel Thomas's own wife was named Dorothy, but police could not find any so-named woman in the neighborhood with a connection to a white male who might be out stalking the street with a gun. Dorothy Thomas had no white male associates nor any romantic attachments in her life other than her late husband, and the Diane/Dorothy trail seemed cold.

Of the two best witnesses to the Harold Green shooting, Linda Snyder had given a detailed description of the suspect's clothing and build, and placed his age as early twenties. She could not determine his race because she had only seen him from behind as he ran from Harold Green's car, and the brim of his hat had been pulled down over his ears, concealing his hair color. Witness Dominic Punturiero, who had provided the description upon which the composite sketch was based, had also said the suspect wore a hat, but he had gotten a facial view, since he had looked up and noticed the man walking in the direction of Green's car just before hearing the shots. Punturiero said the suspect was white, with a very pale complexion, guessing his age as early to midthirties.

None of the witnesses to the McCoy shooting had gotten a look at the shooter's face, but had said the man was blond, which seemed to sync with Punturiero's recollection of a pale complexion. Frenchy Cook and other witnesses to the Thomas murder had put the shooter in his late teens to early twenties, but then again, it had been late at night. Dominic Punturiero was so far the only witness who had gotten a daylight view of the gunman's face.

Glenn Dunn had also been murdered after dark and it might therefore be more difficult for witnesses to give a good description—if any good witnesses could be found, that is. So far they had only the teen, Kenny Paulson, who had seen the shooting happen but still vacillated on whether the gunman was white or black.

For the time being, the police went with what seemed to be the best composite and description they had: white male, thirty to thirty-five, average in every way.

If they couldn't get better details than that, this could be like looking for a needle in a stack of needles.

Coincidentally, reporter Dan Herbeck had written a feature titled "The Buffalo Police Detectives 1980" that had been published in the *Buffalo News Magazine* on Sunday, September 21, the day before the murder of Glenn Dunn. It profiled four of Buffalo's veteran detectives, giving readers some lively insight into each man's life and his individual approach to solving crime. In the introduction, Herbeck noted the differences between true-life detectives and their highly glamorized fictional counterparts. Underscoring the challenges of real-world investigative work, Herbeck wrote, "Even the best detectives admit that the odds of solving a crime are stacked against them. The number of violent crimes in Buffalo is constantly on the rise; the number of policemen has dropped from 1,400 to less than 1,100 in five years." He continued, "The Buffalo police detective, for the most part, is doomed to a life of frustration—a life that becomes an endless stretch of phone calls, paperwork, interviews and loose ends, most of which will never be tied. It is a life of tips that usually lead nowhere . . ."

The composite sketch in the newspaper—combined with the potent tonic of a reward—had right away generated tips from callers. An officer in the Buffalo Homicide Bureau had dutifully typed them up on a P-73 form that was delivered to Chief Donovan's in-box that same night. For the most part, they were the type of pseudo-tips one might expect from an unremarkable sketch and such a generic description. Typical were the call from a man who reported that about a month before, "a white dude who rides a motorcycle, believed to be a member of the Hells Angels, got beat up by a black man" on Genesee Street in a fight over a stolen TV set. The caller thought the unknown white biker was seeking revenge. He'd try to find out the guy's name or license plate and call back. Another came from a woman who refused to identify herself and said only that the composite looked like the owner of a downtown liquor store.

The very last call on the P-73 was different, though. It came from a middle-aged woman named Mammy Brooks, who worked as a nurse at Deaconess Hospital. Ms. Brooks said that a coworker of hers, a young white girl named Gloria, had a teenage brother who had witnessed the shooting at the Tops parking lot. Gloria and her brother are afraid to call the police, Ms. Brooks explained, but she was trying to coax them into doing so. The teenage boy was coming out of the grocery store and saw a white guy walk up to the car and shoot the victim in the head. The boy is afraid to call because he knows who the guy is. Also, the guy is not as old as the news estimates his age. He's in his twenties, and he might possibly live in the area of Genesee Street, in close proximity of the homicide.

Chapter 5
SEPTEMBER 26–OCTOBER 7, 1980

"WEAPON TIED TO Falls Death, 2 City Killings," read a headline in the *Buffalo Evening News* on Friday, September 26. A bullet used to kill Joseph McCoy had been positively matched to a bullet from Harold Green, which had already been linked to the Dunn and Thomas murders.

Now that the four shootings had been scientifically linked, little doubt remained that a serial killer had struck. The greatest fear in such situations, of course, is that the offender will strike again. None of the police officials had yet mentioned this to the press, but it was hardly necessary for a generation raised on syndicated news and national TV coverage of the Son of Sam, Ted Bundy, and the Zodiac Killer, the last of whom had never been apprehended.

Leo Donovan hoped that the suspect would take a cue from some of his homicidal brethren and make contact with police. Preferably to turn himself in, but any contact would have been welcomed. Both of the region's major newspapers quoted Donovan: "I was hoping we'd see some word from him, either a phone call or a letter. If he would talk, maybe we could get him to realize that he's not going to come to any harm if he surrenders, but he has to stop hurting innocent people."

While the killer had so far remained silent, the public had not. Buffalo police had received more than 200 tip calls by Friday morning while

Cheektowaga police had about 125, and Niagara Falls about 50. Each call had to be vetted and checked out. This was in addition to the standard work of recanvassing, witness follow-up, and checking files for prior offenders who might have a history of assaults or violent run-ins with blacks. Press coverage that day included Chief Donovan's speculation that the suspect may be a "psychopath" who hates black people and a plea from Lieutenant John Zaccarella of Niagara Falls. "We're asking the general public to help us," Zaccarella was quoted. "If anyone sees this guy or anyone who looks like him, call the police immediately." The newspapers repeated the suspect description—and, in the case of the *Buffalo Evening News*, the reward being offered—and the calls kept coming.

Phone tips were not the only reaction from the community. On Wednesday night, a white man walking near the scene of Joseph McCoy's murder in Niagara Falls had been stopped by some black residents who spotted a handle protruding from a paper bag he was carrying. Police quickly converged on the scene, only to discover that the item in the bag was a hacksaw the man had just bought at a local store.

The only new information from police was that they were going to try hypnosis on a witness to the Harold Green shooting to see if it might bring forth any new details. According to reports, the witness had suggested hypnosis. With no new solid developments to write of, other than investigators' theory "that the suspect has a grievance, real or imagined, against black men, and he has chosen murder as a means to vent that grievance," the *Courier-Express* conducted an informal survey around the black community to ascertain whether the crimes were causing heightened fear. None of the handful of black men interviewed expressed an undue amount of concern for his own safety, although the article stated that the community was "cautious." One man identified as a retired auto plant worker blamed the shootings on the high unemployment and inflation, coupled with the problems presented by school integration.

The pastor of an east-side church commented that incidents like this often happened in large cities, and that "drinking and the use of dope also may have had something to do with the shootings," while an employee of an east-side tavern said: "Shootings are an everyday thing with me, so I'm always overly cautious to avoid becoming a victim of some nut. The person doing the shooting is the type of animal I would like to run into because he would learn he would be dealing with an animal himself. I deal with psychos every day, so one more nut will be nothing new to me."

On Saturday, September 27, lacking the real name of the gunman, the media gave him one: the .22 Caliber Killer. The *Courier-Express* reiterated that the victims were not linked in any way and that hate for blacks was a possible motive, "a hatred that permits him to kill indiscriminately." The *Buffalo Evening News* quoted Chief Donovan: "The people he has killed, I believe, were killed at random. Whatever reason he chose for picking those people, we have no idea." A separate article offered the opinion of experts that the offender would probably kill again.

September 27 was also the date of two disturbing occurrences, which, in hindsight, might have been considered a jarring preview of things to come.

Glenn Dunn, the first and youngest victim, was buried that morning. A large crowd had gathered in the chill fall air to pay last respects. During the graveside service, two vehicles described as a dark-blue compact car and an old brown pickup truck came driving by. Two white males were seated in the blue car. A mannequin head stained with what looked like blood was mounted on the hood. The driver and passenger of the blue car shouted taunts and racial slurs at the mourners. The brown pickup truck that followed behind had two or more white males, with red coloring on their faces, who also yelled epithets at the crowd. Multiple police units responded to the numerous 911 calls on the incident, but both vehicles were long gone. Officers took a report and remained in the area until the funeral service ended. The Dunn family was visibly shaken by what had happened, as were all the others in attendance at the boy's funeral, as well as the residents of this black neighborhood who had been drawn to their windows by the shouting. No one had gotten a license plate on either vehicle, and police cruising the area did not find any vehicles matching the descriptions.

East of the city, police in Cheektowaga received a call that evening from an assistant manager at the Burger King where Harold Green had been shot. Someone—it sounded like an adult white male—had called the restaurant and said, "I'm leaving you this message, that I'm going to kill another nigger." The assistant manager had hung up and immediately called police and her supervisor, who told her to put on a security man for the rest of the night and to call police when employees were leaving.

––––––––––

One of the most intriguing leads that the Buffalo police received came early on from a detective in Cincinnati, Ohio. Gus Gromke of the Cincinnati Police Department had read about the four unsolved shootings and called the Buffalo Homicide Bureau. Detective Gromke wanted to know if the cases were similar to the recent sniper shootings around Salt Lake City, Indianapolis, and Cincinnati. Several black men and boys had been wounded or killed by ambush attacks from a sniper. In May, a rather prominent civil rights activist named Vernon Jordan had been shot and seriously wounded in Indiana. In June, two black teenage boys had been killed in Cincinnati. And a month earlier, in August, two black men had been murdered in a park in Salt Lake City in the same manner. The guns used were a .44 magnum, a 30.06, and a 35mm. A suspect by the name of Joseph Paul Franklin had been captured in Florence, Kentucky, on September 25, but he had escaped through a window at the police station and was currently at large. Franklin was thirty years old, five feet eleven, two hundred pounds, and had brown hair with blond streaks. He had tattoos, one of them a hammer and sickle on his left forearm. Franklin was apparently a virulent racist and consummate criminal, suspected in a number of other shootings, bombings, and bank robberies.

Buffalo Detective Gerald Dove gave Detective Gromke details on the Western New York shootings and asked for a report on the Joseph Paul Franklin investigation. It was certainly a lead worth following, particularly if Franklin made a habit of traveling the eastern part of the United States in search of black victims and employed a variety of guns in his sniper attacks.

Sadly, there seemed to be no shortage in the country of serial murderers targeting innocent black victims. A prolific serial killer in Atlanta, Georgia, had been claiming the lives of children and adolescents in a spree that had begun in the summer of 1979. There were more than a dozen homicides to date, with the murderer still on the loose. Aside from the race of the victims, though, there were no commonalities between the Atlanta Murders—sometimes referred to as the Atlanta Child Murders—and the .22 caliber killings.

Joseph Paul Franklin seemed a much more promising possibility. However, many in law enforcement had a strong feeling that the .22 Caliber Killer was not likely to be an out-of-town drifter. He seemed too familiar with his surroundings, too confident about his escape routes and his ability to blend in.

————

Sunday newspapers across the state ran stories about the shootings in Western New York. Even the venerable *New York Times* had taken note and reported on the crimes and the progress of the investigation. The local papers meanwhile were filled with prominent coverage of the case, from reports of the harassment at Glenn Dunn's funeral, to community reactions, to speculations about what might happen next and opinions on what should be done.

Police were candid in stating that they hadn't yet had any breaks. The *Courier-Express* quoted Homicide Chief Leo Donovan: "We don't have much to go on. What makes this case so frustrating is that he may kill again. We don't know who he is. We don't know what his motive is." Reporter Erik Brady wrote that most murder cases are a question of whodunit, but this one is a matter of finding whodunit before he does it again. Once more, comparisons with the Son of Sam abounded.

But this was no "ordinary" serial killer; the fact that the three dead and one critically injured victim were all black males—and the assailant a white male—presented an even more insidious, overarching threat to a region already under significant stress. Even now, less than a week into the investigation, fears of racial discord and vigilantism were looming. The big question was whether the shootings were, in fact, racially motivated. If they were—or were even perceived as such—and authorities were not able to provide a swift resolution, what might be the ramifications? Columnist Henry Locke wrote an article featuring comments and concerns from several civil rights leaders in the area, some of whom feared that paranoia might develop in the black community, which could lead to worse incidents. Amid the speculations that a hate group could be responsible and that citizens might start arming themselves for protection against the assassin—or assassins—some took a more pragmatic, though no less cautionary, view. "The sad thing about the questions being raised," said Donald R. Lee, a former president of the New York State Conference of the NAACP, "is that the murderer's actions could possibly trigger some negative reactions between black and white citizens, when in reality it is only some nut out there blowing people away."

Leo Donovan appealed for calm. He also made another plea for the killer to contact him, promising that if he would do so, he would not be hurt and would receive psychiatric care. "The man is sick and he needs help," Donovan said. "Maybe he will realize this. And if he reads this in the paper I hope he will contact me in some way." Then, as if thinking aloud, Donovan continued, "On the other hand he may have a 'catch-me-if-you-can' attitude. That's the whole thing—we don't know what kind of a sociopath or psychotic we're dealing with."

Chief Donovan and Commissioner James Cunningham assured the public that the police were working around the clock. All twenty detectives in the homicide squad were working on the case, in addition to detectives from individual precincts. There were, of course, other homicide cases to be worked, but all city detectives were now also involved in this investigation. Officers were going door to door in neighborhoods around the crime scenes in search of more information. Donovan stressed the need for help from the public. "We're hoping for a break, for some clue to turn up. What we don't want is for someone else to get hurt. We are afraid of not finding a clue until he strikes again."

This fear was shared by some prominent black citizens in the community, who were not content to wait and hope for clues, and certainly not for the killer to strike again. Reverend Bennett W. Smith, age forty-seven, was the pastor of St. John Baptist Church on Goodell Street, in the heart of Buffalo's black community. Known for his passionate and inspirational sermons, Smith had been the pastor of this large church since 1972. Beyond his work as a clergyman—or rather, as an extension of it—Bennett Smith worked actively for civil rights causes and fair housing. He had been a part of Dr. Martin Luther King's famous march from Selma to Montgomery in Alabama. He was a close friend and colleague of the Reverend Jesse Jackson and served as coordinator for the Buffalo branch of Jackson's Operation PUSH, which stood for People United to Save Humanity (later changed to People United to Serve Humanity), an organization devoted to the economic advancement of blacks and black-owned businesses.

In an interview with the *Courier-Express*, Reverend Smith announced a drive within the city's black community to raise a reward fund for information leading to the arrest of the .22 Caliber Killer. He asked that black churches in the area collect donations and turn them in to Operation PUSH, which would hold the money in a special reward fund. Smith noted that while the black community was not in a panic—which he noted was a good thing—the shootings had instilled an underlying sense of terror. The situation called for not only swift action, but also results. "If this man is not caught by Monday," Smith said, "black leaders will have to get together and move on this case."

Bennett Smith already had plans to do so. He told the newspaper that he had a meeting scheduled on Monday with Fletcher Graves, head of the regional office of the US Justice Department's Community Relations Division in New York City. Mr. Graves was flying in for the meeting, which would also be attended by Buffalo Police Commissioner James Cunningham; the district attorney; and Daniel Acker, president of the local chapter of the NAACP. The meeting had come about as a result of a phone call Fletcher Graves had made on Friday to Daniel Acker. According to Acker, Graves had inquired about the killings and asked if he thought it would be necessary to bring the FBI in on the case. Daniel Acker had told the Justice Department official that it would be a good idea, as he felt the FBI "would be able to mount a more concentrated effort to capture the killer."

Acker had expressed his concerns about a police slowdown in the area due to the department's ongoing contract negotiations, adding, "and I know the police are dragging their feet in certain instances. Also, they have more murders than they can handle. So I think any help we can get from the outside would be good."

Asked for a comment, Erie County District Attorney Edward Cosgrove took exception to involving the FBI. He did not feel there were any grounds to do so and expressed confidence in the way the investigation was being handled by Homicide Chief Leo Donovan. Cosgrove did not think Mr. Acker or anyone else should have concerns about "the ability of local law enforcement officials to look into this problem." Adding that he had not been invited to a meeting with the Justice Department official, Cosgrove said, "I would be courteous to anyone who wanted to discuss this, but I would not be responsive to asking the FBI into the case. In fact, I would discourage it."

Daniel Acker had his doubts about the ability of local law enforcement—*any* local law enforcement, anywhere—to successfully handle such an investigation without assistance and oversight from federal authorities. Acker was seventy years old, married, the father of three adult children. He had been president of the Buffalo branch of the NAACP—National Association for the Advancement of Colored People—since 1972. Personally and professionally, Daniel Acker had learned and experienced quite a lot in his seven decades of life.

He had been born and raised in the coal mining town of Williamson, West Virginia. As a young man, he had earned a bachelor of science degree in chemistry and education from West Virginia State University and his master's degree in the same fields at the University of Michigan. He had spent his early career as a teacher, first in elementary school and then as an instructor of chemistry and physics at Liberty High School in his hometown, before opting for a career in industrial chemistry. A chemical plant in West Virginia offered him a position but withdrew the offer when they discovered he was black. During World War II, however, with the government in great need of skilled chemists, he was hired by the Trojan Powder Company in Sandusky, Ohio, and assigned to the Plum Brook Ordnance Works, which Trojan Powder maintained, where he worked on advanced chemical and defense-related developments, including the Manhattan Project.

Acker had moved his family to Buffalo in 1944, when he received an offer from Linde Air, a division of Union Carbide. While he had enjoyed a fruitful career as a chemist at Linde that spanned over thirty years, life in his adopted city had not been without its challenges. When Daniel Acker bought a home for his family in upscale North Buffalo in 1950, hostile neighbors dug up their shrubs. In the 1960s, recognizing the need for decent housing for blacks in the area—and the myriad of obstacles they faced in finding it—he cofounded an organization called HOME: Housing Opportunities Made Equal. Always a great believer in education and an advocate of civil rights and community involvement, Acker had led the charge for the desegregation in Buffalo public schools, filing a class-action lawsuit in 1976 in his role as NAACP president.

Daniel Acker had seen his share of racial hostilities. And he understood all too well—perhaps more keenly than local law enforcement, no matter how sincere and well-intentioned they might be—the threat that a racially motivated assassin on the prowl could pose to victims, both intended and unintended. To both black and white.

———

Police had spent the weekend pursuing leads and questioning more than a few men who had either caught their attention or been brought to it. Interestingly, they had received another tip on the owner of a certain liquor store in downtown Buffalo. The first had come from the anonymous female who had called the homicide bureau, but the source of the second was a police officer who definitely felt the man should be questioned. The liquor store owner not only resembled the Cheektowaga composite sketch, but he had also been making threats that he was going to "get even for what happened to his wife."

Detectives paid a visit to the man, who was white and thirty-five years old. They were somewhat surprised to find him dressed like the suspect described in the Cheektowaga composite. They were even more surprised when the man readily admitted that he looked like the composite, and further that even though he wasn't the shooter, he liked people thinking that he was. He said he had indeed been telling people on the street that he was going to get even for what happened to his wife. When detectives asked what had happened to her, the man pulled out some news clippings to show them. Four years ago, his wife had been shot twice in the stomach by three black males during a holdup. The three perpetrators—two in their late teens and one juvenile—had been arrested. According to the liquor store owner, one of them was still in prison but only had a year to go on his sentence.

Far from being reluctant to speak with police, the liquor store owner talked a blue streak. He told the detectives that he worked days as a physical education teacher at a Buffalo public school and invited them to contact the school's principal to "check him out." He said he did not have a pistol permit or any guns. The detectives searched him anyway.

He bragged about his education and claimed he had helped police in some investigations. He had forty credit hours in psychology courses, he said, and commented, "You know it takes about four years for the mind to snap." When detectives asked what he meant by that, he wouldn't elaborate. He did say that he had been telling people on the street that he was a suspect in the .22 caliber killings. It gave him a feeling of power, he said, adding that he wasn't afraid of any blacks coming after him.

Detective Gerald Dove and his partner meanwhile followed up on the tip call from Mammy Brooks, the nurse who claimed that her coworker Gloria had told her that her younger brother had witnessed the shooting of Glenn Dunn. After speaking with Ms. Brooks, detectives spoke with a supervisor at the hospital who told them that there were two employees named Gloria. One was named Gloria Paulson, and she lived on Floss Avenue.

These details immediately rang a bell with detectives. Kenny Paulson of Floss Avenue had given a statement to police on the Glenn Dunn homicide.

They paid a visit to the Paulson household. Neither Gloria nor Kenny was at home. Their mother said that Kenny had left for the Buffalo Bills football game and wouldn't be back until later. She gave them the name of his employer but said that if they wanted to interview Kenny, they'd have to try and get him some evening, after work.

Harold Green died at 7:45 p.m. on Sunday, September 28. He had never regained consciousness. Now there were four dead men, but no prime suspects.

If the black community had not been in a panic before, the large-print headlines on Monday morning announcing Harold Green's death all but assured they would be now. ".22 Gunman's Fourth Victim Dies." The newspapers reported that though the same gun had been used in all four murders, the possibility existed of more than one shooter. Given the wide discrepancies in witness descriptions of the assailant, the killings could be the work of two or more men working together, with the same gruesome objective.

The murderer of Glenn Dunn and Emanuel Thomas had been described as a young, slight man in his twenties.

Harold Green's killer was said to be a taller man in his thirties.

Joseph McCoy had reportedly been shot by a man with long blond hair.

Leo Donovan had been in this line of work long enough to know that bystanders, even the most well-meaning of them, often see things differently. While he could not dismiss the possibility of more than one gunman, he considered it remote. What Donovan really hoped for was that his men could find a witness who could give them accurate and sufficient details for a new composite sketch—something better than the everyman drawing that was circulating now.

———

Throughout Sunday and the early part of the following week, Buffalo police were checking blue cars. Officers had fanned out in the neighborhoods where Emanuel Thomas and Glenn Dunn had been shot and took down the license plates of nearly every blue car in the area. Based on a witness tip, they were particularly interested in four-door Chevy Impalas.

Door-to-door canvassing on Zenner Street, where Emanuel had been killed, had so far not produced anything but a couple of wild-goose chases. A few teenage boys who had boasted of seeing the shooting to their friends admitted that they had been home in bed and had only heard the shots, or nothing at all. One of the early witnesses at the scene, the teenage girl who had come downtown to give a statement, had fingered her former boyfriend as the shooter. Police had immediately gone to the boyfriend's home and discovered he had an alibi and people to back up his whereabouts at the time of the murder. Further checking revealed that the girl had psychiatric problems.

Another witness to the Thomas shooting, a young man who had given police a description of the shooter's getaway car, went to precinct 16 to report that he had been harassed. He had been walking to the bar at the corner of Zenner and East Ferry when two white men in a light-blue compact car drove by and the passenger said to him, "All niggers should die," followed by "pow." The young man went into the bar, but when he came out a few minutes later, the car, which had been parked on the east side of Zenner facing Ferry, began following him. He ran into a yard and came around the fences in the rear to reach his own home on Zenner Street. He and his mother looked out their window and watched the car go by three times, but they could not call police because they didn't have a phone. His mother thought it was the same car she had seen on the night of the Emanuel Thomas shooting. The only description the young man could give was that both men were white and the passenger looked about thirty years old, had dark hair and a mustache, and was wearing a blue jacket.

Police staked out the area in unmarked vehicles. All marked police cars were instructed to keep away from the immediate location but to cruise nearby streets for any sign of the suspect vehicle. The blue car that the young man had described also sounded very similar to the one used to harass mourners at Glenn Dunn's funeral. Whether the suspects were actual killers or just sadistic tormentors, police wanted to catch them. Despite a lengthy stakeout, however, the compact blue car was never seen again.

––––––––

Detective John Regan spent that Monday knocking on doors up and down Zenner Street in search of witnesses to the Thomas homicide. Regan and his partner, Mel Lobbett, had of course been the first detectives at the scene of the Glenn Dunn shooting. Since the decree had come that all detectives would work on all the .22 caliber cases, Regan, along with the rest of his colleagues—both in and out of the homicide division—found themselves running down leads collectively, portioning their time among each homicide investigation rather than focusing on one. This system had its advantages and disadvantages.

While more detectives meant that more leads could be pursued more quickly, and while each of the dozens of detectives was sharing information with the others, the sheer volume of information to be shared was staggering. Phone tips from citizens now numbered well into the hundreds and came from as far away as Rochester, eighty miles east of Buffalo. This was in addition to calls and leads from law enforcement in neighboring states. In the fall of 1980, mobile phones, texts, and instant messaging were undreamed of tools of a future generation; communication meant landlines, message pads (the paper and pen kind), and typewriters. Sharing information took time, even with the most diligent of efforts. As the .22 Caliber Killer investigation entered its first full week, detectives who had not been present at the crime scenes on the nights or days of—and had not participated in the initial questioning of witnesses—were following up in some instances without the benefit of knowing the full history firsthand, particularly feelings or instincts that aren't recorded on a witness statement.

Thus it had been other detectives, not John Regan or Mel Lobbett, who were assigned to follow up on the tip concerning statements allegedly made by Kenny Paulson's sister to a coworker, and yet two others who attempted another follow-up on Tuesday, September 30, with Paulson's sister. It was some time before Detective Regan even learned of this tip, as it was only one in an ever-growing pile. Though the subsequent detectives were aware that Kenny Paulson had given a statement, they were unaware of Regan's instinctive feeling—shared by Lieutenant Bill Misztal, the first officer to question Paulson at the scene—that the kid had been less than candid.

Later that week, Detective Al Williams was finally able to speak with Gloria Paulson. She said that the only thing her brother had told her was that the shooter had blond hair.

This was not the only instance of conflicting information in the investigation. A young male witness to the Emanuel Thomas murder had told police that he and two friends—brothers who lived with their mother on Zenner Street—had been standing outside at the time and had witnessed both the shooting and the escape of the suspect in the blue car. He claimed that he and his friends had even attempted to chase the car down the street.

When questioned, however, the two brothers insisted that they had been inside their home at the time and hadn't seen or done any such thing. Their mother backed them up. The other witness stuck to his story. He even gave a more detailed description of the car they had allegedly chased, although he altered his recollection of where the suspect's car had been parked.

This was a common and twofold problem for police: witnesses who lied because they didn't want to get involved in a criminal investigation, and others who lied or exaggerated because they wanted to be a part of things. This was particularly true of high-profile cases that garnered a lot of media attention, which the .22 caliber killings certainly had. Determining who was being truthful could sometimes be a gradual, painstaking process.

Tuesday's recanvass of Floss Avenue did turn up one good witness for the Dunn homicide. Barbara Wozniak had given detectives from the sixteenth precinct her account of hearing four loud pops and seeing a hooded figure dart through the fence of the Tops parking lot. She now told it again to Detective Stanley Suszek and Officer Richard Robson, who attempted to get as much detail as possible. Noting that Barbara's house faced the Tops parking lot and the opening in the fence through which the shooter had evidently fled, it appeared she did have an excellent sight line.

On the night in question, Barbara had thought the person she saw running away was a kid who had set off some firecrackers. She had watched only long enough to see him running past five or six houses up the street from hers. In the minute or so she had stood outside and watched the person run, she hadn't seen anyone else either on the street or on porches.

Barbara had not seen his face and could not say whether he had been white or black. For that matter, she couldn't definitively state whether the person was male or female, but judging by the build and the running speed, she thought male. She estimated his height at five feet nine and described his clothing as dark pants and a navy blue or black jacket with a hood. She saw him pull the hood down, as if to keep his head covered.

Barbara Wozniak was cooperative, credible. Her account was good. *If only she had seen his face!*

The composite sketch circulating now seemed to be impeding rather than aiding the investigation. Uniformed patrolmen were devoting a substantial amount of time responding to sightings of the suspect. He was seen at bus stops, grocery stores, and gas stations. Officers would arrive and sometimes find a startled, average-looking white man in his thirties who would dutifully answer their questions. Other times they'd be told they had just missed the suspect or discover that the call had been a hoax. More often, the calls came from panicky citizens who were genuinely afraid of Buffalo's "Son of Sam" and were heeding the advice of law enforcement to contact police if they saw anyone who resembled the description of the suspect—which was quite a lot of people.

The fear and anxiety was by no means limited to the black community. Many whites were almost equally leery of the phantom gunman and his disturbed, esoteric agenda. Anyone who would prowl the streets randomly blasting strangers must have a screw loose, so few people felt absolute confidence in the idea of their own invulnerability. Who knows when a madman might decide to switch targets? After all, David Berkowitz, the real Son of Sam, had at first reportedly attacked only young women with long, dark hair before expanding the scope of his victims.

Undoubtedly, the fear was far more intense within the black community, given the profiles of the victims and the long, notorious national history of racial animosity and violence, of which Buffalo, like so many other American cities, had seen its share. Tuesday's reportage of the crime spree included a prominent article that quoted an unnamed but "well-known forensic psychiatrist" who gave a profile of the killer and a dire prediction in a bold headline: "Loner, Filled With Hatred, Will Strike Again." The psychiatrist theorized that the killings were the result of the man's "prodigious anger and hatred" toward blacks, that he would likely strike again because "the pathology lies in him," and that the murderer did not experience any guilt or remorse. Alongside the composite sketch was the doctor's analysis that the suspect was "sick" but "may well be mentally competent to stand trial, if the legal system ever catches up with him." The article stated that it would be difficult to catch the murderer, who might appear passive to friends and coworkers. According to the psychiatrist, "It's going to take a great deal of sleuthing."

Already there was talk of citizens banding together to help capture the killer. A group of about thirty black residents had formed under the leadership of Grady Davis, chairman of the Buffalo Soldiers Democratic Club, with the intention of acting as a support network that would operate in conjunction with police. Davis and members of the group had paid a visit to Commissioner Cunningham and Sheriff Kenneth Braun on Monday. The purpose of the support network, Davis explained, was as much to divert fear and hostility in the black community as it was to aid in capturing the murderer. Following the harassment at Glenn Dunn's funeral, Davis had received many calls from terrified residents who were convinced that the murders and the funeral desecration were the work of a splinter organization of the Ku Klux Klan. Several black residents had told Grady Davis of seeing "suspicious" whites in their community—which, given the climate, could have meant any white person they hadn't seen before. Some said they planned to buy firearms to protect themselves. Fearing that the situation could spiral out of control, Davis had formed the support network as a means of channeling the agitation toward a positive goal and allowing the community to take an active role alongside law enforcement. What he wanted to avoid, he said, was the possibility of citizens going off on their own and breaking the law out of fear.

Reverend Bennett Smith and Daniel Acker had meanwhile met with Fletcher Graves of the US Justice Department on Monday night and pressed their case for bringing in the FBI. On Tuesday afternoon, Chief Leo Donovan attended a meeting in Police Commissioner James Cunningham's office with Smith, Acker, and Graves, along with a few other black civil rights and religious leaders, an assistant district attorney, and US Attorney Richard Arcara. Donovan explained the scope of the investigation and the commitment of the police to solving the case. All vacations and personal leaves in the homicide bureau had been suspended until the killer was apprehended.

Commissioner Cunningham stated that he would welcome the assistance of the FBI, but that call rested with Richard Arcara, who said he would withhold his decision on formally requesting the aid of the Bureau until the following day, when he would meet privately with Fletcher Graves. Arcara had already briefed the Civil Rights Division of the Justice

Department in Washington on the series of events. The FBI offered the use of its facilities, including its laboratories in Washington, DC. As far as entering the case in an investigative capacity, however, the FBI had no jurisdiction unless a federal violation had been involved.

Covering the meeting in the next day's newspaper, the *Courier-Express* quoted Fletcher Graves's contention that the murders may have been part of "a conspiracy, even a national conspiracy to kill black leaders." He did not explain how the four .22 caliber victims could constitute "black leaders." Nevertheless, he had secured a promise from Commissioner Cunningham that the police department would provide round-the-clock protection for local black civil rights and religious figures if needed.

On the same day, October 1, the *Courier* ran an editorial welcoming the participation of the US Justice Department and Fletcher Graves, and praising the New York state police for taking a larger role in the investigation (which so far amounted to checking on tips from rural areas and offering the hypnosis services of a state trooper who happened to be a hypnotist). The piece criticized the three local police departments—Buffalo, Cheektowaga, and Niagara Falls—for a "fragmented" approach to the shootings and the "seeming sluggishness" in the early stages of the investigation. It ended with a call for all law enforcement agencies to "redouble their efforts to solve these horrible crimes."

Immediately following his Wednesday morning meeting with Fletcher Graves, US Attorney Richard Arcara directed the FBI to enter the ".22 Caliber Killer" investigation. Arcara and Graves had pinpointed a section of federal law that would permit FBI entry: civil rights legislation enacted twelve years before made it a federal crime—with a possible sentence of life imprisonment—for any person to interfere with the federally protected rights of other citizens on the basis of race. Per section 245 of Title 18, these rights included enjoyment of the services and facilities of "any lunch counter, soda fountain or other facility which serves the public and is principally engaged in selling food or beverages." Since two of the victims had been murdered in places that might be construed to fit this definition—Glenn Dunn in a grocery store parking lot and Harold Green at a Burger King—the killer had interfered with their right to public accommodations and had therefore violated their civil rights.

Federal investigators would now be working on the case with the state police, the three municipal police departments, and the district attorneys of Erie and Niagara counties.

Arcara stated that no one individual or agency would be in charge of the investigation; they would all collaborate, as they had in the past on stings and bank robberies. "The law enforcement agencies around here have worked together long enough over the years so we don't have that kind of a problem," Arcara said. "The problem of 'who is the leader.'"

On the heels of this announcement, Erie County District Attorney Edward Cosgrove called for a meeting in his office the next day, where all the various agencies involved would discuss the investigation.

While officials planned meetings and pondered conspiracy theories, Leo Donovan kept his focus on the nuts-and-bolts police work. He remained convinced, based on his experience and the evidence, that the .22 Caliber Killer was one man. He called for a small, unpublicized meeting of his own, one that he hoped might produce results.

They needed a better composite of the suspect. Frenchy Cook had been with Emanuel Thomas the night he was shot and had gotten a close-up, full-face view of the killer. He was the only living person they knew for certain who had. Donovan had Cook brought to headquarters on Wednesday night.

Detective Paul Delano had Frenchy go over his account of what happened again, which was identical to the statement he had already given. They showed him a photograph of a suspect—a man with some personal problems and criminal history who had been brought to the attention of police by one of his former coworkers because of his resemblance to the Cheektowaga composite. Frenchy thought the suspect maybe, possibly, looked somewhat like the man who killed Emanuel, but he just wasn't sure.

They questioned Frenchy about what the shooter looked like, encouraging him to recall specific details of the man's facial features. Using individual parts to build a portrait—images of different size and type noses, eyes, brows, and chins—they worked on constructing a likeness of the shooter, until finally they came up with a second composite.

It looked very much like the first one.

The key difference was that the suspect looked much younger.

The composite was sent to cartography, where a photograph could be made showing the suspect in a fishing hat, a crushed blue cap, and a watch cap.

Frenchy Cook was experiencing a great deal of distress and anxiety over the shooting. After completing the composite, he told officers that he was thinking of going to California out of fear for his own safety. Officers tried to reassure him and hoped that he would stay. His identification could be important if a suspect was arrested.

Leo Donovan was dismayed at the new composite, with its essential lack of difference and distinction from the first. Still, it was a starting point. What he wanted to do was have it shown to other witnesses as soon as possible to see if it jogged memories and, ideally, if any features could be added. One thing of which Donovan was now relatively certain was that the suspect was a younger man. If they could refine the composite with the recollections of other witnesses, it could be a key to identifying the killer, who, Donovan was convinced, was out there in the community somewhere. Despite all the floating theories about multiple gunmen and national conspiracies, Leo Donovan felt the truth lay much closer to home, in the guise of a single troubled white male, who was able to effortlessly blend into the community without drawing attention to himself—because he had done so all his life. The killings had started in Buffalo, and the solution would be found here as well.

For the second time in a week, Madona Gorney wanted to call the police. She had been following the case from the beginning, from the rainy Monday night the previous week when she had returned home from the Tops market and saw the news on TV about the shooting of Glenn Dunn, which she had missed by only minutes. She had, of course, contacted the police the following morning and spoken with officers that day. But now, after seeing the composite sketch in the newspaper and reading all the articles about the shooter possibly being a white man, she felt she should speak to them again. She kept thinking of that lone white man she had seen outside of Tops that night sitting on the railroad ties by the store entrance with the brown paper shopping bag at his feet. Of course, he didn't look anything like the composite. The man she saw had been far younger, and he wore glasses. Moreover, she hadn't sensed any malevolence about him. On the contrary, Madona thought he might be "slow," judging by the dull, blank look on his face.

Madona didn't have to call the police again. John Regan came to her home that Thursday, October 2. She told him about the young white male. He was twenty to twenty-two years of age. He had dirty-blond hair, parted on the left side. She described his eyeglasses—light metal frames—and his clothing—a blue nylon jacket, light-colored shirt, khaki pants, and light-colored sneakers. His face was fuller than the composite sketch in the newspaper. She mentioned his vacant look, the brown paper shopping bag. When Madona had passed him on her way into the store, he had just been sitting there, alone, as though he was waiting for someone. When she came out of the store, he was gone.

Detectives Al Williams and Frank Deubell went to Niagara Falls to have the witness in the Joseph McCoy shooting view the new composite. This witness said the suspect's jaw was not long or angular, as depicted in this new version. She said he was not wearing a hat when she saw him and that his hair was brownish blond, and was between his ears and shoulders in length. His nose was not large, but slender. She couldn't give any more specific facial details since she had only seen his face in profile. He was twenty-three to twenty-five years old, about five feet six or five feet seven, with a slender build. He wore dark pants, a blue- or black-checkered shirt, and some sort of canvas-type shoes.

"We are beginning to realize what we are looking for," announced Lieutenant Frederick Netzel to the media. "We slowly are trickling into one description; a younger guy with blond hair."

Dominic Punturiero, the key witness to the Harold Green shooting, had been summoned to Cheektowaga Police Headquarters to work with an artist on refining the original composite. The sketch had been based on his estimate of the shooter's age at thirty to thirty-five, but when the artist drew thirty-something-type age lines on the face, Dominic said the lines didn't belong, leading police to conclude that the suspect fit the early twenties age range. Dominic was unable to help when it came to hair color, since the shooter had been wearing a hat.

Chief Donovan held off on publicly releasing the new composite. It still looked too much like the first. He wanted to be as sure as possible this time. He hoped more witnesses would come forward, particularly any to the daylight shooting of Harold Green. Donovan shared the belief of his counterparts in Cheektowaga that there must be more witnesses, considering the time of day, sunny weather, and how crowded the area had been at the lunch hour.

Russell Sciabarrasi had contacted Cheektowaga police and gave his account of the strange man wearing "hunter-type" clothing who had sped away in the red station wagon. Russell had noticed some hair sticking out from the man's hat. He described the hair as sandy, brownish blond, more blondish than dark, and it looked stringy, as if it hadn't been washed in a while. The man had a light complexion and medium build. He described the man's fishing hat and clothing as also looking rather dirty. Russell recalled the red station wagon as a late 1960s model, probably a Ford. The license plate may have had the numbers 194.

This information seemed very pertinent. Russell's home was only a block or so away from the Burger King where Green had been shot.

Once again, via press conferences and the media, the police asked for the public's help. This time, they emphasized the need for specifics when it came to suspects: names, addresses, license plate numbers. They encouraged anyone who had been in the vicinity of the shootings to contact them with any information, no matter how insignificant it might seem.

While they were eager to hear from potential witnesses, they also hoped to discourage the obviously pointless leads on guys who just happened to have blond hair and might be a bit off-center. The police had enough to contend with just dealing with the folks who called in to report their grumpy neighbors, former spouses, and "weird" coworkers—all of which had to be checked out, just in case. Then there were the serial confessors, a peculiar though common phenomenon in high-profile murder cases where individuals would, against all reason and logic, call the police—sometimes persistently—to turn themselves in. Scattered incidents of harassment and/or vigilantism were an added drain. A white man complained to police that four young black men had pointed handguns at his car at the intersection of W. Delavan and Delaware and accused him of being the .22 Caliber Killer. According to the complainant, the men had held him at gunpoint for several minutes before speeding off.

Leo Donovan told the press that they still had no viable suspects or solid leads but he felt that one thing that had been accomplished was the prevention of additional killings, thanks to the police departments and the media. In the same straightforward manner in which he shared information with the press, he had also pointedly expressed his resentment of the criticisms leveled at police and the allegation that the investigation had gotten off to a "sluggish" start. Donovan countered that the murder probe had been intensive from the start and remained so. He noted that the Buffalo Homicide Bureau had an exemplary record, with arrests upwards of 80 percent and a 90 percent conviction rate. In a gesture of conciliation—and perhaps realizing that alienating the police department at the beginning of a major multiple homicide investigation that had already attracted national attention was not the smartest move—the *Courier-Express* made a 180-degree turn from their editorial of the previous day and ran a small piece praising "the dogged and devoted round-the-clock work of the Buffalo Homicide Squad, under the direction of Chief Leo Donovan."

———

Not surprisingly, Richard Arcara's dictate that no one would be in charge of the .22 Caliber Killer investigation caused problems from the start. As is often the case with leaderless collaborations, it wasn't panning out as the seamless team effort that Arcara had apparently envisioned. The Thursday meeting called by Erie County District Attorney Edward Cosgrove was attended by officials from all three police agencies as well as the state police, Erie and Niagara County Sheriff's Departments, the US Attorney, and Niagara County District Attorney's office. Donovan and Cosgrove clashed over the latter's call for a news blackout. Cosgrove wanted to appoint Joseph Mordino, an assistant DA and chief of the vio-lent felony offense bureau, as legal coordinator and spokesman. The idea was that Mordino would have sole responsibility for the release of any information regarding the progress of the investigation; police would not communicate directly with the media.

Donovan objected. If he felt that releasing information to the media would help solve the murders, he would do so. Nor was the idea well received by members of the media, who had waited for more than two hours outside the closed-door meeting and were informed of this deci-sion via a press release read by a secretary. Most of the meeting attendees left through a side door in order to avoid questions. When reporters were finally able to reach Joseph Mordino for comments, he had none, except to say, "I'm just getting information today and I'm in the process of digesting it." When they asked police officials about the meeting and the investiga-tion, they dutifully referred the reporters back to Mordino.

Of course, the reporters had their sources anyway, one of whom said that the meeting had consisted mostly of "drinking coffee, smoking ciga-rettes and shooting the bull," which the reporter duly noted in Friday's newspaper.

The news blackout was rescinded the next day. In lifting the gag order, Edward Cosgrove said that Joseph Mordino would continue as "legal coordinator" but that the police agencies could speak for themselves.

Cosgrove also nixed the hypnotist that Cheektowaga police wanted to bring in for their witness to the Harold Green shooting. Hypnotism had to be handled very carefully, he explained, performed only by a licensed physician with the highest credentials in such a practice. Otherwise, any suspect picked out of a lineup by a witness who had undergone hypnosis might not be admissible in court.

A remarkable, though erroneous, report on the .22 caliber killings made the national news on that Friday night, October 3. On the *CBS Evening News*, Walter Cronkite told viewers that Joseph Paul Franklin, wanted in six states for a series of sniper attacks on black men, was a top suspect in the Buffalo area shootings. "That's just not true," said Leo Donovan. It had already been discovered that Franklin had checked into a motel in Florence, Kentucky, on September 23, the day of the Green and Thomas murders, making his presence in Buffalo at the time of the shootings an impossibility. Donovan remained firm in his belief that the shooter was a local man.

To that end—and on the basis of tips and profiles of persons with known racist inclinations—detectives had questioned twelve potential suspects on Friday. None had panned out. Police were also in the process of checking out approximately 2,500 older model blue cars registered in Western New York in the hope of finding the one used by the killer in his escape after shooting Emanuel Thomas.

As the weekend progressed with no promising developments and the phone tips slowed considerably, Leo Donovan gave serious thought to an unconventional method of tracking the killer. The news director for TV station WKBW had previously approached Donovan about calling in the services of psychics. The station had vetted several with successful track records in helping solve homicide cases and had found two individuals in Chicago—one a psychic, the other an astrologer—who would waive their professional fees. If the chief would agree to meet with them, WKBW would cover their travel expenses.

Feeling it couldn't hurt—and well aware of the brick wall his detectives had hit in the investigation—Donovan agreed. The mystics flew into Buffalo and met with Donovan for several hours on Monday. They were taken to the crime scenes. They handled the victims' clothing and the .22 caliber cartridge cases. They told the police that the weapon used in the homicides was "potentially available" to them; it was buried in a plastic bag behind a maintenance building in a cemetery. The spot was marked with a brown or tan stone approximately eight inches wide, with two quartz-like stripes running through it. They gave the police a general area where the cemetery was located, adding that it was in a poor state of repair.

When reporters asked Donovan why he had agreed to such an unorthodox mode of investigation, he said, "We don't have much to go on in this case. I'm sorely in need of information and direction, and I'm receptive to any and all information that comes in, no matter what the source, if it eventually leads to the killer." Donovan added that the psychic, a woman, had made a drawing of the killer that "was not too far off" the new composite sketch police had been working on for a week.

Officers spent the following day searching various cemeteries. They found nothing. Following their meeting on Monday with Chief Donovan, the psychic and the astrologer had been eager to return to Chicago. "There's a criminal out there who is a murderer. If he knows we're on his trail, we can be knocked off too," the psychic explained. They asked the media not to use their names until they were out of town.

Thirteen days had passed since the thirty-six-hour killing spree that had taken four lives. Phone tips had all but dried up. The public furor and panic had subsided. With no real leads and nothing new to go on, detectives revisited the same ground, hoping to turn up anything that might have been overlooked. Officers who had been hurriedly added to the investigation at its height were quietly reassigned to other cases.

As the sun set on Tuesday, October 7, with the sudden, strange rash of murders now two weeks behind them, the people of Western New York perhaps slept a bit more peacefully beneath the waning crescent moon, never suspecting that the worst was yet to come.

Chapter 6
OCTOBER 8–19, 1980

ON THE NIGHT of Tuesday, October 7, Parler Edwards said good night to his lady friend, Alean Carr, at 7:45 and got in the driver's seat of his brown Checker Taxicab. He pulled away from Alean's house at 1102 Ellicott Street in Buffalo and drove off for another night of work. He mentioned to Alean that he had a "special" that night, meaning a regular customer, whom he was to pick up at the suburban Depew Train Station at 2:30 a.m. Though she gave it no thought at the time, Alean assumed that Parler would spend the earlier part of the night at the train and bus stations in downtown Buffalo, where he typically began his evening shifts in search of fares.

As Alean would later tell investigators, Parler was very predictable; a man with structured, routine ways and little variation in his schedule or habits. When Parler left her home on Tuesday night, Alean had every expectation of seeing him the next morning at 8:00 a.m., when he would pick her up to take her to work, and then again at 5:00, after her workday, to drive her home again, as he did every Tuesday through Saturday. Even with his late special fare at 2:30 a.m., Alean felt sure that Parler would be at her home on time the next morning, as always.

Parler W. Edwards was seventy-one years old. Though he was diabetic and had had a rather serious health crisis a year earlier that had landed him in the VA hospital for a time, he was a fit and strong man. He stayed active and controlled his diabetes with a strict diet and abstention from alcohol.

In more ways than one, Parler was a man who knew how to take care of himself. An army veteran and former factory worker, Parler stood five feet nine and a half inches tall and weighed 172 pounds. His gray-black hair was close-cropped with some frontal balding, and he sported a short, trim mustache. He came from the hardscrabble black neighborhoods of Buffalo's lower east side, and for some years had lived in the neighborhood northeast of downtown called the Fruit Belt, so named because of the orchards that had once graced the landscape and its longitudinal streets that bore names such as Grape, Orange, Lemon, and so on. Parler and his wife had raised six children here.

Alean Carr and Parler Edwards had been friends for thirty-five years. They had grown particularly close in the last five years, after Parler's wife died of cancer in 1975. Parler had retired from factory work the same year. Though he drew pensions from both the plant and the army, Parler had purchased a taxi almost immediately after his retirement and embarked on a late career as a cab driver, typically working seven days a week, and almost always at the same familiar haunts.

One of his steady stops was the Howard Johnson's restaurant at 4215 Genesee Street in Cheektowaga, across from the Buffalo International Airport. The staff at Howard Johnson's knew Parler as a regular customer. The overnight waitress saw him in the restaurant in the early morning hours of Wednesday, October 8, as did a fellow cabbie. Parler was sitting at the counter around 1:30 or 1:45 a.m. His cab was parked out front. Later, no one would recall exactly when he left.

At 2:25 a.m., the train from Chicago to Buffalo pulled into the Depew Train Station on Dick Road, three miles south of the airport. An elderly man named Robert Harley stepped off the train. As he entered the terminal, he was surprised to find that his ride home was not waiting for him.

That was odd. Robert and Parler Edwards had been friends for decades, going back to the Depression era. Robert made regular business trips to Chicago, and Parler always drove him to and from the train station. As Robert Harley would later tell police, Parler had driven him to the train station on October 3 for his trip to Chicago and they had arranged that Parler would pick him up upon his return on October 8. Parler had never been late, much less a no-show, which is why Robert waited for him at the station for quite some time—hours, in fact, during which he had repeatedly called Parler's home phone. It rang and rang.

As daylight dawned with still no sign of Parler and no answer by phone, Robert concluded that for whatever reason, Parler Edwards was not coming to pick him up. He called for another cab and went home.

————

At 8:20 a.m. on Wednesday, October 8, a woman named Patricia Krammer pulled into the parking lot of her employer at 195 Sugg Road in Cheektowaga. Patricia worked for Ecology and Environment, Inc., an environmental management firm located at Airport Industrial Estates, a lonely, secluded industrial complex that stood in the shadow of the Buffalo International Airport. Stepping out of her car, Patricia noticed red liquid under her driver's side door. Thinking that her car was leaking some type of fluid, Patricia took a closer look. She went to the passenger's side and saw more red liquid on the pavement and more in front of her car. This had obviously not come from her vehicle. It looked like someone had dumped red paint in the parking lot.

Patricia went inside to her office. After settling in at her desk, she went to her boss to let him know about the mess in the parking lot. She was telling him about the red paint stains when coworker John Rinaldo overheard and said that he too had noticed the strange crimson puddles when he had arrived for work that morning. To him, they had looked like blood. That seemed outrageous, though. This out-of-the-way industrial park was hardly the place where anyone would expect to find something so gruesome. There had to be another explanation.

A few employees went outside to look again. Deciding that it might actually be blood—if so, quite a large quantity—and feeling very ill at ease, they hurried inside to alert manager Donald Zangerle, who came out to look for himself.

Zangerle agreed: the viscous red puddles looked like blood. At 9:14 a.m., he called the Cheektowaga Police Department. Officers arrived within minutes and were shown the area in question, at the extreme south parking lot of the facility. The officers observed the pools. They also spotted what appeared to be several teeth and bone fragments. They immediately secured the scene and contacted their headquarters to request assistance of the detective bureau.

At 9:30 a.m., Captain George Kohl and Detective Ronald Selbert of the Cheektowaga police arrived, soon joined by three other detectives including Detective-Lieutenant Thomas Rowan, commanding officer of the Cheektowaga Police Department's Scientific Investigation Unit.

The partial remains spotted by the first officers at the scene were indeed human, leaving little doubt that the blood must be as well. There were six tooth fragments and seven bone fragments that Rowan identified as from a skull. In close vicinity were torn pieces of cloth, shattered plastic buttons, and a white tissue stained with blood.

Something terrible had happened here.

But to whom? And where was the victim?

The industrial park was surrounded by fields and shrubbery. Behind the parking lot, to the south, were two sets of Conrail railroad tracks running east and west. The blood and bone were at the southeastern edge of the lot, a little more than a thousand feet from the paved portion of Sugg Road. A drain located less than thirty feet from the railroad tracks was also surrounded by blood. The pavement bore bloody tire impressions trailing away from the site onto a gravel road that connected the parking lot with Sugg Road.

The Cheektowaga police immediately began collecting physical evidence and launched a search of the area, including the adjacent fields and railroad tracks. Judging by the carnage, they anticipated finding a body rather than a live victim. They found neither. But in a brush area just off the south edge of the parking lot, where it appeared that several branches had been broken off, they did find a three-quarter-inch metal pipe measuring about twenty inches long. The pipe was stained with blood and hair.

Detectives questioned the employees of Ecology and Environment. Patricia Krammer could add nothing beyond her discovery of the liquid under her car that she had initially mistaken for red paint. The first employee had arrived at 7:10 a.m. He had parked near the middle of the lot and did not see the red pools. The parking lot had been deserted with the exception of two cars belonging to employees of Ecology and

Environment that had been parked there for a number of weeks. He had opened the building as usual and had observed nothing out of the ordinary. John Rinaldo had arrived at work shortly after 8:00 a.m. and parked in his usual spot in the south side lot near the drain. He had backed his car up against the brush in the vicinity of the railroad tracks. Upon exiting his vehicle, he had noticed the red stains on the ground. He also noticed that the weeds at the edge of the parking lot had been knocked down somewhat, as if possibly a car had been stuck there.

None of the other employees had seen anything amiss prior to their two coworkers alerting them to the red substance in the lot. The Allen Bradley Company shared the same building and their employees were questioned as well, with the same results. No one had seen any suspicious persons or vehicles that morning. The night maintenance man for Allen Bradley hadn't noticed anyone or anything unusual the previous evening. One employee at Ecology and Environment told police that the day before, sometime between 1:00 and 2:00 p.m., she had looked out her office window and saw a white male walking on the railroad tracks. She described him as five feet ten to six feet, medium build, wearing a red-and-black–checkered wool jacket, carrying a club or baseball bat. She could only see him from the waist up because of the brush between the building and the tracks. He appeared to be always looking at the ground and walking back and forth, toward Sugg Road, and back in the opposite direction.

Ecology and Environment had a night shift, and police questioned the three employees who had worked the night of October 7. All three had parked close to the building some distance from where the blood and bone fragments were discovered the next morning, and had neither seen nor heard anything out of the ordinary. Because the area was so dark and isolated at night, the building alarm system was always activated when night shift employees were present, meaning that the alarm company had to be notified whenever someone entered or left the building. All employees had left either at or shortly after 11:00 p.m., locking and securing the building behind them. They advised police that the parking lot was not lit at night and that the area where the blood was found would have been extremely dark, and therefore they probably would not have seen anything on the ground if it had been there at the time. All of them felt, however, that they would have noticed any suspicious persons or vehicles in the area because that corner of the lot was usually vacant during the night. It seemed that no one had witnessed anything abnormal until the daylight discovery of the red puddles.

Employees at Airport Industrial Estates were not the only ones who found something out of place when they arrived for work that morning. At the Cayuga Road overpass of the Interstate 90 thruway in the town of Amherst, some two miles northwest of the industrial park and about a dozen miles from downtown Buffalo, two laborers from Ciminelli Construction had noticed something unusual, though not nearly as jolting. At least not at first.

At 7:10 a.m., workers spotted a taxicab parked in some brush on a thruway access road by their construction site. They thought little of it at first, although it was an unusual place for a car to be parked. The access road, which ran parallel to the thruway, was not an actual road, but rather had been cleared out just a few days prior to facilitate movement of equipment back and forth along the thruway at the construction site. The cab had not been there when they had left work the previous afternoon.

A few hours later, when the taxi still had not been moved, construction superintendent Thomas Czerwonka went down to take a closer look. The vehicle looked abandoned. He saw no one inside. Walking around to the rear, Czerwonka saw what looked like blood on the trunk and rear bumper. He reported it to his office and to a thruway toll collector, who called the New York state police.

Trooper E. J. Rybak responded to the scene at 10:20 a.m. He noted the vehicle, a 1979 brown Checker Taxicab, had apparently been abandoned just off the access road, approximately 120 feet down an embankment on the north side of the thruway at milepost 419. It appeared that the taxi had been driven off of the access road into an area of heavy brush and trees in an attempt to conceal it from view. Two small trees had been cut down and placed across the taxi. Rybak noticed the bloody marks on the back of the vehicle as well as a piece of clothing protruding from the trunk.

Investigator Thomas Rash of the New York State Police BCI—Bureau of Criminal Investigation—arrived at 10:50 a.m. Trooper Rash forced open the trunk of the taxi with a crowbar. He took one look and advised his fellow troopers to secure the scene and contact the Erie County medical examiner.

A deceased black male was lying on his left side in a fetal-like position, knees drawn up, with the upper portion of his body facing upward. His head was resting on the spare tire on the passenger's side with his feet toward the driver's side. He was fully dressed, wearing brown pants, a blue shirt, and a dark-blue jacket with black shoes and white socks. He wore a silver wristwatch and a gold wedding band on the ring finger of his left hand.

His body was awash in blood. There were severe traumatic injuries to his head and face. The right side of his skull was crushed. His lifeless right eye was open, pupil in mid-dilation. The left eye was perforated. A large gaping wound in his left chest extended from just above the nipple to his mid-abdominal region. The body was in full rigor, a frozen portrait of ghastly, violent death.

The taxicab registration belonged to Parler W. Edwards, 208 Grape Street, Buffalo. Vehicle registration did not prove the identity of the victim, of course, but it certainly gave police a starting point.

In addition to state troopers, Amherst police officers were also present, since the murdered man had been found within the town limits. The Buffalo Homicide Squad was contacted. Chief Leo Donovan and Detective John Ludtka arrived at the scene at 12:50 p.m., shortly after Medical Examiner Edmond Gicewicz.

Chief Donovan and Dr. Gicewicz examined the body. In addition to the massive injuries noted by state troopers, they discovered that several of the victim's teeth were broken off and missing. When the body was lifted from the trunk, a wallet was found directly beneath. It contained no money but was stuffed with personal papers and documents in the name of Parler Edwards, bolstering a tentative identification of the victim.

Word had filtered through that the Cheektowaga police were investigating the scene of an apparently violent assault—sans a body, but with tooth and bone fragments—in the parking lot of the nearby Airport Industrial Estates. Officers from all three municipalities, along with the New York state police, traveled the two miles back and forth between locations to make comparisons and determine if this was a single crime with two crime scenes: one where the victim had been killed, the other where the body had been left.

Among the state police present were Captain Henry F. "Hank" Williams, area commander of the BCI, and Raymond P. "Sam" Slade, one of the bureau's most noted senior investigators.

Less than twenty-four hours earlier, on the night of Tuesday, October 7, Hank Williams and Leo Donovan had attended a contentious three-hour meeting organized by BUILD (Build Unity, Independence, Liberty, and Dignity), an activist group dedicated to protecting and enriching the lives of black citizens. Held at the BUILD Town Hall on Main Street in Buffalo, the meeting had more than 250 people in attendance and included representatives from thirty-eight different community groups. Daniel Acker had been there along with other prominent local civil rights leaders and Councilman David Collins, who represented Buffalo's Masten District on the east side. Erie County undersheriff Thomas Higgins and Michael Lennon, executive assistant to District Attorney Edward Cosgrove, had also attended.

Though the overall atmosphere in the community appeared to have stabilized in the two weeks since the .22 caliber killings, the mood at the BUILD Town Hall gathering demonstrated that, at least in some quarters, suspicion, mistrust, fear, and anger abounded; much of it was directed against police, governmental authorities, the media, and even fellow black citizens who were not, in the opinion of the organizers, adequately uniting and giving the matter the serious attention that they should.

Ire against law enforcement and officialdom was palpable. Rebukes ran the gamut from frustration to outright acrimony. Veiled accusations of incompetence were voiced along with insinuations that the killer hadn't been apprehended yet because authorities just didn't care.

In response to speakers who declared that the .22 caliber killings were part of a plot to eliminate black people, an attendee named Aris Khan said, "It has been a plot for 400 years and the media have perpetrated the plot." Khan described himself as a Buffalonian who had an interest in bringing unity among black citizens. He called for a boycott against any black-supported community groups, churches, and businesses that had not sent representatives to the meeting.

The organizers had four proposals they wished law enforcement to adopt. The first was the promise of an intensive investigation into the Ku Klux Klan and other neo-Nazi groups in the Buffalo area. Several speakers asserted that if KKK members and neo-Nazis had been sent to jail years ago, as had happened during law enforcement efforts to quash the Black Panther Party in the late 1960s and early '70s, blacks would not be under threat from white hate groups. Despite the absence of any hard evidence, a conclusion had been reached by some that the murders were a coordinated effort by multiple assassins rather than the work of a rogue killer. The Reverend Charley H. Fisher, executive director of BUILD, referred to the murders as "part of an international conspiracy." Chief Donovan told attendees that the intelligence squad of the Buffalo Police Department had been conducting just such a probe in the wake of the killings but had not uncovered any ongoing activity of the KKK or other hate groups.

The second proposal called for the establishment of a people's commission on violence against black persons. The third, a task force made up of African American police officers that would, according to BUILD State of Affairs Committee Vice President Ernestine Robinson, go into action when black citizens came under attack by forces that continued to elude the law. The fourth proposal was to establish funding of anticrime programs that had formerly been funded by the US Law Enforcement Assistance Administration but had since been discontinued in Buffalo and other parts of the country.

The law enforcement officials agreed to discuss the proposals with their superiors. This did little to bolster faith, however, particularly for those who felt they were dealing with a long-standing, endemic problem in the system rather than a current crime wave.

The criticisms had irked District Attorney Edward Cosgrove. He knew the number of man-hours and the resources devoted to the investigation. Cosgrove also well knew both the competence of Leo Donovan's homicide squad and the inherent difficulties of solving the type of hit-and-run, stranger-on-stranger violence that the .22 caliber case presented. Fear and anger were understandable, but they were not the ideal platform for a solution. On the contrary, denunciations and hostile rhetoric could mobilize the community in all the wrong ways.

Edward C. Cosgrove, forty-six, was in his second term as district attorney of Erie County. Over the six years since his first election to the office in 1974, Cosgrove had amassed an impressive record. His office had successfully prosecuted a wide array of challenging cases, from organized crime homicides, to municipal corruption in the Town of Cheektowaga, to the investigation and prosecution of a particularly sensitive and high-profile death of a man named Richard Long at the hands of some off-duty Buffalo police officers. He had established an Organized Crime and Special Investigation Bureau (for sting operations), a Police Counsel Program, and an Arson Task Force, along with fending off attempts by the county legislature to reduce his personnel through budget cuts. Cosgrove had, in fact, increased the number of assistant district attorneys under his command from sixty-five to its current number of seventy-six. While the population had diminished, crime had not; the annual caseload had risen from 30,900 in 1974 to 41,000 in 1979. The conviction rate under Cosgrove could be described as excellent.

Always priding himself on being a man of law and order, Ed Cosgrove had spent two years as a special agent in the FBI following his graduation from Georgetown University Law School in 1959 before returning to hometown Buffalo to enter private law practice. A group of New York congressmen had nominated District Attorney Cosgrove to President Jimmy Carter for director of the FBI in 1977, the same year he had been selected Outstanding Citizen by the *Buffalo Evening News*, an honor that was all the more significant considering Cosgrove was not a man who went out of his way to engage with the press. His most frequent public comment on investigations was the proverbial "no comment." He had an aversion to leaks, particularly of misinformation and what he viewed as too much information. As district attorney, he understood public interest in high-profile cases and tried to steer a steady course along the sometimes ambiguous line between the public's right to know and the need for confidentiality.

Cosgrove was still mulling the feedback he'd been given from the previous night's BUILD meeting when he learned of the gruesome discoveries in Amherst and Cheektowaga. From what he was being told, the circumstances of this crime were entirely different from the shootings.

Still, they had another murdered black man in Erie County; one who had apparently suffered a particularly violent death. And Edward Cosgrove understood immediately, as did Captain Williams and Chief Donovan and all of their colleagues, how explosive the news of this latest murder could be.

This time he would not send an assistant, or wait for reports from police, or allow others to inform him of their observations or developments. Ed Cosgrove left his office in downtown Buffalo and drove to the scene.

———

The body was taken to the Erie County Morgue, accompanied by two BCI investigators. State troopers and Amherst police took possession of the cab and had it towed to the state police barracks for processing while dozens of officers and technicians combed both crime scenes—including the route in between the two locations—searching, documenting, collecting evidence and anything that *might* be evidence.

The two state police investigators who accompanied the body to the morgue made a cursory examination of the victim that included an inventory of items on his person and in the wallet that had been found underneath him in the trunk of the cab. In addition to the gold wedding band and blood-soaked silver wristwatch that had been noted at the scene, the deceased also wore a gold ring on his right ring finger. In his left front pants pocket, there was $74.00 in cash—$44.00 in American currency and $30.00 in Canadian bills, the latter clasped in a metal money clip. An additional $20.00 (American), soaked in blood and wrapped in an Erie County Savings Bank calendar, was found in his left shirt pocket.

The wallet was stuffed with documents. In addition to a standard driver license, a taxicab driver license, and vehicle registrations for the 1979 Checker Taxicab—all in the name of Parler W. Edwards—there were check stubs, bank receipts, credit cards, a Marine Midland Bank cash card, a VA Patient Data Card, membership and discount cards, a Social Security plate (again, all in the name of Parler W. Edwards), and a variety of business cards from local businesses, including three different attorneys in downtown Buffalo. There were also several scraps of paper with names and phone numbers written on them.

An autopsy was scheduled for 5:00 p.m. Meanwhile, two state police investigators were sent to 208 Grape Street in an effort to make a positive identification of the victim and notify next of kin. They found no one at home. Leo Donovan and Detective John Ludtka had proceeded to the morgue after visiting the crime scene in Cheektowaga. Ludtka began calling the phone numbers found in the wallet and was able to reach a man who identified himself as a friend of Parler Edwards. He agreed to try to contact the family. At around 4:00 p.m., two of Parler Edwards's adult children, a son and a daughter, and one of his brothers, arrived at the Grape Street address. The state police informed them of the death of Parler Edwards. The family members would be taken to the morgue to make a positive identification of the body following the autopsy.

Parler Edwards had been stabbed at least seven times. Each of these wounds had been made with a very sharp knife and all were rendered with remarkable force. He had one stab wound in the upper left side of his back, one inch left of center, that measured at least five and a half inches deep, extending into his chest cavity and piercing the left lobe of his lung all the way through. A knife had been thrust once in the left side of his neck, deep enough to incise the underlying bone. Four stab wounds were found on the top of his head, one on the right and three in his left scalp, all four cutting into the bones of the skull. Associate Medical Examiner Dr. Catherine Lloyd noted that the three stab wounds on the left side of Edwards's head were close together and overlay the blunt trauma fractures.

This meant that the knife wounds had been inflicted after the bludgeoning.

Edwards had sustained eight wounds with a blunt instrument to his head and face, all of which had been administered with savage force. Two blows on the back of his head—one in the midline and another behind his right ear—had both penetrated the underlying bone, shattering some of it to particles. There was a missing triangular section of skull through which brain fragments protruded. A massive strike on the right side of his forehead had crushed that part of his skull. He had been hit again next to his right eye, while another blow had shattered the bridge of his nose. There were two injuries on the left side of his face, one just above his eyelid, the other perforating his left eye. A fierce blow to his mouth had knocked out several teeth by the roots.

Edwards had defensive wounds on both of his upper limbs. There were abrasions on the backs of several of his fingers, mainly on his right hand. A small knife wound was present at the tip of his right thumb.

There were contusions on his lips and right cheek, abrasions on both buttocks. His stomach contained a large quantity of partly digested food.

The largest and most distinctive wound on the body was the enormous, gaping laceration on the left side of his chest. Designated as knife wound #7 by the ME, the jagged gash was at least five and a half inches long and one and a half inches wide, exposing part of the left lung. When the jagged edges were brought together, it appeared the wound could have been caused by three separate, overlying thrusts of a knife. Three of his ribs had been excised and a portion of one rib was missing. The wound extended as far as the heart. The pericardium had been cut on the left side with a single laceration. Two clean cuts had been made through the aorta. The pulmonary artery and veins had been incised. Only part of the heart remained; the rest was gone. This last wound had been inflicted postmortem, apparently with the express purpose of removing the heart.

Cause of death was exsanguination—blood loss due to multiple injuries.

The director of dentistry for the Erie County Medical Center examined the mouth and jaws of the victim. In total, there were seven teeth missing, which he compared to the six tooth fragments recovered in the parking lot. He concluded, "Beyond any reasonable doubt, that the specimens are the fragments of teeth from the mouth of Parler Edwards." A forensic anthropologist confirmed soon after that the recovered pieces of bone matched the fractures in the victim's head, positively identifying them as "outer table skull fragments of the skull of Parler Edwards."

Present at the autopsy were seven police officers from four different agencies. The cab and body had been found on state thruway property in the town of Amherst, thus involving both the New York state police and Amherst Police Department. The site of the attack in the parking lot of Airport Industrial Estates was within the town limits of Cheektowaga. The Buffalo Police Department had been alerted because of the ongoing investigation of the .22 caliber killings. Leo Donovan and two of his homicide detectives attended the autopsy. Despite the vast dissimilarity between this murder and the shootings, there was still the similarity— or at least pseudo-similarity—of the victim. From the moment of the discovery of the cab and body, a decision had been made that all four police agencies would collaborate on this investigation. Dozens of officers were scouring the crime scenes for recovery of evidence, now to include a search for the victim's heart.

Among the law enforcement at the autopsy was Detective-Lieutenant Thomas Rowan of the Cheektowaga Police. Rowan would long remember the sense of gravitas and foreboding that hung over the room. As he recalled it, "We had all been at many autopsies by that time in our careers, more so Leo Donovan, who had certainly attended hundreds. But this was so atypical, so beyond the pale of anything we had encountered before. The gravity of what we were dealing with was not lost on anybody.

"It's easy to shoot somebody. It's more difficult to stab someone. When it comes to dismemberment, it takes someone who is psychologically on the evil side of the spectrum, way on the other side of the bell curve of types of offenders. We all understood the impact of having a person or persons out there capable of doing something like this. There was a heavy pall over the room, for both the brutality that had been inflicted on this man, and also because we all understood immediately what the future was looking like."

One of the looming questions, of course, was whether this murder was connected to the .22 caliber killings. If so, it represented an escalation in violence that was as bewildering to contemplate as it was horrifying. "We couldn't dismiss any possibilities at this point. Until we learned what the physical evidence would show, we couldn't rule out anything." Physical evidence—both the collection and scientific analysis of it—was Rowan's area of expertise. While other investigators persuaded witnesses and suspects to speak, Rowan coaxed a voice out of forensic evidence.

Though he was only twenty-eight years old, Tom Rowan had attained the rank of commanding officer of his department's scientific investigation unit. He had joined the Cheektowaga police in 1974, two years after earning his bachelor's degree in imaging technology from the Brooks Institute in Santa Barbara, California. His plan had been to work for the NASA Space Program, as many of his fellow grads had done. Instead, he had returned to his hometown and put his considerable training and skills to work in law enforcement. Having a scientific background had worked to his benefit at a time when crime scene processing was on the cusp of incorporating more advanced technologies. Few police officers had been trained in scientific methodologies, and Rowan's unique background and meticulous adherence to scientific procedures had allowed him to advance rapidly through the ranks. He was frequently called in to collaborate on complex cases with his science-oriented colleagues at the Central Police Services Lab in Buffalo. He was already well familiar with the .22 caliber investigation since he had processed the crime scene of the Harold Green shooting, which had occurred in Cheektowaga.

Prior to coming to the morgue late that afternoon, Tom Rowan had spent the day overseeing the collection and handling of evidence at the Airport Industrial Estates crime scene and had assisted Detective-Lieutenant Michael Melton, his close colleague and counterpart in the Amherst Police Department, at the site of the cab. A massive amount of material had already been collected: blood samples, fingerprints, tire and shoe impressions, and every bit of debris within a wide radius of both locations. At Rowan's direction, portions of the parking lot stained with forensic evidence were jackhammered out. He and Detective Melton had photographed both scenes, as had a state trooper. The stomach contents of Parler Edwards obtained at the autopsy were turned over to him for analysis.

Tom Rowan returned to his lab where he spent a long night—the first of many, as it turned out—examining evidence, listening for the story it would tell him.

His colleagues were meanwhile listening to what the people closest to Parler Edwards could tell them. Parler's family had led them to his close friend Alean Carr, who gave them an account of the perfectly routine evening she and Parler had spent the night before, his habits, and his schedule. Though Parler lived at his Grape Street address, he spent most of his nonworking time with Alean, mainly at her home. Parler's schedule really never wavered, she said. He drove his cab all day while she was at work, then they would have dinner together at her house, watch the TV news, and then Parler would go out to work again. He typically worked till midnight and would always tell Alean if he had a special fare that would keep him out later, as had been the case the previous night. Parler only had two specials; one was a lady who lived in the suburbs, the other was Robert Harley, the retired businessman who made regular trips to Chicago.

Alean described her social life with Parler as very simple, mostly just leisurely rides in his cab on the rare occasions he took a day off. Sometimes they would take a drive to Fort Erie, Canada, and eat at a Chinese restaurant or visit his relatives. Parler was tight with his money, Alean said, but he would buy gifts for special occasions such as birthdays or Christmas. He really didn't talk about his financial affairs, but Alean believed he was receiving two or three monthly checks from the army, including a disability pension. He also collected a pension from the plant in North Buffalo in addition to his Social Security and whatever he earned as a cab driver. She mentioned that he usually kept large amounts of money on him, anywhere from $700 to $800, and he was in the practice of cashing checks for fares and friends.

Alean could offer no suspects or leads for the murder. She described Parler as a very good and decent man, very dependable, a wonderful father who was close to his children. According to Alean, there had been no change in Parler's lifestyle or behavior in the weeks leading up to his murder. Tuesday, October 7, had been like any other day.

Parler Edwards did seem to have a very patterned life. Police spoke with other cabbies, skycaps, and employees at the depots and at the airport, all the locations Alean had mentioned. A number of them had seen Parler in his cab at various times throughout the night in the usual places. One cabbie who had been parked behind him alongside the Greyhound bus terminal in downtown Buffalo recalled that Parler got a fare at about 9:15 p.m. that may have been one or two passengers, possibly white, but all he could remember for sure was a tan suitcase. When asked how he could recall the color of the suitcase but not the number or race of the riders, he replied that he judged fares as good or bad tippers on whether they did or didn't have luggage.

No one had noticed Parler pick up any suspicious-looking fares. It was also mentioned to investigators that Parler was not the type to take chances that way. Parler Edwards was very streetwise, cautious, and savvy—not the sort to let his guard down. Moreover, he carried a heavy lead pipe under the front seat of his cab for protection. Parler's kids had also mentioned the lead pipe that their father kept in his cab. They said it sometimes rolled out from beneath the driver's seat onto the floor.

Parler's special fare, Robert Harley, likewise said that his longtime friend was a streetwise guy and nobody's fool. Like Alean, he stressed that Parler was a good and honest man, a nondrinker, and he could think of no one who would want to harm him. Police interviewed the overnight crew at the Depew Train Station, who confirmed the arrival of the train from Chicago at 2:25 a.m. as well as Robert Harley's account that he had waited at the station for hours. No one at the station had seen Parler Edwards, however. He apparently never made it there.

The victim had such regular habits that police were quickly able to trace virtually all of his whereabouts during his final hours—up until 1:45 a.m., when he had last been seen at the Howard Johnson's restaurant across from the airport, three miles away from where he was supposed to pick up his special fare. Somehow, someway, in that short time span and distance, Parler Edwards had taken a wrong turn and had met up with a person or persons who were not a part of his regular routine.

Or were they?

As orderly as Parler's life appeared to be, his taxicab was not; it was loaded with a mishmash of papers and various items. It would take investigators some time to examine and catalogue all of it, but one thing that had caught their attention immediately was a stack of betting slips that looked like those used in the numbers game, or numbers racket, the illegal underground lottery. A record check at the Buffalo Police Department showed that Parler Edwards had been arrested eight times. Five of those arrests were for assault and had occurred between 1932 and 1966. His most recent arrests had been in July 1969, first for facilitation of gambling and later the same month for promotion of gambling in the first degree and possession of gambling records.

Numbers had been around in poor urban neighborhoods almost since the dawn of poor urban neighborhoods. The game predated state lotteries and worked much like them, but with the advantage of higher payouts and no taxes. Bettors chose three numbers and wagered small amounts of money. The winning numbers were determined by either a drawing or some agreed-upon combination, like the last three digits of the next day's stock market close or total handle at a racetrack. Numbers games were sometimes called the "Italian lottery" because they were ultimately under mob control. The people who took the bets and delivered the payoffs were called numbers runners. Even after the advent of state lotteries, numbers rackets were still in operation throughout the country, and were very lucrative for the people who ran them.

Alean Carr acknowledged to police that Parler had been arrested for his involvement in gambling in 1969 and said that his wife had been very upset with him over it. As far as Alean knew, Parler had gotten out of numbers at that time and had not been involved since. He wasn't engaged in any sort of illicit activity, to the best of her knowledge, although Alean did say that Parler was very tight-lipped about his personal affairs, particularly anything related to his finances.

His friend Robert Harley thought that driving a cab was really more of a hobby for Parler. His grown children agreed. They said their father didn't need the money, that the cabbie work just gave him something to do in his retirement.

Parler had begun driving a cab following the 1975 death of his wife. Could he also have resumed his role in the numbers racket? If so, he certainly wouldn't be the first man with a sideline he kept secret.

On the surface, Parler Edwards seemed much like any other elderly widower, leading a quiet, uneventful life centered around family and long-standing friendships. His manner of death seemed totally at odds with his lifestyle. But the discoveries in his cab and his past could be significant.

Police also learned that Parler always carried three wallets. Only one had been found so far, placed curiously—or perhaps strategically—underneath his dead body. Whoever killed him obviously hadn't been concerned with concealing his identity, nor were they interested in taking his jewelry or the cash in his pockets. The large amount of money he reportedly carried with him had so far not been found.

Whatever the motive, he had not simply been killed, but overkilled.

As Wednesday, October 8, drew to a close, investigators had no suspects, but they did have some questions that would require further digging. In the meantime, they were guarded about releasing details of Parler's death to the public. A brief newspaper article appeared that day stating that an unidentified black man, thought to be a cab driver, had been found dead in the trunk of a car. Police didn't divulge the manner of death or the mutilation, but they did say there was no immediate indication of a connection with the .22 caliber killings. So the grisly murder of Parler Edwards did not cause or exacerbate panic.

Not at first.

———

Tonawanda is another suburb of Buffalo, located directly north of the city, bordered on the east by the Amherst area and on the west by the Niagara River. At 4:29 a.m. on Thursday, October 9, a Tonawanda police lieutenant on routine patrol noticed what looked like a person lying in the parking lot of a boat launch facility off of River Road at the foot of Sheridan Drive. Lieutenant Leroy Lieder stopped his vehicle and got out to take a closer look. Shining his flashlight, he saw a deceased black male lying in a large pool of blood. Lieder radioed for assistance.

A group of Tonawanda police officers responded immediately and secured the scene. The victim, fully clothed, lay on his back in a slightly raised area of the parking lot among some garbage cans. His shirt was drenched with blood. There were gaping wounds in his throat, a long open wound on the left side of his chest. He had lost a massive amount of blood; the pool surrounding him extended north of the body and created a bloody path almost thirty feet long, at the end of which was found a gold wristwatch with a broken band. Six feet away from the body, in the same direction, there was a six-inch buck knife and, further on, a piece of rope. There were bloody tire impressions on the pavement.

The small boat launch facility was located approximately seven miles from downtown Buffalo. The parking lot was bordered on the south by the Tonawanda Water Treatment Plant and on the north by the Erie County Treatment Plan. At the edge of the lot were docks entering directly into the Niagara River. Located within the parking area was a building that housed Walt's Bait Shop. The Huntley Power Plant sat at the river's edge a short distance away on River Road. The area was otherwise isolated, with no homes or businesses nearby. The victim lay in the southeast corner of the lot, approximately fifty feet away from the water treatment plant fence, near some trees, foliage, and five twenty-gallon garbage cans. No wallet or identification was found in his clothing or in the vicinity.

The medical examiner was called. Despite the predawn hour, an assistant district attorney also reported to the scene almost immediately. Other officials and other police agencies would soon follow. Tonawanda had now joined the list of municipalities in Western New York with a gruesome murder of a black male.

Drawings and photographs were made of the scene. It was noted that the boat launch facility was about eleven miles from the site where the body of Parler Edwards had been discovered only hours before. Both bodies had been found in very close proximity to thruway entrance ramps.

The medical examiner made a preliminary examination of the victim before he was taken to the Erie County Morgue, where the body was tagged as a John Doe. Tonawanda police meanwhile spoke with the owner of Walt's Bait Shop, who lived on the premises. The man said he had been out for the evening, arriving home about 4:15 a.m., and he hadn't seen or heard anything out of the ordinary. Two employees of the water treatment plant working the graveyard shift said much the same, though both periodically had to go outside to check machines and log readings at the plant and pump station. The only unusual occurrence had been a car full of giggling teenagers that had raced up to the water's edge at about 11:30 p.m.—tires had squealed, and then the car had backed up and did circles and fishtails near the ramp at the docks before speeding off. At about the same time, however, one of the employees had noticed a white car in the vicinity of the bait shop and a station wagon parked toward the barricade fence, facing the Huntley Plant. Another unidentified car parked next to this car. He had seen the same three vehicles in the parking lot for the past three nights.

At the morgue, a Buffalo police officer took a set of fingerprints of the deceased black male, which were turned over to the evidence unit. A search of the fingerprint file resulted in a positive match to the prints of one Ernest Jones, DOB 3/13/40, of 326 South Park Avenue, Buffalo.

Of the seven law enforcement officers present at the autopsy, four had attended the postmortem of Parler Edwards the evening before: Chief Leo Donovan, Tom Rowan, Michael Melton, and Raymond Motyka of the state police. They were now joined by Detective John Ludtka of Buffalo Homicide, who had accompanied Donovan to the Edwards's crime scenes, and two detectives from the Tonawanda police. For half the assembled lawmen and for Associate Chief Medical Examiner Catherine Lloyd, the autopsy was a surreal repeat of the day before. The victim was a smaller man, five feet three, and weighed 143 pounds. His head, neck, and upper limbs were covered with dried blood. His eyes protruded, pupils in mid-dilation. Blood filled his nose and both ears. He had severe injuries to his head and chest.

Ernest Jones had five incised wounds. Three of these were major penetrating gashes across his throat and neck that had severed both his right jugular vein and his left carotid artery. A large gaping V-shaped slash measured four and a half inches in length and exposed his lacerated larynx. One of the wounds was so deep it had incised the vertebra. His throat had not just been cut—it was mangled. A great deal of blood surrounded all of the neck wounds. There was a superficial horizontal wound beneath his chin that was one inch long and directly in the midline, as if someone had taunted him with a throat slashing before actually doing the job.

The largest incised wound was in his chest. Jagged and open, it was eight inches long with a two-inch-wide gape. His sternum had been cut through. The great vessels to the heart had been neatly cut. His heart was gone. As with Parler Edwards, there was very little blood found in the chest or around the wound, indicating the heart had been removed after death had occurred.

There was a stab wound on the lower left side of his neck and another above the massive chest incision. He had also been stabbed twice in the left side of his back and once behind his left ear. There were two blunt trauma injuries on the back of his head, both on the right side, and two peculiar puncture marks in his scalp. The head wounds were penetrating but not as extreme as those that had been inflicted on Parler Edwards. Ernest Jones had died as a result of blood loss from the massive mutilation of his throat.

Like Edwards, Ernest Jones had several defensive wounds on the backs of the fingers on his right hand. He also had a large amount of undigested food in his stomach. Jewelry and some money ($36.00 in cash) were found on him.

The similarities would not end there.

Shortly before 1:30 p.m., Detectives Frank Deubell and Melvin Lobbett were dispatched to the victim's home. They requested that Ernest Jones's wife and eighteen-year-old son accompany them to the morgue. The body had been cleaned and prepared for viewing as well as possible, with the sheet pulled up over the neck. Mrs. Jones was anguished and inconsolable. She sobbed and clung to her husband's body on the gurney until finally some of the officers gently pulled her away.

She and Ernest had been married for twenty-two years, she told investigators. They had seven children ranging in age from thirteen to twenty-one. The last time she saw her husband alive was at 8:00 the night before, when he had left for work.

Ernest Jones was a cab driver.

———

As with the Parler Edwards crime scenes, police were searching a wide area in and around the boat launch facility, collecting every stray item. Aside from the knife and gold wristwatch that had been recovered within a few feet of the body, they weren't finding anything of significance. According to his wife, Ernest Jones had left home the night before in his taxi. Where was it now?

Detectives Al Williams and John Montondo of Buffalo Homicide were sent to interview the owners and employees of Broadway Cab Company. The owner confirmed that Ernest Jones, whose nickname was Shorty, drove cab #56. Shorty had been driving for him for about six months, he said, and he drove cab #56 exclusively. Shorty leased the cab from him for $35.00 per day and took it home with him. Though the taxi was owned by the company, Shorty had it in his possession all the time and no other cabbies drove it. Cab #56 was a maroon 1976 Chevrolet with a black vinyl top and "BROADWAY LIVERY" decals on both front doors. Williams and Montondo immediately put out a pick-up and hold-for-homicide with the vehicle description and plate number.

According to the owners, Jones did not call in when working or after trips, but it was customary for him to receive calls from the cabstand. The dispatcher on the 4:00 p.m. to midnight shift said they had received several calls for Jones last night, which was typical. Shorty Jones had a lot of specials, callers requesting cab #56 specifically. Williams and Montondo also spoke with the dispatcher on the midnight to 8:00 a.m. shift who said that she too had received a number of calls for cab #56. She had informed the callers that Jones was not working because his name was not on the running sheet. However, she did put the calls out to him anyway in case he was on the air. Neither of the dispatchers had heard from Jones at all during their shifts, although one thought he might've said hello to her, via the radio, when she began her shift. Drivers often did that, but she couldn't remember for sure if Shorty had done so the previous night.

Al Williams and John Montondo were on their way back to headquarters when they heard over the police radio that the cab had been found. At 2:40 p.m., a patrolman from precinct 5 had responded to a complaint call of an abandoned vehicle on Potomac Avenue, a residential neighborhood on the west side of Buffalo. The officer had discovered the red taxi parked at the curb in front of 96 Potomac in a no parking zone. Williams radioed back with instructions to keep everyone away from the cab and not to touch it.

Two officers from precinct 5 were on the scene when Detectives Williams and Montondo arrived minutes later. Al Williams made a visual inspection of the cab while his partner started canvassing the nearby houses.

Potomac Avenue was a one-way street in a working-class, largely Italian neighborhood. The location was a block away from Niagara Street and the adjacent thruway that ran parallel to the Niagara River. It was

3.5 miles from where Shorty Jones's body had been found. Potomac had alternate parking, and the cab had been left on the south side of the street, where no parking was allowed on Thursdays. It was the only vehicle parked on that side.

All four doors of the cab were shut but unlocked. On the metal portions of the exterior driver's side of the car, both front and rear, were marks that appeared to be blood. There was blood on both the front driver side and front passenger side windows. Peering into the cab, Williams saw blood on the metal part of the shield that separated the front and rear seats. There were spots of blood on a cushion in the driver's seat and on the door handle. Hand- and fingerprints were visible on the windows. A set of keys—they looked like car keys—were in the front passenger seat. The meter had registered $9.45.

In a repeat of the previous day, police from different agencies converged on quiet Potomac Avenue to investigate a vicious slaying with dual crime scenes. Photos were taken by both the Buffalo and state police photographers. Chief Leo Donovan ordered that the cab should be towed to the Tonawanda Police Department and touched as little as possible in the process. The tow truck driver hooked it from the rear to avoid having to go inside the vehicle to release the gear lever from the parked position.

Several residents on Potomac had noticed the cab at various times throughout the morning, conspicuous because it was on the no parking side of the street. Its earliest sighting had been around 5:30 a.m. by a man leaving for work. No one had seen who parked it or when. The complaint call about the abandoned cab had come from an anonymous elderly male.

Reporters had been prodding police for information since the discovery of Parler Edwards's body the day before. Officials who wanted to keep the specific details under wraps knew immediately that with the murder of Shorty Jones—another black cab driver found with his heart cut out, killed just a day later—keeping the press at bay would be impossible. It wouldn't be advisable, either. Faced with the prospect of a savage killer on the loose who specialized in mutilation and dismemberment, no one wanted to be accused of withholding vital information from the public about the danger that lurked.

In an uncharacteristic move, Edward Cosgrove had held a press conference at 3:00 p.m. the day before in the Amherst Town Hall, during which he had divulged a number of details about the murdered man found in the trunk of the taxicab. Without giving the victim's name, because the family hadn't yet been notified, Cosgrove said that the victim had been brutally beaten about the head but had not been shot. The murder did not appear to be linked to the .22 caliber killings. He confirmed that the victim had "massive" injuries to the head and face; that he had been beaten in the Cheektowaga parking lot, where police had found bloodstains, teeth, pieces of bone, and human tissue; and that the body, found in the trunk of the cab, had been dumped by the thruway in Amherst. He said there was a "deep, long slash to the left breast," but that it appeared the head injuries were the cause of death. He did not mention the removal of the heart.

Stressing that the victim had not been shot, Cosgrove said that all of the fatal injuries were apparently inflicted by a blunt instrument and that the victim had been dead a relatively short time before the body was discovered. He added that robbery appeared to be the motive. The Amherst and Cheektowaga police departments would conduct the investigation, he said, with Captain Henry Williams of the state police coordinating and Buffalo Homicide Chief Leo Donovan assisting. Cosgrove also informed the press that he himself would be the sole spokesman for information relating to the case, and he'd make himself available day or night.

According to an article in the October 9 morning edition of the *Courier-Express*—printed before the discovery of the second cabbie murder—Ed Cosgrove spent the first twenty minutes of the press conference conveying details of the crime and investigation and another twenty minutes criticizing "segments of the media, some politicians and other self-posturing individuals" for suggesting that local law enforcement was incapable of handling the .22 caliber investigation. "I am personally and professionally insulted when some people suggest that our police aren't doing their jobs," Cosgrove stated. "A terrible disservice is done to the community when self-posturing, divisive, selfish ideas are tossed around for self-serving purposes. The police don't deserve it, blacks don't deserve it and whites don't deserve it." Though he declined to mention names, he acknowledged that some of the individuals to whom he was referring were speakers at Tuesday night's BUILD meeting. He dismissed the suggestion that the murders were connected to the KKK or similar white supremacist groups.

Edward Cosgrove now found himself in the unenviable position of having to release some very frightening details of these two grotesque murders—the press had their ways and sources and would find out anyway, particularly with the number of persons privy to the crime scenes and those with glimpses of information—and he had to do so without instilling further fear. The truth, bad as it was, seemed preferable to the rumors and conjecture that could crop up if the public perceived a lack of candor. Better to reveal the grim facts now while officials were still a step ahead of the rumor mill.

The key here was to simultaneously impart a measure of reassurance for the public, some clear sign that law enforcement was quite literally on the case (or cases), responding en masse, and on the road to making arrests. He called a press conference for that morning. Prior to speaking to the media, Cosgrove spoke extensively with others—heads of local law enforcement, the FBI, and David Brown, chief counsel to New York Governor Hugh Carey. Some key decisions and plans were made.

In the first of four press conferences he would hold in the hallway outside his office that day, Edward Cosgrove confirmed that the body of another murdered black man had been found by the Niagara River and that there were definite links between this homicide and the murder of Parler Edwards the day before. He revealed that the hearts of both victims had been cut out, and in both instances the heart removal appeared to have been done "by someone who knew what they were doing," although not necessarily medically trained; perhaps someone "with a knowledge of hunting." The weapon that was used to make what Cosgrove described as the long horizontal slashes on the chests of the victims had not yet been recovered, nor had the missing hearts.

"The four September .22 caliber murders are not related to the two homicides uncovered yesterday and today," he said. "There is no evidence in any way to connect them." Noting the vast differences, Cosgrove said he didn't believe that the mutilation murders were the work of the .22 Caliber Killer changing his modus operandi. These latest murders appeared "to have been the work of a deranged, mentally disturbed person," he said, "although this is merely conjecture on my part." The only similarity was that all six victims were black males. He added that there was no evidence of "Ku Klux Klan or Neo-Nazi involvement" in any of the deaths. At most, he thought, "the .22 Caliber Killer may have set off some deranged person."

Many in law enforcement agreed that the shootings and cabbie murders were not connected. For one thing, multiple weapons had been used on Edwards and Jones. Multiple weapons in a street slaying almost invariably meant multiple assailants. There were also a number of police who thought the .22 Caliber Killer had left the area by now.

Cosgrove continued releasing information throughout the day. He told the assembled media he had requested that the FBI take a more active role in the investigation and was awaiting word from Washington. (A special agent from the Buffalo FBI office meanwhile told reporters that the agency was analyzing all of the cases for possible violations of civil rights laws, which he said was still a key requisite for full FBI involvement.) Governor Carey had pledged the full cooperation of the state police. The governor had ordered the dispatch of BCI personnel from around the state to Western New York, including five black officers.

The major announcement was the establishment of a "command post" in the office of the district attorney. A task force of more than a hundred police officers chosen from the various agencies had been consolidated into an investigative team, of which the district attorney would be in charge. "I've assumed control of this investigation," Cosgrove said. "I've taken the responsibility of carrying this forward. The investigation of all these homicides is going to be conducted by me, with the New York state police directing, with the assistance of all the police departments involved." The authority for this had come directly from Governor Carey.

Ed Cosgrove would later say that his decision to take charge had been crucial and carried the twofold purpose of solving the murders and preventing all-out racial warfare. The investigation needed leadership and direction. An army of police from separate jurisdictions—some would say competing jurisdictions—were working on the cases. Every army needed a general. The investigation also needed a face, a single individual with authority to whom the community could turn for information and assurance. Optics were as important as the investigative work. As district attorney of Erie County, Ed Cosgrove was the region's de facto chief law enforcement official.

The command post had been put together swiftly but efficiently. Rules of order had been written and a chain of command established. Naming himself, as he had at yesterday's press conference, as the sole source of information with respect to the investigation, Cosgrove further outlined the hierarchy. Major George R. Tordy of the state police was in charge of the "police aspects" of the investigation. Directly under him were Captain Henry Williams of the state police BCI and Chief Leo Donovan of the Buffalo Homicide Squad. The command post had a dedicated space within the district attorney's office. At a cost of $1,000, new telephone lines had been installed to facilitate communication with officers who would be working around the clock on the investigation. There was also a dedicated hotline for information from the public.

The late edition of the *Buffalo Evening News* featured Cosgrove's statements in an article below the front-page fold, following related stories on the murders beneath the bold headline, "2 Black Murder Victims Mutilated." Top center was a large photograph of police and morgue attendants carrying the latest victim (Ernest Jones, though he was not yet identified in the press) on a gurney. The entire front page for Thursday, October 9, was dedicated to coverage of the murders. Among the prominent articles was one in which Assemblyman Arthur O. Eve and the Reverend Charley H. Fisher of BUILD appealed for blacks to remain calm but take heed. "No one should travel unless they travel with someone else," Mr. Eve was quoted. Mr. Fisher said the latest murders have put the black community in a "state of emergency," and likewise advised that people stay calm and not go out alone.

According to the newspaper, Arthur Eve cited a variety of incidents that appeared to be due to the efforts of an organized group to physically and verbally harass black citizens. He encouraged people to report all such occurrences to the police. Eve also made a plea for the Buffalo Police Benevolent Association "to stop its unofficial slowdown and demonstrate to the black community that they are concerned for its welfare." This was a reference to the current contract negotiations going on in the department. Ed Cosgrove had made a similar comment about Buffalo police being hampered by fiscal and labor problems that prevented them from fully complementing the task force. (Police Commissioner James Cunningham responded that there had been no slowdown in the homicide investigations and that detectives were working overtime on the cases.)

Another article featured the theories of a University at Buffalo psychology professor that the killer in the mutilations was a bigot and sadist, and that the .22 Caliber Killer was likely a separate individual, paranoid and acting out of delusion. It was conceivable, he thought, that all the publicity could spawn imitators and more killings.

The murders were no longer just a local story. The prospect of a serial killer had already drawn interest from reporters and journalists beyond Western New York, intrigued all the more because the killings were happening in the same time period as the Atlanta Child Murders and the cross-country spree of racist assassin Joseph Paul Franklin. With the nightmarish murders of the cabbies, seeming more like something straight out of a horror movie than real life, the story attracted even greater attention. New faces appeared at the press conferences, churning out headlines, stressing the urgency, drawing parallels with crimes against blacks in other parts of the country, both contemporary and historical.

While some journalists stuck to straight reporting, others indulged in theory and speculation, often of the alarming variety. As journalist Jonathan Mahler would eventually write in retrospect about media coverage of the Son of Sam case: "The frenzied coverage fanned the growing sense of fear; the growing sense of fear fanned the frenzied coverage." Son of Sam had been a more "typical" serial killer, choosing victims of his own race, mainly targeting women. The Buffalo killings had the provocative twist of apparently being racially motivated, a point repeated over and over, often along with cautionary comments of those who viewed this as an epidemic rather than an aberrant series of murders, unsolved because authorities were indifferent to the suffering of blacks.

The three network affiliate TV stations in Buffalo made the crimes the focus of their broadcasts throughout the day, breaking in with live coverage from the press conferences and footage of police clustered at the crime scenes. In between were recaps, community reactions, and experts opining on what was going through the killer's mind. There were the inevitable comparisons with David Berkowitz, who was serving his six life sentences at the Attica Correctional Facility thirty-some miles outside of Buffalo. Channel 7 enhanced their interview with a psychiatric expert by showing a photo of Berkowitz in the background. A second piece on Berkowitz informed viewers that the Attica inmate had lost his Social Security disability benefits. The only purpose of this minor story, which again featured a photo of the notorious murderer, seemed to be to keep the specter of serial murder alive, or perhaps to warn would-be killers that they might be putting their Social Security benefits at risk.

The big topic was the mutilation of the cab drivers, which drew comparisons with Jack the Ripper. Some reporters were particularly vivid, telling viewers that the attacker "ripped out the hearts" of his victims. One anchor referred to the cab drivers as the "Ripper" victims while another newscaster declared there might be "not one but two crazed murderers on the loose in Western New York." A promo for a late newscast had an anchor tag the big story, "Hunting the hacky hacker!" While all the stations noted Cosgrove's statements that the two killings were not linked to the previous four, some tied them together by observing that all six homicides were being investigated as one. An investigative reporter for Channel 2 attempted to connect the murders to black killings nationally, raising the possibility of "a national conspiracy against blacks."

Amid the plethora of coverage and commentary, the one detail that resonated far and wide was that the two cabbies' hearts had been carved out. Unfortunately, no one had thought to tell the family of Parler Edwards about this detail ahead of time. One of his daughters said later that the family learned of it when they heard about it on TV.

The sensational news spurred a great deal of action. Community and activist groups held emergency meetings. Daniel Acker sent a telegram to Governor Hugh Carey asking him to send the National Guard. Buffalo Mayor James D. Griffin and Reverend Bennett Smith appeared on television together that evening appealing for the community to remain calm, reminding viewers that Buffalo was the City of Good Neighbors.

––––––––––

The night of Thursday, October 9, was harrowing.

The violence began in the late afternoon and went on throughout the early hours of the morning. A shot was fired at a Buffalo Fire Department dispatcher as he drove to work. The bullet hit his car. A man walking on a street nearby was attacked by four men. He was beaten but not robbed. Two men pulled up alongside a man stopped at the intersection of Broadway and Fillmore Streets and shattered the driver's side window of his car before speeding off. The victim was treated for facial cuts at a local hospital. Other motorists had rocks hurled at their cars, shattering windows and lights.

In the most serious incident reported, a young couple sitting in a parked car was approached by two men who said they were narcotics squad detectives. One carried a billy club, the other a gun. When the men failed to produce badges, the couple attempted to flee. The police imposters fired two shots through the rear window of the car before running off.

All the attacks were unprovoked. All happened on the east side. The victims were white, the perpetrators black. "It is probably not prudent for whites to wander into the black neighborhoods at night right now," a police officer at the Genesee Street station told a reporter. "The paranoia on the east side is very widespread. The tension is so thick you can cut it with a knife."

The most jarring incident was the burning cross that scorched the night sky. Twelve feet high, wrapped in old clothing and rags that had been doused with gasoline, the makeshift wooden cross had been propped against a street sign and set ablaze at the intersection of Jefferson Avenue and Brunswick Street in what a reporter called "the heart of the city's black community." It had not burned for long, though. Two police officers had spotted it immediately and knocked it to the ground. As they summoned the fire department, a black man across the street shouted to them, "Leave it burn. Call channel seven and get the cameras down here."

Another black man raced up in a car and took two flash pictures of the officers with the cross.

Police Captain Floyd J. Edwards was the commander of the Cold Spring Station. Captain Edwards, who was African American, filed a report on the cross burning with Commissioner Cunningham. "In the opinion of this captain," Edwards wrote, "because of the size of the cross and the circumstances regarding this incident, the possibility that white people would have put up the cross without being seen by anyone is very remote." Less than ten minutes before they found the burning cross, Edwards reported, two of his officers had passed by the intersection on their way to another call on Brunswick Avenue. The cross had not been there but the officers had noticed a group of six young black males standing in a circle. Driving back past the intersection just minutes later, they had spotted the enormous cross on fire. The six black youths were gone.

"In light of recent newspaper and television coverage of the '.22-caliber killer' and the 'ripper' who knifed two black men to death," Captain Edwards wrote, "the officers feel that this incident was done only to get the black neighborhood up in arms." Some black teens admitted their responsibility for the prank soon afterward, but photos of the charred cross had already gone out over newswires, presumably as the work of white supremacists.

The staged cross burning was particularly vexing to police officers like Clifton Jones and Danny Owens, both of whom were black. Officers Jones and Owens wanted to form a task force of black officers to help not only with the investigation of the killings, but to help keep peace in the black community and prevent further incendiary acts. Stanching the tide of vigilantism was of even greater concern. "Some of the blacks are starting to retaliate," Officer Jones told a reporter. "Our big worry is that some innocent white people are going to get hurt." Pervasive fear, blind rage, and acts of agitation like the cross burning had elevated the situation to crisis levels. The change in atmosphere was palpable. "This isn't the same City of Buffalo we knew one month ago."

Precinct 12 had received a number of calls from black citizens asking how to obtain pistol permits. Officer Jones had already noticed more people carrying guns on the street. Speaking of the smaller crimes and malevolence that the wave of murders had spawned, a veteran police officer cautioned, "There are a lot of crazy people, both white and black, who will use a situation like this to their advantage." Reverend Bennett Smith said that some black men had purchased guns, perhaps illegally, because they would rather have the police catch them with an illegal gun than for the murderer to catch them without it.

The cross burning and overnight attacks were given prominent coverage in the newspapers on Friday, October 10, along with a lengthy article on the front page of the *Buffalo Evening News* about a black auto worker who had come forward and told the *News* that two white men had tried to kill him on October 1. Police Commissioner James Cunningham personally questioned the auto worker after reporters from the *News* brought him to police headquarters. The fifty-nine-year-old auto worker, whose name was not released because, per the *News*, he was regarded as a potential witness to the .22 Caliber Killer and mutilation murders, said that as he was driving home from work around 11:00 the night of October 1, he had been followed by two white men in a beat-up blue Chevy van who got in front of his small car and refused to allow him to pass. After some jockeying on the road, the van headed him off and a club-wielding white man jumped out and shouted, "I'll kill you, nigger." The white man, who, the victim said, "had to be a lunatic," beat on the auto worker's car with the club. When the victim rolled down his window and asked the attacker why he wanted to kill him, the man responded by punching him in the eye. He continued slamming the club against the car and spewing racial epithets, prodding the man to get out of his car. The auto worker said he had been afraid to get out and fight back because he noted that the white man wore a pouch over his right thigh that could've held a weapon. He thought the assailant might be the .22 Caliber Killer. The other white man was still in the van, who just sat there and watched.

Several people had run outside during the commotion, which had happened near the intersection of Hertel Avenue and Military Road in Buffalo. The witnesses backed up the auto worker's account. The assailant was described as a short, stocky, "hippie-like" guy in his midtwenties or thirties with long, fair hair, wearing a baseball cap. According to the

Buffalo Evening News, Commissioner Cunningham said the auto worker gave information that matched what police had already gathered in the murder investigation, including the description of the vehicle. The commissioner had the auto worker speak with homicide detectives and ordered a roundup of the witnesses to his assault. The *News* described this account as "the first tenuous shred of evidence that appeared to link the .22 caliber killings of four and the mutilation of two others, all blacks," though it was unclear what this link might be.

The state police were investigating an incident on October 5 that victims feared might also be the work of the .22 Caliber Killer. A black bus driver had been injured on the thruway, possibly by gunfire. Paul Oberle was driving members of the choir of St. John Baptist Church from Buffalo to Syracuse when a small projectile shattered the lower left windshield of the bus. The incident had occurred eighty miles east of Buffalo on Interstate 90. A small fragment of metal was removed from Oberle's neck at a hospital in Syracuse, where he was treated for cuts on his arm and neck from the flying glass.

Captain Henry Williams of the State Police BCI said it appeared that the shot came from a small caliber weapon, possibly a .22 caliber, if in fact it had been a gunshot; the fragment recovered was too small to ascertain whether it was part of a bullet. The state police could only confirm that it was a piece of metal but were investigating the incident as a possible shooting. Captain Williams noted that a shot would have to have been fired from a wooded area northeast of the thruway and crossed the westbound lane before hitting the bus, which was traveling eastbound. It seemed doubtful that anyone could have passed the bus and set up in a position to shoot at it. Small game season had begun October 1 and the possibility of a bullet ricochet from a hunter had to be considered also. The state police had questioned people in the area, none of whom recalled seeing any suspicious persons or vehicles. Troopers wanted to speak with a black man who told the Reverend Bennett Smith that he had been traveling in his own car behind the bus when another car carrying two white men and a white woman had tried to force him off the road a few minutes before the bus driver was injured. Smith told reporters that the man had given the car's license plate number to police on the night of the occurrence, but Captain Williams said he had been unable to find any officer who may have been given the number.

The .22 Caliber Killer had become the bogeyman. The elusive blond gunman had taken on an almost phantom-like status in the minds of many, feared as the culprit behind every strange occurrence, every threat or menacing act.

Jesse Jackson arrived in Buffalo on Friday, October 10. The Reverend Jackson had come at the request of local civil rights leaders in order to help calm the community. He spoke to a crowd of more than eight hundred people on that Friday night at the BUILD Town Hall. Some off-duty black police officers provided security on their own time because the BUILD office reported receiving a death threat to Jackson from an anonymous caller.

Jackson invoked the name of slain civil rights leader Dr. Martin Luther King as he warned against responding to the murders with violence and retribution, encouraging the community instead to exercise civil power and focus on the larger situation rather than just the current wave of homicides. "Sure we're going to demand to find out who killed six people," the Reverend Jackson told the mostly black audience. "But there's more. We can't just worry about those who killed six men. What about those who killed our dreams? What about those who leave us unemployed? What about those who leave us in slum housing?

"We don't have to fight fire with fire. We don't have to fight lives with lives. We don't have to fight hate with hate. We must change our minds, then change people's minds about us," Jackson said in a rising voice. "There's nothing in the world more powerful than a made-up mind."

The crowd responded with enthusiasm as Jackson continued, "We've got ten million votes to fight with. We must get mad enough and get smart enough to go to the polls and retire some people." He warned that resorting to violence would be suicidal for blacks. "Beware of anybody who tries to define your manhood as getting a gun and getting revenge," Jackson said. "There they are with all those guns, and police, and investigators, and judges. Here we are with women with children and no husbands, trapped in a neighborhood where they can turn the lights out, and turn the gas off, and pull the supermarkets out.

"Don't fall for no funny definitions," the Reverend Jackson cautioned. "Don't drop no vote and pick up no stick, no gun. There's power in that vote. Power." Speaking of the murders, he told the audience, "If we have political power, we can demand the district attorney to take action. If we have political power, we can demand the Department of Justice to take action." Jackson said it was important for the community to come together in the crisis, across all racial and political lines, but added that if the killer was not apprehended "within a reasonable amount of time, then we've got to march in the community where the killers are."

Drawing to a close, the preacher declared, "I am . . . Somebody . . . I am . . ." and the crowd shouted back in unison, "Somebody!" Jackson ended his passionate forty-minute speech by leading the assembly in singing "We Shall Overcome."

Earlier in the day, Jesse Jackson had appeared on a televised meeting and panel discussion hosted at Channel 7 studios along with local religious, political, and civic leaders to discuss the rash of murders. In addition to Jackson, the panel included Erie County Executive Edward Rutkowski, Raphael Dubard of the NAACP, Erie County Sheriff Kenneth Braun, Fletcher Graves of the Justice Department, Earl Clarke of BUILD, and the Reverend Bennett Smith. Jackson and some other panelists criticized Buffalo Mayor James Griffin, District Attorney Edward Cosgrove, and Police Commissioner James Cunningham for not attending the meeting. Jackson said that their attendance would have represented a presence of assurance. "We need the complete moral force of the white community," Jackson stated. He added that the black community had lost confidence in local authorities because blacks "are under the impression that the cops aren't doing enough" to apprehend the killer or killers.

Following the televised meeting, Jesse Jackson and the other panelists proceeded to Cosgrove's office where they met for ninety minutes with the district attorney, Buffalo City Council President Delmar Mitchell (who was acting mayor because Griffin was out of state on a preplanned trip), and Councilmen David Collins and James Pitts. Councilmen Collins and Pitts were both African American and represented districts that were largely populated by blacks. Ed Cosgrove had not attended the panel because he had been on a state police helicopter viewing the crime scenes with Leo Donovan and Lieutenant Sam Slade. Returning from the flight, Cosgrove told reporters that the killer of the cab drivers must've been "very familiar" with the sites where the bodies were discovered because the areas were not very accessible and the murderer therefore "had to know where he was going."

The presence of the Reverend Jackson was not the only major news of the day. Reports were coming in of yet another extraordinary attack on a black male. At 3:30 p.m., a nurse had interrupted an attempted strangulation of a patient on the seventh floor of the Erie County Medical Center on Buffalo's east side. The victim was Collin Cole, age thirty-seven, who was in the hospital's detoxification unit. A nurse passing by Cole's room had noticed the door to his room was closed. She opened it and saw a white male crouched over the patient, who was on the floor. The white man said to the nurse, "He's fallen and hurt himself," before rushing past her and out the door.

Ed Cosgrove spoke to the press at 10:45 p.m. that night to confirm the news. A white male had choked Collin Cole with a ligature and then escaped from the hospital. Cole would likely have been killed if the nurse had not interrupted the attack. Cole received severe injuries to his neck and was in serious condition following emergency surgery. Before lapsing into unconsciousness, Cosgrove said, Cole told hospital security that the white man had said, "I hate niggers" before strangling him in his bed.

Referring to Collin Cole as "the seventh victim" in the string of attacks on black men, Cosgrove said that the nurse and several witnesses described the strangler as about thirty years old, five feet two to five feet four, with blond hair. Cosgrove said it appeared "to be the same maniac" responsible for the .22 caliber killings. Stating that the nurse had given a very good description of the assailant and that her information "jibes with the information we already have," Cosgrove said that a massive manhunt was underway. "It is my belief with the intense effort we have ongoing that we will stop this maniac."

Racial violence had broken out again that Friday even before news of the attack on Collin Cole. A white student at Burgard High School was stabbed that morning by a black classmate. In the afternoon, a car with two black men turned the wrong way onto Elm Street, a one-way street, and ran down two white males. Witnesses claimed that the car had aimed for the white men, one of whom fell off the car hood twenty-five feet past the point of impact while the other had been dragged seventy-five yards. Both victims were admitted to the hospital and police had charged the forty-six-year-old black driver with drunk driving and hit-and-run injury.

Starting around 9:00 p.m., police were called repeatedly to the intersection of Jefferson and Sycamore on reports that gangs of blacks were attacking passing cars with axes and meat cleavers. Whites driving by were pelted with rocks and bottles. A white man from Toronto was dragged from his car by a group of young black males, one of whom hit him with a baseball bat.

A shot was fired at a black cabbie. A van and a car filled with white youths stopped in front of a bar and fired a shotgun blast through the front window, fortunately missing the patrons inside. A group of twelve young black men hurled a cement block at a white police officer driving an unmarked patrol car. It hit the vehicle with such force that it shattered the rear driver-side window and shot across to the passenger window, shattering it as well. When the officer opened his car door, all twelve charged toward him. He sped away.

The city seemed to be going mad.

Bennett Smith denounced the violence during a prayer meeting the following morning at PUSH headquarters that was broadcast over the radio. "Young brothers and sisters are standing on the street corners, throwing bottles at buses and rocks at cars," Smith intoned. "They are only hurting the situation."

Jesse Jackson attended the prayer meeting, which attracted a capacity crowd. Edward Cosgrove had also come, somewhat bravely perhaps, considering the criticism that had been leveled at him by Smith. But the district attorney, well aware of the escalating violence and the fever pitch in the black community, had some things he wanted to say. Bennett Smith introduced Cosgrove as "the man who doesn't know who I am," a reference to the meeting the day before when Cosgrove had turned to Smith and said, "I don't know who you are."

"Mr. Cosgrove has been so busy chasing the Mafia, he hasn't had the time to find out who I am," Smith told the assembly. He reproached the district attorney for rarely visiting the east side and the black community. "Now that he's here, it's a national and local news event."

Ed Cosgrove had handled tough crowds before. Stepping up to the microphone, the district attorney said, "One of the worst things about my job is that I get to see very little of good people and good things. I haven't met you, Mr. Smith sir, because you are a good man." This provoked a grin from Bennett Smith and applause from the crowd. (Jesse Jackson was later heard to remark that Cosgrove had a good speech writer.) Poised and gentlemanly, the district attorney spent an hour speaking to and with the attendees, during which he received rounds of applause in growing frequency as the crowd transformed from suspicious to gracious. At the end of the hour, even Bennett Smith had changed his mind. Smith led the final round of applause for Cosgrove, telling the audience, "Let's support our DA. Let's hear it for our DA!"

Cosgrove actually divulged very little in the way of solid information about the progress of the investigation, other than to say with assurance that the investigation was progressing and that things were looking brighter.

One of the attendees was one of Parler Edwards's sons. When he asked when his father's body would be released for burial, Cosgrove explained that the body had to be retained at the medical examiner's office for the time being due to the ongoing investigation.

Cosgrove scored points by acknowledging that groups like the KKK "actually do exist," adding that police had done a rundown of former Klan members but that no evidence tied the murders to any such extremist group. (Earlier that week, the *Buffalo Evening News* had quoted him as saying that there were no KKK or neo-Nazi groups in the community. Cosgrove denied ever saying this.) The crowd was encouraged to hear that the nurse as well as three other hospital employees had gotten a good look at the strangler. FBI agents were on their way to Buffalo to produce a new composite and assist with the manhunt. The most tantalizing bit of information that the district attorney shared seemed to indicate a breaking development.

"We hope to have some good news soon," Cosgrove told the audience. "There is something very interesting, something very substantial going on right now," he said. He could not elaborate, but told the crowd, "We are preparing search warrants for certain places." When asked if this meant that an arrest was imminent, he replied no but stressed his optimism over the recent development. "I'm a lot more encouraged than I was last night at 10:30."

After the meeting, Bennett Smith was effusive in his compliments for the district attorney, praising him to the press for his appearance at PUSH. Smith took it as a sign that the DA was truly concerned about the black community. Councilman James Pitts took a more reserved view of Cosgrove's presentation. "It was encouraging," Pitts was quoted. "But what we really need is an arrest."

An arrest had in fact been made, though not for murder. The substantial development that had inspired such optimism in Ed Cosgrove was the arrest hours earlier of a local man on charges of driving while intoxicated, or DWI.

At 1:50 a.m. on Saturday, October 11, an Amherst police officer arrested the twenty-nine-year-old white male who gave his address as room 28 at the Grand Motor Inn, 2000 Niagara Falls Boulevard in Tonawanda. In the course of the arrest, the man made what Ed Cosgrove would later describe to the media as "bizarre statements." As recorded by the arresting officer, the man had said:

> He hates niggers and tried to strangle a nigger in a hospital yesterday. If you open up a nigger, it's messy, and that you put niggers in trunks. That he, [suspect], called nigger blood ketchup and that people throw blood on him. Right now he has clothing soaking in a tub at 2000 Niagara Falls Boulevard, Tonawanda, New York with ketchup (nigger blood) all over it, and that further, three days ago, he had blood all over his hands and it hurt when he tried to wash it off. He had recently cut his hair because he had blood in it and could not get it out. He has a sharp knife in his room.

The suspect was booked and held at the Amherst jail for DWI and resisting arrest while Assistant DA Joseph Mordino immediately prepared an application for a search warrant of the Grand Motor Inn and the suspect's 1975 red Chevy, which he personally delivered to the home of a Supreme Court justice for signature. Awaiting the warrants, John Regan and other task force members were sent to the Grand Motor Inn to keep watch on the premises until the search could be executed. Among the items seized were a screwdriver, a pair of shears, a length of wire, and some clothing recovered from the garbage can outside the man's motel room. None of the clothing was bloody—no traces of blood were found on anything—and there was no sharp knife, nothing soaking in the tub. The only red substance noted was paint the man had sprayed all over the TV set and his car.

The suspect was questioned for several hours. Checks of his background were made. He was taken to the Erie County Medical Center for a forensic examination. He had been treated there before as well as at the Veterans Hospital for psychiatric problems. He had called the Amherst police a number of times to confess to crimes. He had also confessed to the latest murders to an Associated Press reporter, who told police that the man also claimed to know that the reporter had committed a murder of his own.

Ed Cosgrove held a press conference Saturday evening, where reporters noted that he was markedly less enthusiastic about the Amherst man. By Monday he said the man had been discounted as a suspect.

———

City streets were much quieter on Saturday than on the two previous nights. The intersection of Jefferson and Sycamore was littered with debris and broken glass, remnants of the violence, but there were no further incidents. While there were two shootings on the east side that night, they were not racially motivated, and there were no new reports of black-white violence. Three factors helped keep the uneasy peace: the damp, cold weather; the visible street presence of extra patrol cars, including several from the sheriff's department in addition to the Buffalo police; and media reports of the attacks that had occurred on Thursday and Friday, which, according to police officers, had kept whites out of the black neighborhoods on Saturday. As one cop told a reporter, "They're nuts if they're going in there now."

While a tense calm had settled over the city, there were two cross burnings over the weekend in the suburb of Lockport. This time it was done by whites, who were arrested and charged with criminal mischief.

Things had clearly not returned to normal in Buffalo, however, and officials rightly recognized the relative peace as a temporary lull rather than a good omen. Mayor Griffin had cut short his trip and returned to Buffalo late Saturday, where he was met at the airport by Police Commissioner Cunningham for an update on the investigation. The mayor, Cosgrove, Cunningham, and a host of local clergy—both black and white—made daily appeals to the community for calm and brotherhood. Cunningham told the press he was confident the .22 Caliber Killer would be captured soon. Rewards for information were upped into the tens of thousands of dollars. The task force operated 24/7, pursuing every lead.

Still, the only thing that could really bring about any sort of a return to normalcy would be an arrest. That hadn't happened. And despite assurances to the contrary, none were on the horizon.

Perhaps the most tragic act of retaliation occurred on Tuesday, October 14, the same day that city officials, in an attempt to forge respect and camaraderie throughout the larger community, declared a twenty-one-day period of mourning for the six murder victims. Terence Lee Mills, age thirty-seven, was an urban planner at the Central City Restoration Corp. in downtown Buffalo. Mills had earned his law degree from the prestigious George Washington University, where he had been an honors student. Instead of pursuing a potentially lucrative legal career, Terence Mills had chosen to return to hometown Buffalo and devote himself to the revitalization of the city's poorest and most blighted neighborhoods. Mills left his office at around 6:30 that Tuesday evening and was walking toward his car when he was stopped by two black men. One of the men showed a knife and demanded money. Mills handed over his wallet. He raised his hands in the air and told the men, "That's all I have." The black man with the knife took the wallet. Then he plunged the knife into Terence Mills's chest.

The two men ran away. Witnesses said that the man with the knife jumped into a cab at nearby Niagara Square. Terence Mills told police what happened to him before dying in a hospital a half hour after the stabbing. Police later found his wallet, credit cards, and a knife with the inscription "007" in a sewer.

The killer was Larry Barnes, age twenty, nickname "Too Tall" because of his six-foot-four height. Barnes went to an east-side pizzeria that night and bragged to friends that he had "yoked" a white guy and showed off the bloody knife to prove it. "And I'll yoke another one if I have to," Barnes declared. Barnes and some others felt the killing was justified; a white life violently taken in exchange for the black men who had been snuffed out. Some congratulated him for doing the right thing.

Not everyone agreed that murdering an innocent white man was the right thing to do. Informants quietly went to the police and told them what they had heard at the pizzeria. Larry Barnes fled to California. He was indicted in absentia and arrested a year later in San Jose by the FBI. He eventually pled guilty to first degree manslaughter and served seventeen years. Barnes refused to name his accomplice, and the second man was never apprehended.

The mother of Terence Mills said that of the scores of sympathetic calls and letters of condolence she received, the ones that meant the most to her had come from the many black residents at Willert Park, the inner-city housing project that Terence had been working to revitalize at the time of his murder, expressing sorrow and telling her how grateful they were for all that her son had done for them.

———

A Unity Day rally was held on the afternoon of Sunday, October 19. Five thousand people of different races and religions gathered in downtown Buffalo to show solidarity. They wore black ribbons in remembrance of the murdered men. They held hands and vowed that good would triumph over evil, and that the community stood as one. Mayor Griffin and other politicians gave speeches. Religious leaders offered prayers and words of hope. Bennett Smith spoke of a mighty resurrection and a glorious ascension, when all races would walk together in peace.

Newspapers heralded the success of Unity Day. The remarkable turnout showed the promise of a brighter future. The glow of goodwill had warmed and inspired.

It was a day of great hope and community bonding for the people of Buffalo. The last they'd see for a while. As Western New York entered the 1980 holiday season, peace and unity would be as elusive as the killer or killers themselves.

Chapter 7
OCTOBER 20–DECEMBER 21, 1980

ONE AFTERNOON IN the fall of 1980, a boy named Bobby Grot left his school, which was PS 43, and walked up to the corner of Lovejoy Avenue. There was always a crossing guard at Lovejoy because it was one of the main streets in the neighborhood. After the guard helped him cross the street, Bobby, who was eleven, went and sat on a bench to wait for his friend so they could walk home together.

Somebody else was already on the bench, a guy Bobby had never seen before. To Bobby he looked like a cool older kid, past high school but still a kid. He wore an olive-green army jacket, the kind like on the TV show *M*A*S*H*, and he sat perched on the top edge of the bench with his feet on the seat. Bobby sat down at the other end to wait for his friend. The cool older kid looked at him and smiled.

"What's your name?" he asked.

"Bobby," the boy answered. "What's yours?"

"JC," the older kid said. "Like Jesus Christ."

That gave Bobby a little jolt. What a weird thing to say, and really disrespectful. Bobby was an altar boy at St. Francis. People he knew didn't talk that way, comparing themselves to Jesus Christ. Bobby could just imagine what the priests at St. Francis would do if they heard that.

The older kid started talking to him, kind of rambling about something, but Bobby wasn't really listening. He didn't want to talk to a guy like this, even if he did look cool. The guy kept on talking, even though Bobby avoided looking at him and didn't say anything back. Later, Bobby wouldn't remember what he said, since Bobby had decided to just tune him out. Whatever it was, though, the guy seemed pretty animated, like he was trying to make a point or something. He kept talking and Bobby started to feel anxious. He wasn't exactly scared, because the guy in the army jacket wasn't threatening him or anything, plus they were on a bench right on Lovejoy Avenue across from the school and the city pool. The weather was pretty nice and there were other people around, although he and the older kid were the only ones on the bench. There were some firemen hanging out in front of the fire station just a few yards away and the crossing guard was still around somewhere, so Bobby didn't feel like he was in danger. Still, he wished that his friend would hurry up and get there or that the older kid would just go away, or at least stop talking. Couldn't he tell that Bobby wasn't listening to him anyway?

The only two things that Bobby would remember about the conversation, if you could call it that, were the first thing the guy said—the remark about Jesus Christ—and the last thing he said, because that's when Bobby got scared.

Leaning toward Bobby so that their faces were only about a foot apart, the guy pointed down at the street and said, "Do you know what those bricks are for?"

Bobby looked down. The boy was pointing at an area near the curb where some of the asphalt had worn away, exposing the bricks underneath. "Do you know what the bricks are for?" He seemed upbeat, like he was about to reveal something really exciting or important. Bobby was a little curious, so this time he answered and said no, he didn't know what the bricks were for.

"They're there so you can pick them up and throw them at niggers."

Bobby felt his stomach tighten. He didn't know what to say. The older kid was white, and so was Bobby, but Bobby wasn't used to hearing people talk that way. His parents had taught him better. Only bad people said terrible things like that. Plus, it was scary. Not just what the guy in the army jacket had said, but *how* he said it, like he was really proud. That's when Bobby decided he was leaving. He wasn't going to stay on this bench with this older boy anymore, even if it meant he had to go stand on the sidewalk somewhere.

Bobby Grot got up and started walking. He walked past the guy on the bench, who stared at him as he left. Bobby wasn't comfortable just standing on the sidewalk. He wanted to be away from the guy on the bench, so he kept walking and went inside a store a couple blocks away. The whole thing had upset him. He was glad he never ran into that guy on the bench again after that.

Eventually Bobby would see the scary older kid again, and he would recognize him right away. But fortunately for Bobby, they only met in person that once.

––––––––––

Parler Edwards had died within two hours of eating his last meal. Tom Rowan had taken the stomach contents to a forensic laboratory in Binghamton, New York, for analysis and to the University at Buffalo, where they were examined by a botany professor. Edwards had a mixture of vegetables in his stomach that indicated his last meal had been a salad. The toxicology screen showed no presence of drugs or alcohol. Ernest "Shorty" Jones also had a large quantity of undigested food in his stomach, showing that he too had eaten shortly before his death.

Second autopsies were performed on the bodies of Parler Edwards and Ernest Jones in an effort to gain as much forensic information as possible, including a more precise idea of the weapons that had been used on each victim. Dr. Michael Baden was the deputy chief medical examiner for New York City, perhaps best known as the pathologist who had re-autopsied victims of the 1971 Attica Prison uprising. Baden had come to Buffalo along with Dr. Homer Campbell, a forensic odontologist from the University of New Mexico, and Dr. Campbell's wife, Karen Tober, a forensic anthropologist, the weekend following the discovery of the bodies. The examinations provided little insight beyond what the original medical examiner, Dr. Catherine Lloyd, had already given. Dr. Campbell determined that the instrument used to inflict the wounds on both victims had to have been as sharp as, or sharper, than a surgical scalpel. The odd puncture wounds in Ernest Jones's skull could have been made by a screwdriver.

One of the first mandates of the task force had been the establishment of an evidence team to collect and process anything found at the crime scenes or subsequently that could be of evidentiary value. It was decided that the same group of scientific analysts would be immediately dispatched to the scenes of any future murders that could be related to the six. The evidence team consisted of a half-dozen members culled from the different agencies who would collaborate and share their scientific findings. Assigned from the state police were investigators Raymond Motyka and Thomas Rash; from the Amherst police, Lieutenant Michael Melton and Detective Michael Summers; Deputy Charles Fink from the Erie County Sheriff's Department; and Tom Rowan from the Cheektowaga police.

The search for evidence had literally been conducted from land, sea, and air. In addition to the wide grid searches done at the scenes and the use of a helicopter, police divers had searched the Niagara River near the boat launch where the body of Jones had been found in an effort to find the weapon or weapons. Ponds near the crime scenes had been drained. Roofs of nearby buildings had been searched. Metal detectors had been used to scan the ground. All to no avail. Working with the physical evidence they did have—blood, fingerprints, tire impressions—the evidence team was assisted in their analyses by crime labs of the New York state police and Buffalo police as well as the FBI laboratory in Washington, DC.

The cabs of both Edwards and Jones had been exhaustively searched by the task force as well as by a special unit brought in from the FBI. Each and every item found anywhere inside, every scrap of paper or loose penny trapped between seats, was catalogued and secured. Both cabs had been partially dismantled. Tires from each were shipped to the Washington FBI lab for comparison with bloody tire impressions taken from the pavements and casts of impressions left in the soil.

A total of twenty-one latent fingerprints and palm prints were lifted from the cab of Ernest Jones. The bloody palm print on the rear driver's side window was identified as belonging to Jones. Two latent fingerprints were lifted from the trunk lid of Edwards's cab. The prints would only be valuable evidence, of course, if police had suspects to compare them to.

Among the FBI personnel that had been whisked to Buffalo that first weekend were two special agents who authorities hoped could help shed light on the appearance and persona of the killer. One was Horace Heafner, a noted forensic artist who had been with the FBI for close to twenty-five years. Heafner had been brought in to reinterview witnesses and develop a new sketch of the suspect. The other was John E. Douglas, who had been with the Bureau for ten years and was currently an instructor at the FBI Academy in Quantico, Virginia. At age thirty-five, Douglas was considerably younger than many of the senior agents, but he had already made his mark, primarily in the burgeoning field of criminal profiling.

Profiling was an investigative tool initiated in the FBI in 1970 by Howard Teten, a criminology instructor for the National Police Academy in Washington, DC. Prior to joining the Bureau in 1962, Teten was a seasoned police officer in San Leandro, California, with a keen interest in the study of criminal behavior, particularly aberrant criminal behavior, and how such knowledge could help identify suspects in unsolved crimes. Integrating a knowledge of forensic science, crime scene analysis, and abnormal psychology, criminal profiling is a method of hypothesizing the age, background, lifestyle, and character traits of likely suspects by scrutinizing details of a crime scene and the actions of the perpetrator and then comparing them to known profiles of offenders of similar crimes. Teten had been inspired by the work of Dr. James A. Brussel, a New York psychiatrist who, in 1956, had provided police with a detailed personality profile of New York City's "Mad Bomber," an elusive terrorist who planted homemade explosives around the city for more than a decade. When George Metesky, the so-called Mad Bomber, was apprehended in January 1957, the analysis provided by Dr. Brussel had proven to be uncannily precise, down to the type of clothing the suspect would wear. Howard Teten and his Bureau colleagues had further developed the art and science of profiling, which had since become key course work for agents in training and the cornerstone of the FBI's Behavioral Science Unit.

John Douglas, as a young agent and instructor at Quantico—in fact the youngest instructor at the FBI Academy when he had been appointed in 1977 to teach hostage negotiation and applied criminal psychology— had taken criminal profiling a step further by going straight to the source in violent crimes: speaking at length with perpetrators themselves. As the FBI had sent him around the country to teach criminal psychology classes, Douglas had used his spare time to visit various prisons and interview as many violent offenders as possible, focusing on those convicted of serial rapes, arsons, and homicides. He noted commonalities in their backgrounds and personality traits and paired them with facts about their relationships and past professions to develop a character study, or criminal profile.

Though profiling was still a relatively new and controversial technique, it had gained momentum as profiles submitted on some notable cases had proven to be remarkably accurate. More and more police agencies were willing to give it a try, particularly in cases that had stymied law enforcement. John Douglas had provided profiles in fifty-nine cases in 1979. Requests for his services for this year had doubled.

On October 12, 1980, three days after the discovery of the second murdered cab driver and three weeks after the .22 caliber shootings, John Douglas delivered a psychological profile to the task force. The first and most extensive part of his report dealt with the October 8 and 9 mutilation murders of Parler Edwards and Ernest Jones.

"There are many ways to kill or have someone killed," Douglas wrote. "The underlying motivation of the offender is typically expressed by his crime. The presence or absence of anger, rage, frustration and guilt can be observed in almost all criminal acts.

"The motivation behind the killer(s) is obviously to kill blacks. However, this offender is not satisfied by just the process of killing his victims. He must totally consume them and take a part of them that for one reason or another is needed by him. Cases reviewed and personally profiled have found other cases throughout the United States where offenders have taken heads, hands, breasts, blood and genital organs. The crimes are heinous and irrational. However, behind this madness is an offender who is 'mission oriented.' He will rationalize his acts as justifiable.

"Your offender is paranoid in his thinking and may be experiencing symptoms of delusions and/or hallucinations. This disorder was not created overnight. The disorder has been slow and insidious, commencing probably in his early to mid-twenties. He will have a prior psychiatric history where in all probability he has been treated for the disorder known as paranoid schizophrenia. What this diagnosis signifies is an individual who may be delusional as well as experiencing hallucinatory symptoms.

"The crime scenes reflect rage, over-control, as well as overkill. The offender comes prepared with his 'kit.' His kit will include his weapons as well as perhaps containers, box, jar, etc., to transport his 'souvenir.'

"The crime scene also reflects that the hearts of his victims were cut out post-mortem. He had *time* to do his mission. The personal feeling here is that he is illogical in his thinking, disorganized and careless. He does not necessarily want to get caught, but he is sloppy and careless during the commission of the assault.

"The drop sites are areas that are known to your offender. He either resides, has been or is employed nearby, or has family members in this vicinity. Most cases fitting this pattern will find the offender not owning a personal vehicle. If he does, it will be an older model and not properly maintained."

Douglas provided the background of the offender. "He comes . . . as a product of child abuse, a broken home, alcoholic parents (one or both), absent or passive father, a possessive mother who may have had incestuous relationships with him as a child. In school he was average to above average in intelligence; however, he never really made the grade. He was and is passive, introverted and withdrawn. He has a poor self-concept and may have had a serious injury or illness. He does not verbally communicate well with others and avoids coming into direct contact with anyone. He may be a veteran of one of the armed services; however, he would have been discharged early in his career for medical reasons or failure to adjust to military life."

The profile advised that the offender would keep a hidden diary that could contain incriminating statements and that he probably lived alone. "If [he] were married, it was for a very short period of time. The wife will be considerably younger either chronologically or in maturity at the time of their marriage. Your offender, if employed, will be involved in menial occupations."

Delving into the area of criminal history, Douglas wrote: "Within close proximity to all of his prior residences, you will find cases of mysterious fires, voyeurism and animal torturing or experimentation. As stated earlier, he was not created overnight. Police or agencies involving black political movements may have received letters from your offender in the past. The letters will be rambling, disorganized, and statements made by him will be prejudiced and without any basis or foundation.

"Your offender lives in a world of fantasy. His fantasy will make him perform certain ritualistic acts that will be unexplainable, even by him. He will return to the crime scenes. The motivation for his return is to relive and heighten his past heinous behavior. Secondly, he will frequent the cemetery and communicate verbally with his victims and may in fact plant items at the cemetery plot to include his victims' heart."

Douglas gave detailed suggestions on interrogation techniques for the suspect, including the ideal time and place (at night, in a nonthreatening environment) and the angle and distance at which interrogators should sit. He advised giving the suspect a pad of paper and his choice of black, blue, or red pens to write down his thoughts or confession. "He should be told that you understand him and empathize with him. Your approach should be that you know he did the homicide, but allow him to tell you how he did it and why. You can also verbalize that there may be another part of his personality that he does not know and maybe the both of you can reveal who this other personality is.

"Care should be taken here not to put words into the mouth of the suspect or provide him with information that only the investigators and the murderer would know to be true." He advised that a thorough background investigation on the suspect should be conducted prior to the interview. Having such knowledge would serve the dual purpose of establishing a rapport and the ability to either discount or credit statements made by the suspect, who would be delusional.

"Three behavioristic patterns have been observed by similar offenders in the past. They will turn towards religion, alcohol and/or drugs. This behavior is to the extreme, and his participation in these activities will be to the extreme. Law enforcement should view this behavior as a defense mechanism utilized by the offender as a means of coping with his bizarre and irrational criminal act.

"He may attempt to become overly rigid in his personality and will often times involve himself in mentally exhaustive and repetitious behavior patterns, known as obsessive compulsive behavior. The offender feels he is losing control over himself and he will attempt repetitious acts in order to repress his unwanted thoughts and memories of the crimes. Extreme orderliness and neatness will oftentimes be observed at their residence."

Douglas summarized his findings. "Your offender is probably a white male in his late twenties to early thirties. He is paranoid in his thinking and mission oriented. He is a loner, withdrawn and nocturnal." He reiterated his opinions that the suspect would have a prior psychiatric history, come from a troubled home, and keep diaries of his innermost thoughts. Douglas contended that the offender may have attended the victims' funerals, and if so, his behavior had been inappropriate.

Douglas offered a final thought regarding the removal of the victims' hearts: "He will either preserve the heart (refrigerate, alcohol, etc.) or consume it. If the victims' family members continue to request the killer to return the heart, he will probably in fact do so, if he has not consumed it. It will be delivered to the crime scene (place of assault), residence of the victim, or cemetery grave plot."

The final pages of the profile addressed the .22 Caliber Killer. John Douglas saw pertinent differences in the two sets of homicides. "The question one asks," he wrote, "is whether the first four cases of homicide are related to the last two. Does or can the modus operandi of the homicidal personality change? These questions cannot be answered simply.

"The first four cases lack what we call pathology. There is nothing out of the ordinary done to the victims that we know of either prior to or after death. What may be pathological is the offender's determination to extinguish black men. This pathological disorder may be a subtle one and may not show up as readily as in the last two cases.

"This is the type of individual who will join hate groups or even groups who have positive values or goals. They will be similar in personality even if their goals are different. They begin to run into psychological problems somewhere between their early to middle thirties. They develop a highly systematized delusional system that may at times sound very convincing if one accepts its basic premises. People close to these individuals will eventually find these people obsessed with a mission, and if you are not with them in their ideological beliefs, they believe you are the enemy.

"The method and style of the homicides where the .22 caliber handgun was utilized appears to be organized and very rational in the mind of the killer. Generally, the personality of this individual will differ slightly from the offender pictured earlier in the first part of this report.

"This individual fits the personality style of an assassin who is also delusional but who does not experience any of the hallucinations. He generally will be older and more articulate. He also is 'mission oriented' and likes to let the community and world know that he is responsible for his crimes. Generally, he will print or type letters setting forth his mission and send them to the local media and/or the case coordinator. His rationale for killing is that of the paranoiac who feels that no one in the past has listened to him attentively, and now because he has been ignored for so long, must do it all alone. I say alone, because once again, offenders committing crimes as demonstrated in the four shooting incidents generally act alone.

"As stated earlier, the absence of any pathological crime scene data makes for a most difficult crime scene analysis. If we heard from this offender through written communiques, it would assist in my analysis.

"Whether or not all six homicides are related is a difficult question. They could be related if we see overt signs and precipitating factors in any suspects developed who during this period of time experienced a severe amount of stress. Stress caused by something either real or imagined. Stress that became too heavy a burden to bear."

John Douglas did not reveal any of the specifics of his report to the media. The profile was kept confidential from all but key members of the task force. The one comment Douglas did make to the press was that his profile pointed to two different killers.

In his report, Douglas noted the importance of victimology in drawing a profile. Knowing as much as possible about the victims beyond their sex, race, and ages had a bearing on an offender profile, as it did, of course, on the investigation as a whole. Background on the cab drivers had been limited at the time Douglas had been brought in. He had prepared his psychological sketch of the murderer of Parler Edwards and Ernest Jones based on the basic data investigators were able to provide and on the presumption that both men had been targeted because of their race and gender. The more investigators learned, however, it looked less and less likely that Edwards and Jones had been random victims of a homicidal stranger.

Ernest "Shorty" Jones had been arrested eight times. Between 1958 and 1966, Jones was arrested four times on assault charges and once for petit larceny. In 1970, he had been charged with two counts of first degree rape. His most recent arrest had occurred in April of 1978 for felony assault. He had no convictions.

Parler Edwards also had eight arrests, although his were entirely separate from, and unrelated to, those of Shorty Jones. So far there was no definitive evidence that Edwards and Jones knew each other, and the number of arrests on each man's rap sheet appeared to be coincidental. What might not have been coincidental was the white pad with three-digit numbers that had been found on the dashboard in Shorty Jones's taxicab.

Tracing Shorty's last movements had been nearly as easy as tracking the routine life of Parler Edwards, though for very different reasons. Whereas Edwards was a discreet man with set ways and a quiet social life, Shorty Jones was his opposite. Shorty had a lot of friends and acquaintances, many of whom had seen him on the last day and night of his life, and more of whom were aware that Shorty used his cab to run numbers. Among other things.

In contrast to staid Parler Edwards, whose connection to the numbers racket was thus far circumstantial and historical, Shorty Jones had spoken freely and even proudly about his criminal endeavors, at least with some people. One longtime acquaintance claimed that Shorty had told him point-blank that he used the cab as a front for his illegal enterprises. In addition to numbers, Jones sold drugs—mainly marijuana and pills, although one regular customer said that he could get "almost anything" by making a phone call—and he pimped prostitutes. One of his associates told police how Shorty had driven him down to Chippewa Street and pointed out "his" girls. Another friend said Shorty kept a collection of photos of his hookers in a bag in his cab. (This explained the black satchel with images of unknown females that investigators had found.) Shorty also had a couple of girlfriends. One steady lover in particular stood out.

Zoe Fontaine was twenty-three, white, and worked as a night waitress at a diner northeast of downtown. Zoe's coworkers were well aware of her relationship with Shorty, who often stopped in for coffee and usually drove Zoe and another waitress home. According to her coworkers, Zoe had been distraught over Shorty's death because they were "very close." Their relationship had apparently not been a secret. According to Shorty's brother, even Shorty's wife knew about Zoe.

Zoe spoke candidly—and tearfully—with police about the relationship. Though Shorty maintained ties with his family, she said, he had been living with her for the past six months. They had first started dating in 1970, when Zoe was thirteen and Jones was thirty. They had gone out together off and on over the last ten years but had been going steady for the past seven months. According to Zoe, she and Shorty were planning to be married in October 1981.

She acknowledged that Shorty sold drugs, mainly at the Perry Projects, though she couldn't—or wouldn't—name his customers or suppliers. The previous July he had brought a bag of marijuana to the apartment, and Zoe had helped him divide it up to sell. Shorty told her that he had stolen it from someone, but she didn't know from whom. As for numbers, she said that he placed bets regularly but insisted he wasn't a runner.

Zoe related two incidents that had occurred in the days immediately before Shorty's death. Close to midnight on the Friday before he was murdered, Shorty was driving Zoe to work in his cab when a rusty dark-blue van stopped alongside them at a traffic light. The van's driver, a white male with light hair, hollered at Shorty, "Hey nigger, what are you doing with that white girl?" Shorty started to say something back, but Zoe stopped him. When the light changed, they and the van had turned in different directions and that was the end of it. Two days later, Zoe was working an overnight shift when, somewhere between 3:30 and 4:00 a.m., she noticed a white man sitting at the counter who kept staring at her. She described him as about five feet four, in his thirties, with dirty-blond hair, pale skin, and a scar on his face. As he stared at her, she said he had a weird, evil look about him. Two seats away from him sat another white man, this one with brown hair and a wide mustache. She saw them talking and got the feeling that the two men knew each other but were trying to pretend like they didn't. Shorty came in about 4:20 a.m. and sat down with Zoe at the far back counter. He kissed her, and Zoe noticed that the blond man was staring at them with what she again described as a mean, evil look. About twenty minutes later, Shorty got up to leave and said he'd return before her shift ended. As he passed the counter, Zoe saw the blond man look at Shorty, then put his head down and mumble something. Shorty walked outside to his cab and the blond man followed him. Zoe saw him saying something to Shorty, who shook his head no. Shorty got in his cab and rolled his window up about three-quarters of the way. Blond man was still talking and Shorty was still shaking his head no as he drove off.

The blond came back into the restaurant. Zoe went to wait on a table and when she came back a few minutes later, both the blond and the man with the mustache were gone. A few minutes after that, another waitress told Zoe that Shorty had just called and said he wouldn't be coming back after all, that he'd see her after she got off work at 8:00 a.m. because he didn't want any trouble to get started at the restaurant. He said that the guy who had followed him out told him to come up to his room at the Travelodge so he could "blow him up." The waitress also told Zoe that she had overheard one of the customers tell the blond man that he looked like the .22 Caliber Killer and he had responded that he was.

Shorty had picked up Zoe at about 8:35 a.m. As they were walking from the restaurant, someone started hollering at them from a second-floor window of the Travelodge, which was next door to the diner. She looked up and saw a person standing at the window through the partly open curtains, but she didn't have a clear view. Zoe was concerned that it might be the man who said he wanted to blow Shorty up, so she urged him along. They went to their apartment and stayed there until they went to dinner that night at 8:30.

Zoe had not seen either of the men since. The last time she saw Shorty was at 6:45 p.m. on October 8, the last day of his life. He told her he was only working until midnight and that he'd meet her either at the restaurant or at the apartment. She never heard from him again. At 4:15 p.m. the next day, as she was preparing supper for him at the apartment, she heard on the radio that he'd been killed.

Zoe hadn't been concerned when Shorty didn't show up as planned, she explained, because he had a relative who was in the Navy Reserve or a similar organization and he often drove this person to some basin in Tonawanda, and Zoe had assumed that this was the reason Shorty did not return the morning of October 9. Investigators noted this information. Though it seemed an odd hour to drive someone to a Naval Reserve function, it tended to establish that Jones made periodic trips to the Tonawanda waterfront area. Whether or not this had any bearing on the fact that his body was discovered in a small boat launching facility remained to be seen.

Midnight seemed to be when the trail went cold. At around 2:00 p.m. on his last day, Shorty picked up one of his special fares at her home and drove her to the Ellicott Square Building in downtown Buffalo. The fare was a woman who said she knew Shorty well. He picked her up again after she concluded her business downtown, at which time the woman noted that his mood had changed. He no longer seemed to be himself. She explained that Shorty was normally a very happy-go-lucky person and it was apparent that something was bothering him. They chatted briefly on the drive home, and Shorty said that he would be at her baby's christening the following Sunday and that he'd be bringing Zoe with him.

Shorty had visited with another of his specials at her home at around 5:00 or 5:30 p.m. They sat in his cab talking for about twenty-five minutes until Shorty got a call for a fare and left. She had anticipated seeing him again at around 7:30 p.m. when he would drive her to bingo, but her husband had ended up driving her instead. She had called the cab company at 9:30 that night requesting Shorty to drive her home but was told that he was not in his cab. That was very unusual, she said, since Shorty always stayed in, or very close to, his cab. She continued calling for him up until about midnight, to no avail.

Shorty spent fifteen minutes at the diner with Zoe, leaving at 6:45 p.m. He then went home to see his wife and family, leaving around 8:00 p.m. The next confirmed location was the Little Harlem Hotel on Michigan Street. Employees said that Shorty was there at about 10:00 p.m. when a fight erupted between two black females and a black male cab driver. The argument was over some money, possibly cab fare, that was owed the cabbie. Shorty had intervened as peacemaker. The police had been called, but the two females left with Shorty in his cab before officers arrived.

The last sighting of Shorty alive and well had been at the Sunoco gas station on Broadway and Jefferson. From 11:30 p.m. to midnight, Shorty and a fellow cabbie had hung out, watching TV on a portable that Shorty had. They had both been sitting in their own cabs. Shorty showed him a bankbook for a joint account he had with Zoe. When they parted, Shorty had placed the portable TV, bankbook, a camera, a pocketbook-type holder containing photographs, and an undetermined amount of cash in a green cooler. Shorty placed the cooler in the trunk of his cab on the left side. Investigators had found the cooler in the trunk with all of the items inside that the cabbie had described, except for the portable TV and the money.

The cabbie said that Shorty usually carried a substantial amount of cash with him, anywhere from $800 to $1,000. He didn't see Shorty with any weapons that night or on any other occasion. He added that right after the homicides of Edwards and Jones, talk among people on the street was that the murders were over a beef in the numbers racket.

The task force hadn't found anyone who either saw or heard from Shorty Jones after midnight, though different people had tried to reach him. Among those seeking cab #56 was an employee at the Little Harlem Hotel who had called the cab company at 1:00 a.m. Shorty usually drove him home from work. Though the dispatcher had put the call out over the radio, Shorty had not answered, nor had he answered radio calls from his own daughter, who had tried to reach him between 1:00 and 1:15. The next sighting of Shorty Jones had been the discovery of his body at 4:29 a.m. in the parking lot of the Tonawanda boat launch; his taxi was found that afternoon on a residential street in Buffalo over three miles away.

An intriguing detail about Shorty's cab was the location where it had been abandoned, in front of 96 Potomac Avenue. This address was two houses down from where Zoe Fontaine's father and brother lived. Another of Shorty's girlfriends had contacted the task force to suggest that this should be looked at "very carefully."

Zoe's father claimed that he had not seen the cab on the street that day. Zoe's brother told police that he knew Shorty as his sister's boyfriend. He said he had never been inside Shorty's cab, but he admitted seeing it parked near his home that morning and had noticed what looked like blood on it. He said he had not been sure whether it was Shorty's cab or not. The brother voluntarily gave police his finger and palm prints, which didn't match any that were found on the cab.

Detectives Williams and Montondo had learned that Shorty Jones carried a gun, a small automatic .380, which he usually kept in a zippered bag somewhere in his cab. Shorty's wife confirmed that he had such a gun, but she had not seen it in a long time. Zoe told police that Shorty had stopped carrying the gun a few weeks prior to the murder, and that he had ceased doing so at Zoe's urging. She had been afraid he might get in trouble for having it. Zoe said that Shorty was carrying a knife the last time she saw him—she had felt it in his jacket pocket when he kissed her good-bye. The knife she described sounded like the one that had been discovered a few feet from his body.

None of the people who knew Jones could offer any suspects for his murder. A check of his bank records showed that he had four joint accounts; three with his wife, one with Zoe Fontaine. The accounts with his wife all had balances of less than $5.00. The account he shared with Zoe had a balance of $402.20.

Police also checked the bank records of Parler Edwards and found that he had a savings account at a local bank with a balance of almost $19,000. He also had a Canadian bank account. Edwards's finances appeared very robust, particularly for a man whose work pension check was $112 per month. Then again, Edwards also drew Social Security and pensions from the army, plus whatever he earned as a cab driver, and he was reputedly tight with his money.

Shorty's wife admitted that he was a numbers runner in a follow-up interview with investigators. He took bets for fares and friends, and had to drop the slips off, but she didn't know where. She felt that his involvement was minimal and that he was not an upper-level person in the operation. He had told her that he didn't want to become heavily involved because people wanted credit and he felt it was more trouble than it was worth. She said any money would've been kept in a cooler in the cab's trunk.

The Jones murder investigation presented a number of red herrings. Drugs. Prostitution. Mistresses. Gambling. Racial hostility over a white girlfriend. Jones had begun driving a cab in February 1980, roughly coinciding with the resumption of his steady relationship with Zoe Fontaine. His drug sales had lately expanded beyond marijuana and pills to include PCP, the white powder known on the street as "angel dust." By most accounts, his behavior on the last day of his life had been unusual, particularly his failure to answer any calls that night, even from his special fares (some of whom were also drug and betting customers). By the time his daughter had tried to reach him around 1:15 a.m., Shorty may have been dead. Further canvassing of residents on Potomac Avenue turned up a man who believed he saw the cab parked there at 3:00 a.m., although he wasn't positive. Then there was the statement from Shorty's friend regarding his sudden demeanor change in the early afternoon of October 8, when it appeared that something was bothering him. Whether what was bothering Shorty was hearing word of Edwards's death could only be speculated. If this was the case, though, Shorty would've somehow known the fate of Parler Edwards before the news had been made public.

Aside from the shared traits of race, gender, and profession, the only other common denominator with Edwards and Jones was their alleged link to numbers. As the days of October passed and investigators delved further, the notion that both were actively involved in the Mafia-controlled numbers racket—and likewise had been deliberate victims for somehow running afoul of the organization—took on ever greater viability, and appeared much more plausible than the prospect that a deranged white man had somehow convinced two very streetwise cabbies—neither of whom were on call at the time—to drive him to remote locations in the dead of night.

Zeroing in on the final movements of Parler Edwards was a far more linear task. Armed with the information concerning the time and contents of Edwards's last meal, investigators questioned employees of the Howard Johnson's. The restaurant had not been busy in the early morning hours when Edwards was last seen there. The overnight cook recalled seeing two black males in the restaurant in the early a.m. but could not identify them. He said he didn't make a salad for anyone but advised that a salad could have been made by the waitress on duty.

Only one waitress had worked that overnight shift. She recalled seeing Edwards in the restaurant but didn't recall the exact time and denied having made a salad for him. Investigators learned that it was against restaurant policy to prepare special orders, such as a salad, during the shift in question, and theorized that this could be the reason that the waitress denied making the salad, if in fact she had done so.

The waitress was questioned extensively at the task force command post as to her actions and observations during the time preceding the presence of Parler Edwards in the restaurant, while he was there, and after he left, with negative results. The questioning officers noted that she appeared to be very nervous, uneasy, and evasive, and generally uncooperative during the entire duration of questioning, leading them to believe that she was not entirely truthful in her answers and that she could possibly have supplied pertinent information concerning the activities surrounding Edwards's presence in the restaurant.

A subpoena was served on the manager of Howard Johnson's, directing her to turn over all sales slips issued by the waitress during her shift that night. With the slips was a handwritten note from the waitress stating "0-voids, 0-missing, and 0-overrings." The sales slips were numbered sequentially. Curiously, one was missing. The manager couldn't account for this because the slips were checked daily, she said. When officers went back to the restaurant to question the waitress again, they found she no longer worked there. According to the manager, she just stopped showing up for work one day.

———

Among the people who placed both Edwards and Jones as actively involved in the numbers racket was, interestingly enough, Collin Cole, the victim of the strangling attempt at the Erie County Medical Center on October 10. Police had been eager to speak with Cole, but interviews kept being postponed due to his medical condition. Cole had emerged from surgery the night of his attack in "very serious condition," according to the briefing Ed Cosgrove had given to reporters, and remained in the intensive care unit. Questioning by investigators had to wait until doctors deemed him well enough.

Collin Cole had, however, given a statement to hospital security after the attack. The assailant had left Collin unconscious with marks on his neck, facial lacerations, a bruised eye, and blood on his right ear. Upon regaining consciousness thirty minutes later, Collin had told the head of hospital security: "A white man came in my room. He was wearing a white shirt, dark brown pants, had blond hair, and blue eyes. He was about 5'8" tall. He said to me, 'I hate all you Niggers. I hate all you Niggers. I hate all you Niggers. I'm gonna kill you.'" The security officer asked Collin if knew his assailant or any reason for the attack and he responded no. Doctors decided it was necessary to perform an emergency tracheotomy due to the excessive swelling of his neck muscles.

There had been a delay in reporting the incident to Buffalo police, so Collin was in surgery by the time officers arrived. Normally, an assault at a county medical center would not have been reported to them at all, but the decision was made to do so because of the ongoing .22 Caliber Killer investigation and that this had involved an attack on a black man by a white man. Detectives Mel Lobbett and John Regan had arrived with a state police investigator. They questioned the staff and had the patient's room photographed and dusted for fingerprints.

The nurse explained that she was passing by Collin Cole's room at 3:30 p.m. when she noticed the door was closed. The door had been open when she'd passed by on her earlier rounds. Entering the room, she saw the patient on the floor with a white man standing over him. The white man told her that the patient had fallen out of bed and hurt his head. As she approached to assist the patient, she asked the white male why he did not call for help, whereupon he fled the room and hurried down the corridor in the direction of the elevators, catching the attention of some other hospital staff along the way. The nurse was shown a composite of the .22 Caliber Killer. She said it closely resembled the man.

Other members of the task force had been called in along with Assistant DA Joseph Mordino. Deciding that the assailant could possibly be the .22 Caliber Killer, the details were relayed to the command post. Cole had been under heavy guard since, and security throughout the Erie County Medical Center had been bolstered in the wake of the attack. At the request of County Executive Edward Rutkowski, the county legislature had allocated $24,000 for the immediate hire of additional security officers.

Collin Cole was not unknown to police prior to the dramatic and much publicized strangulation attempt. He had a considerable rap sheet dating back to the 1960s, mostly for prostitution and loitering, though he had been convicted on a grand larceny charge in the late 1970s that involved the beating of an elderly man. Collin had done time for that offense and had in fact just been released from Attica Prison in January 1980. His most recent arrest occurred in April. Collin was a homosexual and transvestite who made his living as a prostitute and female impersonator on Chippewa Street in the city's red-light district. His street name was Wilma. In his younger years, according to some vice cops, he had passed for a fairly good-looking woman, and Wilma was not averse to rolling johns for extra cash, beyond the fee for services rendered. A prominent forensic psychiatrist for the county had contacted police and suggested that Collin's activities prior to checking into the hospital at 11:20 a.m. on October 9 should be checked. In a meeting with investigators on October 20, the psychiatrist, who specialized in criminology, advised police to take a careful look at Cole in regard to the slayings of the two cab drivers, and further that he should be looked at as a potential suspect in the homicides and even in his own assault. In observing the case, the doctor had found what she labeled as remarkable similarities in the victim and suspect syndrome.

Since a nurse had interrupted the assault and witnessed a white man with a cord in his hand fleeing Collin's room, the legitimacy of the attack was not in question. Police certainly needed to speak with Collin about what had happened as well as anything he might know about Parler Edwards or Shorty Jones. Collin was in the know when it came to street vice. In addition, one of Jones's associates had told investigators that two weeks before his murder, Shorty had complained that a black male he referred to as "Drag Queen" owed him money. The informant didn't know the identity of Drag Queen but Shorty had voiced this while they were discussing narcotics. Collin Cole had been admitted to the Erie County Medical Center on October 9 for a drug overdose.

Ten days passed before investigators were able to communicate with Collin. In the first of his interviews with John Regan and Investigator Richard Cryan of the state police, Collin confirmed that he knew both Edwards and Jones and had been a passenger in both of their cabs in the past. Shorty, he said, would transport him around the city and never charged the fare. Shorty dealt in marijuana, cocaine, and PCP, according to Collin, and he pimped for both white and black girls and for homosexuals, in addition to using his cab to run numbers. He had last seen Edwards and Jones about two weeks prior to the murders. As for the attack on himself, at first he claimed he had nothing to add about the man who had tried to strangle him.

Investigators spoke with Collin on multiple occasions. He didn't seem to have a problem talking with police, but getting reliable, consistent information from him, particularly on the strangulation attempt, was proving no small task. When shown the latest composite drawing of the .22 Caliber Killer, he at first said it looked similar to his attacker but later stated it didn't resemble his attacker nor any of his tricks, most of whom were black. By turns he could be flirty or capricious. As a witness, he was tiresome. Captain Henry Williams at one point wearily remarked to him, "You know, Collin, I'd even crawl in bed with you myself if you'd give me a straight answer."

On October 24, John Regan and Richard Cryan spoke with Collin again about anything he might remember of the attack. After about an hour, Collin revealed that he knew the man who had strangled him. He and the man, who here shall be called Darren, had met a few years ago when they were doing time at Wende Prison, and Darren had come to live with Collin at the Royal Arms Hotel on Utica Street after his release from Wende. Darren was a burglar and had accumulated about $2,700 in heisted cash. Collin had walked out on Darren and taken the $2,700 with him. He didn't see Darren for a while, until the afternoon of October 10 when Darren confronted Collin in his hospital room about the betrayal and then tried to strangle him.

Officers retrieved some mug shots, including Darren's, and brought them to Collin's room. He picked out Darren's mug shot as the man who had attacked him and, in the presence of family members, gave a deposition.

Though the attack on Collin Cole had been hastily folded in with the task force, coming just a day after the two horrific cabbie murders—and because of knee-jerk fear that the blond strangler could be the mysterious blond assassin—there were a number of factors from the outset that tended to cast doubt on the .22 Caliber Killer scenario. Skipping the question of why a hit-and-run gunman would opt for strangulation, and count on getting lucky enough to find a black male in a room by himself at the county hospital, why would a killer looking for a random victim go up to the seventh floor, so far up from the convenience of any easy escape route to the street, particularly when there were many black male patients on the lower floors of the hospital?

Despite what had been announced to the press and the public, the three prime witnesses to the attack on Cole—the nurse and staff members who saw the suspect flee—had described a man who looked markedly different from the descriptions of the .22 Caliber Killer. All three said the man had bright yellow blond hair, not dirty blond. All, including Cole, said he had blue eyes. (None of the .22 Caliber witnesses had given an eye color.) The strangler, described by witnesses as five feet two to five feet four, also seemed to be much shorter than the September shooter, although Cole had initially pegged his height at five feet eight. Then there was the other detail that came to light: someone had asked for Cole's room number before the assault.

Ed Cosgrove had been in a no-win situation with the Cole attack. To withhold all information on the incident would've created suspicion and mistrust in sectors that were already apprehensive about his commitment to the investigation, especially if the attack could later be definitively linked to the September shootings and/or the cab driver murders. In the interest of keeping the community informed—and demonstrating that the task force was responding immediately to any suspicious white-on-black attack—he had called the press conference that night. Based on information from the nervous hospital employees, and perhaps some details that had been lost in translation, the announcement was made that the strangler appeared to be "the same maniac."

The story had instantly blown up. Reports of the attack on Collin Cole referred to the nurse as the "star witness in the series of brutal slayings." Hospital staff who had witnessed the attacker flee—or believed they had—were reportedly receiving twenty-four-hour police protection, including an elderly hospital volunteer who claimed he saw a blond man in the employee locker room two hours before the attack and feared it might've been the strangler/killer.

Though Ed Cosgrove continued to state at press conferences that no connection had been established between the shootings and the cabbie murders, the notion that all six murders as well as the strangulation attempt were the work of the .22 Caliber Killer had nonetheless been firmly ingrained in the public's mind. Details in fine print aside, the narrative had been established: all seven crimes were related, all were racially motivated.

The crimes were, after all, being investigated collectively by the task force, giving the impression they must be connected, while headlines and broadcast news touted *the* murder probe, consistently referring to "the six killings" and citing Collin Cole as the "seventh victim," all of which further played upon the primordial fear of an invincible bogeyman capable of all manner of brutality, able to slip effortlessly into the shadows once his evil deeds were done.

Cosgrove was asked daily by the media whether a link existed between the two sets of murders. When the question came up again at a press conference in mid-October, Cosgrove stated, as usual, "There is no evidence to link them," but added, "Are we concerned that there might be a relationship between all of the slayings? Absolutely!" The *Courier-Express* translated this into a bold headline: "DA Won't Rule Out One Killer; Previously Refused To Consider Any Tie In All 7 Incidents."

The single slayer theory created a problem for FBI artist Horace Heafner as he tried to create a new composite sketch. Heafner had met with a dozen witnesses from the shootings and the hospital attack, and reconciling all the conflicting information was proving a challenge. Explaining the delay in releasing the new sketch, a source told the media, "We have so many different descriptions that it would probably hurt a prosecution if they were released now." After several days' work, the FBI released five sketches in late October that were dutifully broadcast and published on front pages. One sketch showed the suspect with straight, short, light hair while three depicted him in different hats, and one in profile with longer hair. The description was a white male about five feet six to five feet nine, in his early to midtwenties, clean shaven, with dirty-blond hair and a slender build. It was noted that the sketch was not supposed to represent the subject in the same manner a photo would, but to give a general description of his features.

Once again, there was very little to distinguish what Cosgrove called the "new and improved" sketch. While the DA expressed satisfaction with the FBI rendering, there were many in law enforcement and the general populace alike who did not find it either much of an improvement or particularly helpful. As one dismayed black resident was later quoted in a local newspaper, "Do you know how many white people look like that?"

More daunting to investigators was that there was no guarantee the sketch represented one suspect. Faced with all the conflicts, the FBI had done their best to produce a "boiling down" of descriptions from witnesses to several different crimes. In other words, the facial characteristics— quite possibly of more than one individual—had been melded into an overall portrait.

Cosgrove stressed at press conferences that the composites should not be construed as a photographic likeness. He believed that the new sketches were much more accurate than the first had been and hoped they would "awaken recognition of someone with the same general features." He felt confident that the sketches would generate a new flow of information to the command post.

On this last point he was correct. The hotline was flooded with calls, all of which had to be checked out. This influx of new "leads" on the amalgamated blond bogeyman privately caused frustration for the most informed detectives, who knew damn well they had three separate cases on their hands.

———

Edward Cosgrove had decreed strict confidentiality for the task force, and thus the emerging details on Edwards, Jones, and Cole were not released during his press conferences. Reiterating that he himself was the sole source of information, he played his cards very close to the vest and insisted that all those in and around the task force—which had grown to 185 members—do the same. As one law enforcement official had told inquiring reporters outside the command post, "I can't even tell you what sandwiches we're ordering for lunch." But the media had their sources, of course, and they were definitely eager to report something more than same old accounts of the daily closed-door meetings of various politicians who had little to offer aside from restating their grave concern over the slayings.

On October 22, the *Buffalo Evening News* ran a story headlined, "Taxi Killings May Be Linked to Betting War." Similar stories and whisperings began to crop up, revealing the discovery of the policy (betting) slips that had been found in the cabs and some details on the connections and criminal histories of the last three victims. An October 24 article in the *Courier-Express* divulged that Collin Cole might know his attacker and that the assault had occurred following an argument.

By the next day, newspapers reported that probers had ruled out a single slayer. Sources inside the investigation had tipped them off that all evidence indicated the shootings, cabbie murders, and strangulation attempt were three separate cases. News stories revealed that Edwards and Jones were numbers runners and that both had worked for the same cab company in the past, "a company well known to police for trouble," one source was quoted. Ernest Jones "was known to keep company with a white woman" and his blood-stained taxi had been found "not far from where this woman's father lives," while longtime prostitute and street crime virtuoso Collin Cole had been "involved" with the man who tried to strangle him with a telephone cord.

Murders over a numbers racket dispute obviously didn't fit the narrative of a white racist assassin or a national plot to eliminate black men, nor did an altercation between two ex-cons over stolen money and spurned affections. For some, that was a problem.

The premise that all the crimes had been the direct by-product of racial hatred was by now a theme in which many individuals, black and white, were heavily—and publicly—invested. Eroding or otherwise wresting this concept away, even in the interests of truth, was no longer an option for some, particularly those devoted to what they viewed as the greater crisis at hand. To that end, the victims had been eulogized as symbols and martyrs of all that was wrong in society. The Catholic priest who conducted the funeral service for Shorty Jones had spoken of him as a peacemaker who had helped quell racial tensions in the Commodore Perry Housing Projects, saying that it was ironic "that a man who did so much to restore peace between black and white citizens should die in what is believed to be a racial incident." The priest blamed Shorty's death on a sick assailant. "He caught this sickness from somewhere and we as white brothers and sisters may be passive or active carriers of the disease that convey support to this sick killer," he said. "The unequal housing, education and employment opportunities for our black and brown brothers convey to the sick person support that he is justified for his sick ways." Calling for change and an end to racial slurs, he told the mourners, "If we don't actively try to put an end to those racist conditions, then we are supporting the actions of this sick person and others like him."

US President Jimmy Carter had taken a special interest in the case. Briefed by New York Governor Hugh Carey and Senator Daniel Patrick Moynihan on the "calm but serious situation in Buffalo," Carter had mobilized additional federal resources and personnel. As a result of the president's intervention, Charles P. Monroe, deputy director of the FBI's criminal division, and Drew S. Days III, assistant US attorney general in charge of the department's Civil Rights Division, were dispatched to Buffalo to review the investigation. Monroe had played a key role in the FBI's probe of the sniper attack on civil rights activist Vernon Jordan earlier that year. Speaking at a press conference at the Buffalo Airport, Monroe said that civil rights "is an area of my expertise." The FBI still had not made a determination on whether the civil rights of any of the murder victims had been violated.

With so much focus on civil rights—still cited as a key requirement for the FBI to assume jurisdiction in the case—and the foundation firmly cemented on the platform of racially motivated slayings, the revelation of facts that cast doubt on this premise were met with resistance and even outrage. Following reports that Collin Cole knew his assailant, the Reverend Bennett Smith went to see Collin at the county medical center. Smith emerged from the meeting and announced to the press that Collin Cole did not know his attacker. "Mr. Cole substantiated that the assault on him was the result of a racial encounter. He had never seen the man before and did not know him," Smith said.

"There is a mentally disturbed person out there somewhere who has killed six black men," Bennett Smith angrily told reporters. "There may be more than one killer responsible. But the murders have all been directed at black males out of hatred for blacks and for no other motive."

Smith and other black leaders lambasted the press for revealing details of the victims' criminal histories. "Blacks don't care about that," Smith snapped. "Catch the killers. We don't want to read the background of the victims." They also resented the questioning of victims' family members by investigators, though this was standard procedure in any homicide investigation. Tempers flared again when Ed Cosgrove conceded at one of his press conferences that he could not rule out the possibility of a black assailant in the cab driver murders.

John Douglas of the FBI was experiencing a similar pushback in Atlanta, where he had been called to develop a suspect profile in the Atlanta Child Murders. Investigators there had been looking for a white offender. When Douglas concluded the offender was black, as he would later recall, "They didn't like it." His predictions and suggestions were dismissed as crazy. (Eventually, each proved to be true.)

The murders in Buffalo and Atlanta had thrust both cities into the national spotlight. In both cities, the killings had unleashed widespread fear—and set the great wheel of racial politics in motion. Bloodshed and racial discord were always hot topics. Buffalo Mayor James Griffin appeared on the ABC news program *Nightline* for a broadcast dedicated to the unsolved homicides in Buffalo and Atlanta. Host Ted Koppel pressed him on whether he thought the murders in Western New York were connected to the Ku Klux Klan or neo-Nazi groups, as asserted by some black leaders in Buffalo who were also interviewed. Griffin responded that he agreed with District Attorney Edward Cosgrove that the murders were the product of a deranged mind.

Speculation that the killer was psychotic had become another bone of contention. Cosgrove had been assailed by members of black activist groups and the NAACP for characterizing the killer as deranged or maniacal, although Bennett Smith had been quoted by a journalist from *Newsweek* as saying, "There is no doubt the killer is mentally deranged, that premeditation is involved and that the killings are racially motivated."

When Ed Cosgrove was asked at a press conference whether his comments might give an attorney a ready-made defense in the event of an arrest, he answered, "Any self-respecting lawyer who takes on this case would be insane himself if he didn't entertain insanity as a defense."

This provoked resentment and anger from individuals who were already dissatisfied with Cosgrove's handling of the investigation. Officials of the NAACP called for a federal takeover. Hazel Dukes, state president of the NAACP, had flown in from New York City for a meeting with Cosgrove and a briefing on the investigation, after which she told the press, "I'm unhappy with the investigation here. It has been 27 days since the first murder and the killer still has not been captured. We will continue to request and push for federal intervention and an investigation independent of local efforts. No stone should be left unturned." Dukes said she would also continue to press for "intensified efforts" by Cosgrove's office.

While no arrests had been made, the task force had unquestionably put forth intense efforts. Every lead, tip, and avenue was being followed. Scores of white men were questioned. As one Buffalo police captain later recalled, "They pulled in every white guy who was a little bit off." By mid-October, two men who had been reported to the task force by tipsters had committed suicide. Another man who thought he was under investigation—erroneously, as it turned out—cut his wrists. He had recovered and moved from the area but kept calling Buffalo police to ask if he was still a suspect.

The whole spectacle had dredged up the weird and the depraved. Someone had left a heart on a shelf in the public library. Buffalo police responded to the 911 call and questioned two young women working there who said that when they had returned from a twenty-minute break, a black male had approached one of the women, pointed at the shelf, and said, "Look at that, someone left that. Someone left that for you." Based on the description, the library security guard said the man sounded like a "bummy" type guy who was always hanging around the library. The heart was small, about two and a half inches long, and confirmed by the medical examiner as not human. It was transported to the morgue for further analysis.

The command post received a call one night from an anonymous male who said that "seven more niggers would be killed." The call was traced to a bar on Genesee and Jefferson Streets; Leo Donovan immediately dispatched officers. There were two pay phones inside and one outside the bar. The owner and barmaid hadn't paid attention to who might've used the phones but said there hadn't been any white patrons in the bar at all that night.

The task force was also receiving calls from police agencies across the country with suggestions that the cab driver murders could be cult killings or the work of small subversive organizations dedicated to the occult.

The NAACP and other black activist groups were pushing vigorously for a federal inquiry into a connection between the murders and the Ku Klux Klan. The Buffalo FBI office had so far ruled out such a probe. Fears of a KKK link or conspiracy were not mere paranoia. In recent years, in reaction to the civil rights victories of the 1960s and subsequent federally mandated school integration and busing, the Klan had experienced a resurgence in membership and nonmember support that was by no means underground nor restricted to states in the deep south. In September 1980, robed Klansmen marched in Southington, Connecticut, and held two nights of rallies and cross burnings, reportedly attended by some eight hundred people, to celebrate the installation of the state's first Grand Dragon.

In April, three Klansmen in Chattanooga, Tennessee, had injured five middle-aged black women in a drive-by shooting that followed cross burnings. Violence erupted in the city that summer after an all-white jury acquitted two of them and convicted the shooter on a reduced charge. *Newsweek* published an article on October 6 that detailed the growing paramilitary and weapons stockpiling activities of the Klan in cities across the country. By the end of 1980, it was estimated that KKK membership around the United States had grown to ten thousand members with one hundred thousand nonmembers donating money, attending rallies, or reading their literature. While these numbers represented only a sliver of what the Klan had been in its heyday in the 1920s, when membership had reportedly numbered in the millions and in some areas had effectively controlled state and local governments, it was nevertheless a significant and menacing surge, particularly since new young leaders of the KKK such as Bill Wilkinson, so-called "Imperial Wizard of the Invisible Empire," were eschewing the secrecy and hooded anonymity of their forerunners in favor of public marches and active recruiting.

In the waning months of 1980, as the hunt for serial killers preying on blacks was underway in Buffalo and Atlanta, Wilkinson had plans to appear on *The Phil Donahue Show* on television and was giving an extensive, no-holds-barred interview to Wayne King of the *New York Times* for a Sunday magazine feature. Titled "The Violent Rebirth of the Klan," it was published in the *Times* magazine on December 7, 1980, and profiled other Klan leaders in addition to Wilkinson. Some of the new KKK chapters were attempting to rebrand themselves not as racist but simply as "pro-white," obviously hoping to lure those who felt disenfranchised by shifting demographics and the lagging US economy, playing on fear and vulnerability, as all adept cult leaders do. A few branches were even opening their ranks to Catholics, a group the Klan had long sought to eradicate, or at least suppress. There had been no groundswell of Catholics responding to this magnanimous offer, however, and the KKK had not seen any appreciable uptick in membership in cities with large Catholic populations, which Buffalo had.

Buffalo police had in fact investigated the possibility of a link to the KKK or neo-Nazi groups. In early October, Detectives Harold Frank and Matthew Parsons had traveled to Syracuse to meet with a former Buffalo resident who supplied them with information on a small group of avowed Klan members in Western New York, led by a resident of the east side of Buffalo named Karl Hand. According to the informant, a few years prior, Hand and a half dozen of his friends, who were all white males currently in their early twenties, had proclaimed themselves the "protectors of Schiller Park," a neighborhood on Buffalo's east side. The group met often at a particular member's home to discuss their philosophy and talk about "getting" people, which meant assaulting black males. The group had on numerous occasions attacked black males in the neighborhood and engaged in fights to protect "the kids," presumably white kids, from area blacks. The informant said that the group had been in such fights during the summer of 1980. They kept a store of KKK literature and attempted to distribute it. He never heard them talk of killing anyone but said that about three years earlier they had been responsible for fracturing the skull of a black male with a length of pipe in the Genesee Street-Schiller Park area. Asked about any weapons the members might have, he said they had all types of knives as well as firearms, and that some time ago police had seized a number of firearms during a raid of the home where meetings were held.

All the members were heavy beer drinkers, but as far as any taverns where they might hang around, the informant said they had been banned from most bars in the area. Two years earlier they had held a family picnic in Emery Park that was sponsored by the Ku Klux Klan during which the men shot at paper cups with a pellet gun and practiced throwing knives and hatchets into a tree. The group's leader, Karl Hand, was constantly preaching his Nazi philosophy. He often praised Adolf Hitler as someone who had the right solution.

Karl Hand and several of his associates were already known to police. Far from being under the radar, Hand spoke openly of his beliefs. He stood on street corners trying to pass out his racist literature. He had immediately been a person of interest in the .22 caliber shootings but was eliminated as a suspect when it was learned that he had been hospitalized for a kidney transplant during the time the shootings occurred. He had been discharged on October 6, a day prior to the murder of Parler Edwards, but it didn't seem likely that a man who had undergone such a serious surgery would have the strength to carry out a sustained and brutal attack the following night. Hand's followers had also been closely checked, but all were confirmed as either in police custody or out of state at the time of the murders. Leads on others with a history of racist philosophies and affiliations had been pursued but led nowhere.

A postal worker turned in a business card from Knights of the Ku Klux Klan that he had found stuffed in the coin return of a pay phone at Genesee and Bailey. The card read, "Racial Purity Is America's Security," and had a mailing address and phone number in Louisiana. The postal worker told police he had been approached over the summer by a white male in his sixties driving an old blue car who asked him to distribute the cards to all white families on his route. The postal worker said he had been approached two or three times over the past year about passing out material of a similar nature, each time by different individuals. He had always refused.

Klansmen and Nazi sympathizers aside, the murders and their resultant publicity had emboldened some racist behavior from individuals who ran the gamut from the potentially dangerous to misfit lost souls. Detectives Paul Delano and Harold Frank paid a visit to a teenage student at Erie Community College (ECC) who had penned an ominous poem. The poem had been brought to their attention by the postal inspector's office, as the young man had written it on the outside of an envelope that he then mailed. It read:

The .22 Caliber Killer is at ECC,
So all of you Niggers stay clear of me.
If I see you, you'd be dead.
I will shoot you in head.

If I see you in the Hall
I'll spray your brains all over the wall.
I'm so vicious you will see
If you thinks that's really shitty
I'll kill every nigger in the City!

When they interviewed the teen at ECC he admitted writing the poem on the envelope but claimed he had copied it off a desk at the school, though he couldn't remember which one. He thought the poem was kind of neat and thought that his brother might enjoy it. The teen said he had a poor relationship with his father, who had told him that he thought the killer was doing good. When asked if he was under psychiatric care, he replied no but added that he felt he might have an emotional problem with his father. He said he had no friends and described himself as a loner. Detectives took additional information and did some checking on the young man and his father but ultimately ruled them out.

Police were also sifting through crank calls, threatening notes left on cars, and letters received by police headquarters. Among the correspondence that bore scrutiny was a small envelope postmarked from Rochester addressed to "Buffalo Police, Buffalo New York." Inside was a note on lined paper written in a slanting print:

Stop me before I kill
More but I dinint cut out
No Hearts. Somone other
did those.

There was no way to determine from whom it had come or assess the legitimacy. It was kept at close hand in the homicide squad in case the writer made contact again, but he or she never did.

———

While the task force continued laboring behind a veil of secrecy, fissures that had erupted around the city were widening into chasms. Though no sustained incidents of racial violence on the streets had occurred since the weekend following the cabbie murders, undercurrents of resentment and mistrust had boiled up on both sides of the racial divide. And there was no question that in some quarters, despite the best efforts of clergy and perpetual sound bites from officials who praised the community for sticking together, a division of us-versus-them was emerging along racial lines. The climate of fear had not so much birthed racial antagonism and suspicion, but had rather unearthed that which had lain dormant.

Newsweek published an article on October 27, 1980, about the spree of murders in Buffalo and Atlanta. Under the headline "The Fears of Black America," it summarized the crimes and touched on other killings of blacks across the country over the past year. The article began with a quote from Stanford University historian Kennell Jackson that perhaps best illuminated a collective feeling: "When you pick up the newspaper and read about this black being killed here and another black being killed there, it does something to your psyche, something bad. It leads to the perception that it's suddenly hunting season on blacks again."

A random phone survey of three hundred black families in Buffalo had been conducted in mid-October. Fifty-two percent thought the police were doing a good job of trying to solve the murders. When asked if they thought "an extremist group" was responsible for the six murders, 28 percent responded yes, 27 percent said no, and 43 percent declined to answer. Sixty percent said they feared for their personal safety.

Fear had taken root in the white community as well. Fear of riots and reprisals, and a redux of the week in June 1967 when a portion of the east side of the city had been torn asunder in what the *New York Times* described as "a four-day rampage by Negro youths." Gangs of angry blacks, as many as 1,500 individuals in total according to an estimate from the *Times*, had roamed the ghetto setting fires, breaking windows, looting, clashing with police, and attacking whites indiscriminately. Scores of people were injured, more than one hundred arrested. Assemblyman Arthur Eve had urged an end to the violence but referred to the riot afterward as "only logical" as a result of high unemployment, slum housing, and poor relations with the police.

The great divide in perception had never been more apparent than in the aftermath. While many blacks blamed the riot in large part on poor relations with the police, Buffalo Police Commissioner Frank Felicetta had disagreed, saying that relations between his department and the city's one hundred thousand black residents were excellent and expressing surprise that the race riots then sweeping the country had similarly broken out in Buffalo. "I would have been willing to bet anything that we would never have had a riot here," Felicetta was quoted.

Arthur Eve had countered, saying of the police, "They're bigoted. They live in the suburbs and have no idea what goes on in the Negro areas nor any respect for the people living there." The viewpoints had been so strikingly divergent that one visiting government official had wondered aloud if the opposing sides were talking about the same city.

———

Edward Cosgrove met daily with black leaders and community groups, making himself readily available as he had vowed to do from the start. With no real progress to report on the investigation, however, he was increasingly met with skepticism and reproach. Cosgrove was not the only target of ire, but he handled it with more fortitude than some.

Police Commissioner James Cunningham was accused by some black officers and personnel at BUILD of not providing police protection for the Reverend Jesse Jackson during his visit. Cunningham responded that "other than the president of the United States, no dignitary has been given more protection than we gave to Reverend Jackson." The commander of the special services bureau claimed that Jackson never had less than eight plainclothes officers with him in addition to security from Cheektowaga police and the sheriff's department. Cunningham reacted angrily over Jesse Jackson's public criticism of him for not attending the panel discussion at Channel 7. Cunningham shot back that Jackson's entire visit had been staged by the TV station for publicity, which caused anger from black activists who insisted that Jackson's visit had helped calm a tense situation that might otherwise have turned violent. Cunningham refrained from attending most public meetings on the probe, inciting more rebukes. "I have always said that there has never been a killer apprehended at a news conference," he snapped. Mayor Griffin met with community groups but faced similar criticism for not holding regular press conferences on the murder investigation. Griffin said that he agreed with Cunningham that there were more than enough press conferences going on.

In addition to the fiery criticism the district attorney was taking from black leaders, his office also heard from citizens who were outraged over the investigation for starkly different reasons. He received complaints from people who felt that too much time and resources were being consumed by the probe. A few were blatantly hateful. One particularly virulent letter read, in part:

> What is the matter with the people of Buffalo? Five members of the despicable nigger race are killed and the town goes absolutely schizophrenic! I didn't see the town declare unity day for the multitude of white cops murdered by niggers . . . and all the elderly couples and singles beaten or robbed by niggers, including me!!! Damn them! Let them know the fear we've experienced for years at their hands. I am seeing, along with a large number of others, a sad case of nigger coddling, reverse discriminatory treatment!! I hope he gets 20 more before you catch him. It'll make life a lot more bearable for all of us . . .

At the end of October, two new resources were established. The first was the Rumor Control Unit, a call center installed at city hall at the direction of the US Justice Department "to provide facts and dispel rumors about the investigation of the murders of six black men, and any related racial incidents." According to the director, the first five calls they received were from persons concerned about whether rioting would break out when the official twenty-one-day mourning period was finished. Days before, some black leaders had warned that it might be difficult to maintain calm in the black community after the mourning period ended unless a suspect was captured.

The second innovation was the establishment of a second tip hotline for the murder investigation. The first hotline that had been set up at the DA's task force remained in service and was open to all; the new hotline, operated at the office of the US Attorney, was a private number intended for the use of blacks only.

Assistant Attorney General Drew S. Days had ordered the second hotline at the request of black leaders who claimed it was necessary because of black mistrust of the police department. The hotline would be manned by black community leaders, who would pass the tips directly to the FBI field office and to the district attorney. The number was unpublished, presumably given out privately to black citizens via community groups. According to Bennett Smith, blacks felt that tips they phoned in to the DA's hotline just ended up in the wastebasket. The second hotline would have a built-in system to keep black leaders informed on the status of each tip.

Mayor Griffin decried the whole thing as a bad idea. Griffin felt all information should be channeled through Cosgrove's office and that a second hotline would do more harm than good. Ed Cosgrove made no public comment on the matter. For the first time since assembling the task force, he did not hold a daily press briefing.

Politicians in Erie County were meanwhile conferring with politicians in Albany about the reward fund. At a press conference at the Buffalo Chamber of Commerce, it was announced that the reward had grown to $100,000, with the city, county, and chamber each contributing $25,000 and the remaining $25,000 raised from private donations. But there was a problem: state law prohibited the city from offering more than $1,000, and the county was capped at $5,000. Meetings were held to try and figure out a work around this dilemma. The common council passed resolutions. Advisory panels were formed. The matter would be brought before a special session of the state legislature in late November.

Drew Days had declared that the six murders and attempted murder of Collin Cole had to be dealt with on two levels: a strong push to apprehend the killer or killers, and a strong assurance to the black community that all was being done to that end. The task force members—John Regan, Mel Lobbett, Al Williams, Sam Slade, Tom Rowan, and their 180 fellow lawmen—also had to deal with the investigation on two levels: continuing the dogged, day-to-day, hands-on police work that was the only hope of ever solving the crimes, and avoiding the backbiting political sideshow it had all become.

Among those who shunned the politics and the spotlight were the families of the victims. They offered few, if any, public comments and had essentially receded into the realm of bit players in the spectacle of high drama swirling around them. For those who had loved the dead boy and the five dead men, the echoes of grief swelled high above the cries of acrimony, or even the calls for justice. No matter who would be arrested, no matter who would be elected or reelected, no matter who would eventually collect the reward, for them the end result would forever remain the same. Glenn, Harold, Emanuel, Joseph, Parler, and Shorty were never coming back.

———

On November 9, Ed Cosgrove announced that a new composite of the .22 Caliber Killer would be released soon. "We have a little closer and finer look at the person who is responsible for the .22 caliber killings," he stated during a radio broadcast. FBI artist Horace Heafner was creating a new composite on information from "six or seven" witnesses that had been put under hypnosis.

Reporters at the unveiling of the new sketch appeared a little baffled. It looked no different than the last. "It's of the same individual," Cosgrove conceded. "It's a refined view of the earlier composite." He pointed out that the nose was a bit narrower, the face more slender, with "a little more maturity around the eyes." Age, height, hair color, and clothing remained the same.

November passed into December with no significant developments. Merchants and restaurants around the city experienced a sharp decline in business. Dread of the .22 Caliber Killer and street crime in general—although the former had not resurfaced and the latter had dropped significantly—kept people away, particularly after dark.

As Christmas approached, some black leaders decided that more needed to be done to express dissatisfaction over the lack of any arrests in the killings. On December 17, the Black Leadership Forum, a coalition of area clergy, activists, and politicians that had formed in early October in the wake of the murders, held a press conference to announce a boycott of downtown stores. Leaders were asking "all self-respecting black people and other citizens" not to make any purchases at any of the stores on December 22, 23, and 24 in protest of the unfruitful manhunt.

Lillian Meadows, a black activist and senior citizens advocate, sharply disagreed with the boycott. She pointed out that many of the stores employed blacks. She didn't want to see them lose their jobs, and didn't see how a boycott would help matters anyway. Initiators of the boycott insisted that it was a means of showing "concern" that the investigation had apparently ground to a halt.

There was little that Ed Cosgrove or anyone else could say to argue that the murder probe had stalled. They were still investigating, still questioning the occasional person of interest, but none of the two thousand leads they followed had panned out. On the same day that the Black Leadership Forum announced the boycott, Cosgrove submitted an itemized list of task force expenses to the county legislature. The highest expenditure was $17,555.57 for installation and maintenance of computers used to code, store, and organize 160,000 pieces of information related to the investigation. The "command post" expenses totaled more than $9,800.00 and included over $4,000 in payments to informants, transportation, and meals and lodging for witnesses. Medical experts and consultants had been paid $7,800.00 to date. The total came to $35,204.11.

The task force expenses were published in the newspaper, noting that the probe had so far failed to produce any arrests.

As 1980 drew to a close, task force members felt the keen burden that the cases of the past fall had grown as cold as the winter winds that swept across Lake Erie. Several times they'd thought they had a suspect in their grasp. But they were wrong.

The task force would continue into the new year. They would start anew, follow more leads, go wherever the trail led them, though many believed it had gone irretrievably cold.

They thought at least that the killings were over.

But they were wrong.

PART TWO
THE MIDTOWN SLASHER

It is a man's own mind, not his enemy or foe, that lures him to evil ways.

—Buddha

Chapter 8
DECEMBER 22–28, 1980

MANHATTAN WAS AWASH in holiday spirit. Or at least in holiday decorations.

Of New York City's five boroughs, Manhattan shines as the tourist destination, the place that even locals refer to as "the City." At Christmastime, the main plazas and public squares are decked in lights and giant, lavishly decorated Christmas trees, complementing the glow from festive store windows and the clanging bells of Salvation Army volunteers situated on corners.

The man in the wire-rimmed glasses was a stranger in Manhattan, as were many of the people who thronged the streets on this Monday morning. Outwardly there was nothing about him that drew attention or set him apart from the millions of others who hurried along the sidewalks or ran to catch the trains. He surely wasn't even the only one with a knife concealed in his jacket.

John Adams, age twenty-five, was not a stranger in the city. He lived on 153rd Street up in the Bronx and commuted to Manhattan on the trains. At 11:30 a.m., Adams was exiting the subway at Fourteenth Street and Seventh Avenue. He didn't notice the white man in the wire-rimmed glasses passing by in the opposite direction. Not until the white man suddenly sidestepped in front of him, hit him hard in the chest, and kept going.

It took John Adams a moment to realize what had just happened. *He stabbed me . . . he stabbed me!* John clutched the area around his heart. Warm blood oozed through his winter coat and over his trembling brown fingers. He turned and saw the white man quickly boarding the IRT number two train. And then John Adams collapsed.

———

Ivan Frazer, age thirty-two, was another of the city's millions of commuters. At 1:30 p.m., Frazer sat on the E train from Queens westbound for Manhattan. When the train stopped at Ely Avenue, a young man wearing wire-rimmed glasses and a salt-and-pepper cap took a seat across from him. Frazer glanced up from his newspaper. The young man, whom Frazer later described as maybe about twenty-two and very innocent looking, had sat down between two women and seemed to be trying to flirt with them.

The young man in glasses asked both women for the time. One stayed mute and turned away. The other told him the time but kept her eyes forward. Ivan Frazer found this kind of cute, the way the young man was trying to strike up a conversation with girls on the subway. Ivan smiled at the young man and he smiled back, then looked down. Ivan went back to reading his newspaper.

The young man wasn't having much luck with the ladies. He seemed to be out of lines after asking for the time, and they weren't paying him any mind. One of the women got up and left. A few minutes later, the train stopped at Fiftieth Street and Fifth Avenue, and the young man stood up. Both hands were in his pockets as he stepped forward to leave the car. Ivan saw the young man's hand coming swiftly toward Ivan's chest. He instinctively raised his left arm to ward off the blow.

Startled, and wondering why in hell the guy had done that, Ivan jumped up from his seat and lunged after the man, throwing him up against the door. The young man jumped off the train and Ivan followed.

"What's going on?!" Ivan asked.

The young man stood facing him, shaking. He looked down at Ivan's hand. Then he slipped his own hand into his right jacket pocket, pulled out a knife, and began waving it around.

People on the subway platform started running away. Ivan looked down and saw that his left hand was hanging, bleeding. And then Ivan ran too.

———

At 3:30 p.m., Luis Rodriguez, age nineteen, was walking on Madison Avenue between Fortieth and Forty-First Streets when a white man with wire-rimmed glasses jumped in his path.

"Give me your wallet," the man reportedly said.

Luis stopped short. Witnesses weren't sure if the victim handed over the wallet or if the white man grabbed it from Luis's jacket before or after plunging a knife into Luis's chest. The white man ran away.

Luis turned slowly. "I've been stabbed," he cried out. "He took my wallet."

He fell to the pavement.

———

At 6:47 p.m., Antoine Davis, a thirty-year-old from Brooklyn, was attacked at Thirty-Seventh Street near Seventh Avenue.

At 10:40 p.m., Richard Renner, age twenty, was assaulted as he entered a candy store on Forty-Ninth Street between Broadway and Seventh Avenue.

Sometime after 11:00 p.m., Carl Ramsey was attacked on the subway at Thirty-Third Street between Seventh and Eighth Avenues.

All three died shortly after being stabbed in the chest. All three were black males.

———

Captain John Meehan was commander of the third detective zone in mid-Manhattan. On Tuesday, December 23, Captain Meehan was conferring with several of his detectives on the series of stabbings that had taken place the day and night before. While stabbings in the city were not an anomaly these days, there were some very notable similarities in these attacks, four of which had been fatal.

Luis Rodriguez had died in the hospital. All he could tell police was that the man who knifed him had taken his wallet. Antoine Davis,

Richard Renner, and Carl Ramsey died before making any statements. Witnesses to the different attacks, however, had given a description that sounded remarkably like the same suspect: a white man in his thirties of medium build, five feet seven to five feet ten inches tall, 150 to 160 pounds, wearing wire-rimmed glasses.

All the victims had been stabbed in the chest with a single thrust. All the attacks had occurred around midtown Manhattan. Aside from Luis Rodriguez, the assailant reportedly said nothing to the victims before suddenly plunging a blade into them and then hurrying away.

Manhattan detectives also had two strangely similar reports from black men who had been stabbed on the subway the previous day but survived. John Adams, attacked at Fourteenth and Seventh, was recovering at St. Vincent's Hospital after a four-hour surgery to repair the knife wound near his heart. Ivan Frazer had been treated for the stabbing of his left hand. Both survivors described an unprovoked attack by a small but strong white man in wire-rimmed glasses who fled without a word. That made six victims within about a twelve-hour span. Five black men and Rodriguez, who was a dark-skinned Hispanic.

There were no connections among any of the victims.

Captain Meehan recalled the teletype reports from Buffalo about the spate of shootings of four black men in September by a white man. He decided it was worth a call to compare notes.

Meehan called Erie County DA Edward Cosgrove and Captain Henry Williams of the state police BCI, both of whom were very receptive to the information. Cosgrove and Williams noted everything Meehan told them and immediately made arrangements for two of their task force members to travel to New York City the following day.

On Christmas Eve, Mel Lobbett and William "Joe" Cooley, senior investigator for the state police, boarded a plane for New York. They met with Captain Meehan, who then assigned one of his detectives to work with the visiting lawmen from upstate.

Joe Cooley had joined state police in 1962. Melvin Lobbett had been a Buffalo police officer since 1961, a detective since 1973. Cooley and Lobbett had both been consumed by the .22 Caliber Killer investigation for the past three months. Catching the serial killer was top priority for law enforcement in Western New York, one they'd been pursuing vigorously, which is perhaps why they were dismayed by the attitudes they encountered among their downstate counterparts.

As Cooley recalled, the New York detectives didn't seem to put much stock in a possible connection with the Buffalo murders. They didn't even seem particularly alarmed about the attacks that had occurred in their own jurisdiction, as Joe Cooley perceived it. The files were scant—brief statements from witnesses, a photo of each victim, and a composite of the suspect drawn by one of their police artists. Granted, only a couple of days had passed since the stabbings, but there was something just a little too casual, a little too dismissive about the way New York seemed to view the whole matter, as if the attacks were routine rather than a possible sign that a serial killer could be roaming the state. After a while, Joe Cooley couldn't hold back.

"Is this a normal thing in New York?" he asked. "A bunch of guys getting stabbed in one area in a single day?"

"No, it's not normal," the detective answered.

"Then you do have a problem," Cooley said. "And it might just fit with ours, because we've got a problem."

Still, the NYPD detectives were skeptical. The Buffalo killer shot his victims. The guy with the glasses stabbed them. The attacks were months apart, and Buffalo and New York City were 450 miles apart. And none of the Buffalo witnesses had said anything about a guy wearing glasses, whereas all the New York witnesses had mentioned it.

Cooley and Lobbett didn't feel that glasses versus no glasses meant much, nor even gun versus knife—not when so many other details were lining up, particularly the hit-and-run style of attack on black men by a guy with dark-blond hair.

The New York composite did look markedly different than any of the .22 Caliber Killer sketches. In addition to the wire-rimmed glasses, it showed a man with a much rounder face, very short hair, a more prominent nose, and full lips.

Though there were assurances of a continued exchange of information, Joe Cooley left Manhattan feeling that the NYPD wanted nothing to do with them. He also felt that New York had a bigger problem on their hands than they realized.

There may have been some Manhattan detectives who tended to agree, especially when another black man was attacked in a subway on Wednesday. This victim sustained no injury, as he successfully fought off the knife-wielding attacker. The description of the fleeing assailant matched the details supplied by the other victims. By the time the New York detectives got wind of it, though, Joe Cooley and Mel Lobbett were on their way back to Buffalo.

If New York law enforcement was not yet persuaded that they had another serial killer, their local press was. They had already given him a name: the Midtown Slasher. Even the *New York Times* gave the slayings front-page coverage on December 24, though they demurred from using the Midtown Slasher moniker.

While Captain Meehan had his doubts about a connection with the Buffalo killings, the NYPD was definitely considering the prospect that the stabbings had been racially motivated. They received sixty calls from the public after news of "the slasher" hit the papers. A team of detectives was assembled to question witnesses and interview other recent stabbing victims.

Though the New York newspapers brought up the .22 caliber killings and reported that Meehan had been in touch with authorities in Buffalo, Meehan commented only that information had been exchanged, and further that the NYPD could not say definitively that the slashings were related, much less linked to any murders in Western New York. Ed Cosgrove gave much more weight to the possibility of a connection. "We are aggressively pursuing the similarities between the knifings in Manhattan and the .22 caliber slayings," he told the media. "The random manner in which the victims were chosen, the boldness of the attacks, the blackness of the victims and other similarities which we are not prepared to discuss," he was quoted, "cause us to feel the same man may be responsible." Cosgrove said that his team was following every aspect of the New York investigation and that his task force was as interested in each development "as much as if we were conducting it."

By late Christmas Eve, John Meehan and his detective squad felt reasonably certain that the six or seven Manhattan knifings were connected, but they were even less convinced of a link to the Buffalo slayings. Some

THE MIDTOWN SLASHER 157

of their witnesses viewed composites of the .22 Caliber Killer and said the gunman didn't resemble the slasher at all.

New York papers wrote of the rampant crime that plagued the city and the weariness of New Yorkers who faced threats day in and day out. "A month ago, one kept one's eyes peeled for a large black man brandishing a white cane," wrote the *New York Times*. "Now it's a small white man wearing wire-rimmed glasses."

By the weekend, both New York and Buffalo law enforcement officials told reporters they had discounted a link. The task force had even checked to see if any of the six Buffalo murder victims had been in New York City at any time before the murders. They had also consulted with authorities in Atlanta and other cities with similar unsolved homicides and bold assaults, concluding that the murders in New York bore the most resemblance to those in Buffalo. Ed Cosgrove told the press that there were no new developments in the investigation, and that while the task force had initially thought the murderer in New York City could be responsible for the killings in Buffalo, that lead had not panned out.

Si-lent night.
Ho-ly night.
All is calm,
All is bright . . .

He sang the Christmas carol, over and over again, as he walked the unfamiliar streets. Back and forth, round and round, he walked without aim, but not without purpose. He watched for signs, and when one came, he descended into the subways and got on the trains. Or he left the subways, reemerging on the sidewalks to walk and sing "Silent Night" some more, and see if there was a church.

He stopped often in churches; very many churches—even long afterward, he'd be able to name a lot of them—where he would pray. He prayed all the time. He slept in a church basement.

He didn't like this city. Days had gone by, and he was tired. He hoped that he'd done enough on this mission. He really wanted to go home for

Christmas. His feet hurt very badly, and the seminary had turned him away. Again.

All the time, he looked for signs.

On Christmas morning, it was finally okay for him to go home. He put on his dress greens and went to catch a bus.

Chapter 9
DECEMBER 29–31, 1980

THE STREETS OF Buffalo were icy on the morning of Monday, December 29.

Sattler's Department Store at 998 Broadway, east of downtown, was one of the city's biggest and most popular retailers. Across the street sat the Broadway Market, a collection of ethnic food vendors and specialty shops housed in a structure that took up an entire block. Stores were preparing to open their doors on this first Monday after Christmas, ready for the bargain shoppers, gift returns, and folks stocking up for New Year's Eve parties.

By 7:15 a.m. there were already a few pedestrians heading up and down Broadway, many of them employees bound for Sattler's, while others made their way to or from the city bus stops. There was a bus stop right in front of Sattler's and another further west, at Broadway and Fillmore.

Alice Wanot arrived fifteen minutes early for her 7:30 a.m. shift at Sattler's. With a little time to spare before she had to start work, she decided to drop a letter in the mailbox at the corner of Broadway and Gibson, about a half block past the store entrance. On her way to the mailbox, Alice, who was fifty-seven years old, saw a black man standing in the doorway of the Sattler's Pet Shop. As she would later tell the police, she was afraid to walk by him. But then she noticed a white man in the next doorway and she figured it was safe to walk to the mailbox. At about the same time, she saw two of her fellow employees coming across the street toward the store. She felt safer then and didn't pay any more attention to the men in front of the store. All she could remember was that one of them wore a plaid jacket and the other had glasses, but she couldn't recall who was wearing what. She knew that one was a black male and one was a white male.

Coworkers Dorothy Muldowney and Gloria Topper got off the bus at Broadway and Fillmore at about 7:20 a.m. and walked together down Broadway toward Sattler's. Both ladies were walking very carefully, keeping an eye on the sidewalk because of the icy conditions. As they crossed Gibson Street, Dorothy heard someone running. She grabbed her purse tighter, afraid it might be a purse snatcher. She glanced up briefly and saw a white male, probably in his twenties, as he dashed by.

Gloria also heard someone running. She looked up and saw the young white man running quickly toward them. She thought it was very stupid for him to be moving so fast like that, with all the ice. He slipped and almost fell, but caught himself and kept going at a rapid pace. She figured he was probably rushing to catch a bus. She looked back and caught a glimpse of him turning the corner and running north on Gibson Street.

Neither Dorothy nor Gloria noticed the man's clothing, other than that he wore a hat. They didn't notice anything more until a minute or so later, when they got a little closer to Sattler's and saw a body lying on the ground.

Around the back of the building, a young shipping clerk had parked his car in the lot behind Sattler's. At about 7:25 a.m., while still in his car, the shipping clerk saw a man come running into the parking lot from Gibson Street, coming from the direction of Broadway. The man vaulted over a guardrail and crossed the lot, exiting onto Beck Street and into another parking lot. From there he cut across at an angle toward Mills Street and disappeared from view.

At about the same time, John Raszeja parked his car in front of Sattler's near the corner of Beck. His passenger, a female coworker, stepped out of the car. She was opening the door of 998 Broadway when she heard a voice say, "Help me." She turned and saw a man staggering toward John. Thinking he was probably a drunk, she continued into the store. John

Raszeja didn't hear a cry for help. All he saw was the man who staggered into the street and collapsed in front of his car.

Bus driver E. W. Johnson normally stopped at 998 Broadway each morning at 7:24, but he was running a little behind today because of the weather. As he pulled up and opened the bus door, a man rushed forward, pointed at a figure lying in the street, and told him, "I think he's been stabbed!"

Officers were on the scene within minutes, along with an ambulance. Medics were unable to raise a pulse on the victim. At 7:35 a.m., the patrolmen radioed homicide.

Detectives arrived at 7:45 and were directed to the body of a black male, covered with a white sheet, lying face up on Broadway about four feet from the curb. Lifting the sheet, they noted a stab wound in the man's neck and a small pool of blood by his head. He was wearing a plaid winter jacket over a rust-brown colored suit with a vest and a tie. He was dead.

Whatever had led to this stabbing, events must've unfolded very swiftly—and quietly. John Raszeja had stayed with the dying man, who had collapsed in front of his car. Raszeja had sent his son into the store to call police and shouted to employees approaching the building to do the same. The victim had not said anything.

The man who alerted the bus driver told police that he had been standing on the sidewalk, watching for the bus, when the black male had shouted, "I'm stabbed!" before staggering over to where he had collapsed. He hadn't seen the stabbing take place and hadn't noticed anyone else around. Not one of the several Sattler's employees who had either already arrived for work or were walking toward the building at the time reported seeing a scuffle or hearing any type of argument or confrontation.

The shipping clerk described the man who had run through the parking lot as white, about twenty-five to thirty, probably closer to thirty, wearing a dark-brown woolen ski cap. He couldn't tell the color of the man's hair because the cap had been pulled down over his ears. The man seemed to be about five feet nine to five feet eleven with a medium build.

The shipping clerk hadn't noticed if the man wore gloves, nor had he noticed his trousers, but he said the man wore one of those green army jackets with pockets all over, like a fatigue jacket.

Dorothy Muldowney and Gloria Topper gave statements to the police about the white man who had run past them, but they were unable to give a description. The only thing Gloria could add was that she thought the white man had been wearing glasses.

Anita Adams called the police. She heard on TV that a black man had been stabbed in front of Sattler's and she was afraid it might be her husband, Roger.

Detectives Al Williams and John Montondo went to see Mrs. Adams at her home in the lower flat at 342 Gibson Street. Her husband had left for work as usual at 7:15 a.m. He walked around the corner to the bus stop in front of Sattler's for the ride downtown to his job at National Fuel. She described the plaid jacket and rust-colored three-piece suit he'd been wearing and showed the detectives his photo. They confirmed that the victim probably was her husband. Mrs. Adams called her mother and asked her to go to the morgue to make the identification.

Anita and Roger Adams had been married four years, and they had a daughter turning three in February. Roger had also become a father to her eight-year-old son from a previous relationship. They had been living in California for the past few years and had moved to Buffalo about fourteen months ago. Roger had started his new job at National Fuel the past November.

Roger, who was thirty-one years old, had grown up in Chicago, his wife told them. He had not been in New York City recently, or perhaps ever. Her husband rarely went out alone, and when the two of them did socialize, it was typically to visit relatives. Anita Adams had been heartsick when she heard the news about the stabbing. Roger had commented to her that he was the only black who caught the bus in the morning in front of Sattler's. Their eight-year-old son had been watching television when they showed the body of a man being wheeled into an ambulance and had said to his mother, "That looks like my father's arm."

Melvin Lobbett attended the postmortem that morning. Roger Adams had been stabbed in the left side of his neck from right to left, downward and backward. The wound was three-quarters of an inch in length and three to four inches deep. The blade had transected the left internal jugular vein and cut through the left side of his carotid artery and subclavian vein, then into his chest where it terminated in the apex of his left lung.

The second stab wound penetrated his right chest and went through his right lung. This wound was also three to four inches deep.

Roger Adams had bled to death almost instantly.

Lobbett noted that both wounds appeared to be twisted. Roger had four small contusions on the back of his right hand that could have come from his fall to the pavement. The ME did not classify them as defensive wounds. From all appearances, someone had taken Roger Adams completely off guard and thrust a knife deep into him twice.

The task force had immediately gone into action. Searches of the area and questioning of witnesses turned up nothing, except for accounts of a white man possibly wearing glasses and a green army jacket who ran away from 998 Broadway over the icy pavement.

Edward Cosgrove placed a call to New York City. They had not made any arrests in the Midtown Slasher case and they hadn't had any similar attacks since Christmas Eve.

Tom Rowan and the scientific investigation team reported to the morgue and to the murder scene for collection of forensic evidence. The blood on the street and on the victim's clothing had all come from Roger Adams. Despite the limited amount of evidence to test and analyze, it was a long night for Rowan. At home that evening, the enormity of the situation hit him hard. Perhaps it was the terrible incongruity of the blood pool and crime-scene tape in front of the twinkling windows of Sattler's Department Store, merrily decorated for Christmas, or the Happy New Year signs visible from the Broadway Market as the evidence team photographed the crimson-streaked snow that marked the final jerking steps of Roger Adams as the life bled out of him. Perhaps it was the sheer exhaustion of the eighteen-hour days he had already poured into the investigation, or the desolate feeling that the random, pointless killings had not ended. As Tom Rowan would recall many years later, "I cried twice in this investigation. Once was the night that we found Parler Edwards and the second time was after the autopsy of Roger Adams. I had become involved in the case with the murder of Harold Green but it really hadn't hit me at that time. It was early on and there was so much to be done in terms of processing the evidence. By the time Roger Adams was killed, time had passed and I had learned a little more about the victims and interacted with some of the families. We had spent the last few days reviewing the reports on the New York City murders. And it all came down on me that night.

"My wife came into the room and said she had never seen me cry after coming back from a crime scene. I had been to so many at that point. But for once, I just couldn't stay in investigator mode. I kept thinking about Roger Adams, what a nice guy everyone said he was, what a nice family he had. The existential part of me took over and all I could think was, what is going on here? What kind of inhumanity is this?"

Tom Rowan was not the only task force member feeling consumed by events and by questions without answers. Al Williams had another sleepless night, disturbed and preoccupied by thoughts of what had happened and where it would all lead. *Who is this guy? Who is he? Why here? Why now? Why?*

Edward Cosgrove had been careful with his comments to the press on Monday. While affirming that the task force was investigating the murder of Roger Adams—which appeared to be an "unprovoked, motiveless attack on a black man, similar to the situation in New York City"—he said he wasn't sure if there was any connection between either the .22 caliber killings or the Manhattan murders. On the following day, news came in of a strikingly similar murder in Rochester.

Wendell Barnes, a twenty-six-year-old black man, was stabbed in the chest on the morning of Tuesday, December 30, as he waited for a bus at 172 East Main Street in Rochester. He staggered into a restaurant and collapsed, dying shortly afterward in the hospital. Witnesses described the assailant as a white man wearing a red or maroon ski cap, a three-quarter length green jacket, and glasses. He stabbed once and ran. The only new detail was that the man had some beard stubble, like a five o'clock shadow. They said he seemed to run with a limp. The Sattler's shipping clerk, the only person in the Roger Adams slaying who had gotten a clear, extended view of the white man fleeing, had also mentioned that the man ran "funny."

Cosgrove's task force was not alone in their interest in this slaying, which had occurred about seventy miles east of Buffalo. Captain John Meehan in New York City had also taken serious note. His detective squad wanted all the details from Buffalo and Rochester. The composite prepared by Rochester police bore a strong resemblance to the New York City composite of the Midtown Slasher, including the glasses. *Jesus, did they really have a knife-wielding assassin roaming the state?* At this point, no one in law enforcement was discounting the possibility. Meehan told the press that they'd take help from anywhere they could get it, adding, "Our main goal right now is to get this guy off the streets before he hurts somebody else."

———

On the afternoon of Wednesday, December 31, Albert Menefee left his home at 91 Laurel Street in Buffalo and made the short walk up to the Main Utica Tobacco Shop at 1381 Main Street. Stepping inside the store from the icy sidewalk, Albert, who was thirty-two years old, spotted his friend Claudia. Albert and Claudia were old friends who hadn't seen each other in a while. They wished each other a happy new year and chatted for a few minutes. As they stood in the store talking and joking around, Claudia absently noticed another patron—a white man wearing a green coat—standing nearby, looking at the magazine rack.

Claudia had to go outside to wait for the bus. Albert suggested that they get together sometime soon and Claudia wrote her new address on a matchbook for him. She said good-bye and went outside. Albert bought a pack of cigarettes and then stepped out himself. As he walked through the door, a man approached him and asked for the time. Albert looked down at his wristwatch and answered, "4:04." He glanced up and saw that the man was not looking at the watch, but instead was staring intently at his face. The next thing Albert Menefee felt was a blow to his chest.

That son of a bitch, Albert thought. He was about to ask if he wanted to fight but the man was already moving away, crossing Main Street. The light hadn't changed yet, but the man walked into Main Street anyway, stopping traffic, and he kept looking back at Albert. That's when Albert felt the warm blood spreading across his shirt.

"I've been stabbed!" he cried out. "Stop that man!"

Claudia turned when she heard Albert's voice. She'd been standing with her back toward the store, waiting for the bus. She looked at Albert and he said it again: "I'm stabbed!"

She laughed. "Come on, Al. Quit bullshitting."

"I'm not bullshitting," he said, grabbing his chest. He pointed to the man who was now running down West Utica and shouted, "Somebody stop that motherfucker!"

Claudia looked and saw the man in the green coat as he shot down West Utica and turned the corner at Linwood, disappearing from sight.

Albert Menefee stepped back into the store and repeated that he'd been stabbed. He kept one hand clutched over his heart, and with the other he pointed at the fleeing white man. One employee called an ambulance while another dashed over to nearby precinct 6 to summon police. Claudia had followed Al into the store, trying to help and wondering how this could have happened. They had been talking and laughing just a moment before. Maybe a minute had passed between the time she walked out of the store and Albert had cried out. How in the world had he been stabbed? In the middle of Main Street, no less. There were people all around.

At 4:10 p.m., the tobacco shop clerk rushed into precinct 6 and told the desk officer that a man had been stabbed. Detective Sergeant Francis McQueen rushed over and found that an ambulance and two patrolmen were already on the scene. Lieutenant Philip Ramunno was in the back of the ambulance trying to speak with a black male who lay on the gurney.

Albert Menefee had to be rushed to Buffalo General Hospital. Lieutenant Ramunno made the ride with him as other detectives followed and still more rounded up witnesses at the scene. Albert was semiconscious by the time he reached the emergency room. Before being rushed into surgery, he told the officer and the attending doctor that he had been stabbed by a white man who walked up and asked him the time. The last thing he said before being whisked away was, "He looked like the picture."

———————

At the scene of the attack, a female clerk at the store told police she had looked out the window and saw a white man punch the victim in the chest. Neither of the two male employees had gotten a view of the attacker's face, although one glimpsed his profile as he fled. All three agreed on his escape route, that he had cut diagonally across Main and then down West Utica. Witnesses at the bus stop also agreed on this, as well as on the general description of the man. No one had seen a weapon. A pick-up had been put out by responding officers: white male, five feet nine, wearing a green field jacket and red knit cap.

The incident was immediately all over the news. Police received a phone call from a woman who reported that the suspect had run in front of her vehicle. She said he was running hunched over with a choppy gait, looking from side to side, with his right hand in his jacket pocket and his left hand holding the right outer pocket.

In the waiting room of the hospital, the family of Albert Menefee was interviewed by police. His mother and two cousins told investigators that Albert had been employed by the City of Buffalo tax assessment department for the past two years. He rode the bus to and from work every day. He was unmarried but had a steady girlfriend. They said he was a homebody who didn't go out much, but a friendly type who would speak freely with strangers and got along with whites and everyone else. They couldn't offer any information on any recent problems or anything else in his background that might aid in the investigation.

Albert was moved to the intensive care unit that evening following surgery. The attending physician informed the officers who had remained at the hospital that he was guardedly optimistic about the patient's survival. Albert had a single stab wound of the heart, right of the midline, just below the sternum. The knife had passed through the right ventricle of his heart and pierced the inferior vena cava. The doctor estimated the length of the blade as at least five inches. The surgery had gone as well as possible and the victim could recover as long as no complications set in. The physician cautioned, however, that the national survival rate for this type of wound was 5 to 10 percent.

The police were given a bag containing most of the victim's clothing, which they took for analysis and evidence. One officer had already typed "Albert Menefee Homicide" in the subject line of a report he submitted that night to Leo Donovan.

Albert had said that the man who stabbed him looked like the picture. He must've meant the composite sketch. *But which one?*

———

Edward Cosgrove ordered roadblocks set up on major streets leaving the city and at bridges and the airport. He had given this directive following the stabbing of Albert Menefee: "Shut down the city!" Other members of the task force didn't see much point to this plan, never mind the logistics of blocking every avenue and bridge in the second largest city in New York on New Year's Eve—in hopes of catching a man who, as far as anyone knew, fled on foot. The command went largely unheeded.

The district attorney was not the only one with a seismic reaction. Reverend Bennett Smith said that his belief of the past September was coming true. Smith told Henry Locke of the *Courier-Express*, "I said then, and I'm saying it now, the attacks on black males were like an indoctrination ritual that was taught by some hate group. The assailants could have been trained in some secret camp on how to kill a black man and to make their getaway. It could be happening because of black men marrying white women, and the killers feel threatened that their supposedly super race is in jeopardy."

Smith said that no matter who was behind the murders, whether the Klan or neo-Nazis or others, the situation had forced black men to go on the offense. "New Year's Eve will be a bad time because many black males will be armed," Smith warned. "They feel the best defense is a better offense."

Daniel Acker echoed the charge of a national conspiracy to eliminate black men and asked that law enforcement agencies should "double and triple their efforts to come up with an arrest" while some black citizens opined that if the victims had been white, the killers would have been behind bars months ago.

Cosgrove called for the FBI to take a more extensive role, to tie together the work of law enforcement in Western New York, Rochester, and New York City. Responding to inquiries from the press, James P. Turner, acting assistant attorney general for civil rights, stated that the Bureau was already "fully involved," assuring that all the reports were going to FBI headquarters where they're being "properly coordinated." Justice Department officials restated their position that the FBI could not assume control of the case unless violations of federal rights had been established. Homicide by itself was not a federal violation. Special Agent John Thurston of the Buffalo bureau office told reporters, "Obviously, we have to find out who murdered someone to find out if his rights were violated." In other words, the Bureau, while being "fully involved," would wait until local authorities had apprehended and charged a suspect before determining whether they would take over the case.

The year 1980 came to an end. The temperature in Buffalo at midnight hovered around fifteen degrees Fahrenheit, clear and cold. Police, out in force around the city, may have been nonetheless grateful for the biting air that night, which sometimes helped keep people indoors. Amid the street patrols and the distant sounds of celebration far beyond the doors of the command post, Edward Cosgrove had one fervent resolution for the new year: to stop this madman before he killed again.

He was out there. He was out there, somewhere.

Chapter 10
JANUARY 1–APRIL 13, 1981

IT WAS BETWEEN 3:30 and 4:00 a.m. and still bitter cold when Kim Edmiston returned home from a New Year's Eve party. Kim lived alone in the lower flat of a two-unit house at 116 Hamilton Street in a section of Buffalo known as Black Rock. The party had been held at a friend's house in Kenmore, a first-ring suburb just a short drive away.

Kim was twenty-one years old, a petite young woman at just under five feet four, with long brown hair. She hadn't had much to drink at the party, and she had stayed for some time afterward to help with the cleanup, so she was sober in the wee hours of New Year's Day as she drove through silent streets in a not-so-silent car. Kim had been having trouble with her own car—it wasn't always starting up for her—so on the previous afternoon, knowing she'd be going to the New Year's party, she had switched cars with her dad, who promised to take a look at hers. Kim was driving one of her father's winter beaters, an old Dodge Dart that literally squeaked and rattled as it chugged down the road. For all its conspicuous noise, the Dodge still ran well and that was all that really mattered, since she definitely didn't want to get stranded on a cold night like this. Kim would always feel especially grateful that she had used her father's car that night and that she'd been completely sober, keeping her wits about her. If not, the outcome of what was about to happen to her might've been very different.

She was nearly home, driving south on Tonawanda Street, when she saw what she first took to be a boy or a teenager. He appeared as a slight figure, very thin and not very tall, jogging down Tonawanda Street. He wore no hat, no gloves, and just a lightweight jacket.

That's weird, Kim thought as she drove by him. How strange that this young guy was out there by himself, jogging down the street in the dead of night, especially without proper winter clothing. She figured he must be running home from a neighboring house or something, then dismissed the sight altogether.

The Dodge made a squeaking right turn onto Hamilton Street. Kim headed for her usual parking spot, at the corner of a dead-end side street that intersected with Hamilton, almost directly across from her apartment. Halfway down the block, as she was about to turn left onto the dead end, she glanced at her rearview mirror and saw the jogging boy again. He had turned onto Hamilton Street and was coming up behind her. She wondered if the sound of her squeaking car had caught his attention. Or maybe he was coming this way anyhow and it was just coincidence.

She made the turn, parked, and shut off the engine. She kept an eye on the rearview mirror and waited for him to pass. When he didn't, she turned to look. He was standing on the sidewalk directly across the street from her, about six to eight feet away, staring at her. *Oh shit, what is this about?* Kim thought. He stood with an unusual posture: legs apart, fists clenched at his sides in some sort of a power stance, like a military bearing. *What's he going to do, this little jerk?* He didn't speak. He didn't move. He kept his eyes on her and she kept her eyes on him as she sat frozen in the driver's seat. She glanced away for a moment and when she looked again, he was walking toward her.

Kim started the car, threw it in reverse, and peeled away. She drove to her mother's house, about a mile and a half away. Parked in the driveway at her mother's, and feeling out of danger, she hesitated to get out and ring the bell. Kim's youngest sibling was only two years old. The baby would surely wake up. Kim didn't want to wake them, especially since nothing had really happened. She even felt a little foolish. It was just a strange teenager, probably drunk from a New Year's party. He looked so young and wispy that Kim thought she probably could've fought him off herself, if it had come to that. She decided to drive around for a little bit and then head back home. He must be long gone anyway. Nobody would hang around in temperatures like this in such a thin coat.

It was about fifteen or twenty minutes later when she pulled into the same parking spot on the dead-end street. She looked around carefully and saw no one. She shut off the engine, grabbed her purse and a plastic bag that held her shoes, and got out of the car. She padded toward her apartment, dodging occasional patches of ice as she crossed Hamilton, her winter boots making dull thuds on the pavement.

She was about halfway across the street when a bad feeling suddenly came over her. She paused and looked over her shoulder.

If it hadn't been for the bitter cold air, she wouldn't have seen him.

At first, she didn't see anyone; then, looking back at the apartment building on the corner diagonally across from her house, she saw rapid plumes of breath coming from behind the edge of the building. Someone stood hidden in the shadows, visible only by the exhalations of warm breath forming vapor clouds in the freezing air.

Kim had no voice. She ran for her apartment. She ran very fast, but he ran faster.

Her front door was at street level and she had her key in the lock when he caught her. He slammed into her from behind, knocking her into the heavy oak door. He grabbed her arm and whirled her around so they were face-to-face. He shoved her back against the door. That's when she realized that this was not a boy, but a man, probably around her own age. His skin was pale, his hair dark brown. He had a long, thin nose. He stood only a few inches taller than she, but he was much stronger, more powerful than his slight build would suggest as he loomed above her in the frigid gloom. He had her helplessly pinned with her back pressed against her own front door.

He's going to rape me . . . The thought hammered through her head again and again. Acute terror rendered her mute. She could not scream. She could not even speak. All she could do was think, the shrieks in her own head rising to a fevered pitch. *Oh, my God, I'm about to be raped* . . . *and there's nothing I can do* . . .

He clutched her and drew her to him so that they were nose-to-nose. Then he pushed her back sharply, bouncing her off the door. He reached again and did the same thing twice more. Then he let go, took a step back, and stood there, staring into her face. Or at least toward her face.

Kim looked at his face. And oddly, very oddly, it almost seemed like he wasn't looking at her at all. He didn't have the salacious expression of a rapist. He didn't have *any* expression. He looked emotionless, detached. Not at all like a man in an aggressive standoff with a captured young woman. He looked more like someone in a trance, a sleepwalker stalled in the random stimuli of an overarching dream.

He didn't say a word. No commands, no warnings not to scream. Nothing.

He stepped back about a foot or two. Then he made a strange gesture; he raised both of his arms up slightly from his sides, palms open and out, as if to say, what now? I've got you; what are you going to do now? That's when Kim saw the knife.

In his right hand, he held a knife with a blade a few inches long. He held it out at his side, parallel to his body, the blade slightly tipped up. It looked like a hunting knife with an upward curve at the tip. He still didn't say a word. His silence frightened her almost as much as the weapon.

Kim didn't know where this was going, but she knew something bad would happen. Nobody pulls out a knife for no reason. This was going to turn physical again. His pause had given her a chance to think, and the sight of the knife had helped bring back her voice. She was cornered, but she had a makeshift weapon of her own. With her arms now free and some space between her and the attacker, she clutched the drawstring of the plastic bag in her hand. Inside the bag was the pair of Bastad clogs she had worn at the party. She whipped the drawstring around her wrist a couple of times until there was no slack, then held up the bag and shook it at him.

"Come on!" she said.

She thought she could deflect the knife with a swing of the heavy wooden shoes. The moment he started toward her, she'd be ready with her best shot.

But his feet didn't move. He cocked his head at her, the way a dog might when it hears a foreign or confusing sound. He looked amused. He started laughing. He laughed loudly, like a crazy person. He tipped his head back, as if he were bellowing laughter at the sky. The moment his eyes were off her, Kim reached over and turned the key, still in the lock of the front door. One turn to the right, and the door opened. Her whole weight had been against the door, and she fell into the hallway flat on her back. The entrance hall was very small, with a staircase on the left leading to the upper apartment and the door to Kim's ground-floor unit on the right. As she lay on her back, he started to come through the front door. She raised her legs and kicked the door with both feet as hard as she could.

The door hit him and knocked him off balance, maybe onto a patch of ice. She heard him fall. And that's when he spoke the only word she'd hear him utter all night: "Dammit!" Or maybe it was "Shit!" One of the two. She'd never be sure of the precise word, only that he uttered a single, frustrated curse.

Kim screamed for the woman who lived upstairs—"Cindy! Cindy! CINDY!"—as she scrambled to her feet. Grasping the keys, she opened the door to her apartment and lurched inside, slamming the door behind her and locking it. She ran to the phone and called the police. Afterward she stood shaking; her eyes trained on the front door, tensed and ready to run. She listened but heard nothing other than the sound of her own panting. He hadn't followed her in. She hoped he had run away.

Three large windows in her living room faced Hamilton Street. As afraid as she was to look out, she had to assure herself that he was gone. She crept over to a window and carefully lifted a slat on the Venetian blinds.

There he was, pacing back and forth in front of her windows. He had one arm raised above his head, extended slightly forward, the knife gripped in his fist. He held it with the blade pointed downward, as if he were about to plunge it into something. He marched back and forth, back and forth, knife high in the air, like he was on some sort of military maneuver. Declaring battle.

What the hell?! Kim thought.

He jerked around and scanned the windows with his eyes. The blank look of earlier was gone. He looked angry. Very angry, and intense. His eyes darted up and down the windows, all around, as if searching for a weak spot, determined to find a way in. Kim feared he might just decide to smash a window, injury to himself be damned. She threw open the blinds with both hands and yelled, "Cops are coming!"

He stood there and stared at her.

Oh my God, she thought. *That didn't scare him. What am I going to do?*

She grabbed the phone and dialed police again. When she looked back out the window, she saw him running away toward Niagara Street.

She begged the police to please hurry. She hung up the phone and went into the bathroom, the only room in her apartment without a window. She locked the door and barricaded herself inside. Crouched in the small room, she stayed alert for the slightest sound. After a few minutes, she couldn't take it anymore, the waiting, the straining to hear, her nerves rubbed raw. She started shouting for her upstairs neighbor until she heard movement upstairs, then finally a knock on her door and her neighbor's voice calling her name. She bolted out of the bathroom and opened her front door.

"Kim, what's going on?"

"I don't know! There's some maniac out there!" She pulled the neighbor inside and locked the door behind them.

"How long ago was this?" the police officer asked.

"About a half hour ago," Kim answered. She described the man's looks, his actions. She told them he acted "military." She didn't know how else to describe it.

The officer seemed a little skeptical. He kept asking if she was sure this wasn't someone she knew. Kim got the feeling the officer thought it was some kind of domestic dispute, even though she kept insisting that she had never seen the man before. She couldn't explain why he hadn't tried to rape or stab her, when he could easily have done either; she didn't know why he marched in front of the building instead of trying to break down the door, or why he had waited for her outside in the freezing cold. The whole incident was as bizarre and unfathomable to her as it sounded to anyone else. She couldn't explain the why, she could only tell them the what.

Kim told the officer that she felt like the man had been toying with her, like the whole encounter was spontaneous and amusing to him, at least until she hit him with the door. He obviously hadn't expected that. She even got the feeling that he'd had no intention of really hurting her until she had taken control of the situation and slipped away from him.

It was only then that he seemed to become enraged, and God only knows what would've happened if he'd gotten a hold of her after that.

Kim asked the officers if they were going to go look for him. The reply was that they'd have a car drive around. Now Kim was angry. The police struck her as very nonchalant about the whole thing. "You're not even going to *look* for him?" The officers assured her that the man must be long gone by now. There was nothing to worry about. Keep the doors locked; get some sleep; call us again if you need us.

She locked the doors behind the officers, silently fuming that precinct 13 was useless.

The first light of dawn had broken. There would be no sleep for Kim or the girl upstairs, who took the story a lot more seriously than the police had. They left the house together, making sure each got to her car safely. Kim Edmiston drove to her mother's house. She didn't return home for two days.

She felt paranoid for many weeks afterward and kept her guard up whenever coming to or leaving her apartment. The thing that frightened her most was the thought that he must live in the neighborhood, somewhere very close by. There seemed to be no other explanation for his light clothing that night. He couldn't have walked, or jogged, from any real distance, dressed like that. Who would wander around in just a cloth jacket when the temperature was only a few degrees above zero? You'd have to be out of your mind.

———

Calvin Crippen had to work on New Year's Day. Luckily for him, he didn't have to report until the afternoon.

Calvin, who was twenty-three, worked at McDonald's on Bailey Avenue and Genesee Street on the east side of the city. He lived at 12 Hertel Avenue on the lower west side of Buffalo and rode the bus to work. Calvin arrived at the bus stop on Niagara Street near Hertel shortly before 3:00 p.m. He was the only one at the bus stop, which was not a surprise, since so many people were off work for the holiday. The temperature had hit twenty-seven degrees—the warmest it would be all day, and an improvement over the previous night—and a light snow began to fall. Calvin carried his work shoes in a plastic bag.

It was close to 3:00 when Calvin noticed another man approaching the bus stop. The stranger walked from between some parked cars at the curb and headed in Calvin's direction. Calvin paid him little mind until he heard the man speak from behind him.

"You fucking nigger."

Calvin turned around. The man had a hunting knife raised in his right hand. He lunged at Calvin, who instinctively swung the bag with his shoes to bat the blade aside. The knife sliced into the bag. Calvin pulled back and frantically swung again. He hit the man on the side of his head, causing him to lose his balance.

Calvin turned and ran up Niagara Street toward Hertel. He looked back once and saw the man running down Niagara in the opposite direction.

It might've been the only time Calvin felt grateful to hear a white guy call him a nigger. Otherwise, he would never have turned around.

Joe Cooley and Melvin Lobbett were at precinct 13 taking Calvin Crippen's formal statement.

Calvin had come to the precinct with his parents to file a report. The moment the desk officer heard the details and description of the suspect, he called the task force. Mel Lobbett questioned Calvin and pecked out the answers on a typewriter.

"Can you describe this man that attempted to assault you?"

"He was a white male, late twenties, about five foot eight, 160 to 165 pounds. Medium build. Unshaven about three days. It appeared to me that he was starting to grow a beard. A goatee type, brownish color. He had a regular Buffalo accent. He had a red skull hat. A little hair came down on his forehead in the front. He wore a dark gray and black jacket, wool, buttoned from top to bottom. Brown pants. Black shoes. White dingy socks on. No gloves."

"Can you describe the knife to me?"

"It was a hunting knife. The blade was wide. About six to seven inches in length. I didn't really see the handle that good."

"Were there any other persons on the street or nearby at the time?"

"No."

"Did you say anything to this man?"

"No."

"Did you see where this person came from?"

"Just from behind the car."

"How far away was the man from you when you first saw him?"

"About three feet."

"Can you identify this man if you see him?"

"Yes."

"Did you ever see him before this afternoon?"

"No."

"Do you think you injured him?"

"I think I gave him a good shot," Calvin replied. "I think the end of my shoe struck him."

Joe Cooley showed him sketches of the .22 Caliber Killer. Calvin looked them over and said, "The one with the watch cap, but the eyes are smaller than the one that attacked me."

While Cooley and Lobbett interviewed Calvin Crippen at the police station, Al Williams and Frank Deubell were in the intensive care unit at Buffalo General Hospital speaking with Albert Menefee.

Albert's survival seemed nothing short of a miracle. Doctors were still continuously monitoring his condition, but they expected him to recover. Albert's spirit was as strong as his heart. He wanted to speak with detectives, the sooner the better. Barely out of surgery, he had written a note to his family members that echoed what he had said to the first officer about the attack: it was the guy he saw on television who got him.

Detective Williams asked him about this. Albert replied that he had been referring to a composite sketch shown on TV the day of the Wendell Barnes stabbing in Rochester. He described how the man had approached him and asked for the time, then landed a blow on his chest that Albert at first took to be a sucker punch. "I can take a punch," he told the detectives, "but I felt the prick and noticed the blood."

Albert's description of the attacker was very precise. He placed the white man's height at five feet eight. Albert himself was five feet nine, and the assailant, who had faced him squarely prior to the stabbing, was only an inch shorter. Albert had been wearing sunglasses, but it appeared that the man had light hair. He said the man's eyes were light colored, either hazel or gray, and that he needed a shave. It looked like he had about a two-day growth of beard. He placed the man in his late twenties or early thirties and said he had a worn-out look, kind of tired looking with bags under his eyes, as if he had been out drinking. The man had a long nose, like the actor Danny Thomas. The only aspect of his description that varied from the witness accounts was that Albert thought the man had been wearing a soft felt dress hat, a dirty gray color.

On the matter of the man's coat, Albert was absolutely certain—it was a green army field jacket. "I was in the military and I know that the military makes the clothes to fit the man, and his fit him."

He agreed with witnesses on the man's escape route and added that the man ran funny, with an awkward gait, like a senile old man. He said he'd be able to identify the man if he ever saw him again, but didn't relish the idea of another encounter.

———

Larry Little, age fifty-two, was up early on Friday, January 2. At 6:20, he was outside his home on Monroe Street on the east side, brushing snow off his car. As he cleared the windshield in the predawn light, he turned around in time to see a white man come up from behind and swing at him with a knife. The knife grazed Larry in the neck, but he dodged in time to avoid being cut. Larry bolted and the white man chased him, both of them sliding around in the falling snow. The man must have dropped his knife, though, because instead of trying to stab him again, the white man picked up a stick and began beating Larry on the head and face. Larry lunged at him and they both fell in the snow.

They grappled and Larry bit the attacker on the leg. Larry then got up and ran and so did the white man, but this time he ran away instead of pursuing. The attacker jumped into a green Pontiac and took off down Monroe Street. Larry followed him for a short distance, but he couldn't make out the whole license plate number.

Larry Little rushed inside and called police, who responded in force and spent a good part of the morning sifting through the snow with rakes in search of the knife. They didn't find one. A squad car drove Larry around in the hope of spotting the green Pontiac, or at least one like it so they'd have the model. Larry estimated the auto year as mid-70s and said part of the license plate was 446. The DMV produced lists of green autos with 446 in the license plate numbers.

On that Friday afternoon, funeral services were held for Roger Adams. There were several white mourners at the service, neighbors and close friends of the Adamses who came to pay their respects and offer support to Roger's wife and two young children. Albert Menefee's family had informed police that Roger and Albert were cousins through marriage, and though police considered this, they ultimately determined that the relationship had no bearing on the attacks. They had also confirmed that Roger was no relation to the New York City stabbing victim with the same surname.

Edward Cosgrove told the press he felt optimistic that police would capture the stabber that weekend. He was encouraged that they had surviving victims to ID the suspect—they were bringing in FBI artist Horace Heafner once again to make yet another composite sketch—and they now had a partial plate number and description of the assailant's vehicle. Police Commissioner Cunningham shared the DA's optimism. "We know what he looks like," Cunningham said. "We know what he's wearing, and we even know what he's driving. He can't be lucky forever."

Asked whether he thought the stabbings and the .22 caliber killings were connected, Cosgrove pointed out the similarities in style of attack and victims, but said he didn't know if all were done by the same man. On a connection between the Rochester and Buffalo knife attacks, Cosgrove was unequivocal. "This person has struck on five successive days," he said. "It's my hope and prayer he doesn't strike again tomorrow."

No one connected the attack on Kim Edmiston with the stabbings, least of all Kim herself, despite the fact that it had happened close to where Calvin Crippen had been ambushed hours later. It hadn't registered with the media and went unreported in the press. Kim was white, female, and though the man had brandished a knife, he had not tried to stab her. Kim had also gotten a close-up, extended view of her attacker, and he looked nothing like any of the composite sketches.

———

No stabbings or attempts occurred over the weekend or on the days that followed. Authorities were closely monitoring city bus stops and now had a new concern. Some armed black men were taking the initiative to place themselves as decoys in hopes of capturing the killer. Councilman James Pitts, who referred to the men as bounty hunters in his comments to the press, said that they were after the reward money. The common council had approved a $25,000 reward on the Tuesday following the knife attacks. Leo Donovan expressed his disapproval of the bounty hunters and warned that anyone found in possession of an illegal weapon would be subject to criminal charges and possibly ineligible for reward money even if he captured the killer. Donovan stressed that inexperience and panic on the part of self-styled bounty hunters could lead to innocent people being hurt.

Cosgrove met with Councilman Pitts and black leaders on Wednesday to update them on the investigation. There were no hot leads. The new sketch prepared by Horace Heafner looked virtually identical to the sketches he had made of the .22 Caliber Killer the previous fall. This seemed to solidify the theory that the .22 Caliber Killer and the stabber were the same man.

Those who suspected that the Klan or neo-Nazis were behind the murders rather than a single "psychopath," as Cosgrove and officials kept reiterating, had their fears bolstered by news of an upcoming spectacle in downtown Buffalo. In December, Karl Hand had applied for a permit to conduct a neo-Nazi demonstration in Niagara Square right in front of Buffalo City Hall. Hand had distributed pamphlets seeking "100 White Men with Guts" to join him downtown on January 15, the birthday of Martin Luther King Jr.

Hand, who claimed to be the information officer for the Western New York region of the National Socialist Party of America and a former national organizer for the Ku Klux Klan, told reporters, "We chose Martin Luther King's birthday to accentuate the irony that blacks are always belly-aching about preferential treatment but at the same time they have had Supreme Court decisions that have run against the white majority. They discriminate against us in jobs, promotions, scholarships. By choosing this date, we can draw attention to this fact."

In response to Hand's plan, a coalition of black activist groups distributed a flyer calling for "1,000 Black Men with Guns" and planned a counterrally in Niagara Square on the same day and time. They called themselves the Martin Luther King Day Memorial Rally Coalition and applied for a permit to demonstrate. The city denied permits to both, igniting a legal firestorm on both sides. Civil rights organizations lambasted Mayor Griffin for denying the Martin Luther King Day Memorial Rally their first amendment rights while the ACLU made the same charge on behalf of Karl Hand. City lawyers defended the permit denials as necessary to avoid violence in light of current racial tensions. The Buffalo common council voted unanimously to seek a legal means to prohibit the Nazi demonstration, but a federal judge refused to enjoin the rally. Both demonstrations, which organizers on either side claimed would be peaceful, would be allowed to proceed.

Denied any legal remedy to prevent the head-to-head rallies, Mayor Griffin and city and county leaders planned an official gathering in nearby Lafayette Square on the same day (though a few hours later) as a memorial celebration in honor of Martin Luther King. They also planned to have a large police presence in Niagara Square during the two unsanctioned rallies.

Mayor Griffin and Commissioner Cunningham asked the media not to overplay the neo-Nazi demonstration. Griffin dismissed Karl Hand as a flake and encouraged others to view him similarly and not give him or his proposed rally too much publicity. Nevertheless, Hand's rally sparked what the *Washington Post* later described as "an orgy of overreaction," writing that local television stations "treated the event like the coming of World War III," while the police commissioner assigned over three hundred law enforcement officers to be present at the demonstration. In the days preceding, Hand was interviewed and quoted in numerous newspapers, including the *New York Times*.

On the day of, Karl Hand stood in front of city hall beside a statue of Millard Fillmore and held a placard reading WHITES HAVE RIGHTS. By most reports, he was the sole demonstrator, though some accounts said there were as many as two others. By contrast, a few hundred counterdemonstrators showed up across the way. Commissioner Cunningham estimated that there were about seven hundred people at city hall, with half the crowd made up of police and press. The city-sponsored memorial for Martin Luther King held in Lafayette Square attracted over a thousand people. Senator Daniel Patrick Moynihan attended along with other state and local officials. Mayor Griffin and County Executive Ed Rutkowski designated 1981 as "the year of understanding" in Buffalo.

Though Karl Hand told reporters he was not disappointed by the turnout—or lack thereof—for his rally, it had unquestionably failed, at least insofar as gathering supporters. From a publicity standpoint, Hand could arguably claim somewhat of a victory, much to the chagrin of Mayor Griffin, who complained that the press had given "an awful lot of credibility to a couple of nuts."

There were no violent confrontations and no arrests related to the rallies, except one: Karl Hand was arrested afterward by federal officials on weapons charges. The feds found the firearm after Hand told a reporter he had a gun for protection.

Despite the outcroppings of racial hostilities that had sprouted amid the media maelstrom surrounding the killings, the rejection of Hand's white supremacist movement ran true to historical precedent in Buffalo. The Ku Klux Klan had quite literally been run out of town in 1925 during the time period when the KKK was experiencing a wide resurgence in other cities across America. The arrival of Klan operatives in 1921 and the instant public backlash against them helped elect Buffalo's first Catholic mayor, Francis X. Schwab, a former brewer, who won the election despite being under federal indictment for violations of the Volstead Act (commonly known as Prohibition). The Klan's short-lived and tumultuous presence in Buffalo was marked by threats and violent confrontations, mostly against Klan members and sympathizers. Mayor Schwab was believed to have played a role in the ransacking of Klan headquarters that resulted in records being stolen. The Klan membership list was put on public display at police headquarters. The KKK shuttered their office soon after and left town. They had not been a viable organization in Buffalo since, and the recent probe of neo-Nazis and groups with similar philosophies had turned up nothing but a handful of random renegades.

A far more important occurrence on January 15, 1981, was the letter sent by New York state police to scores of firearms examiners across the country. As detectives had questioned and eliminated suspect after suspect, technicians at the Buffalo Police Services lab had conducted meticulous examinations on the ballistics evidence. The letter summarized the four .22 caliber killings and key findings that had since been made. The fact that empty shell casings were found at the homicide scenes was indicative of a self-ejecting, or semiautomatic, type of weapon. While several types of commercial ammunition had been used in the killings, the rifling characteristics of the recovered bullets were identical:

> Number of land & grooves - 6
> Direction of twist - Right
> Approximate land width - .045"
> Approximate groove width - .076"

There were no gross imperfections on the rifle impressions of the bullets. The firing impression was wedge shaped and measured approximately .07" in width. This appeared to be an unusually wide firing pin, as the impression widths were consistent on all the recovered cases. One edge of the impression had unique gross markings, which were photographed and included with the letter. Inquiry of the Crime Laboratory Information System indicated the following possible weapons: Ruger pistols, Ruger 10/22 rifles, Walther pistols, or Starr pistols. Of these, the Ruger 10/22 rifle produced a firing pin impression that was most consistent with the evidence cartridge cases. If the weapon used had, in fact, been a 10/22 rifle, it would have to have been cut down to a concealable size.

The letter requested that any examiner coming in contact with a .22 caliber weapon that produced a firing pin impression resembling the photograph should contact Captain Henry Williams at the DA's task force.

In early February, Sam Slade traveled to the Sturm-Ruger plant at Southport, Connecticut, in an effort to establish with certainty whether a Ruger 10/22 rifle was the weapon used in the .22 caliber killings. Engineers at Sturm-Ruger provided Slade with some valuable information. Firing pins for the 10/22 rifle and the various Ruger pistols had not undergone any significant structural change since the weapons were first produced. Blueprints and a comparative analysis showed that firing pins for the pistols were somewhat smaller than the 10/22 rifle firing pin. This meant that Ruger pistols could be eliminated as weapons used in the homicides. While this helped narrow the field, there had been more than a half million Sturm-Ruger 10/22 rifles produced since the model's introduction in 1964.

Blueprints and several sample firing pins were sent to the Buffalo police lab for further analysis. The lab confirmed that the Ruger 10/22 firing pin impressions were the most typical when compared to the evidence shell casings, but lab director Robert Perrigo informed Leo Donovan that he was reluctant to state categorically that the 10/22 rifle was the gun used in the homicides. They were still testing and evaluating Starr and Walther pistols in an effort to eliminate them as weapons of interest.

While the evidence team zeroed in on the make and model of the gun, their counterparts were once again stymied when it came to finding who had used it. February turned to March with no further attacks of the .22 Caliber Killer/Midtown Slasher, which was the only positive news other than the recovery of Albert Menefee. After thirteen days in the hospital, Albert had been released in good condition. He faced ten to twelve weeks of post-discharge rehabilitation, after which doctors expected him to be fully recovered and back to normal. Albert had beat the odds. During a press conference following his release from the hospital, he thanked the emergency and surgical teams that had saved his life. When asked for his feelings about the attack, Albert said, "I'm not angry about the situation. I'm just sorry that I missed out on the New Year's cheer."

While neither Albert Menefee nor Calvin Crippen expressed bitterness or complaints about the investigation, Edward Cosgrove faced deepening disapproval from black community leaders, some of whom were calling for his removal as head of the task force. Arguments over the investigation and Cosgrove's leadership had spilled into city government, sparking heated sessions of the common council between members who expressed continuing faith in the task force and those who bitterly denounced it as an abject failure. At the end of February, three council members with varying views sponsored a resolution requesting that Vice President George Bush come to Buffalo to review the inquiry.

Cosgrove had continued meeting with black leaders despite the votes of no confidence. He kept them apprised of developments, mainly concerning the number of suspects being questioned or otherwise checked out. In March, he announced he was rolling out phase two of the investigation. This meant little to those who had been thoroughly unimpressed with phase one.

The task force had, in fact, gone through hundreds of suspects, culled from tips and from records of violent offenders from around the state. The Department of Criminal Justice Services in Albany had produced a list of 495 persons with a "violent bent" who had been arrested in Erie and Niagara County over the past three years and who somewhat matched the composite sketches. The list was cross-referenced with registered owners of .22 caliber firearms and owners of vehicles matching those variously described by witnesses. Albert Menefee and Calvin Crippen had been brought in to view suspects, but both were positive that the man who attacked them was not among any of those shown to them by police.

Forensic and lab work had not been limited to ballistics. A double-edged diver knife seized from the home of a man the task force had labeled as "psychotic and a racist" had been sent to the FBI lab in Washington, DC, for tool mark comparison with cut tree limbs found at the site of Parler Edwards's cab.

The Buffalo investigation was not the only one growing colder as the weather grew warmer. New York City and Rochester were also at dead ends with their cases. Though New York City detectives and some task force members had all but dismissed a link between the .22 caliber killings and the stabbings—or even a connection between the New York City and Western New York knife attacks—others in law enforcement weren't ready to discount it, seeing markedly strong similarities in the *nature* of the attacks that transcended the particulars of weapon. Profiler John Douglas felt that all the knife attacks were likely the work of a single offender, regardless of the geography. He also felt the .22 Caliber Killer and Midtown Slasher could indeed, from a profiling standpoint, be the same man. Douglas remained convinced that the cab driver murders had no connection to either the shootings or the knifings.

The mutilation murders of Parler Edwards and Shorty Jones were still very much a part of the task force inquiry, and, in some minds, inextricably linked to the .22 caliber murders. Collin Cole meanwhile had recovered from the strangulation attempt and resumed his life as a street hustler. The investigation into his attack had quietly faded away. Collin appeared to have little interest in the pursuit of justice on his behalf, and his varying stories and total lack of cooperation would've made it an exercise in futility. It seemed that Collin and Darren, the person he had named as his attacker, had patched things up. Darren had since been arrested in Pennsylvania on an unrelated charge. Rumor had it that he and Collin were going to move to Florida together as soon as Darren got out of jail.

Phase two of the investigation involved reinterviewing several witnesses, including Shorty Jones's girlfriend, Zoe Fontaine. Buffalo police had found and arrested a black male named Leonard Hersey who was in possession of Shorty's missing handgun. John Regan and Paul Delano showed the gun to Zoe, who became very upset to see that the police had it. Zoe said she had felt guilty about talking Shorty out of carrying the gun. She felt that if he'd had the gun with him, he would still be alive. Zoe admitted that she gave the gun to Leonard a few days after Shorty was killed. She and Leonard had lived together for a number of years prior to the resumption of her relationship with Shorty. Zoe said she was in love with Leonard again and had given him the gun for protection. She also said that she thought the police had killed her boyfriend, Shorty Jones. When asked why she thought this, she replied, "Because no one has been arrested for his killing."

State police investigators also reinterviewed Zoe on a separate occasion about Shorty's drug and gambling activities. She didn't offer much on either subject, and still insisted that Shorty wasn't a numbers runner. Zoe did mention one thing that might've been of great interest to investigators had it not been buried in the voluminous stacks of paper in the Jones file. She mentioned that on October 8, Shorty had discussed the death of Parler Edwards with her. Shorty had told her that he didn't know Parler Edwards and never had any dealings with him.

Zoe had last seen Shorty at 6:45 p.m. Parler's family had not identified his body at the morgue until 7:00 p.m. His name had, in the meantime, been withheld from the press. This meant that Shorty Jones knew that Parler Edwards had been murdered before the victim's name had been made public.

In early spring, a teletype on the murders was sent once again to law enforcement nationwide. Investigators hoped that maybe someone, somewhere, might have a new lead to offer. Maybe the reminder would jog a memory or match some newly discovered offender in some other jurisdiction.

They could only hope.

The task force had covered and recovered the same ground in Western New York countless times over the past seven months, to no avail. Task force members had traveled to Atlanta to compare notes and see if there might be a connection. They had considered an endless roster of suspects that included some who were remote at best. They had even made inquiries about a disturbed young man named John Hinckley, who had been arrested for shooting President Ronald Reagan and three others in Washington, DC, on March 30 with a .22 caliber revolver. Some investigators were now quietly admitting that the case might never be solved.

The one factor perhaps equally encouraging and frustrating for any detective is the certain knowledge that no matter how cold or confounding a case, the potential to solve the mystery always exists. Nothing happens in a vacuum. There are answers. Elusive as they may be, they are out there. The challenge, of course, is finding the person or persons who can provide them.

Many years hence, after all was said and done, John Regan would look back with rue and antipathy when he thought of Kenny Paulson, his first witness to the first murder. "If he had only told us that night, when Glenn Dunn was shot, none of the rest of it would've happened," John Regan would later say. "If he had just told us that it was Angela's brother."

PART THREE
THE QUIET MAN

"I'm afraid I can't explain myself, sir. Because I am not myself, you see?"

—Lewis Carroll, *Alice in Wonderland*

Chapter 11

"CHRISTOPHER ... CHRISTOPHER ... CHRISTOPHER ..."

There he goes again, thought Private First Class Corwin. The prisoner lay with his hands clutched to his head, rolling rhythmically from side to side in his bed as he cried again in a low beseeching voice, "Christopher!"

PFC Corwin was a military police officer stationed at Fort Benning, Georgia. His current assignment was to stand guard round-the-clock on a fellow soldier, Private First Class Joseph Christopher, who was confined to the psychiatric wing at the Martin Army Community Hospital.

PFC Joseph Christopher had been in the B4 ward of the base hospital for a few days. Where he was supposed to be was in the stockade. Private Christopher had been arrested by the military police on January 18, 1981, for allegedly stabbing another soldier. It was now April, and prisoner Christopher's three months in military police custody had been eventful, to say the least.

Christopher was in the stockade awaiting court-martial when he stopped eating. His weight plunged by thirty-two pounds in a little over a month, necessitating medical treatment. That had been his first admission to the B4 ward back in early March. He had spent four weeks in the hospital and was sent back to the stockade on April 3. He didn't stay long, however. He was readmitted to the psychiatric ward on April 10, this time following emergency treatment for a self-inflicted wound.

That act of self-mutilation had prompted the army to classify Private Christopher as a suicide risk. As a result, an MP had to watch him at all times. PFC Corwin had to follow Joseph Christopher wherever he went.

191

He had to escort him to and from meals, the latrine, and wherever else he might go on the ward, although Private Christopher rarely moved anywhere these days. A large portion of Corwin's shift entailed sitting in a chair by the prisoner/patient's bed.

Joseph Christopher slept a lot. He shuffled to the bathroom. Everything he did, on the rare occasions he did anything, seemed to be in slow motion. On the occasions when he did finally wake up, he would often go through this routine of holding his head in his hands and rocking back and forth in his bed muttering, "*Christopher . . . Christopher!*" in a plaintive moan.

PFC Corwin's first name happened to be Christopher, but it was not Corwin that the patient/prisoner was calling when he went into this routine; Joseph Christopher didn't even know the name of his guard, despite the fact that Corwin stood or sat right next to him, usually in a chair directly next to his bed, in eight-hour shifts, day in and day out, and despite the fact that Corwin had also guarded Christopher in the stockade and had intervened on occasion when he had "conflicts" with other prisoners.

Private Christopher had never spoken to Private Corwin. Most of the time, Joseph Christopher didn't seem aware that anyone else was in the same room, or even the same universe, for that matter. He seemed to dwell in his own head, which, based on his behavior, appeared to be a very desolate place indeed. When Joseph Christopher would go into whatever routine this was, the rocking and squeezing his head and calling "Christopher," over and over again in despair, it was apparently his own name he invoked in that mournful chant.

So it came as a surprise to PFC Corwin when Christopher finally spoke to him. Corwin was sitting dutifully in a chair by the side of the bed when he noticed that the patient was awake and looking directly at him.

"What's your name?" he asked.

"Private First Class Christopher Corwin."

There was a pause.

"PFC Corwin, do you realize I was a mass murderer in Buffalo?"

Corwin didn't react. This wasn't the first time he'd heard a prisoner say something outrageous. And this was, after all, the psychiatric ward. When he finally responded, he said, "Christopher, I really can't believe that."

"Well, I was," the prisoner/patient said.

"I refuse to believe that," Corwin said.

"It's true." He spoke slowly, remotely. "I killed seven people in Buffalo and I killed some people in New York."

Corwin shook his head. "I still don't believe you, Christopher. At ease. Go back to sleep." A command of "at ease" in the military means "relax." In this context it meant "shut up."

The prisoner/patient lay quiet. There was a long pause. Corwin noted the distant look on Christopher's face. Finally, Corwin said, "Christopher, I hope to God not. Why would you kill people?"

"No reason. I had no reason," he answered in the same slow voice. "I just did it."

PFC Corwin wasn't sure what to think, either about the statements or Joseph Christopher himself. Christopher's first stint in the stockade had lasted forty-six days, during which he had twice assaulted a fellow prisoner, made an escape attempt that involved trying to stab a guard in the eye with a pen, and had his nose broken and tooth fractured by guards as they fought to drag him off to a segregation cell.

When he wasn't acting combative, he was acting weird. Christopher's mellow moments could be almost as unnerving as his erratic violence. He spent a good portion of his stockade time in administrative segregation, or solitary confinement, due to his unpredictable nature. Alone in his cell, he would sometimes spend his time quietly writing letters to his family or reading the Bible. Other times he would sit and stare at the ceiling with a grin on his face, pointing his finger at the overhead light. That could go on for hours. Guards would overhear him laughing or carrying on a conversation, but when they looked, no one else was there. It was also during these times, when he appeared to be mentally elsewhere, that he would compulsively masturbate, which seemed all the more strange because when he shared a cell with other prisoners, he would scold them for even talking about sex, partying, or anything else that offended his deeply religious sensibilities.

There were times when Christopher sat still and silent on his bunk, staring down at the floor looking crushed and despondent. Then there were times when he appeared normal, looking and behaving much like any other guy, maybe a bit quieter and more reserved than most, but a regular guy all the same.

You just never knew what to expect with him, which is why guards and prisoners alike had learned to be cautious around Private Joseph Christopher, or avoid him altogether when possible. His behavior could be so bizarre, so contradictory, and so utterly incomprehensible, there were more than a few people who wondered how the hell he had gotten into the army in the first place.

They knew for certain that Private Christopher's problems, whatever they might be, were not a question of combat fatigue or post-traumatic stress disorder, at least not as a result of military service. Christopher had only been in the army since the previous November. He'd been arrested and thrown in the stockade after only two months as a soldier. He hadn't even made it out of basic training.

This is why PFC Corwin was not at all sure what to make of Private Christopher's remarks about being a mass murderer. The prisoner/patient said nothing else during the remainder of Corwin's watch. It was such an outrageous claim; and why was Christopher talking about having killed people so far away, in Buffalo and New York, when they were in Georgia? It didn't make a lot of sense. Then again, nothing about Private Christopher made much sense. Corwin decided to report the conversation to his guard commander and let his superiors handle it however they saw fit.

PFC Corwin was not the only person at Martin Army Community Hospital who had to report a strange conversation of late with Private Christopher. Captain Bernard Burgess was a staff nurse on the B4 ward. On Friday, April 10, Captain Burgess had conducted an intake interview with Private Christopher upon his readmission to the hospital. The question-and-answer session had been fairly routine—Burgess, along with most of the staff in the hospital psych ward, was already acquainted with Joseph Christopher because of his very recent one-month stay in their facility. Burgess wanted now to gauge Christopher's state of mind, if he could. According to the emergency room report, Christopher had used a razor blade to make a ten-centimeter circumferential cut around the base of his penis. Suturing of the wound had required several stitches. Following treatment, doctors had him transferred to B4 immediately for psychiatric evaluation.

Burgess asked Private Christopher how he was feeling. He didn't get much of a response, which wasn't unusual when it came to this patient, although Burgess noted that Christopher seemed more alert than he had on some previous occasions. The captain let a silence ensue, hoping that the private would speak of his own volition about whatever was on his mind. Christopher appeared calm rather than agitated, and Captain Burgess hoped that if he didn't press, the patient might open up and talk about why he had injured himself. The psychiatric ward staff had learned the first time around that pressing Christopher for answers didn't work. He seemed very mistrustful of everyone. Maybe this time, Burgess hoped, the patient could communicate his thoughts and feelings a little better. After writing down all of the basic intake info—religion, next of kin, medical issues—Captain Burgess asked the patient if he had anything he wanted to add or if he had any questions.

Christopher spoke in a soft voice. His affect was flat. He asked Captain Burgess if he was aware of some killings that took place in Buffalo or New York City that had been reported in newspapers and on TV. Captain Burgess replied no.

In the same flat voice, Joe Christopher said, "When I was home on leave, from December 18 to January 2, I killed some people."

"How many?" Burgess asked.

"A total of thirteen."

"How did you kill them?"

"I shot some with a gun and stabbed some others," the patient replied. "I know they knew I did it because my picture was in the newspaper."

His voice remained soft and dull, his face unanimated.

"Where did this happen?" Captain Burgess asked.

"In Buffalo and New York City. Fifth Avenue. My friend said there was a picture in the newspaper that looked like me," Christopher said.

"This happened while you were on leave?"

"When I was on Christmas leave," Christopher said. "I did it because I felt that I had to. Something came over me and I couldn't control it."

Burgess asked him to elaborate on what had compelled him, but the patient couldn't explain. Burgess thought for a moment. The last time Christopher was in the psych ward, Burgess recalled Christopher saying that stabbing the solider in the barracks—the offense that had gotten him thrown into the stockade back in January—was the worst thing he had ever done in his life. He reminded Christopher of what he'd said then.

"That wasn't the worst thing," Joseph Christopher answered. "This is worse. I want to call the police and tell them I did it."

Nurse/Captain Bernard Burgess wasn't sure what to think. Christopher asked again if he could call the police. Burgess asked Christopher to wait in the hall.

Once the patient exited the nurses' station, Burgess went and spoke to Captain Allen, the head nurse, and told him what Christopher had said, including that Christopher wanted to call the police in Buffalo or New York. Captain Allen instructed Burgess not to let the patient use the phone. Captain Allen would speak with his superiors and they'd address the situation on Monday.

Burgess got Joe Christopher from the hall and brought him back to the nurses' station. He told Joe that he wouldn't be able to call the police right now. The patient looked blank and didn't argue.

"I don't want to talk anymore now," Christopher said.

Joseph Christopher got up and shuffled off into the hallway. Bernard Burgess did some paperwork. Burgess wrote down some details of their conversation, noting in his report that Christopher maintained the same dull affect throughout their entire interview. He noted, "Need to check out patient story on Monday, further information needed. Talk to patient again tomorrow."

———

Lieutenant Dorothy Anderson was another nurse assigned to the B4 psychiatric ward. On Saturday, April 11, Lieutenant Anderson wrote in her nursing notes that patient/Private Joseph Christopher was reluctant to have her change the dressing on his wound. That was understandable. A male staff member took care of it and reported to Anderson that the wound appeared to be healing normally.

Later in the afternoon, nurse/Lieutenant Anderson checked on Christopher and asked how he was doing.

"What do you think is going to happen to me?" Christopher asked. "I just want to go back to my people."

Lieutenant Anderson was unaware of anything he'd said the night before to Captain Burgess but found Christopher's words understandable nevertheless, considering his predicament and his obvious psychological distress.

She noted in her report that day that his affect was bland and flat; that he did not attempt to injure himself again; that he ate all his dinner and was cooperative, even helpful. He spoke little, which was of course not unusual, and she knew from experience it was best to let him speak if and when it suited him.

Christopher had already let Lieutenant Anderson know that he did not trust her, which was in keeping with how he seemed to feel about everyone on the ward, staff and patients alike. She remained attentive and friendly, and allowed for him to come and talk to her if he chose.

Anderson made note that her primary goal with the patient was to help him find ways to control his behavior. He obviously had serious difficulties—starving himself, self-mutilation, ill-conceived escapes. Private Christopher certainly did himself a lot of harm.

On Monday morning, April 13, Lieutenant Anderson ran the group therapy session on the ward. Joseph Christopher did something out of character at the meeting. He became agitated while Anderson was speaking to another patient in the group and he interrupted.

"How can you tell him he has problems?" Christopher asked angrily.

Since it was rare for Christopher to participate at all, Lieutenant Anderson turned her attention to him. "Should we be discussing something else?" she asked.

"I want to discuss where I'd rather be right now," Christopher said.

"Where is that?" Anderson asked.

"In New York. In the Adirondack Mountains."

By this time, Lieutenant Anderson had read the nursing notes that Nurse Burgess had written about things Christopher had said on Friday evening. Something about killing people in New York. It dawned on her that the patient might've said such things as a ploy to get back home. He had once asked what it would take for him to be transferred from Fort Benning to a veterans' hospital in Buffalo.

"How bad do you want to be back in New York?" Anderson asked him. "To what lengths would you go to get back to New York?"

"What do you mean?" he asked.

"Would you lie, or say someone in your family was ill, or anything like that?"

"I'm not going to answer that question," Christopher said. He seemed angry with her.

About an hour after group therapy ended, Lieutenant Anderson was at the nurses' station preparing medication when Joseph Christopher approached her. Patients were not allowed in the nurses' station. She asked him if there was something he wanted to talk about.

"No, I don't have anything I want to talk about. I have something to tell you." He asked if she knew anything about him committing a crime.

"Did you commit a crime?" Lieutenant Anderson asked.

"Yes. I killed some people."

"How many people did you kill?"

He paused and thought about it, then said, "I'm not sure about the number."

"Were they all male, all female, or were they mixed?" Anderson asked.

"They were all male," Christopher answered.

"When did this happen?"

"In December, around Christmas."

"What was the time span?" Anderson asked.

"I don't know what you mean."

"Did they all take place in December or was it from December to January?"

Christopher thought about it for a bit. "From September to January."

"Then the last person you killed was in January?" she asked.

"Yes."

"Were the people all black, all white, Puerto Rican, or mixed?"

"I don't know," he said.

"What do you mean, you don't know?"

Christopher thought again. "None of them were white."

"Then they were all ethnic?" she asked.

"Yes."

"Why did you do it?"

"There were reasons," Christopher answered.

"I don't understand," said Lieutenant Anderson. "What reasons?"

"I knew this was something I had to do," he told her. "There were signs that told me I had to do this."

"Did somebody tell you to do it?" she asked. "Did you hear voices or something that told you to do it?"

"No," he answered. "There were just signs. I knew it was something I had to do."

"Why are you telling me this?" Anderson asked. "You told me outright that you don't trust me. Why are you telling me?"

He looked at her and said blankly, "I wanted you to know." He turned to leave. "That's all I have to say," he told her. He walked out to the dining area behind the nurses' station and sat down in a chair.

After a moment or so, Lieutenant Anderson followed him. She had to keep an eye on him anyway, as he was under one-on-one watch.

"Why are you staring at me like that?" he asked.

"Am I staring at you?"

"I just want to know why you're looking at me like that."

"I didn't know I was looking at you in any particular way," she answered.

Joseph Christopher fell silent. Nurse/Lieutenant Anderson remained with him for the rest of her shift, but he said nothing else.

Anderson reported the conversation to Captain Allen, who spoke with his superior officer about what Private Christopher had said to the two nurses. They notified the deputy provost marshal, who in turn contacted the army's Criminal Investigation Division, known as the CID.

Sergeant Thomas Carr of the CID reviewed the army's records on Private Joseph Gerard Christopher. For a man who had only been in the service for five months, Christopher had quite the dossier.

Joseph G. Christopher was twenty-five years old. He had enlisted in the army on September 16, 1980, in Buffalo, New York, which was listed as his place of birth and civilian home. According to his enlistment papers, he stood five feet eight inches tall, weighed 170 pounds, had brown hair and hazel eyes. He had scored high on the military entrance exams but had chosen infantry. He had passed his medical exam on September 19 and had reported to Fort Jackson, South Carolina, for processing on November 13. He had arrived in Fort Benning, Georgia, on November 19 for basic training, assigned to company A, Fourth Battalion, First Infantry Training Brigade.

On January 18, 1981, approximately two weeks before he would've completed basic training, Christopher had allegedly attacked Private Leonard Coles, a fellow soldier in his platoon, and inflicted two knife wounds in the victim's chest. Private Coles had been treated at Martin Army Hospital, recovered, and had since been released. There were several witnesses to the attack. Motive unknown. Private Christopher had refused to make any statements.

January 21, 1981

Well good morning mom. I cannot say things are fine because I am in Jail. I am charged with aggeravetted assault do not go telling anyone not any of my sister at all it is a pretty seious charge so I might end up doing some time or get toussed out of the army I do not know I only talked To a consulear not a lawer they are sending to defend me I will have to send those packetages back to you cannot have anything. Mom about the trees in the country call that guy back and try to get out of the contract or the propert[y] will be worthless . . . What that place need is me to take out firewood and clear out all the apple trees if they cut the trees you might as well sell the place also the money he gave you is no were close to what wood is worth these day please try. write soon PS they finally got the Hostage

Love

Joseph Christopher

January 18 was a Sunday. At 10:30 a.m., men in the second platoon were milling around building 4877, a two-story, wood-frame barracks. It was near the end of quiet time, when recruits are allowed to socialize, write letters, or relax as they like.

Private Leonard Coles, age twenty, had spent the late morning talking with friends in the barracks. Around 10:40 a.m., the platoon was instructed to fall out for formation. Recruits headed to their wall lockers. Coles stood facing his open locker when he felt someone grab him from behind. "When he actually grabbed me, I thought it was somebody playing," Leonard Coles later recalled. "But when I felt something hit me in the chest and I saw the blade go up, then I knew it wasn't playing."

Men in the barracks heard Coles shout, "What's going on?!"

Private Coles instinctively pushed back against his attacker and spun him around, shoving the man against the lockers. The attacker pushed forward and Coles reached up and grabbed the man's upraised wrists. The knife quivered in the attacker's right hand as the two men locked in a vibrating grip, the attacker pushing forward and Coles pushing back.

Private Anthony Bulger heard the commotion from across the bay. He looked and saw two men standing, facing each other, wrestling. The two grappling men knocked into a bunk and fell to the floor.

Private Bulger ran over to break up the fight. Several men had heard the noise and came to see what was going on. Private Coles was sitting on top of another man who struggled beneath him. "I didn't know who it was until we hit the floor," Leonard Coles said later. "That's when I got hit in the side. I knew he had stabbed me. He tried to keep the knife in me but I grabbed his hand and pushed it away. He tried to stab me again and I grabbed his wrist that the knife was in. That's when I looked up and saw that it was Private Christopher."

Coles held one hand against Christopher's face and pinned Christopher's right elbow to the floor with the other. "I was shouting and Christopher was screaming," Coles recalled. "I know I used profanity but I don't know what I said."

As Private Bulger intervened, he saw the weapon in Christopher's hand. "Help me!" Bulger shouted. "This guy has a knife!" Another soldier ran to Bulger's aid and they scrambled on Christopher as he thrashed and fought.

Private Charles Getz had been standing in the middle of the bay when he heard the yelling and saw men running toward the lockers. Getz went over and spotted Coles on top of Christopher. He grabbed Coles by the belt and pulled him off. That's when he saw the blood on Private Coles's fatigue shirt.

Private Claude Coleman got there in time to see Leonard Coles standing, clutching his side, and he heard Coles say, "I've been stabbed!" Coles ran off and Private Getz followed after him.

Bulger and another soldier were on the floor trying to restrain Private Christopher, who was screaming incoherently, crying, jerking his head from side to side "as if he was out of his mind," as one witness stated. Claude Coleman saw Christopher's body shake, as if he was having a convulsion. The two soldiers were trying to get the knife out of Christopher's hand but he had it gripped as if for dear life. A third man jumped in and grabbed Christopher's flailing left arm. They struggled and shouted at him, but as all three would tell the CID later that day, Private Christopher did not seem to be aware of what was happening or where he was, and he didn't appear to recognize anybody around him, even though they were all men in his platoon.

They managed to pry the knife from his hand and one of them shouted for someone to fetch the drill sergeant.

Christopher eventually stopped struggling under the weight of his three barracks mates. He sobbed and wailed and whimpered, and though he was surrounded by men he knew in a place he'd been living for weeks, his eyes darted wildly in petrified shock, like a man who suddenly awakes to find himself cast into a lake of fire.

The one detail that left the deepest lingering impression on some of those who witnessed the incident up close was the look of Joseph Christopher. As Claude Coleman described, "It was a really disturbing thing to see, the way he cried and was so scared and out of it. Like watching somebody's mind break apart right before your eyes. The memory stays with you, even if you wish it wouldn't." Three decades afterward, one of the men who had held Christopher to the floor that morning said, "The main thing I remember is the crazy look in his eyes. It was a wild, scared, crazed look that I'd never seen before. I literally had nightmares about it for years after. I've only seen that look one other time in my life, when I saw a deer that had been hit by a car. It was a young deer and both its front legs were broken, and it had that exact same look in its eyes, this maniacal look of terror and confusion."

———————

Dear Carlo
I am not doing very well
I got myself in a lot of trouble
They have me in the stockade
charged with aggervated Assualt
with intent to comit murdure
I need a good lawyer, I am not
very good at asking for favors
please help me. I go to Court marshell
in 30 to 40 days From January 19 1981 also
my mail has not been comeing please have
some get in contact with me
Sincerely your friend
Joseph Christopher

———————

Sworn statement of Private J. Cloud. "Christopher walked up to Coles from behind while Coles was standing at his wall locker. Christopher put his left leg between Coles's legs, grabbed Coles from behind by putting his left arm around Coles's chest, and started hitting Coles in the chest with his right hand. I couldn't see them from the front and that's why I don't know if Christopher had the knife in his hand at that time but I think he did."

Q: Why did Christopher attack Coles?
A: I don't know. Coles never said anything to him and I was with
    Coles all morning. Except for this morning about 0700 hours,
    that was the first time I saw Christopher and probably the
    first time Coles saw him too.

Q: Did anything happen at 0700, or any other time, that would have made Christopher angry with Coles?

A: Not to my knowledge. At 0700 hours, me and Christopher were just getting off duty from the Reactionary Force. Coles was at the barracks at that time.

Q: How far away were you standing from Coles and Christopher when they were fighting?

A: About four feet. My wall locker is behind Coles.

Q: Where had Christopher been prior to the incident?

A: At the other end of the barracks where his bunk is located.

Q: Had Christopher and Coles been in arguments prior to this incident?

A: Not to my knowledge.

Q: Do you know where Christopher got the knife?

A: Probably while serving at the mess hall. I think he was working as a server there last Wednesday (14 Jan 81).

Q: Is there anything you would like to add to your statement?

A: Yes. Christopher might have mistaken Coles for me. Last night, 2100 [hours], 17 Jan 81, I saw that Christopher had wet his bed and I kidded him about it. He didn't say anything to me at the time. That was while we were on the Reactionary Force. No one else knew about the incident. I think the knife was in his wall locker and he did not get a chance to get to it until he saw me with Coles in the barracks. Christopher usually stays by himself and doesn't talk to people much.

———

The knife had a white handle and was eleven inches in overall length with a six-inch silver blade. It was a non-folding, kitchen-type knife. The mess hall shift leader confirmed that it looked identical to a knife he had first noticed to be missing the night before.

Statements from all the witnesses were consistent in that Christopher had not said anything to Coles either prior to or during the attack. No one was aware of any tension or previous interaction between the two men, least of all the victim himself.

Private Leonard Coles had been admitted to the base hospital in stable condition and underwent surgery for two stab wounds: one in his right upper chest area and another on the left lower lateral chest. There were no serious internal injuries and only a minor injury to the spleen. Coles was interviewed by the CID and said he didn't know why Christopher had attacked him.

Private Juan Feliciano usually walked to and from church on Sundays with Private Christopher. On the morning of January 18, Feliciano and Christopher had walked to church at about 7:45, at which time Feliciano observed that Christopher was extremely nervous and shaky. Normally Christopher didn't say much, but on this morning the two of them had a conversation. "We were talking about military life and other subjects. We also talked about people messing up in the platoon," Feliciano told the CID. Private Christopher had remarked that he was tired of everyone messing with him, and that "if anyone fucked with him, they would not be fucking around anymore." Christopher had not mentioned any names. "We went to church and after church was out I didn't see Christopher anymore. When I was walking back to the barracks, I heard that there had been a stabbing. I later found out that Christopher had stabbed Coles."

According to Private Feliciano and others in the platoon, Private Christopher was very religious. Christopher was a Catholic and attended mass every Sunday. He also carried a Bible and red prayer book everywhere he went, including the mess hall and the latrine.

Dear Mother
Today is Sunday January 31, 1981. Went to chaple service this morning the chapilin gave a good sermon it kind of hit home and, I pray that God grants me the grace to be a good and wise Christian from this day on.
About my situation I am hear Because I stabed someone pretty bad
They harassed me until I snaped I guess because I keeped
to myself and read my Bible and prayed
I just could not get away from it and when they noticed
they tried to get closer to me trying to make out like a wimp

and a fagut they keeped harassing me It was craze. Mom
is it not normal to need time to be able to relax.
Please talk to Mr [Carlo] Bianchi tell him that if he dose not know
a good lawyer that I asked you to talk to Mr Becker
I should of wrote him first but I was kind [of] upset[.]
ever since dad passed I have gone to him for conculing
like my father. Mom would you please show him this
letter to explain my situation
about the readers digest I would like them very much.
I have two but can not do the skill builders because
they are not mine. I would like very much to have
good reading and writing skills. I think if I go to jail
I going to classes for reading and writeing. This army
is good for building your body but I do not want to be
superman. I just want to live a simple life.
I just got the letter I thing you wrote first after I told
you that I was in here [stockade] the one you said was mushy
I started to cry I love you so much It hurts.
Erternal love
Joseph

The CID wanted to determine a reason for the assault.

They spoke with Joseph Christopher's commanding officers, who described him as a quiet recruit, unremarkable, neither particularly good nor particularly bad. Kept to himself. Did not cause problems.

The men in Christopher's platoon all said the same thing: he was very quiet, kept to himself, read his Bible all the time. He meditated a lot. He did not socialize or build friendships with anyone, nor did he get into arguments or fights. The same word was used over and over again in describing Joseph Christopher: loner.

Officially, prior to the assault on Coles, there were no issues with Private Christopher.

The only thing that struck the CID as a little off was the degree to which Christopher had apparently avoided camaraderie. That was a little unusual, particularly in an infantry training brigade, where soldiers typically build friendships and are encouraged to do so; in combat, these are the people you will rely on and who will in turn rely on you. No one in Christopher's platoon even knew where he was from.

The stabbing of Private Coles had, of course, become the hot topic of conversation in the barracks and had piqued interest in the quiet recruit. A few details on Private Christopher began to emerge.

Private Claude Coleman, one of the witnesses to the Coles assault, learned that Christopher was from Buffalo. Coleman had perhaps had more interaction with Joseph Christopher than anyone else—which wasn't saying much, insofar as really knowing anything about him. Claude Coleman had discovered early on how difficult it was to forge any kind of a friendship with Private Christopher.

Coleman had first encountered Joe Christopher back in November, the day they were inducted into the army. "I noticed him because of his hair," Coleman would recall. "It was very short, like he already had a military haircut. He was also wearing sandals. That caught my attention too." At Fort Benning, Coleman and other recruits had tried talking to Christopher. "He seemed aloof. Later on I didn't think he was aloof, I thought he was just being very careful. But why or careful of what, we didn't know."

Throughout basic training, Coleman had only one conversation with Christopher and it occurred soon after their arrival at Fort Benning. "We were in the woods on a field exercise. Joe and I were sharing a shelter-half [pup tent]. As we were going to sleep, Joe asked me where I was from. I told him I was from a little town in upstate New York that he'd probably never heard of, a town outside Buffalo called Cheektowaga.

"That sparked his interest and he started asking me all kinds of questions; what I did before the Army and all that. Then I asked him, 'Hey, where are you from, man?' He said, 'Upstate New York,' and I asked him whereabouts. He said to me, 'Just shut up and go to sleep, man.' I'll never forget the way he said it, like kind of matter-of-fact. Just told me to shut up and go to sleep. And that's the last thing Joe ever said to me."

The next contact of note that Coleman had with Christopher was during pugil-stick training, a combat exercise in which two recruits use long padded weapons to simulate fighting hand-to-hand with a rifle. "Joe got carried away," Coleman remembered. "He just kept coming at me, like he wanted to beat me to death. The drill sergeant stopped it and he said to Joe, 'What's wrong with you?'"

Months afterward, Claude Coleman would be asked if he thought Joseph Christopher's behavior toward him had anything to do with race. Claude was half-black, half-white. "I didn't think so. It's not like Joe was any friendlier with the white guys."

That would be the consistent refrain from everyone in the platoon: no one had ever heard Christopher make any racial remarks or display animosity toward blacks. Private Christopher just seemed to want to avoid *everybody*. Right from the start, it also seemed like he didn't want to be in army. Which made everyone wonder why he had joined in the first place, and what kind of a guy he really was.

February 4, 1981
Dear Mom
I have not heard anything about a court date except
that I am going to get a genral court marshall what
ever that means
Please tell me if you talked to anyone about a lawyer
I rather be in prision then in this stockade.
I pass my day in pray
I am relieing on Gods Grace to help throw this ordeal
I don't know what will be I only pray. I put cotton in
my ears it helps a little but I am always keyed. your
letter are presents from heaven
I Honestly Love You
Joseph

Major Donald Morgan of the Fort Benning JAG office had been assigned as Private Christopher's attorney. Major Morgan was having a lot of difficulty working with his client. Private Christopher would not communicate with him. Christopher was suspicious and guarded, and he wouldn't discuss his case, no matter how Major Morgan tried to assure him of the attorney-client relationship and establish a rapport.

The only person at Fort Benning who Christopher would speak to was Father Michael Freeman, the Catholic chaplain, who visited him in the stockade at Private Christopher's request.

Christopher's legal problems had only compounded since he'd been sent to the stockade, as evidenced in summary reports of his first three and a half weeks in custody:

29 Jan 81   Involved in altercation with and attempted to assault another prisoner in mess hall.

5 Feb 81   Involved in second altercation with [same prisoner] and assaulted him in mess hall. During process of being placed in Administrative Segregation, assaulted guard; minimum necessary force used to subdue, Christopher sustained injury to nose. Transported to MACH[1], refused treatment, returned to Admin Seg.

11 Feb 81   Attempted to escape from custody while at MACH Mental Hygiene Clinic; bolted from doctor's office and attempted to stab guard in eye with pen.

Christopher was also steadfastly refusing to eat, for reasons he would not explain.

————

Dear Mom
Today is Friday 13 February 1981 I decided that I am going to eat what ever they put on my tray
Mom I know that you would like to come down here but I do not want you to spend the plain fair and pay for accomadation . . .
I am kind of depressed and my letter probably reflect that

————

1   Martin Army Community Hospital

mom I seem to me that I am a fool
each time I turn or talk to someone I feel depressed latter
think I said the wrong thing and will get myself in more trouble
and you would not believe the stuppid things I do I pray that
god someday maks me a fool no more
I Love You All
Joseph

Dear Mom
Today again being friday [February] 13 I am not going to stick
to my decidtion to eat everything they put on my tray take lunch
and feel bloated and I get bad feed backs most of this
Probally dose not make sense but this place is turning
so I do not know what is the thing to do when I use to talk to
Mr Biachni He told me he use to eat a apple in the morning
and meat at night. I can do 55 pushups now and 75 sittups
mom I am sorry I must be a weak person This place in hard
on my head I pray and pray
Take the money I have and come see me visiting day is
sunday do not spend your monies I know that holding you
will give me the strenth I need do not worry I am not thinking of
hurting myself or anything but I am very lonely
I sorry to cause these hardship mom really I am . . .
I have to hold fast to my dreams or I will never be able
to say I lived and I know I live because I feel intence Love.
Always
Joseph

───────────

Digging deeper, the CID learned that the attack on Private Coles was not
the first time Christopher had caused a buzz in the platoon. He had done
other things that raised eyebrows—and eventually, fists.

More than once, he shaved his head with a razor. When asked why,
he said he couldn't afford the haircuts. Other times he said he didn't want
anyone else cutting his hair. He would sometimes get up and walk around

the barracks after lights out. One night when he was on fireguard duty, when he was actually supposed to be patrolling around the barracks, a fellow soldier had awakened to find Christopher standing by the bunk, staring at him. The nocturnal wandering apparently became so frequent at one point that some of the men had a hard time getting a good night's sleep, dozing and waking because they were uneasy around him.

One incident stood out from the rest and marked a moment when feelings about Private Christopher surged from wariness to hostility.

"I KNOW I'm not SEEING what I'm SEEING!" the drill sergeant thundered.

The platoon stood in formation, silent and at attention.

The drill sergeant was wild with fury, disbelief. "Are you *FUCKING KIDDING ME*?!" He glared, eyes ablaze, veins bulging as if to pop, screaming to shake the earth. *"ARE! YOU! FUCK-ING! KID-DING MEEEEEEEE!"*

It wasn't bluster. The drill sergeant really couldn't fucking believe what he was seeing. Neither could anyone else.

January. Weeks now into basic training. And there, in formation, out between the barracks for the whole goddamned base to see, stood a private wearing shower shoes. Dressed in uniform but with shower shoes—flip-flops—on his feet instead of boots.

To make it worse, the stupid bastard was standing in the front row. Not in the back, where he might've had at least a slim chance of getting away with it, but in the goddamn first row, where nobody passing by, including officers and other platoons, could miss it.

"Private Christopher!" The drill sergeant charged forth, growling, snapping, baring his teeth like a pit bull about to maul a Chihuahua. "Are you a wise guy?! Are you the stupidest motherfucker on the face of the fucking earth?! Coming to MY formation in SHOWER SHOES! WHERE ARE YOUR FUCKING BOOTS?!"

Joseph Christopher stood wide-eyed, clueless, like a student who suddenly realizes, too late, that he's handed in the wrong assignment and the teacher is angry.

"He said something about having to wash his feet, or his boots were wet, or something like that," Leonard Coles recalled. "In those days, it was mass punishment. If one guy screwed up, the whole platoon got punished. They took Christopher inside to the drill sergeant's office. The rest of us got a ten- to fifteen-minute punishment session, doing push-ups, sit-ups.

"When they released him back to the barracks, guys were saying to him, 'What the hell were you thinking, man?' and 'Oh, you're special, huh?' He got a lot of flak for a couple days. The drill sergeant was embarrassed, the whole platoon was embarrassed. It was a big thing.

"Right then and there, I knew something wasn't right with him," Coles remembered. "We already knew this guy was weird, but *that* weird? That was an unforgettable day."

If Private Christopher didn't grasp exactly how upset his fellow recruits were with him that day, he found out at night after lights out.

A blanket party is a group attack, an unofficial form of corporal punishment inflicted on a recruit who is deemed a fuck-up or undesirable by his fellow soldiers. The victim is restrained by having a blanket held tightly over his body and face to keep him from fighting back (and from identifying his assailants) while others beat him with blunt objects, such as bars of soap encased in socks. Blanket parties usually happen in the barracks after dark, when the victim is asleep in his bunk, as was the case here. According to men who were in the barracks when it happened, there were about twelve guys who participated in the beating.

"I saw them do it to him after dark," Claude Coleman remembered. "I didn't see them planning it, but I saw them do it. I'm sorry to say they did. There was no way anybody could help him. He just had to lay there and take the pain." It bothered Coleman, who felt the blanket party was unjustifiably cruel. "I mean, this guy was mentally ill. He had serious problems that wouldn't have been obvious to anyone on the street, but it was clear by now that something was wrong much deeper in his psyche. He needed to be taken out of the military—out of society, as it turned out—but to torture the guy like that? He didn't deserve that."

Another barracks mate spoke of the blanket party and the treatment of Private Christopher in general: "Guys picked on him before then, knocking his hat off, smacking him in the back of the head. We'd go to mess hall and no one would sit with him. I avoided him myself. I always got a weird feeling from him so I kept my distance and so did the people I hung out with. There were guys who tormented him, though. He was a fuck-up, a weirdo, and there's little or no sympathy for fuck-ups. It's just like high school. Most of the guys were just over high school age, late teens, early twenties. Not much compassion for the oddball."

January 11, 1981

Mom if you wondered why my voice sounds funny over the phone, it because tear come to my eyes when I hear your voice or write to you. It makes me feel so good. I do not have much to say except that I try to say the rosary at night and always pray that you and everybody is ok please tell them I send my love.

truly

Joseph G. Christopher

Leonard Coles recalled that the frequency of Christopher's strange behavior had stepped up after Christmas leave, leading up to the shower shoe debacle and the stabbing. "When we got back from Christmas, that's when he was weirder than ever. He started carrying the Bible with him everywhere, even to KP duty, which he seemed to love.

"And that was strange too. Most of us didn't want KP, washing dishes and peeling potatoes. Our MOS (Military Occupation Specialty) was 11 Bravo. We were infantrymen and KP was a nuisance, but he seemed to like it. One of the platoon sergeants even brought it up once, said to him, 'Christopher, maybe you should've chosen an MOS as a cook.' Come to find out later that he was stealing stuff from the kitchen. He had a stash up under the barracks, a survival kit. The CID was trying to figure out when and how he did this."

Coles remembered other oddities. "Joe accused someone of taking something from him, shaving cream, soap, something real common that we all had. He thought someone went into his wall locker. That complaint went all the way up to the platoon sergeant. One night he was caught in the latrine shaving all the hair off his body, under his armpits, everything. Another time they caught him in there reading the Bible after lights out. We thought he was doing whatever he could to get attention. I started to think he was trying to get put out of the army. At one point, there was talk about whether he could be transferred to another platoon but we were close to graduation and he had completed everything he needed to go on to the next phase.

"That became another source of concern because the next phase was AIT, Advanced Individual Training, where you have more liberty. Everybody was like, okay, he's weird enough with restrictions on him, how weird is he going to get *without* restrictions? We were moving on to weapons qualification and that made us nervous, since now we're going from a guy being weird around the barracks to being weird around a weapon."

Dear Mom
I spoke to someone that you wrote to
please try not to worry
I know that it is hard but I know
that God will see me and guide me . . .
I have fasted since noon Friday except for an apple
Saturday morning and I am not going to eat until
Monday morning.
Mom I lay here awake half the night, saying the rosary
planning and dreaming about starting over. I have made
plans for the house too! It's the only thing that
makes me feel good.
Mom I have found out that I can live on meat Apples
and I love soup I will learn to hunt with a bow I know that
I can find a job if I have to I also need to find a good woman
This world is not going to beat me I am not insain I know what
I need to be happy I have asked God to make it happen for me.
also I want to learn how to make candals when the sun does down

I will have my meal by candle that is what I think freedom is
In God I trust
Joseph
Just writing this last part of this letter has unkeyed me
They have bein on my case about not eating my fingernail
and skin are in good condition so I do not think I have
any deficience
see you love you
Joseph

---

5 Mar 81   Admitted to MACH Ward B4 for observation after periodic refusal to consume meals.

28 Mar 81   Escaped from custody while on work detail in day room of Ward B4 at 0955 hours. Apprehended by military police at 1930 hours.

3 Apr 81   Released from MACH Ward B4 and returned to detention facility.

8 Apr 81   Placed in Admin Seg using minimum necessary force after several instances of refusing to obey guards' orders.

The men in his platoon had seemed loosely divided into two camps when it came to Private Christopher: those who bullied him and those who avoided him. Private Coles had been in the latter. Coles had not participated in the blanket party. The question then remained why Christopher had attacked him—and so brazenly.

It seemed that a rational explanation might not be found. It also became increasingly obvious to the army that an attorney was not the only type of professional help that Private Christopher needed.

A prisoner screamed.

He shared a cell with Joseph Christopher, who had just been released from segregation that morning, April 10.

Christopher had gotten hold of a razor blade. Though he wasn't using the blade on his cell mate, the man was nonetheless frantic. "Guards! Guards!" the cell mate screamed. "He's cutting his dick off!"

———

Mom This is the last letter I am
writing I am not strong when
I open my mouth the word
are twisted they are shaped by who ever I am
talking to good by to you my trusted friends I knew you
since I was nine or ten good by
good by

———

On April 14, CID Agent Tom Carr spoke with nurses Bernard Burgess and Dorothy Anderson. He took sworn statements from them. He spoke to Private Christopher, or tried to. Christopher replied to every question with: "I don't want to talk about it."

Carr reread a teletype that had recently come over the wire at CID. It concerned a series of killings of black men in Buffalo and New York City that had occurred in the fall and winter of 1980–81.

Private Joseph G. Christopher of Buffalo was white. The victim of the barracks stabbing, Leonard Coles, was black, as was Private Cloud, who may have been Christopher's intended victim. The prisoner whom Christopher had attacked twice in the stockade was black, as was the guard whom he had fought. Christopher had used a pen to stab a Puerto Rican guard, hitting the guard above the right eye.

Agent Carr picked up the phone and called the Buffalo Homicide Squad.

Chapter 12

THERESE CHRISTOPHER WORRIED about her son. Things were terribly wrong, and to make matters worse, he was nine hundred miles away from her.

Therese was fifty-three years old, a diminutive woman with red hair turning gray. She lived in a gray clapboard house on Weber Avenue on Buffalo's far east side, a pleasant if prosaic neighborhood lined with similarly modest, middle-class homes on small parcels of land. Therese had lived her whole life in Buffalo, and in this home for almost twenty years, since 1962, when she and her husband, Nicholas, had bought the four-bedroom house and moved in with their four young children. Nicholas had died five years earlier, in 1976, at which time their three older offspring—daughters Sophia and Lorraine, and son Joseph— were in their twenties. The youngest child, Angela, had been in her early teens.

The loss of Nicholas had been a cataclysmic blow for the family. They had fared all right financially, since Therese worked as a registered nurse and received her late husband's veteran's benefits. But emotionally, psychologically, the family had lost its master and guide. Nicholas Christopher had been a strong man, a dominant figure who presided over his household with conviction and unshakeable self-assurance. His wife Therese was a gentle soul, sweet and spiritual, who looked up to her husband and relied on his judgment. She depended on him so greatly that she hadn't even learned how to drive a car until after his death (her niece Louise gave her driving lessons after Nick passed away).

The presence of Nicholas still permeated the home. His work benches in the garage and basement, his myriad tools (he had owned every crafting instrument and power tool imaginable), his hunting gear and gun collection, all had been kept intact. Lights were kept low or off in the living room, where a photo of him sat atop the mantle with votive candles before it that were often lit.

Despite the ubiquitous visual reminders, though, the absence of Nicholas still seemed to be all too painfully felt, and much mourned, by the family he'd left behind. Now more than ever, perhaps, Therese may have longed to have Nick with her to decide how best to handle the crisis with their only son, confined in a faraway army stockade down in Georgia.

Therese had been stunned when she received the letter from Joe back in January telling her what had happened. She had never known Joe—Joey, as they had fondly called him—to be violent. He had had struggles in his young life, and of course there had been the adolescent phase of rebellion, but even that had been comparatively mild—much less than some parents had to contend with, for sure—and there had never been anything like this; never any real trouble, certainly never anything criminal. The fact that Joe now stood charged with a crime, and such a serious one, was unfathomable. The fact that it had happened in the army made it doubly heartbreaking. She'd had such hopes that the army would be the solution to Joe's problems.

All through the summer of 1980, Joe had been very depressed. He couldn't find steady work. He seemed always preoccupied, troubled and down on himself. It reached the point where he became uncommunicative to the extreme, sometimes going for days at a time without speaking or even acknowledging when others would speak to him. He had enlisted in the army last fall, about two months after he turned twenty-five, which made him a little older than many new recruits but still young enough to embark on what Therese had hoped would be a positive and fulfilling new course for his life.

Joe had called home on January 17, the day before he'd been arrested. He had sounded very upset during that phone call. He told his mother that he missed home and that things weren't going very well, although he didn't elaborate. He broke down and cried. He mentioned that he had a night detail and probably wouldn't be able to make it to Mass the next day.

Then came the bad news about his arrest, and the letters—the bizarre, unsettling letters to her, to his sisters, and to neighbors that scared her more than anything else.

Being away from her son in his time of distress was hard, but it was equally difficult for Therese to be in the dark about what was happening with him, or in him. Her only source of information was Joe's letters home, which had become so rambling, so disjointed, and very disturbing as a reflection of his state of mind.

To most people, his letters were bewildering. To a mother with a background in psychiatric nursing, they were not only alarming, but telling.

Therese had done a lot of reflecting herself. She had come to the realization that Joe's problems ran much deeper than she'd thought.

Therese Christopher's two devotions in life had always been her family and her church. Therese came from a sprawling Irish household of ten children in which she was one of nine daughters. Her husband Nicholas had also been born in Buffalo, a first-generation son of Italian immigrants. Therese and Nicholas Christopher had lived their lives surrounded by a multitude of family at the center of which, of course, were their own children. Their oldest daughter, Sophia, was married with babies of her own and lived a few blocks away. Lorraine and Angela lived at home with Therese, as had Joe until he left for the military.

Up until Joe ran into such trouble in January, Therese had spent much of her waking hours in the comfortable routine she'd always known, dividing her time between her nursing job at nearby Deaconess Hospital and at St. Lawrence Roman Catholic Church, around the corner from her home. She now spent a good portion of her off hours seeking help for her beleaguered son. In February, she began writing to various people at Fort Benning. One of the earliest letters she penned was a frank, heartfelt plea to Joe's commanding officer in which she explained a little of her son's background and his behavior leading up to his enlistment in the army, along with some conclusions she had since come to concerning the nature of his problems:

Dear Sir,

I am writing to you in regard to my son, Joseph G. Christopher, who was arrested on a charge of "aggravated assault" and is in the post stockade.

I feel you should know that there is apparently a possibility that he has become a manic-depressive schizophrenic. I say this because I have worked with people with this illness in my training as a registered nurse at Gowanda State Hospital. I have noticed in the last two or three years that he has been more and more intro-spective, asocial and self-deprecating. His personality seemed to start changing drasticly after the death of his father.

His dad died at the age of 54, after two open heart surgery operations . . . I think he blames himself for his father's death because he had argued with him about the way repair work should be done on our house, etc.

His father had known that his life would be short because of his heart problem and was often impatient with Joe and seldom complimented him on any job that he had done.

She wrote of Joe's depression over the past year and his unemploy-ment; that he had broken up with his girlfriend and had taken to visiting his father's grave on a daily basis. She described how Joe had denigrated himself repeatedly the previous summer, telling his mother that he was no good and wished he was dead.

She explained that Joe's decision to enter the army had come about from a suggestion his late father had made years before. Nicholas Chris-topher had served in the infantry during World War II. Joe had once asked his father what he should do after high school and Nicholas had suggested the army, thinking the discipline would be good for him. Joe had, in fact, tried to enlist some years before but had been turned down because of a hernia. Joe had saved money for an operation and tried again after the hernia was surgically repaired.

Because he had been unable to find steady work, Joe hadn't been able to contribute monetarily to the family. Though she hadn't needed his money, Therese wrote, Joe had felt it was his responsibility to care for her and his two sisters. Being unable to do so made him feel inadequate.

She detailed how Joe had radically changed his diet in the past year, fasting for days at a time and then eating only raw vegetables, uncooked oatmeal, and bread that he would bake himself. To her surprise, he also became very religious. She believed he was having a mental breakdown brought on by a post-traumatic grief reaction to the death of his father and an improper diet. In closing, she wrote:

> I am sorry for what Joe did and I cannot imagine what provoked it, but I think he needs psychiatric & medical help as well as the help of a good lawyer. I would greatly appreciate your help in this matter and would appreciate hearing from you either by mail or by phone.

The responding officer suggested that Therese write to Major Morgan, Joe's military attorney. She did so a few days ahead of the February 17 preliminary hearing, at which time it would be decided whether or not Joe would be court-martialed. She gave Major Morgan much the same information—apparently, Joe would tell him nothing at all—in the hope that it would be helpful to Morgan in understanding Joe's "long and deep-seated state of depression." She added some of Joe's good points as well, mentioning his skills in carpentry, mechanics, and welding, and the fact that he'd become very religious. She stressed that Joseph had never been in any trouble and that the assault charge was still a matter of confusion to her.

Therese also wrote of something she'd recently learned; last summer, Joe had confided to a friend that he feared he was "going crazy."

Peter Tramontina had been Joe's best friend for a decade. They had grown up together and Peter still lived in the neighborhood. Peter had come to see Therese after hearing about Joe's arrest. Joe had written a letter to neighbor Carlo Bianchi asking for help finding a lawyer. Carlo and Lydia Bianchi were an elderly Italian couple who had known Joe and Peter since they were kids. As a teenager and adult, Joe had often helped the Bianchis with tasks like home repairs and shoveling snow. The Bianchis wanted to help, but they hadn't known what to do. They were older and their English wasn't the best. Mrs. Bianchi showed the letter to Peter, who then went to Therese. She told him about the situation in Georgia, which stunned Peter as much as it had the family, and that's when Peter told her what Joe had said the previous summer, about his fear that he was losing his mind. Peter had suggested to Joe that he get medical help. Joe had stopped confiding in Peter after that.

Peter had noticed some strange behavior from Joe on the rare occasions when he saw him. On hot summer days, Joe would be bundled up in heavy clothing. And there was the thing with his hair, how he'd suddenly started cutting it so short, sometimes nearly shaving his head bald.

———————

Therese remained largely unaware of what was happening down at Fort Benning. She managed to glean some information as it became clear to the army that her help would be needed in deciphering—and hopefully managing—her son's erratic behavior. She learned that Joe had stopped eating while in the stockade and that it reached the point where he'd had to be tube fed. The tube feeding had apparently so traumatized him that he went to the other extreme, gorging himself at times and grabbing food off other people's trays. In addition to placing him in the B4 ward for observation and group therapy, the army had him seeing a psychiatrist, Major Eleanor Law. Therese wrote letters to Major/Dr. Law and spoke with her on the phone. She gave her the overview of Joe's background and further detailed some of the changes they had seen in him.

Within the past year, he had suddenly developed a strong aversion to the nickname Joey. He insisted on being called Joe or Joseph instead. That seemed an odd turnabout because nearly everyone—family, friends, neighbors—called him Joey and always had. While home on Christmas leave, he had yelled at one of his sisters for calling him Joey. Therese hadn't thought much of it at the time. Perhaps he just felt that "Joey" was too infantile and he wasn't a child anymore. The sudden objection to his lifetime nickname wouldn't have amounted to anything by itself, of course, but there were other things.

All through the spring and summer of 1980, in addition to his self-doubts and self-loathing, Joe seemed beset by anxiety and odd apprehensions. There were times when he would be gripped by an ephemeral fear that he wouldn't or couldn't explain, and he wanted his mother to sit and hold his hand. He asked her what the difference was between right and wrong. Sometimes he told his mother that he didn't understand how she could still love him.

Joe had begun retreating from people before this. He broke up with his girlfriend with whom he had been living and moved back home in late 1978, when he was twenty-three, and stayed in the house more and more of the time. In March of 1979, he had been fired from his maintenance job at Canisius College. Except for a brief stint at Carhart Photo some months later, Joe had been unemployed since.

For reasons that were difficult to discern, he had lately become overwhelmed with renewed grief over his father's death, though it had occurred years before. He seemed to have grown somewhat obsessed by it. He said he could no longer stand to be around his friends whose fathers were still living because he felt jealous of them.

Joseph, who was twenty years old when Nick passed, had been very close to his dad. Nick had been a scoutmaster for Joe's Boy Scout troop. His father taught him many trades—how to make or repair this or that—and took him hunting and fishing. Then there was the cabin.

When Joe was a boy, Nick purchased some land out in the country, in a place called Ellington about sixty miles outside Buffalo. Together, father and son had built a two-story cabin on the property, complete with electricity and plumbing. The Christophers had spent many summer weekends at the cabin, which was Nick's pride and joy. Joe had always loved being there, and when he got older and could drive, he'd take his buddies out for hunting and camping.

That had caused a problem at one point when Joe was in high school. Nick had given Joe an old car to drive himself to and from school— Therese explained that there had been a lot of racial tension in the city schools at the time, the early 1970s, because of the new integration policies, and Nick let Joe drive because there was a lot of fighting on the bus. Joe started skipping school and taking his friends hunting instead. When Nick discovered this, he was furious. He flew into a rage and smashed the stock of Joe's prized shotgun, which Nick had given him as a gift for his sixteenth birthday. According to Therese, the fight had ended with both father and son crying and hugging.

Therese believed that Joe's issues with food had come about from an irrational sense of guilt he felt over his father's death. Joe had convinced himself that his arguments with his father and his failures as a son had exacerbated Nick's heart condition, which Therese assured him had not been the case. His father's heart problems had been a result of having contracted malaria while in the army during World War II. Nick had required a salt-free diet, and thus salt had never been used in their home. Joe's distaste for army food could've come about initially because he found the food too salty. The self-imposed deprivation, she felt, could be Joe's way of punishing himself.

Therese asked Major Law if it was okay to send Joe some items he had requested. He wanted some wool socks, a book on learning to play guitar and guitar strings, and a pair of bowling shoes. Therese knew she couldn't send the guitar strings but asked if it was all right to send him the socks and bowling shoes. Joe had written that he didn't feel comfortable wearing shower shoes.

Therese tried to keep Joe's army troubles quiet, but word of his arrest and mental breakdown had spread. Leigh Chamberlain Sr., whose sons had been close friends of Joe back in high school, called her to ask about Joe, as had Donna Vanalden, Joe's former girlfriend. Therese had politely rebuffed their inquiries and wouldn't give them his address, explaining that Joe couldn't have contact with many people right now. Therese and her daughters meanwhile kept writing to Joe, offering encouragement and love.

One of the few people outside the family whom Therese would speak to about her son was Laverne Becker, her next-door neighbor. Mr. Becker, whose nickname was Red, was a middle-aged bachelor who had lived on Weber Avenue even before the Christophers, and had known the family since the day they moved in. Nick and Red Becker had become close friends.

Red had always been very fond of the Christopher children and was particularly close to Joe. Red had taken Joe under his wing after Nick's death, trying to somewhat fill the role of substitute father. Red and Joe had spent many hours sitting on the older man's porch, talking. They had exchanged some letters after Joe joined the army, early on, when Joe's letters were ordinary, optimistic, filled with the usual chatty-type things a young soldier might write home. Red had later received letters that he could barely understand. He gave them to Joe's mother.

Therese told Red that she wished she had recognized Joe's depression earlier and gotten him some help. She had believed that all he really needed was a good job. She had thought that if Joe just had that—a steady, respectable vocation—everything else would smooth out for him.

Obviously, she had been wrong. And now she wasn't sure what to do, other than to keep praying and keep imploring her son to work with the psychiatrist and his military attorney—particularly the former.

Though she had accepted that her son was ill, the crime of which he stood accused—ambushing and stabbing a man—still mystified her. Brashness and bellicosity had never been threads of Joseph's personality. He had rather been almost the antithesis of aggression, much to his father's chagrin.

————————

Nicholas Christopher was a man's man; a consummate outdoorsman, hunter, craftsman, and gun collector. Nick was not physically imposing in stature—he stood only five feet six and weighed over two hundred pounds—but in mind-set and bearing, he was every bit the alpha male. He was a man who knew his own mind and wasn't afraid to speak it. He had worked for the city as a maintenance man, and had always earned his living by the labor of his own hands.

Though raised in the city, Nick preferred the sovereignty of pristine countryside and the rugged pleasures of living off the land. He once owned a horse and always kept hunting dogs. Along with his considerable skills in carpentry and construction, he had developed talents in both wood and leatherworking, and made hats and purses from leather. The only modern technologies that really interested him were tools and firearms, and he kept an extensive collection of each.

He had married Therese in 1950 when he was twenty-nine, a little older than was customary for men of his generation to marry, and in July of 1955 they had their third child and only boy, Joseph.

Nick had been very involved in his son's life. He spent a lot of time with the boy, teaching and instilling in him the same passion for the outdoors, and sought to shape him into the man he thought he should be. The father-son devotion appeared to be mutual. However, as can often be the case when a strong-willed man pours his undivided efforts into an only son, there were conflicts.

Joseph and Nicholas were polar opposites in temperament. Joey was a docile boy, quiet and retiring, and not particularly competitive. He wasn't assertive. He wasn't a leader. He wasn't Zach.

When Joe was thirteen, his pretty cousin Louise had married Zach DiFusco, a strapping young man who had just graduated from the Buffalo Police Academy. Zach was perhaps everything Joey wished he could be: tall, confident, popular, and personable—and very well liked by Nick. Prior to becoming a police officer, Zach had served in the army during the Vietnam War.

Zach shared his Uncle Nick's interest in guns. He visited the Christopher home often and participated in many spirited conversations about army days, firearms, and the world in general. Joe was included in these friendly talks, but being much younger and less experienced, he naturally couldn't contribute on the same level and did more listening than talking. This wouldn't necessarily have been a bad or unusual thing for a teenage boy with much to learn from older males, had Nick not constantly upbraided him in front of Zach—and anyone else—for all the character traits he felt Joey lacked.

Nick's admiration for his nephew had not been lost on Joey. Nor, apparently, was the realization on Joey's part that he would never be Zach's equal when it came to some of the hypermasculine traits his father held dear. Though Joey got along well with his cousin, Zach's presence seems to have unintentionally added further stress to his already marginalized self-image. Now Nick had a living example of the kind of son he *really* wanted.

Nicholas Christopher's two major frustrations in life seemed to be his ailing heart and his quiet son. Long before Zach DiFusco married into the family, relatives recall Nick complaining incessantly about Joey: He didn't try hard enough. He screwed up, again. He did nothing right, as far as Nick was concerned. The frustrated father seldom missed an opportunity to regale others with accounts of Joey's latest failure, whether it be a Boy Scout project, a new skill Nick was trying to teach him that he wasn't mastering fast enough, or his lackluster schoolwork. The berating happened in front of Joey, who never reacted with anger or talked back. He simply looked wounded when his father embarrassed him, face flushed and silent as he waited helplessly for the first opportunity to slip away.

People who knew the family could not understand why Nick was so relentlessly critical of his son. In most people's estimation, Joey never did anything to provoke such ire. Neighbors thought of him as a fine boy, always polite and particularly considerate, the type of kid who shoveled snow out of people's driveways without being asked. Perhaps Nick felt the harsh treatment would toughen the sensitive boy, or maybe he just wanted his son to be a carbon copy of himself. Whatever the reason, if he had hoped to inspire his son with vituperation, he had badly miscalculated. At a young age, the disapproval and humiliation had reduced Joey to an often solemn child, diffident and self-conscious, with a personality at times reminiscent of a whipped dog. He seemed to fear being noticed or getting too close to others, lest he do or say the wrong thing and be injured yet again.

Joey's problems in school added fuel to the blaze of insecurity. He had a learning disability and had to repeat second grade after failing math and English. His teacher was a nun at St. Lawrence who attempted to correct his academic underachievement by means of a ruler and punishments like kneeling on a hardwood floor. Because he would've been assigned the same teacher, Therese enrolled him in public school for his second go at second grade. He passed and returned to St. Lawrence the following year. Third grade there had been fine, maybe because the teacher wasn't a nun. By the end of fourth grade, however, the nuns informed Therese that he would be held back once again.

Catholic school clearly wasn't the proper educational setting for Joey. Beatings with a ruler are not the recommended course of action for a learning disability. Therese withdrew him from St. Lawrence permanently and put him in public school.

The learning disability was hard to pinpoint. The problem did not appear to be his intellect. During his middle school years he consistently scored 95 on IQ tests. In retrospect, his early difficulty in school may have been attributable to markedly impaired vision. According to his army enlistment medical exam, his uncorrected vision in both eyes was 20/200, corrected to 20/25 with prescription lenses. In other words, without glasses, he was so nearsighted that he classified as legally blind. This could certainly have inhibited his ability to keep up with the class, particularly in an era when teachers routinely taught lessons by writing on a blackboard.

The early failures had severely undercut his self-confidence and he viewed himself as an incapable student thereafter, which became a self-fulfilling prophecy. Over his parents' strenuous objections, he dropped out of high school in his junior year. Nick never forgave him.

By his mid-teens, Joey had begun passively rebelling against his father. He made friends with peers who lived nearby—Peter Tramontina and the Chamberlain boys—and started spending more and more time away from home, sometimes staying for days with the Chamberlains. He started smoking and at seventeen, he got tattoos on both arms. Friends recall that his father had been unhappy over this. He also discovered a passion apart from any of his father's—cars.

Joey loved cars, especially fast ones. At sixteen, while still in school, he got his first job as a lot boy at Gene Emser Motor Sales on Bailey Avenue. Gene Emser and his crew considered Joe an excellent employee, very conscientious, hardworking, with a great attitude. He loved the job. He burst into tears when Mr. Emser told him he had to let him go at the end of the summer. Emser felt very bad about it, but he needed someone full time and Joe had to go back to school.

Mr. Emser also rented a garage on Weber Avenue a couple doors down from Joey's house and Joey started hanging around there, working on cars and meeting some of the guys who raced at Lancaster Speedway. By all accounts, Joey had a natural aptitude as a mechanic. He bought a 1967 Camaro, painted black with orange cobwebbing on the sides. He took great pride in the car and washed it daily. He'd only had the Camaro a short time when it was stolen.

On May 21, 1976, Nick died of pneumonia following heart surgery. His wife and children were at his hospital bedside when he passed. When the family returned home, they found that their wall clock had stopped at the minute of Nick's death. Joe talked of this eerie occurrence many times over the years. Even in death, it seemed, his omnipotent father had the ability to stop time.

Therese wanted to visit her son. She and her daughter Sophia made plans to go down to Georgia. In his stream of letters, Joe wavered on whether he wanted them to come or not, one moment telling his mother how much he needed to see her and then writing, often in the same letter, that he didn't want her to spend the money. Though his letters were contradictory and nonsensical, one thing that seemed clear was how alone and isolated Joe felt.

Thank goodness for Father Freeman.

Father Michael Freeman was a Catholic priest and army chaplain at Fort Benning who coincidentally was from Buffalo and, as luck would have it, had once been assigned to St. Lawrence Church, although the Christophers hadn't known him at that time. Joe was eager to talk to a priest. He asked to see Father Freeman often and spoke freely with him.

That gave Therese comfort. At least Joe had one person in the army he could turn to. Therese got in touch with the good priest, who seemed sympathetic and willing to do whatever he could to help. She sent a packet of Joe's letters to Father Freeman so he could better understand her son's fears and delicate state of mind. She mailed them along with a handwritten note:

Dear Fr. Freeman

These are the letters that Joseph has written since he was in the army. Please use them as you see fit to help in his defense. I think they show how unsure he is of his decisions and how lost, confused and helpless he feels. The letter to his sister especially shows how desperate he is in trying to find someone he can trust to talk too.

Thank you for all your efforts in our behalf. Trusting in God's help and yours, I remain

Gratefully yours

Therese Christopher

She had no idea Joe's letters would be turned over to the CID.

As Easter of 1981 approached, Therese felt more alarmed than ever. Joe mailed a religious medal back to her, one that his sister Sophia had given him, along with his copy of *The Way*[2] and photographs of his family. That made Therese fear he had given up. Perhaps he felt that the army had been his last hope for a meaningful life, and now that it had gone up in smoke, so must he. Maybe things had already gone irrevocably wrong for Joe long before and Fort Benning just happened to be the site of impact, like a plane with a failing engine that sputters and coasts a few miles more before the final, inevitable descent. The more she recalled, the more the peculiarities in his behavior might have been harbingers of something much more than depression—his suspicions that people were sneaking in the house and stealing from him; sleeping with a shotgun in his bed because of a sudden fear of intruders; his strange compulsion to hide spoons and forks all around the house; walking around wearing camouflage and a rumpled army jacket with his hair shorn off, even before he enlisted, as if he were already on active military duty.

Even his late embrace of Catholicism, which had delighted Therese, had been intense and irrational; going to church every day, then announcing

---

2   A book on spirituality written in 1934 by Josemaria Escriva, founder of a Catholic religious organization, who said of it, "The 999 points which make up *The Way* were written with yearnings to see Christ, the Light of the World. Anyone who reads it with the same yearnings will not have opened this book in vain." While millions of copies had been sold by 1981, the book was variously described by Catholic leaders as "something more than a masterpiece," to "a bizarre amalgam of traditional piety, penitential discipline, and crude popular moralizing . . . Its readers are exhorted to childlike simplicity, to silence and discretion, and to orderliness; they are encouraged to pray to guardian angels and to the souls in purgatory, and to bless themselves every day with holy water. But they are also urged to acquire professional competence, to stand out from the crowd, to lead and to dominate."

Joseph Christopher, age two.

Joe Christopher, age seven,
with his sister.

Joe Christopher, age twenty-two.

Shooting victims Glenn Dunn, Harold Green,
Emanuel Thomas, Joseph McCoy.

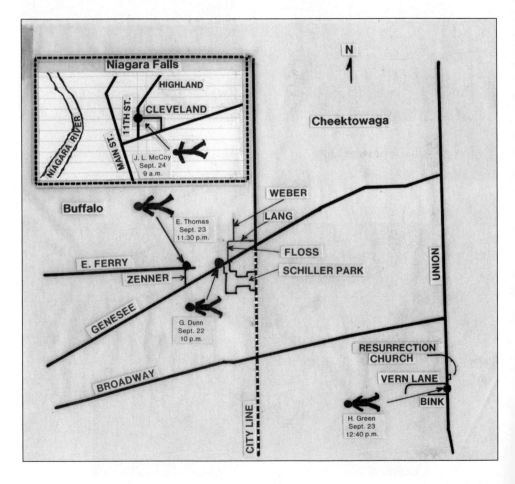

Map showing locations of the .22 caliber shootings in relation to Christopher's
Weber Avenue home. (Photo courtesy of Buffalo *Courier-Express* archive, E. H.
Butler Library, SUNY College at Buffalo)

District Attorney Edward Cosgrove at a press conference. (Photo courtesy of Buffalo *Courier-Express* archive, E. H. Butler Library, SUNY College at Buffalo)

Composite sketches of the .22 Caliber Killer. The sketches were published and broadcast numerous times during the investigation.

The Christopher cabin in Ellington, New York. It was a father-and-son project—
Nicholas and Joe built the cabin together when Joe was a boy.

Joe's bedroom as
photographed by
police in April 1981.

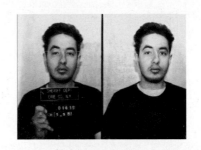

Mugshots taken at the time of Christopher's return to Buffalo, May 1981.

Private Joseph Christopher photographed by police at Martin Army Hospital, April 1981.

Therese Christopher at Fort Benning after her son's arrest. (Photo courtesy of Buffalo *Courier-Express* archive, E. H. Butler Library, SUNY College at Buffalo)

Edward Cosgrove (back row, center) with task
force members at Niagara Falls Air Force Base for
Christopher's extradition. (Photo courtesy of Matt Ortiz)

Homicide Chief Leo Donovan leads a shackled Joseph Christopher. (Photo courtesy of Buffalo *Courier-Express* archive, E. H. Butler Library, SUNY College at Buffalo)

Christopher led into court for arraignment wearing ski mask and shackles. (Photo courtesy of Buffalo *Courier-Express* archive, E. H. Butler Library, SUNY College at Buffalo)

Lineup in Buffalo. Joe is second from left. (Photo courtesy of Edward Silvestrini)

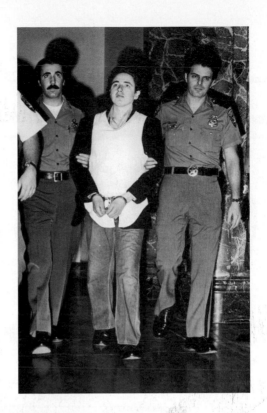

Christopher in bullet-proof vest, escorted by deputies Mondo LoVecchio, left, and Salvatore Castiglione. (Photo courtesy of Buffalo *Courier-Express* archive, E. H. Butler Library, SUNY College at Buffalo)

Christopher unmasked. (Photo courtesy of Buffalo *Courier-Express* archive, E. H. Butler Library, SUNY College at Buffalo)

Tom Toles cartoons poking fun at the composite sketch. (Photo courtesy of Buffalo *Courier-Express* archive, E. H. Butler Library, SUNY College at Buffalo)

Joseph Christopher

Your Honner

I have been interviewed by five Doctor!
Mr Molnar, Mr Wadworth, Mr Joseph, Mr Rubenstin
and an oriental men who's name I do not recall.
Two of witch found me competent, two incompt-
ent and one was undecided, opt to totheir
test in a theiapotic enviorment. In that they
only spent short minutes of time with me. Hence
I was adjudicated to Mid hudson P.C. After
a period of approxamitly two and a half months
I was found competent, by five Doctor and also
an indepennend Doctor. In New York states
number one ranked theiapotic Center. I, their
now being a prepondevence of evidence, nine
Doctors supporting my position an two not. Will
not be aparty to another Test or feel a need
for a hearing, because the result of the
pervious did not support the prefevence
of someone else

I coralate my position to a man that
wins a trip in Las Vagas, was sent their
takes the house and comes back. An
acquaintance possiably haveing interest in say's
Hay how bout me and you go to Atlantic City
I'll provide the tranportation, how is that!
how about! how about! Sincerty
Joseph Christopher

Joseph Christopher's January 1982 letter to the court, protesting
his commitment to Mid-Hudson Psychiatric Center.

Detective Melvin Lobbett.

Thomas Rowan, commanding officer of the scientific investigation unit for the Cheektowaga police and ranking officer on the task force.

Defense attorneys Kevin Dillon, left, and Mark Mahoney.
(Photo courtesy of Buffalo *Courier-Express* archive, E. H.
Butler Library, SUNY College at Buffalo)

Al Ranni, prosecutor.
(Photo courtesy of
Buffalo *Courier-Express*
archive, E. H. Butler
Library, SUNY College
at Buffalo)

Frank Bress, Christopher's first defense attorney in New York City.

David Jay, defense attorney, told the jury his client suffered from "Madness. Absolute madness." (Photo courtesy of Hope Jay)

Sean Hill,
defense attorney.

Dr. Brian Joseph,
psychiatrist.

Surviving victim
Leonard Coles in 2016.

Detective
John Regan.

Thomas Eoannou, for-
mer prosecutor turned
defense attorney, in 2016.

Stabbing victim Albert
Menefee. His recovery
from a knife wound to
the heart was described
as a medical miracle.
(Photo courtesy of
Buffalo *Courier-Express*
archive, E. H. Butler
Library, SUNY College
at Buffalo)

that he was going to enter a seminary and become a priest—after he had already joined the army. Perhaps Therese should've recognized the signs earlier for what they were. But what mother wants to admit her child has lost control of his mind?

She believed that her son's illness was caused by extreme stress and poor nutrition, and further that if they could get Joe home, where he would have the support of family and friends, his mental problems could be successfully treated.

The knife attack at Fort Benning, Therese believed, had been a tragic, isolated aberration. Joseph did not have a violent nature. Of this she felt certain. He was a compassionate and kind soul, sensitive and humble. He had never wanted to dominate or cause harm. All Joe had ever really wanted was love and approval.

———————

April 19 was Easter Sunday. Therese prayed very hard that weekend. She prayed for her son, and she prayed for the man he had injured. She asked for God's divine help and blessing, and a resolution for her anguished son.

At 3:30 p.m. the following Wednesday, April 22, unexpected visitors arrived at her home. Therese Christopher opened her door. Before her stood a man, with several more behind him gathered on her small front lawn and driveway. Therese didn't know the man at the door but she recognized him from television.

Edward Cosgrove stepped forward and spoke to her, and life as Therese Christopher had always known it came to an end.

Chapter 13

SOMETHING VERY ODD was happening on Weber Avenue.

Bob Schmitt lived at 94 Weber with his wife and children. His car was in the shop that Wednesday and Bob's father had picked him up from work to drive him home. As they turned onto Weber, they noticed cars parked on both sides. They couldn't even find a parking space.

They pulled up in front of Bob's house, across the street from the Christophers'. As Bob stepped out of the car, he noticed that there were a lot of people coming in and out of the Christopher house, a lot of men he had never seen before. Some were carrying bags out of the house, but they definitely were not movers.

Bob stepped inside his front door and his wife, Cheryl, met him there. She asked if he knew what was going on. He was about to ask her the same question.

All Cheryl knew was that two detectives had come to the door about a half an hour before and asked if she knew Joe Christopher. She replied that she did. She told them Joe was in the army and they told her, "Yes, we know that." They showed her a picture and asked if she could identify it as Joe Christopher.

"Yes, that's him," Cheryl had replied nervously. She had no idea why they were asking about Joe, and they never said. After showing her the photo, they thanked her for her time and left.

The Schmitts were not the only neighbors who noticed the sudden invasion of their normally sedate street. It was hard to imagine anyone living on Weber Avenue who *didn't* notice. People stepped out on their

232

porches, peering up and down at all the unfamiliar vehicles and at the gathering crowd of unfamiliar faces clustered in front of the Christopher house. The cars parked up and down the block were unmarked and the men wore shirts and ties and holstered guns. Police.

One woman looked out and saw that the street had been blocked off at both ends. News trucks were pulling up beyond the barricades.

This was surreal. What could possibly bring this onslaught of police and reporters to quiet little Weber Avenue?

She looked over at the Christopher house, and suddenly it dawned on her. She turned to her husband and said, "Oh my God . . . it's Joe. He's the killer!"

———

A young man named Dave arrived at the Christopher home. Unlike the phalanx of men who were already there, he had been expected. Dave was dating Angela. As he recalled that frenzied day, "I went to pick her up and it was like a swarm of bees around a nest. I thought, what the hell is this? It scared the hell out of me. I went in the side door and these men kept asking me who I am. They wouldn't say who they were. Finally I had to show them my ID. One guy showed me his ID and asked what I was doing there. I told him I came to pick up Angela and he said I'd have to wait for her out front, so I went and sat on the front steps.

"She finally came out a while later. She was pretty upset. I asked her what was happening and she said it had something to do with her brother. I hadn't known her for very long at the time. I didn't even know she *had* a brother. I didn't know they had a firing range in the house, either."

The firing range in the Christopher basement would be mentioned many times by the media. In actuality, it amounted to a portable bullet trap and a disorganized clutter of reloading equipment and gun parts. Nicholas, Joe, and others had fired weapons down here, however, and that made the cellar a focal point of the search.

The unfinished basement, with its pale-yellow cinderblock walls and maze of pipes running along the low ceiling, looked ordinary in most respects. There was the usual washer and dryer, chest freezer, mishmash of old furniture and aged household items long forgotten. The only distinguishing feature might've been the sheer volume of things packed within.

Cabinets and numerous shelves built along the walls were crammed with a staggering number of tools large and small, various outdoor equipment, and many boxes and varieties of ammunition. There was a desk and long, wide workbench, both piled high. Above each, affixed to the ceiling, hung several jars filled with screws, bolts, and miscellaneous hardware.

Tom Rowan had been assigned to the basement. He and a half dozen other officers searched down here, primarily on the lookout for a specific type of ammunition and a specific model of gun, while their colleagues searched a bedroom on the floor above.

Therese Christopher sat at her kitchen table with DA Cosgrove and Investigator Sam Slade while more than a dozen law enforcement officers delved through her home. Edward Cosgrove had politely introduced himself at the door and presented two search warrants; one for her house and garage on Weber Avenue, the other for the cabin in Ellington. Detectives spotted a detached shed in the backyard on Weber and an assistant DA was dispatched to secure a third warrant.

Therese retrieved her rosary beads and sat placidly with the rosary clutched in her hand. Both Slade and Cosgrove spoke kindly and gently to her, reassuring that the officers would finish as soon as possible. Other than to confirm that Joseph Christopher of Fort Benning, Georgia, was her son and asking that she direct them to his bedroom, they did not ask her any questions.

A gun cabinet in a hallway off the kitchen contained four rifles and boxes of ammunition. A few feet away was Joe's bedroom, a small, sparse room with off-white wood paneling on the walls. An old and thinning liver-colored carpet covered the floor. In one corner sat a low single bed with a small nightstand beside it. To the right of the bed was a shallow closet with no door. In another corner was a chest of drawers and some wooden chairs in a haphazard stack. The room had a single window and the walls were bare except for an indistinct framed print on a side wall, a nature photograph tacked above the bed, and the mounted head of a buck hung directly opposite and facing the bed. Everything within—furniture, lamps, the scant linens—was worn and mismatched, colorless and somber. The joyless effect was so complete that it felt almost staged, as if a set designer had been told to craft a room that reflected suffocating despair.

The rest of the first floor, while not as dismal, was not particularly cheerful. Low ceilings and wood paneling in the living and dining areas gave the home a somewhat dark and closed atmosphere. Then there was the living room memorial to Nick. The prominent photograph of the late Nicholas Christopher, surrounded by vigil lights, was described by the officers as a shrine or altar, and a few found it macabre. As Joe Cooley recalled it, "It struck me as very unusual, and a little morbid, frankly. The dim living room with this shrine to the father as a sort of centerpiece. The whole effect was as if you were in a funeral home."

Tom Rowan didn't feel the shrine was morose but it did strike him as a significant psychological indicator. Rowan, who had taken FBI courses in criminal profiling, viewed the memorial as a clue to the dynamics of the family. As he recalled, "An absent father is important in the positive or negative development of the son. This was an artifact that conveyed the feelings of someone in the household. We didn't totally understand what the significance was, but we knew it was noteworthy. It was photographed and mentioned in reports." Assessing the character and psyche of their subject was a matter of great interest to the task force.

The April 14 call from Sergeant Tom Carr at Fort Benning to Buffalo police had immediately drawn serious attention. Carr had related Christopher's statements to the nurses about having committed murders in Buffalo and New York City. He explained the nature of the charges that the army had pending against Christopher. Carr also advised that Christopher was under psychiatric supervision and would probably never go to trial due to insanity.

Christopher's army records showed that he had not been in service at the time of the fall of 1980 murders and he'd been on leave during late December through the early days of January. Buffalo homicide requested fingerprints and photographs of Christopher from the army and checked their own files in the meantime.

Joseph Christopher had no criminal record. He had last owned a vehicle—a pickup truck—in 1979. The only local government documents on him, other than his birth certificate and school records, were his pistol permit application and its subsequent suspension.

Christopher had applied for and received a license to carry a pistol in 1978. His application listed his date of birth as July 26, 1955, and an address on Kail Street in Buffalo. He was self-employed as a handyman doing home repairs and remodeling.

On April 1, 1980, he had gone to precinct 16 to report that one of the weapons on his permit, a .22 caliber automatic Beretta pistol, was missing. He told the police that sometime in February, he had placed the gun in a green army-style backpack that was hanging in the basement of his Weber Avenue home. When he searched the backpack on March 31, the weapon was missing. The police report was forwarded to the county pistol permit administrator. Two weeks later, Joseph received a letter informing him that his permit had been suspended and that the remaining eleven handguns registered on the permit had to be surrendered. The following month, Joseph sent a letter stating that he had turned over his permit and all of the handguns to Buffalo police officer Zach DiFusco.

The task force started with Officer DiFusco. Summoned to the district attorney's office for questioning, Zach said he had known the Christopher family for about thirteen years and that Joseph was his cousin by marriage. He described the Christophers as solid, stable people. Joe had two older sisters: Sophia, who was around twenty-eight, and Lorraine, who was a year older than Joe. Lorraine lived in an apartment that Nicholas had built years before on the second floor of the Weber Street home. Joe's younger sister, Angela, was eighteen.

Zach described Joe as a normal kid, a bit moody. Joe had given his father a lot of heartache when he was alive, as Nicholas had felt that Joe didn't live up to the expectations he had for a son. As Zach understood it, Joe suffered feelings of guilt after Nick passed away. He had become withdrawn. Asked about the weapons collection, Zach said most of the guns were kept in the cabinet on the first floor or in the cellar. His uncle always had a lot of firearms, both long guns and pistols.

The army had overnighted a package that included some photographs taken of Joseph at Martin Army Hospital. They showed the photos to Zach, who was stunned at how much weight Joe had lost. Asked about

Joe's appearance, Zach said he had always worn his hair short and was clean shaven. They asked Zach to take a look at the composite sketches of the .22 Caliber Killer and see if he could make a comparison. He really couldn't, which wasn't much of a surprise, since the task force couldn't see the likeness either.

Investigators also contacted Zach's wife, Louise, who described Joe much the same way as her husband. Both the DiFuscos had been surprised when Joe went into the army the previous November. Louise recalled that Joe had become very religious in the last couple years and had even talked about becoming a priest.

They were asked if any members of the family ever had any difficulty with blacks or harbored any notable racial resentment. Louise recalled that several years ago, when the two older girls were in high school, one of them had become interested in a black male who was in her group of friends. Nicholas had come home one day to find the black man at the family residence and he was quite upset over this.

As for Joe, he had black friends. Zach mentioned a couple of black guys who Joe hung out with at Costanzo's Bakery. One he remembered in particular was named Louis, who went fishing with Joe a lot. As far as Zach and Louise knew, Joe was a normal person and had normal relationships with his family and everyone else. He had a girlfriend who he had lived with for a while, a couple years back. They thought her name was Donna.

Donna Vanalden was listed as a reference on Joe's pistol permit application. Donna had a permit herself. On Good Friday, investigators paid a call on her mother. They assured her that her daughter was not in trouble but emphasized that Donna should contact them immediately.

The Monday after Easter, Joe Cooley and Mel Lobbett interviewed Donna at her apartment. Donna Vanalden was a slender, attractive woman with auburn hair. She was in her midthirties and lived alone.

Joe Cooley did most of the talking while Mel Lobbett took notes. They asked if she owned a gun and she said yes. They asked if she had a permit for it and she said yes. They asked if she knew Joseph Christopher. She said yes and wanted to know why they were asking. They told her they were investigating the .22 caliber killings. Donna laughed. They explained they were following up on all leads and needed her full cooperation.

Donna thought this was ridiculous. The police must've really run out of options if they were investigating Joe.

Cooley and Lobbett were not laughing, however. They wanted to know everything she could tell them about Joe, and they obviously knew a few things about their relationship already. They asked how long she and Joe had lived together. She told them from about April 1977 to late November 1978. They had been introduced in early 1977 by a mutual friend, Peter Tramontina. The investigators wanted Peter's phone number and she gave it to them. Joe Cooley asked if he could use her phone. He dialed Peter's number and left a message for him to call the state police.

Donna started to feel nervous. *What is this?* Joe wasn't even in Buffalo. And even if he was . . .

They asked if Joe used drugs. They asked how she got along with members of his family and if anyone kidded Joe about his relationship with her, since she was nine years older. They wanted to know about his employment, his guns, if he was ever violent or had any perversions. They asked a lot of questions and Donna was afraid she'd be taken downtown if she didn't answer, although she wasn't sure why she should be afraid. It was the shock of it all, really. Two cops in her home, asking all these questions about Joe Christopher, of all people! The whole thing was crazy.

Her mind flooded with thoughts, memories. Donna answered everything she could. Telling the truth could only help Joe because the truth was very good, for the most part.

He didn't move in all at once. It had been gradual, though it was fairly soon after they met. He would come over and bring a few things, stay for a day or two and then return home. They had never officially decided to live together; it's just how things progressed.

Donna had needed some work done in her house. There was a door that needed hanging and the bathroom needed remodeling. She asked Peter if he could do it. Peter agreed and said he'd bring along his friend Joe, who was really skilled at that sort of thing.

That certainly proved true. Donna was very impressed with the work—Joe had ended up doing the whole thing himself—and surprised that he wanted to charge her so little for what was obviously a professional-grade job. She wanted to pay him more but he refused. She didn't want him to feel like she was taking advantage of him, especially since she definitely wanted to hire him again. She asked if she could at least take him out to dinner and he agreed.

Joe had immediately been fascinated that Donna was a certified pistol instructor. A girl who liked guns! She even belonged to a gun club. They had a lot to talk about. She told him about the club and offered to take him to the range where they practiced, at Canisius College, and introduce him to the other members. They went on a Sunday and he joined. He took some courses, and before long he was an NRA certified instructor himself. Donna was very impressed with him as a teacher, especially how attentive he always was to firearm safety.

He brought her to his house and showed her his father's gun collection. His father's guns meant a lot to him. Actually, in Donna's view, everything his late father had ever owned seemed to mean a lot to him. All of Mr. Christopher's tools and personal belongings in the basement and garage—and both were absolutely loaded with his things—were left exactly as they'd been at the time of his death.

The guns held a special place with Joe, because obviously the collection had been dear to Mr. Christopher. Joe had been in a hurry to get a pistol permit so he could register the handguns in his own name. He asked Donna to put the guns on her permit in the meantime and she did. Joe was afraid that otherwise they would go to his cousin, Zach DiFusco, who was a cop. Joe didn't want that to happen. He was afraid Zach might sell them. Joe considered the guns family heirlooms and wanted them all to stay in the family.

He became a little preoccupied by this, and was upset when his mother once mentioned that she wanted to give one of Mr. Christopher's prized firearms to Zach. He was adamant that his cousin should not have any of his father's guns. Donna gathered there had been some sort of a sibling-type rivalry between Joe and his cousin for the affections of Mr. Christopher. She'd gotten the impression that Zach had been the more favored of the two, even though Joe was Mr. Christopher's own son.

Donna didn't believe that anyone in Joe's family was critical or disapproving of her relationship with him. She got along well with all of them and described Mrs. Christopher as very kind and soft-spoken, a person who never yelled at her son or anybody, even when Joe was sarcastic toward her. Donna had never met Mr. Christopher, as she hadn't met Joe until almost a year after his father's death. His memory was very much alive, however. Perhaps too much so. As time went on, Donna felt the family dwelled on Mr. Christopher's death and never put it in the proper perspective. Joe used to spend a lot of time at his father's grave, just sitting there as much as a couple of hours at a time. He seemed to be on some kind of guilt trip regarding his father's death, although she didn't know why.

As for drugs, Joe smoked marijuana often and he had experimented with speed and acid. He had once injected Valium and got hepatitis. Donna couldn't stand any of that; she never used drugs, and though she wasn't judgmental about his use, she had made it clear from the start that she wanted no part of it. He always respected this and never used anything in front of her nor tried to persuade her to partake.

Joe had a difficult time holding jobs in spite of the fact that, in her opinion, he was an excellent mechanic, very handy, and there was very little he could not do. He and Peter had worked as unarmed security guards during a strike at one of the local factories. When that ended, he had done some freelance work in auto mechanics and home repair, but nothing seemed to last. She had helped him get a job in the maintenance department at Canisius College. That had lasted a little over a year until he was fired for sleeping on the job.

When asked if Joe had any difficulty with blacks or any discernible racial hatred, she answered with a definite no. On the contrary, Joe became very friendly with a black coworker at Canisius named Ernie. They partied together all the time, got stoned, and socialized extensively. Joe and Ernie eventually had a falling out some time ago but she didn't know what it was about. It might've been because Joe got fired and Ernie didn't, but she really didn't know. In any event, Joe had never expressed any racism or any strong feelings about race.

Toward the end of their relationship, Joe became very preoccupied with something that was obviously bothering him, but he wouldn't discuss it. She couldn't speak with him; there was very little conversation; he just drifted away. He would go out at times and walk for hours all around the city, and on a few occasions, he was gone all night. She didn't think he went to bars because he wasn't really a bar person, and for that matter he didn't drink much either, just a 7 and 7 once in a while. He had never been out-of-control drunk.

Their breakup had been amicable. No hard feelings on either side. He moved back home and they kept in touch sporadically. He never explained why he wanted to end their relationship. On the occasion of the final breakup, he had broken into body-wracking sobs and was apparently very confused and in great distress. She felt bad because she would've liked to help him with whatever difficulty he was obviously experiencing.

The last time she saw Joe was about May of 1979. It had been a very unusual encounter.

She had called and asked him about some parts for her car. He told her to come over and he'd put them on for her. He looked very different. He was very thin, almost gaunt, and he had a brush cut. He was wearing his father's old clothes and just had a strange look about him. She asked him what was wrong, you look like hell, why are you dressed like that? He didn't answer right away. He told her to follow him into the garage to get the car parts. When they stepped inside, he shoved her against the wall and pinned her with his forearm. He said, "You're here, let's make it, let's not waste time." He was grabbing at her and at the same time trying to undo his own pants. This was a shock; Joe had never been aggressive. She told him to stop, that it was over, she didn't want any of that. He was overpowering her and he was very strong. The look in his eyes was something she never saw before. She was afraid of what she saw.

She wasn't kidding or joking with him. She told him again to knock it off, it was over between them, and he told her, "No one's here," and wouldn't stop.

Finally, she screamed and told him, "Get away from me! I'm getting married, get off!" She wasn't really getting married; she'd only said that to get him to back off because she was scared. He stopped grabbing but he did not let her go. He grinned at her, and it was weird and frightening. She had no idea what was going through his mind. Joe had never acted like this before.

She shoved him away and said she was leaving. As she stepped out the door he said, "Wait . . ." She stopped and turned to look at him. He still had that awful, frightening grin. "So you're getting married," he said.

Joe wanted to know to whom and she said it was immaterial. She told him, "Let's just remember what we had. What's wrong with you?"

He said, "Let me get you the parts for the car," and suddenly, he reverted back to the way he was. The grin was gone, the crazy, menacing look wiped away. In an instant he was Joe again, as if someone had flipped a switch. As if the few minutes that had come before had never happened.

Sometime later, she told Peter about it. Peter told her it didn't surprise him because Joe had recently had a similar altercation with another woman. Peter told Donna he was concerned about Joe because he was acting funny.

Donna told the officers that other than the changes she saw in him near the end, Joe's behavior during their relationship had been normal. Other than the preoccupation with his father's death and his eventual withdrawal from people, she wasn't aware of any abnormalities. She only recalled one odd incident when Joe, who was quite the camera buff, asked her to go to Forest Lawn Cemetery and pose among the tombstones so he could photograph her. She felt that was sort of weird. The officers asked to see the photographs and she showed them. She said she still felt spooky about it and didn't understand the significance.

They asked if she had any photographs of Joe and she brought a few out. Cooley picked up a couple of them and took a closer look. He asked if he could use her phone.

Mel Lobbett made small talk with Donna while Cooley made a call. She was smiling and nodding politely at Lobbett when she overheard Cooley say, "We got something and it looks like the break." Donna suddenly felt cold. Lobbett continued talking but she didn't hear a word he said. *Break? What is he talking about?* she thought.

Cooley hung up. He said they'd be going now and thanked Donna for her time. He said he'd like to take a few of her photographs. She said that would be okay as long as they were returned. They thanked Donna again and told her not to talk to anybody about any of this.

After they'd gone, Donna felt upset, a little shaken. She went over the conversation again and again in her head, especially those last ominous words she had overheard. *We got something.* She had no idea what that could've meant.

Did they really suspect Joe of being the .22 Caliber Killer? Had she said something that made them suspicious? Why did they want her pictures? They were only snapshots of Joe and some other people at the cabin.

Maybe she shouldn't have told them about the incident in the garage. It was so wildly out of character for Joe anyway. But it had popped into her head as they kept asking over and over again about his behavior and she had been afraid not to tell them. They were going to talk to Peter, and what if he told them and she got in trouble for not saying anything?

Donna had never been questioned by police before. She found it intimidating, even though they had been very courteous. She hadn't meant to say half those things, most of which struck her as irrelevant and silly anyway. They had asked so many questions as one hour had become two, and they had this way of asking things, putting forth the same question over and over, rephrasing it a little each time, and before you knew it you were so far down the rabbit hole—and feeling somehow like a trapped rabbit, even though they were being so nice—and you knew there was no escape until they decided to let you go.

And they'd asked if *Joe* was a good hunter. He was, but not as good as they were.

Alone in her apartment, with the strange discussion with the officers swirling through her mind, Donna thought about things that they hadn't asked and wouldn't have been interested in anyway.

She called him Chris. She called him Joe when they were around other people but when they were alone, it was always Chris. He liked that. He called her babe, and that was one of those sweet things between them, these nicknames they had for each other that were only for the two of them.

His mother and sisters called him Joey. She could tell that irritated him, that they still used his little-boy nickname. He never complained though, which was typical. Joe never went off on anybody, family or otherwise. He just got quiet when he was mad. He'd get a certain look on his face but he rarely said anything.

It wasn't so much the nickname that bothered him but what it seemed to represent; namely that, in Joe's view, they still thought of him as a boy instead of the grown man he was. No one would think to call Zach "Zachy."

He didn't like it when his mother asked Zach's advice. Joe thought his mom and sisters should be coming to him if they needed anything and it seemed like they didn't unless it was some little house or car repair. He was the only son and the man of the family now, and he should be consulted on family decisions and not be viewed as just a handyman. He would confide in Donna these little complaints and frustrations, all of which seemed perfectly ordinary to her. What family doesn't have their little resentments and rivalries?

She wondered about Mr. Christopher at times. Joe had such an attachment and spoke of him in such glowing terms. Once when they were down in the basement of his parents' home, he showed her a broken shotgun that his father had smashed when Joe did something that displeased him. About two-thirds of the shotgun's stock was missing. Donna wondered why Joe had kept it.

Joe liked taking her out to the cabin in Ellington. They'd even taken Donna's sister and her kids out there on a couple of occasions. When he was outdoors, in the vast fields of rural New York or hiking the Adirondacks, he was truly in his element. He could never take enough nature photographs, as if he wanted to preserve every moment spent in rustic land. Joe loved the cabin, and another little family tension had arisen when Mrs. Christopher wanted to will it to her grandson, who was just a baby. That hadn't gone over well with Joe at all.

Still, the frictions in Joe's family seemed pretty par for the course. The jealousy of his cousin might've been a little childish, but everybody's got their hang-ups. Donna had otherwise found Joe mature for his age, except for maybe the stupid thing with smoking pot and dabbling in other drugs. He'd never been obnoxious when he was stoned. He and Peter would just get silly and laugh a lot when they were high, and Joe got more talkative and joked around. It seemed like a manageable flaw when balanced against all of his other good traits. Her first impressions of Joe had been what a gentle and thoughtful man he was. He was a protector, and that extended to Donna as well. He made her feel safe. Other men she'd known had made her feel anything but. How ironic that her youngest boyfriend had also been the most calm and considerate.

The nine-year age difference between them hadn't bothered him, but it had bothered her, and though in hindsight she felt a little ashamed to admit it, she'd been embarrassed by the relationship because he was so much younger. She had sometimes downplayed it to her friends, hesitant to admit the level of their involvement or to introduce him. He had once come to her office and asked for her. He'd been working on a little project, repainting and fixing up her car, and he wouldn't let her see it until it was all done. On the day he finally finished, he was too excited to wait for her to come home from work. He wanted to show her right away. She went outside with him and told him how great it looked. Fresh paint, polished chrome. He was very proud. When she got back to her office, a coworker asked, "Was that Joe?" Donna felt self-conscious admitting that yes, that was her boyfriend, and at the same time she felt guilty about her ambivalence, all the worse since Joe had just done this sweet thing for her.

Eventually, she grew more comfortable taking him to work parties or functions with her friends. Nobody seemed to care about the age thing but her. Donna's mother adored Joe.

Because he was younger—maybe too much younger than she, in her view—Donna had perhaps always had it in the back of her mind that the relationship would end at some point. Therefore when it did, she had been neither resistant nor surprised. Her overriding emotion in the breakup was concern for Joe.

He started changing around August of 1978. Suddenly and without warning, he became very distant and in his own head all the time. Joe had always been a quiet person but there had never been a silence between them. He stopped talking and often looked very grave and distracted. She asked him what was wrong. Sometimes he would tell her, "Nothing," and shake his head, other times he answered, "I don't know," and he had an anxious look about him. He would never explain, but she could tell whenever it became too much for him—whatever *it* was—because that's when he would go out and walk and walk, as if trying to walk his problems off or at least outpace them, or maybe just to exhaust himself to the point where he could fall into a deep sleep.

Three months after it started, he called her one day at work. "I can't do this anymore," he told her. She went home and found him in a very emotional state. He said he had to leave, had to move back home. He couldn't explain it; he just had to go. The remarkable thing was his distress, as if the breakup was giving him more pain than he could endure. But if that was the case, why was he doing this?

Donna was sad when he left, but also a little relieved. Something very heavy was going on with Joe, obviously, and if he wasn't willing to let her in, there was no point in going on together anyway.

She'd never been able to figure out the scene in the garage, what could possibly have come over him. She didn't think he was stoned—she'd heard he quit the drugs, and this didn't seem like a drug thing anyway. As she'd walked down the driveway that day, away from him, she had hesitated at the side door of the house. She had an instinct to go inside and talk to his mother, explain what had just happened and tell her, *something is wrong with Joe.* But how could she tell his mother? How embarrassing. Ultimately, she decided not to say anything and just left. She'd later regret that decision for the rest of her life. *Maybe if I had said something . . .*

It occurred to Donna after the police had gone that the garage incident had not been the last time she'd seen Joe after all.

It had been about 3:30 a.m. when Joe had called at her home, crying, sometime in March 1980. He asked her to pick him up near a lounge on Bailey Avenue. When she got there, he was sitting on the curb in front of a car dealership. He looked like he was in bad shape. He sobbed and told her, "I'm all nuts'd up." She didn't know what to do. It wasn't drugs or booze—he was sober. She thought he was having emotional or mental problems. He seemed to be coming apart.

She took him for some food and calmed him down. He asked if he could come back and live with her. She told him that was impossible, that it was over. She felt very concerned about him, but she had another boyfriend at the time. She dropped him off at his mother's house, and later worried that she had left without seeing that he got inside.

He called once more sometime after, another desperate plea in the middle of the night. She could make little sense of what he said, he cried so hard. *Something is wrong . . . something is wrong in my head . . .*

What do you mean? she'd asked. He sobbed, *I don't know, I don't know . . .* The fear in his voice. She talked him through as best she could, but she just couldn't do anymore. She had no idea what he was trying to tell her. It made her heart ache to hear him so lost and frightened, but she simply didn't know what to do. They'd been apart for over a year now. She couldn't keep going to his rescue.

She kept tabs on him from afar. Peter or her nephews would run into him occasionally, although it seemed to be more by chance. From what she heard, Joe seemed to be closing in on himself and avoiding everyone, even Peter. One of her nephews had run into Joe on the street during the summer of 1980 and spoke to him. Joe didn't seem to know who he was.

Donna wanted to put all these sad and worrisome things out of her head. She didn't want to remember the bad times. There'd been so much more that was very good, quite wonderful, actually, before this unfathomable change. He'd been good to her. To everyone. And in their quietest moments alone, no one had ever made her feel safe and relaxed like Chris.

They would lie in bed and he would rub her back, and they would talk about the day and whatever was on their minds. He often talked about the responsibility he felt for his mother and sisters, how he wanted to take care of them, and how he worried that he would never be able to fill his father's shoes. Donna didn't quite understand why this weighed so heavily on his mind. She'd assure him what a fine man he was, and tell him there was no reason why he had to fill his father's shoes. She told him good things about himself, true things, and though sometimes he smiled and warmed to the praise, she sensed his doubts—not of her sincerity, but of himself. No matter how close they seemed to be, there was a subtle yet palpable emptiness in Joe, a lonely void that she couldn't help him fill.

And that was the thing about Joe that was good and bad. He could give comfort, but he seemed unable to receive it.

Joe Cooley and Mel Lobbett returned to the task force with the photo-graph of Joseph Christopher holding a Sturm-Ruger 10/22 rifle.

The following morning, Tuesday, April 21, Lobbett and state police investigator Thomas Rash boarded a plane for Georgia. An FBI agent met them at the Columbus Airport and drove them to Fort Benning.

They met with CID agents and reviewed Private Christopher's file. They interviewed the nurses at the psych ward. They spoke with Lieu-tenant Colonel Levine, staff psychiatrist at the Martin Army Hospital. Dr. Levine told them that Joseph Christopher was a very sick individual, medically and psychologically, and in need of help. Christopher was uncommunicative. He would not answer questions or talk with anybody unless he initiated the conversations. According to Dr. Levine, Christo-pher avoided direct questions and direct answers. Christopher had once asked him if it was better to lie or tell the truth.

On three separate occasions, Dr. Levine said, Christopher had made homosexual propositions: once to Dr. Levine, another to a psychiatric staff security member, and once to a patient. In the last instance, Chris-topher had said something to the patient about going to the latrine for a blow job. He had said this in the middle of the ward loud enough for anyone to hear.

All of these propositions had been blatant and out in the open, which could've been the whole point of a desperate contrivance. Homosexuality had been declassified as a mental disorder by the American Psychiatric Association in 1973, but it was still grounds for removal from the military. There was no question that Christopher wanted out of the army. He also wanted to stay out of the stockade. Statements such as those he'd made could assure that he remained in the hospital psychiatric ward. Though there were undoubtedly homosexuals in the army, men who really desired sex with other males were hardly open about it. On the contrary, una-bashed propositions were almost a sure means of making sure it *wouldn't* happen, as any soldier stating such a thing would be separated and closely watched until he received the almost certain discharge.

Lobbett and Rash apprised Dr. Levine of the homicides in Buffalo and showed him the psychological profile prepared by the FBI. After reading it, Dr. Levine expressed amazement at how accurately much of the profile fit Christopher. The doctor then expressed some concern about the security of Joseph Christopher while in the hospital. Later that afternoon, the army moved him from the hospital back to an isolation cell in the stockade.

Christopher's army lawyer, Major Donald Morgan, informed Lobbett and Rash that they did not have his permission to speak with his client. Further, Major Morgan had visited Christopher and advised him not to answer any questions from either the Buffalo investigators or the CID.

Lobbett and Rash contacted the task force with their findings at Fort Benning thus far. Edward Cosgrove filed for the search warrants on Wednesday morning, and shortly after, police had descended on Weber Avenue and the Ellington cabin.

Hours passed in the gray clapboard house of Therese Christopher. Except for when she was asked to unlock cabinets in the basement, she remained at her kitchen table. Sam Slade stayed with her, more to say a few gentle words to her once in a while than anything else. Looking back on that day, Tom Rowan felt it was fortunate that Sam had been there with Mrs. Christopher. In addition to being an outstanding investigator, Sam had a knack for making people feel at ease. He was a genuinely compassionate man, and there wasn't a cop in that home that day who didn't feel sympathy for Mrs. Christopher. As Joe Cooley recalled it, "You had to feel sorry for her. This poor lady. Her kid is bonkers, and now we're tearing her house apart. She was very calm and cooperative, but you knew this was eating her up."

Night had fallen by the time the searchers left Weber Avenue. As soon as the barricades came down, searchers of a different kind invaded the street. So began what one resident described as a "month-long infestation of reporters." They knocked on doors, barged down driveways, and made phone calls to many of the neighbors. They'd soon be followed by curiosity seekers—or worse.

Life had suddenly changed dramatically for everyone on Weber Avenue, especially for the shocked and heartbroken in the Christopher home. The glare of notoriety had only just begun.

———

The following day, Therese Christopher wrote a letter to her son.

> Thurs. April 23rd
> Dear Joe,
> I just want you to know I'm at ____ for a couple days until all this hullabaloo is over. Please excuse me for not writing sooner. I was a littl[e] upset when you sent back your medal and the book "The Way" that you had wanted with you. Sophia has talked to Major Morgan and we know what has happened down there.
>
> I am sorry you felt so depressed and please know that we all love you and could never believe the things they are trying to say about you. We have not given any information to the press & they are making up totally unfounded stories gleaned from people down there & rediculous fantisies.
>
> I am wearing the medal you sent home and it does help me to feel closer to you because I know it was last worn by you.
>
> Don't worry about us here at home we know with God's help it will all be worked out for the best. I prayed Holy Saturday that this burden would be lifted from you and that everything would be resolved. If this was the Lord's answer he sure threw us a thunderbolt didn't he? Spiritually I am with you in my every thought and prayer. I wish I could be there with you but I know the press would [be] right on my neck if I dare come near you.
>
> All our neighbors are sticking up for you and Father White was over and said that he had talked to the Catholic chaplain about a month ago and asked him to do all he could for you. He also said he was going to write to you.
>
> No matter what happens Joe please know that we all love you dearly and need you to be in our lives just as we want to be in yours. Remember: "God so loved the world that He gave His

only begotten Son, that whomsoever believeth in Him should not perish but gain everlasting life." You, Dear Son are also my only begotten son and I love you dearly.
Mom

———

On April 29, the grand jury returned a three-count indictment against Joseph Christopher for second-degree murder in the deaths of Glenn Dunn, Harold Green, and Emanuel Thomas.

Chapter 14

KEVIN DILLON CAME from a family steeped in legal tradition. Dillon was a thirty-one-year-old criminal defense attorney with a firm in downtown Buffalo that already bore his name: Dillon & Cataldi. Kevin was the oldest son of Justice Michael F. Dillon, a presiding judge of the State Supreme Court Appellate Division and formerly an Erie County District Attorney. Three of Kevin's uncles were attorneys in Western New York and his cousin James was an assistant district attorney. The name Dillon, therefore, was one that was already quite familiar in Buffalo legal and political circles, which perhaps added a further bit of excitement to an already sensational matter when the press learned he would be defending Joseph Christopher.

Therese Christopher had hired him to represent her son on the weekend following the search of her home. In the few days that had passed between the search on Wednesday and Dillon's entry into the case on Sunday, news of a prime suspect in the .22 caliber killings had already exploded in the media. Though he yet knew almost nothing about his client or the evidence against him, Dillon was well aware from the moment that the suspect's distraught mother came to see him that this would be an enormously complex and highly public case. Judging by news accounts, the prosecution appeared to already be operating in high gear. He informed Therese that he would need co-counsel and immediately contacted his friend and colleague, Mark Mahoney.

Mahoney was also thirty-one years old with an office in downtown Buffalo. Like Kevin Dillon, he had received his law degree from the

University at Buffalo Law School. Both had done their undergraduate work at Catholic institutes—Dillon at Canisius College, Mahoney at Notre Dame—and both came from large Irish families. Each was a superior young jurist. The similarities ended there.

They were near opposites in temperament and style, Dillon having a more subdued and tempered approach, Mahoney a more intimidating presence in a courtroom who wouldn't demur from unleashing a razor-sharp retort on a prosecutor when the situation warranted. They had never tried a case together before. As Kevin Dillon would soon after tell a reporter, he and Mahoney worked well together and their differences complemented each other. Dillon acknowledged they would "argue like hell on some points," which he felt made for robust legal teamwork.

Mahoney would not hesitate to say he could never see himself being a prosecutor. He was a staunch defender of rights, and viewed the defense position as the guardian of the constitutional and fundamental rights afforded to all. His legal sensibilities were therefore immediately on alert upon learning that the search executed upon the Christopher home had been sparked by statements made by Joseph while he was under care at a psychiatric facility.

Managing the wildfire press and publicity that had already engulfed Christopher presented an added challenge and was by no means an insignificant matter. Joseph Christopher had been identified by name in a television newscast on the same night his family home had been searched. This had immediately set off his widespread identification on TV, radio, and in print. Before Dillon and Mahoney had even been retained to represent him, the media had disseminated details of items confiscated during the searches and his arrest in the army on charges of stabbing a black soldier. On April 25, the day before Therese Christopher hired Dillon and Mahoney—and before Christopher had even been charged in any of the Buffalo murders—the *Courier-Express* reported that "Christopher bragged to nurses about the shootings and stabbings of Buffalo-area blacks." If ever there were a case where defense attorneys had to hit the ground running, this was it.

Melvin Lobbett and Thomas Rash had returned to Buffalo from Fort Benning on April 24. In addition to the nurses and staff psychiatrist, they had interviewed witnesses to the Coles assault, the guard whom Christopher had stabbed with a pen, and the stockade commander, Captain Raiford Ames, who discussed Private Christopher's time in confinement. Ames explained that Christopher had lacerated his penis while in a second-floor cell and that another prisoner had witnessed this. Ames further confirmed the written reports the army had provided of Christopher's conduct during his incarceration in the stockade: that Christopher had refused to eat, was very depressed, and had problems with guards and other prisoners. Ames told investigators that this was very unusual behavior for a person in confinement in the military. He added that Christopher was a loner and read the Bible. Christopher did have one friend in the stockade; another prisoner named Robert who was also from Buffalo. Robert had since been discharged from the military for possessing and selling marijuana and had returned to the Buffalo area. Lobbett and Rash relayed this information back to the task force, who promptly interviewed Robert.

"I was in the brig for about three weeks when this guy by the name of Joseph Christopher came for stabbing a black guy in his company for calling him a fag," Robert told the investigator. "Somebody told me that he was from Buffalo and I started talking to him and I found out that he at one time worked at Deaconess Hospital in Buffalo where I used to work. He worked in the kitchen but I didn't know him then." He described Christopher as about five feet nine, "very thin, with a small frame and large hands and a large head. He wasn't into drugs but was heavy into religion. By this I mean he was into spiritual stuff, meditating all the time, used to take his red prayer book with him to chow. He told me that he was a Catholic and he wore a scapular around his neck.

"He was a loner and didn't smoke or use alcohol and was very adamant about the fact that he didn't use drugs. He was extremely interested in survival training, nutrition, physical fitness and emergency medical training.

"Once we were in the cell block and he told me that he and a friend of his from Buffalo 'wasted some niggers.' I don't remember if he specifically mentioned where, but after he said this to me I told him that I didn't want to hear about it and I thought it was bullshit. I didn't want to hear anymore about it because he was already in for attempted murder and I didn't want to get involved anymore than I had to. While we were in the brig, Joe also attacked another black, a guy who had a big mouth. Joe went after him twice."

Returning to the topic of Joseph's friend, Robert stated, "Christopher said that this friend of his in Buffalo used to sit around his apartment and talk about survival, EMT training, and nutrition. He mentioned his name but I can't remember it right now.

"Christopher never talked about broads or where he used to go out to have a good time like everybody else, and in fact used to bitch at other guys for talking about drugs or broads and fooling around. I don't think that he was a homosexual but I don't think he was a completely normal. I mean that he would never give a woman a tumble.

"He told me that he had been to New York City recently and also that he either met someone from boot camp there or that his buddy from Buffalo met him there. He said that he didn't like New York City but didn't say anymore about it."

The investigator inquired whether they had ever discussed weapons and Robert responded that they had. "Joe and I talked quite a bit about weapons, especially handguns. I seem to remember him telling me that he owned a handgun but can't remember what kind. He didn't display a lot of expertise regarding handguns but acted like he was interested in them. I have a strong interest in guns so he and I talked a lot about them. I'm sure those conversations also included knives.

"Joe also used to tell me about a hunting camp that his dad owned in the town of Ellington. He told me that his dad used to take him there for the usual things, hiking, fishing, and camping. He really liked his dad. I got a lot of negative vibrations from Joe regarding his mother but I can't pinpoint why."

Back at Fort Benning, Lobbett and Rash obtained permission to search the belongings of Private Christopher. They seized a black beret, two black plastic-framed glasses (military issue), one pair of gold wire-framed glasses, and a Greyhound bus ticket issued December 11, 1980. Christopher had departed Fort Benning by bus on December 19 for

Christmas leave, at which time he had been wearing a green dress A uniform and black army-issue raincoat. Per training regulations, Christopher had no civilian clothing in his possession.

He had purchased a round-trip ticket. The packet indicated he had traveled through North Carolina and Virginia to Washington, DC, and through to New York City, though the last coupon—from Washington to New York—had not been pulled. According to the bus route schedules, he would have arrived in New York sometime on December 20. The return portion of his bus ticket was unused.

Christopher had been observed at the Columbus Airport by a platoon sergeant on either January 2 or 3. The official company records indicated that he had returned to his basic training company on January 2, 1981, at 4:50 p.m.

In the company of CID agents, Lobbett and Rash had visited Private Christopher in the stockade. Agent Carr explained to Christopher that he would be photographed by two investigators from Buffalo. He was removed from his cell and Lobbett and Rash proceeded to take twenty-three color photographs of him wearing various pieces of clothing and different hats. Christopher cooperated without protest.

A few minutes into the photo session, he turned to Investigator Rash and asked him who he was. Rash explained and Christopher's reply was, "Yeah." Minutes later, Christopher asked to see the identification of Rash and Lobbett. They both complied. Christopher examined the IDs, then wanted to grab and inspect Lobbett's badge. Lobbett showed him the badge but wouldn't allow him to hold it. He seemed much more interested in seeing the badge than in anything else that was going on.

Lobbett asked Christopher, "Do you wear tinted glasses?" Christopher removed the wire-framed glasses he was wearing, looked at them, then replaced them. He did this twice. He gave no verbal answer.

After the photos were taken, Mel Lobbett told Christopher that he and Rash were returning to Buffalo and asked if there was anything they could do for him. "Do you want me to talk to your mother, Therese, your sisters, or Lydia Bianchi?" Christopher stood mute.

Lobbett wrote in his personal observations of Joseph Christopher that he was "ashen-looking. He walked slowly in a shuffle—everything

Christopher did was slow. He appears to be heavy in the chest and small in the buttocks." He noted a tattoo of a snake on his left forearm. Both investigators described Christopher's short hair as curly and dark brown with a reddish cast. Lobbett was of the opinion that Christopher bore a resemblance to the Rochester composite and appeared slightly younger than the New York City composite. Thomas Rash felt that Christopher resembled a composite when he was photographed wearing dark-rimmed glasses, a ski cap, and an army fatigue jacket. He wrote that Christopher was cooperative in all phases of photographing him, that he had a blank stare throughout, and seldom spoke.

The last person Lobbett and Rash interviewed was Father Michael Freeman. They spoke with the Catholic chaplain at the stockade in the presence of Captain Raiford Ames and Agent Tom Carr. The priest explained that he had met Private Christopher within a day or two after his arrest and initial confinement to the stockade. Father Freeman had been told that there was a soldier at the detention facility who had asked to see a priest. Learning that the solider was from Buffalo, which was Freeman's hometown also, Father Freeman had visited Christopher and had a discussion with him at that time, which he felt might interest the investigators.

Father Freeman said that Christopher had been very depressed and nervous, which led the priest to ask him if he wanted a psychiatric evaluation. Christopher replied that he did. Christopher had spoken of his background and problems he was having in his infantry training brigade. According to Father Freeman, Christopher had released him to speak with doctors or anyone else who could help him.

As Freeman related the conversation, "It was just on his background. From a broken home, feeling of guilt that he had over the death of his father. The anger he had in reference to blacks and minorities. He felt persecuted by them. I thought that might be from where he went to school. That he could never get along with them. He reflected on how he was being picked upon by the blacks in infantry training. They were calling him a faggot and picking on him, not giving him any peace of mind.

"I went back over his situation at home, how he got into the army. He mentioned that he had broken up with his girlfriend and he was depressed about that. He thought that maybe he wanted to be a priest and he went down to New York City for a period of time. He wanted to enter a seminary. The seminary wouldn't accept him. After being in New York City for a while, he returned back to Buffalo. He reflected on wanting to get into the army and a depression he was in, and not wanting to associate with his relatives. There was a going away party which was also his birthday party and he refused to be with his relatives. He'd rather be alone."

Speaking of what Christopher had told him about his experience in the army and the circumstances of his arrest, Father Freeman said, "Again he reiterated the blacks picking on him. He was using a knife to defend himself against one who called him a fag." This was the second time investigators had heard that Christopher told someone he stabbed Coles for calling him a fag. The CID had interviewed all the witnesses to the stabbing as well as other men in the platoon and company officers. None could recall any interaction whatsoever between Christopher and Coles prior to the assault.

According to what police had learned so far of Christopher's family, Freeman's statement about Christopher having come from a broken home also seemed to be in error, though whether Christopher had actually said this or Father Freeman had somehow misinterpreted one of his statements could not be determined.

Father Freeman told the investigators that he felt the conversation he'd had with Christopher could be helpful to them because of the situation in Buffalo and the fact that Christopher had been there at the time. He added, however, that Christopher had made no statements at all about any violence in either New York City or Buffalo.

"You mentioned his anger at ethnic races. He definitely has a problem dealing with ethnics?" Lobbett asked.

"With blacks," Freeman answered.

"With blacks? Specifically blacks, okay, because of certain things that happened in his lifetime related to blacks?"

"He wouldn't go into exactly what it was in Buffalo," the priest answered. "I picked up more that it might be a school situation because of a white being a minority there."

Lobbett asked, "Father, did you see Joseph Christopher today?"

"I did," Freeman replied. He had visited Christopher about an hour before but Christopher had not said anything to him.

"Does he appear alert?" Lobbett asked.

"He's alert, more so than at other times I've talked to him. Again, that could've been because of the starvation he was on, the not eating. He did not want to talk today. I never brought up Buffalo, I never brought up New York City or Rochester. I told him I was there—originally I had intended to go down to see him after Easter anyway. I called the hospital and found out he was back here [the stockade].

"My whole conversation with him today had to do with asking him to cooperate and to talk to people. You know, whatever he wanted to talk about either with Dr. Law or to myself or to law enforcement officers. If he'd do that, it might help with his problems. Because he isn't cooperating with speaking to people. He's clamming right up."

Recalling his earlier conversations with Christopher, Father Freeman said he had never mentioned the .22 caliber killings nor any shootings or stabbings in Western New York.

"Did he say anything about New York City?"

"Nothing other than the fact that he was there. He went to New York City to join a seminary and no seminary would have him, obviously. If he was as disturbed talking to them as he was to me, he wouldn't be able to pass the psych test."

While Lobbett and Rash worked down in Georgia, the task force interviewed every person in Buffalo they could find who had ever crossed paths with Joseph Christopher. Prior to the search, investigators had quietly interviewed some of his neighbors, former employers, and friends, including Joe's closest friend, Peter Tramontina, who had been interviewed at length at the district attorney's office.

Peter explained how he'd become aware of Joe's arrest in the army, how Joe had written a letter to the Bianchis who had in turn contacted Peter. He had visited Joe's mother, who was very upset about Joe's situation and didn't know what to do. Mrs. Christopher had given Peter the number of a chaplain in Fort Benning and Peter had tried to contact the chaplain on a few occasions but had been unable to reach him.

Peter confirmed what Donna Vanalden had said about Joe having withdrawn from people over the past couple of years. Peter explained that from their mid-teens to early twenties, he and Joe had been the best of friends and were together most of the time. Lately, however, Joe didn't seem to have any close friends. Peter had periodic contact with him but they were never as tight as they'd once been. Peter had seen Joe four or five times between September and November 1980, including the night before Joe left for the army when they had gone out for pizza and beer. The last time he'd seen Joe was around January 2, when Joe was home on leave. Joe had come over to Peter's house and they had engaged in small talk. Joe had mentioned that he was having difficulty adjusting to army life but he didn't get into any detail.

Asked about Christopher's background, Peter said that Joe had taken his father's death hard and felt guilty for the way he had treated his father. Peter had noticed the biggest change in Joe after his breakup with Donna, after which Joe seemed to isolate himself from everyone, as if he was just done with people.

He acknowledged that Joe had once used a lot of marijuana and also used speed. He confirmed the incident of Joe injecting Valium and subsequently coming down with hepatitis. Joe had quit all of that, however, about the same time he started his unofficial withdrawal from society.

Peter was asked if he was aware of any acts of violence perpetrated by Christopher in the past. He qualified the use of the term "violence." However, he did relate the two incidents he was aware of where Joe had become aggressive with females, Donna being one of them.

Investigators questioned Peter about Nicholas Christopher's gun collection. He acknowledged that Joe had come into possession of the firearms after the death of his father. Peter was asked if he remembered a 10/22 Ruger rifle being among the collection and he responded yes. He explained about the bullet trap in the Christopher basement and recalled that he and Joe had fired the weapon down there and at the property in Ellington. Peter was positive of the identification of the Ruger 10/22 because he remembered the cylinder sheath clip. Investigators showed Peter a cylindrical clip from a Ruger 10/22 and he identified it as similar to the one he had seen and used at the Christopher residence.

Joe had told Peter about losing a Beretta handgun. Joe had been concerned that the loss of the weapon might cause him to lose his pistol permit and thereby the control of the weapons that had been the personal property of his father, which he definitely wanted to keep in the family. Joe had ultimately thought that the Beretta was stolen from the basement by a black male utility meter reader.

Joseph Christopher had been an auto mechanics major at Burgard High School, a vocational school on the city's east side. He had dropped out in his junior year, in January 1974, at the age of eighteen. He had graduated eighth grade from Public School 82, where records showed he had been an average student, earning Bs or Cs in all subjects except physical education, in which he earned an A, and music, which he failed for lack of effort. Other than a high number of tardies and absences in eighth grade and high school, his disciplinary record was average and unremarkable.

His first job out of high school had been as a bus boy at the snack bar at Deaconess Hospital. He had only worked there from early February to late March 1974. According to the hospital, he had walked off the job when told he had to wear a uniform.

He then worked as a furnace cleaner and repairman for ABD Heating. The owner and a longtime employee both recalled Christopher as a good worker who showed up on time, and never had any complaints about him. The owner said that Christopher had actually worked for him twice, as he had quit at one point and said he was going into business for himself in the auto parts line. This hadn't lasted long, however, as the owner recalled that Christopher had come back to work for him about two weeks later. He worked for the company for less than a year. They said that Christopher was a "hotrodder" and drove a black Camaro. Asked if he had ever shown any animosity toward black people or had any problems with blacks, both said no. They were asked about any guns Christopher may have had but they knew of none. They told the investigators that if they were looking at Christopher as possibly being the .22 Caliber Killer, he looked nothing like the composite. Christopher was a short, stocky guy with curly, kinky hair.

Investigators spoke with another man in the same industry who had employed Christopher on a freelance job. He had known Joe for about seven years but had last seen him two years before, when Joe had done some body work on his truck. He had, in fact, asked about Christopher just a couple of weeks before when he had attended an anniversary party for his former business partner, Leigh Chamberlain Sr., and his wife, and had run into Peter Tramontina. He was interested in having Joe do some more body work on one of his vehicles and asked Peter about him. Peter told him Joe was in the army. The man could offer little else, but told the officer that if they were looking at Joe as being involved in the .22 caliber killings, they were "barking up the wrong tree." Christopher looked nothing like the sketches and his hair wasn't blond.

The task force paid a call at the home of Leigh Chamberlain Sr., whose two older sons, Leigh Jr. and Scott, had been close friends of Joe Christopher and Peter Tramontina. The Chamberlain family had known Joe since the boys were in their early teens, when Leigh Jr. and Scott befriended him in Boy Scouts. Leigh Jr. was the same age as Joe and Peter. Scott was a year younger. The Chamberlain boys had also attended Burgard High School. For many years, the four youths—Joe, Peter, Leigh, and Scott—had been together constantly. Joe spent a lot of time at the Chamberlain home, staying for days at a time. After high school, the boys had eventually drifted apart. Leigh Jr. had moved to California a few years earlier. Peter and Scott were both married.

Leigh Sr. had given Joe his first job in the heating business. Joe had worked for him part-time, cleaning furnaces, for about a year and a half. He described Joe as a terrific worker, cooperative, and no trouble whatsoever. Joe rented a garage from a neighbor up the street from his mother's house and always worked on cars on the side. Chamberlain said he liked Joe but that you couldn't get close to him. He'd always been a very polite and cordial young man, but distant.

Leigh Sr. acknowledged that Joe was a gun enthusiast and he was aware of the large collection he'd inherited from his father. Asked whether

Christopher ever carried a knife, Chamberlain said Joe would carry one when he went hunting or fishing, but normally he never saw him with a knife. Investigators asked whether Christopher's emotional makeup had changed after the death of his father. Chamberlain replied yes, but said that he wasn't speaking from personal knowledge, only what he'd heard from Peter Tramontina shortly after the death of Nicholas Christopher. Peter had described Joe as "living like a hermit," spending stretches of time alone at the cabin in Ellington.

Leigh Sr. had visited the cabin in the spring of 1980 when he, his son Scott, and another young man had gone fishing out there with Joe. He'd last seen Joe a couple months afterward, in June 1980, when Joe had taken his daughter to a wedding. Chamberlain's daughter was asked about this evening, specifically about Joe's attitude and the car he drove. She said he had picked her up in a blue, newer-looking car that he'd said he'd borrowed from a friend, but she didn't know the make or model. She thought Joe Christopher was weird, mostly because he didn't drink or smoke and only drank orange juice while they were out. She commented that he had really "calmed down" from his earlier days.

It was the weekend before Easter when the Chamberlains had heard that Joe was in some sort of trouble in the army. Scott Chamberlain had learned about it from Peter at the anniversary party. Leigh Sr. said he had phoned Joe's mother but she would tell him nothing. He wanted to write to Joe, but Mrs. Christopher wouldn't allow it.

Neighbors on Weber Avenue had not been able to add anything of value to the investigation. Without exception, they all described the Christophers as a nice, ordinary family and Joe as a quiet, courteous young man. Most everyone in the neighborhood seemed to know Joe but no one seemed to be particularly close to him, with perhaps two exceptions: Laverne Becker, the middle-aged bachelor who lived next door, and the Bianchis, the elderly Italian couple to whom Christopher had written his desperate letter back in January asking for help finding an attorney.

Carlo and Lydia Bianchi had been among the first people investigators had interviewed after receiving the information on Christopher from

Fort Benning. In broken English, they said they both felt sorry for Joe and the fact that he was in trouble. They constantly referred to him as a "very, very good boy," a "nice boy, not in peace with himself." They thought of him as moody; whenever they asked him what was wrong, he would say nothing. The Bianchis explained that Joe had worked for them around the house doing odd jobs, cutting grass, painting, etc. Mrs. Bianchi said that they received two letters from Joe while he was in the army: one in the beginning, when he first went away, in which he seemed happy, and the second when he was in trouble. They had spoken with his sister after the second letter and told her that they couldn't answer the letter due to their problems writing in English. They had apologized but felt that there was nothing they could do.

Asked if Christopher had ever indicated any dislike for blacks, they responded no. On the contrary, Mrs. Bianchi recalled that Joe had defended blacks when she had voiced complaints about them.

Investigators also visited a middle-aged woman who had purchased a blue 1970 Chevy from Joseph Christopher. He had sold her the car in August and she produced the vehicle registration showing that she had registered the car on August 14. Since the blue car had been in her possession at the time of the murders, the matter was not pursued further.

The task force had been unable to interview Laverne Becker, the next-door neighbor, until after the search of the Christopher home. Investigators visited him where he worked, at the Pepsi bottling plant. Becker had lived next door to the Christophers since the family moved in back in 1962, when Joe had been seven years old. Mr. Becker spoke highly of Joe. He'd been fond of him since he was a little boy and considered him the son he'd never had. Joe had come to say good-bye and had given him a kiss on the cheek before he left for the army.

Mr. Becker was asked if he had received any correspondence from Joe since he'd been in the military. He said that he'd received a few letters prior to the 1980 holidays and recalled the letters being "high and low." Asked to explain, he said that one letter would be very nice and yet another he could hardly understand. Becker was asked if in any of these letters Christopher had expressed a desire or intention to go to New York City over the Christmas holidays. Mr. Becker didn't recall that as being the content of any of the letters. However, Mrs. Christopher had told him about letters from Joseph that mentioned something about going to New York City or Yorktown or some such place. He couldn't remember specifically where. According to what he'd heard from Mrs. Christopher, Joseph wanted to see about going into the Jesuits or the monks or something like that. He wanted to surprise his mother and enter the religious life. Becker believed that this was supposed to take place over the Christmas holidays, but he was unsure. He no longer had any letters from Joseph, as he had given them all to Mrs. Christopher.

Mr. Becker was also asked about the possibility of any of the Christopher girls having been assaulted or injured by any person, in particular a black man, during the past years. Becker recalled no such incident. He was asked specifically if any of the girls ever suffered a broken jaw or any such injury. Again, his reply was negative.

The question of whether any of Joseph's sisters had been assaulted by a black male had come up in the wake of publicity generated by the search. Police had received a couple of anonymous calls. One came from a person who claimed that one of the sisters had been raped by a black man. Another told a police officer that Joseph Christopher "had two or three older sisters" and that one of them was involved with a black male and had a baby by a black man, and that when Nicholas Christopher found out about this, he died. The person further said that Joseph had gone into seclusion since the father's death and had moved his bedroom furniture into the basement, and that he stayed down there by himself since the death of his father. (Police had already searched and photographed the Christopher home. There was no bedroom furniture in the basement.) The tipster believed there was a possibility that Joseph was killing blacks because he thought his sister's relationship with a black male had caused their father's death.

A search of police records turned up no incidents of any females in the Christopher family having been assaulted by a black male, nor by anyone else. People who actually knew the family well told authorities that they had never heard of any such thing. Zach DiFusco, who was called in for further questioning, also stated that he was unaware of such an occurrence. Zach said that to the best of his knowledge, none of the sisters had ever been involved with a black male or had a black baby. The allegation that Nicholas Christopher had died upon learning that one of his daughters had a black baby was patently false. Nicholas had died of long-term heart disease.

Investigators knew the circumstances of Nicholas Christopher's death to be as Zach claimed. They had obtained a copy of his death certificate and had, in fact, even visited the plot where he was buried to check it for signs of disturbance—like maybe a buried .22 caliber sawed-off Ruger rifle.

The searches of the Weber Avenue home and the Ellington cabin had yielded no such weapon. Authorities had not seized any firearms at all, in fact. The only guns found at Weber Avenue were a 16-gauge Remington semiautomatic shotgun, a .30 caliber US carbine rifle, a 30.06 Winchester rifle, a 20-gauge Browning Magnum semiautomatic shotgun, and a starter pistol, none of which were within the scope of the search warrant (or of the investigation). Serial numbers of the four long guns had been recorded and special file checked, with negative results. No firearms were found at Ellington.

The majority of what was seized in the searches was ammunition and spent shells. At the Weber house, police had taken a total of nine boxes of various .22 caliber ammunition. They had also confiscated a cigar box with ten spent .22 caliber casings, a pistol barrel, a Ruger rotary magazine, two gun stocks, and debris from the bullet trap. They took six knives, a black knit watch cap, a leather hat, and a fatigue green army-style jacket that appeared to have flecks of blood on the sleeve. The jacket and hats had been recovered from Joseph's bedroom.

In Ellington, they took three boxes of bullets and sixty-one expended cases of .22 caliber ammunition found on the property. They also cut down a tree that had a number of bullets lodged within. A section of the tree was taken for processing. All items seized were transported to the Central Police Services lab by noon on April 23. The following day, state trooper Terry Rodland personally delivered a number of the items to the FBI lab in Washington, DC.

While the task force interviewed known friends and acquaintances of Joseph Christopher, John Regan had one person in mind that he wanted to speak to, and that was Kenny Paulson, witness to the Glenn

Dunn homicide. From the moment Christopher's name had surfaced as a suspect, Regan had thought of Paulson. Glenn Dunn had been shot in the parking lot at Genesee and Floss, approximately three-tenths of a mile from Christopher's home. Joe Christopher lived on Weber Avenue. Kenny Paulson lived on Floss. Weber was the next street over from Floss.

Detective Regan paid a call on Kenny at his home. Regan asked him if he knew Joseph Christopher. Kenny said he'd never heard of him. He might possibly have seen him around, he said, but he didn't know him by name.

Kenny insisted that he didn't know the assailant and didn't get a good look at his face. Regan had him describe again how the man had left the scene of the homicide. In Regan's opinion, it would be nearly impossible for Kenny not have seen at least a partial portion of the shooter's face, either a side view or full frontal view.

Regan noted in his report that Kenny Paulson was extremely nervous when questioned as to his knowledge of the homicide and whether or not he knew the shooter, either from the neighborhood or personally. Paulson said that he'd be glad to take a polygraph test to remove him from any contact in the case.

John Regan concluded the interview and left. But he wasn't done with Kenny Paulson.

Angela Christopher was in her senior year of high school. She hadn't gone to school on the day after the search, or on the following day. In the aftermath of that surreal invasion, she and her sister Lorraine were living with a sense of caution.

They had taken their mother to stay at an aunt's house to shield her from the reach of reporters and give her the opportunity to seek legal help for Joe, the burden for which, of course, had fallen solely on Therese. There was no peace of mind to be had at Weber, with the steady knocks on the door, the constant ringing of the phone, and the people who drove by the house to shout vulgarities or fling M-80s into their driveway.

Though it had been well publicized that Joseph was incarcerated down at Fort Benning, Georgia—and hadn't yet been charged in any of the

Buffalo or New York crimes—that didn't stop some people from venting their spleen at his home on Weber Avenue. For his sisters, who were still reeling from the turmoil of the past few months with Joe's breakdown in the army and their mother's distress, this sudden notoriety and the constant presence of strangers lurking around their home was not only frightening, but nearly as inconceivable as the idea that their brother was under suspicion for murder.

Angela could not reconcile the sudden nightmare they were living with anything she knew of Joe. He had always been the protective older brother, quiet and inconspicuous, but always there. The seven-year gap in their ages had cast Joe into a paternal role when it came to Angela, particularly after their dad died. It was a duty he'd always embraced and fulfilled well. She'd been very young when Nicholas passed away. Joe had been twenty. It was Joe who came looking for her on summer nights if she wasn't home by the time the street lights flicked on. It was Joe who warned two obnoxious neighborhood boys not to pick on his sister or her friends; who made a bicycle for her out of parts he found and cobbled together because they couldn't afford to buy a new bike; who patiently taught her to parallel park when she was old enough to go for her driver's license.

When they spent time out in the country, back when their dad was alive and taking the family to Ellington for summer vacations, Joe would take her with him when he went to bale hay at the farm down the road and let her pet the horses while he worked. They'd head back to the cabin when it started getting dark and he'd tease her and say he'd leave her behind if she didn't keep up with him. She walked faster, though she knew he'd never really do that.

He'd once made her a snow fort in the backyard at Weber when she was seven years old. He carved it out of a snow bank. It had two rooms with an entrance on the top and on the side. He sculpted a bed and drew in a kitchen and sink. (When Joe made something, he really *made* something.) He'd done all that for her, to give her something special to play in. She loved it. She loved him. He was a normal brother. A very good brother.

To Angela, it seemed like the change that had come over Joe in the time before he'd left for the army had happened virtually overnight. One day he had been his same self, a young guy who wore a leather jacket and went out with friends and kept a messy bedroom. The next day, so it seemed, the jacket was gone, his bedroom hollowed out and stark, and in place of socializing and doing things he'd always loved, like taking photographs and working on cars, he was wearing corduroy pants with a white shirt and going to church every day with their mother. Angela had asked him once, "What the hell happened to you?" He told her to shut up. Then there was that strange thing he did, when he took all the Tupperware and hid it down in the basement. Angela had found it and teased him, "Hey whack job, I found the Tupperware." He flew off the couch and chased her up the stairs.

That silly thing hadn't seemed like much at the time. Even his sudden interest in going to church, or keeping his room so bare and tidy. None of it seemed to her like a big deal in the grand scheme of things. Nothing to really cause concern, and certainly nothing to spark the type of suspicions that had brought the police to their home. Never, throughout any of these shifts in behavior, had Joe ever been cruel or antagonistic, much less violent, toward anybody. How anyone could think her brother was capable of the kind of wanton destruction the authorities suspected was just beyond comprehension. Worse yet, there were people—strangers—who seemed to interpret the search of their house as proof enough that Joe must be the long-sought killer.

And so the family home had suddenly become an object of widespread curiosity, if not outright persecution. A marked place, filmed and photographed and mentioned daily on front pages and TV news. The two young women inside found themselves forced to live as if in a fortress, curtains tightly drawn, on guard for whatever might happen next. They worried about their brother, about their mother, about who might be stepping up on their front porch this time to peer through the windows. They could only wait and pray for the time when it would all finally die down. But that would prove to be a long, long wait.

———

"Joe Christopher and I were genuinely good friends. We worked, socialized, exercised, and went fishing together." Ernie Smith had been Joe's partner on the maintenance crew at Canisius College. Ernie was thirty-six years old, an affable man who had left Canisius soon after Joe had and presently worked as a salesman for an auto dealership. He and Joe had worked the midnight to 8:00 a.m. shift together for the duration of Joe's employment at the college.

Ernie had been brought to the DA's office for questioning two days after the news hit that Joe was a prime suspect in the serial murders of black men. Like all of Joe's other friends, Ernie said that he couldn't see Joe as the so-called .22 Caliber Killer. He also told investigators that Joe had never exhibited any racial hatred. Ernie didn't believe Joe was a racist. He further felt that if Joe was a racist, and particularly antiblack, he would know, since Ernie himself was black.

"We were close friends for about sixteen months, since he started at Canisius until about May of 1978," Ernie stated. "He was always with me, Donna, or Peter Tramontina. I ate at his [Donna's] house, his mother's house, and he ate at mine with me and my woman, Melanie. On one occasion, I moved to a room over Little Harlem on Michigan Avenue and Joe helped me move."

Joe sometimes picked Ernie up for work in his pickup truck. They often went out together to shoot pool or have a drink, although Joe wasn't much of a drinker. Ernie acknowledged that the two of them used to get high, though Ernie limited himself to marijuana. "We smoked together but I never got into any other drugs like he did. I was never around him when he was shooting up."

Ernie also described how the two of them were into physical fitness. "Joe is very strong. We used to work out regularly at Kessler Center, two to three hours a day. We fooled around and wrestled. Joe is two or three inches shorter than me and a little lighter, but he was strong. I could handle him but no way was it easy." Ernie thought it bothered Joe that he couldn't handily win their wrestling matches. "He was using a lot of weight on the Universal, trying to build himself up. He could use 140 pounds pressing, reps, etc. over a two to three-hour workout," Ernie stated. "He used the 140 easy. I only used 90. Joe could easily bench press 180 pounds."

Asked further about their social activities, Ernie said, "Once in a while, Joe would want to go fool around with street girls but we never picked any up. I had a lot of girls—I used to have a different girlfriend every other week like that. Joe never seemed too interested in getting down with them although he could have, I didn't care." Joe was with Donna at the time. Asked about that relationship, Ernie said, "I never made it with Donna. I never tried or even talked like that, although it's in the back of my mind that Joe maybe was afraid I might. I was never alone with her. She was a nice lady, very kind to me, and Joe really loved her. I never kidded with Joe about Donna because I had it in the back of my mind that he was the kind of dude that wouldn't think twice about messing you up over his old lady.

"Towards the end, he was complaining that things were not good at home with Donna, that she was pissing him off. He complained about this guy who owed her money, maybe about $1,000 or so. She had loaned the guy some money or something and Joe was mad that she still had to go see him or work for him.

"Joe tried to score with this black girl who worked with us at Canisius. She turned him down. Later I started going with her and that made him mad. I think she and Joe almost came to blows. She told me that she wasn't going to hook up with that whitey."

Ernie had visited the cabin in Ellington. He'd also viewed Joe's firearms. "He was very proud of his gun collection. Showed the guns to me many times. He had special holsters and everything and almost always had a gun with him, either on him or in his car." Explaining how their friendship had ended, he said, "When Joe and I fell out, he accused me of stealing his buck knife, which I didn't. We went down to his truck and found it. It was like he wanted an excuse to start an argument." Like others, Ernie had also noticed what seemed like an abrupt change in Joe's personality. The knife incident strained the friendship. "After that, we were just about through. Then I had a little fight with a guy at Canisius, a white guy. I gave him a shove and knocked him down. Later Joe came to me and said, 'You're supposed to be a big man.' I told him to cut it out and I walked away. I didn't want to fight with Joe, his knives and his guns."

According to Ernie, Joe seemed to change toward everybody. Joe refused to speak to anyone at work for a period of time. Later, the situation changed and he would speak only to the white workers. Ernie guessed that Joe was jealous of Donna's relationships with other men. It was hard to figure out what was up with him. His behavior just grew odd. Joe was caught sleeping on the job three times. The third time was the last straw. He was fired.

The last time Ernie saw Joe was in the late summer of 1980. Ernie had been outside the auto dealership where he worked when Joe came walking down the street. They spoke. "He said he was walking to a friend's house. He was telling me that he had lost his girl, his truck, and his job because of a drinking spree and that he was trying to get himself together for the past week. I got called on the intercom. When I came back, he was gone."

––––––––––

Melvin Lobbett and Thomas Rash headed back to Georgia on Monday, April 27.

There were several reasons for this. The searches had not yielded the proverbial smoking gun—nor much at all of evidentiary value, according to preliminary tests that had been conducted throughout the weekend. A source told the *Buffalo Evening News* that ballistics tests performed at the Central Police Services lab "don't look too promising at this point." In addition, witnesses to the .22 caliber killings and the Buffalo stabbings, including victim Albert Menefee, had failed to pick Christopher out of a photo lineup that included some of the twenty-three photographs that Lobbett and Rash had taken during their first visit to Fort Benning. Commenting on these disappointing results, the source told the *News*, "It makes things a lot harder."

Christopher's fingerprints had already been compared to the latent prints lifted from the cabs of Parler Edwards and Ernest Jones, with negative results, though this information was not disseminated to the media.

The only thing that tied Christopher to any of the crimes so far were his confessions—made to nurses at a psychiatric facility following a time when he had starved himself, stared at lightbulbs for hours, and cut his penis with a razor blade.

New York City detectives had traveled to Fort Benning on April 25 to do some investigating of their own. This spurred a sort of unspoken competition between the two jurisdictions, mainly on the part of the Buffalo task force. Christopher was the most promising suspect they'd had in months. They didn't relish the idea of New York City possibly making a case against him first, in essence pulling the fish from their net. But perhaps the most compelling reason for Lobbett and Rash to hurry back to Fort Benning was the news that Joseph Christopher had reportedly asked to speak with police.

The CID had stayed in contact with the task force and let them know of some interesting developments that had taken place following the departure of Lobbett and Rash. Over the weekend, Captain Raiford Ames, commanding officer of the stockade, had conversations with Christopher relative to the crimes. In addition, the CID had learned of the statements Christopher had made to PFC Corwin, his guard at the hospital.

Lobbett, Rash, and two detectives from New York City met with Raiford Ames in the presence of the CID. Ames said that on the afternoon of Friday, April 24, guards informed him that Christopher, who was in a segregation cell, wanted to see him. He directed the guards to bring Christopher to his office.

Christopher wanted food. Ames believed that Christopher was going to proposition him. Ames had read a hospital report that stated Christopher had previously made a homosexual proposition to a staff member in order to get a sandwich, and he'd further heard that guards had told Christopher that this was the way to get special favors from the confinement officer. Ames said he had therefore warned him against it right away. "I told him, 'Look, Christopher, I'll do whatever I can to help you while you're in here as long as it is within the regulations, but don't make a homosexual proposition to me because it won't profit you. I'm not homosexual. I don't know if you're homosexual but making a proposition towards me won't gain you anything.' And I asked him was he homosexual, and he said no. So he didn't make the proposition. But that's how we really got started in our conversation."

Christopher had ended up spending the better part of the afternoon in Captain Ames's office. Ames had some food brought in and let him eat his fill as they talked. Captain Ames, who was black, was aware of

Christopher's statements to the nurses and that Christopher was being investigated as a suspect in the New York murders. Everyone at the base was aware of it by this time, as both local and out-of-town press had converged on Fort Benning.

As Ames explained his Friday afternoon conversation with Christopher, "He and I discussed different topics, from racial issues to religious preferences and things of that nature. But I never did approach him directly about the Buffalo incident or anything relating to charges he's facing or he's allegedly involved in, acts that he allegedly admitted to. But I do feel that during the course of our conversation, during his stay here in the office, there was a sense of rapport developed between us where he felt, 'Maybe I can talk to this guy,' because trust was mentioned, and at the onset of the conversation he mentioned, 'Well, I don't trust anyone. I don't have any friends. It's like the world is against me.' And I said, 'Well, I can imagine how you feel, especially facing what you're facing, but don't feel as if you're a Lone Ranger because I don't trust anyone either. As a matter of fact, I don't trust you.' And he let me know that he didn't trust me. And I told him I felt it was best to be that way."

Ames asked Christopher if he had anything against blacks. Christopher told him no. He asked Christopher if he had come to the office to kill him and his answer to that was also no. What Christopher did want, aside from food, was to get out of segregation, back into the general inmate population. Ames told him that wasn't possible.

Their conversation had ended when a female friend of Captain Ames came to his office for a prearranged dinner date. He had introduced Christopher to his female friend. She joined the conversation and at one point she asked Christopher if he had really killed people in Buffalo. He had responded, "People say I did."

The following day, Ames said, he was off duty but had come in for a walk through of the detention facility. He stopped by Christopher's cell and had a brief conversation. "I was just more or less summarizing what had taken place Friday, because that's the first time I really had any prolonged contact with Christopher," Ames stated. "He asked me whether or not it would be possible to get some additional cereal, have the wheat taken out of his diet, and things of this nature. And he asked me whether or not I could contact Chaplain Freeman. And I told him yes, I would, I'd look into all the requests that he made.

"We tried to contact Chaplain Freeman Saturday but we weren't able to. The soonest we could reach him was Sunday morning. Chaplain was in the middle of the service so he had one of his assistants call us back and let us know that after that service, he would come over and pay Christopher a visit."

Father Freeman had come to the stockade and spent some time with Christopher. Ames didn't know what was said, but he had suspicions. As Captain Ames explained, "Chaplain Freeman and I, up until this point had a very open relationship as far as the discussions he had with Christopher, because he [Freeman] felt it was general in nature and he felt obligated, being somewhat an assistant to the confinement facility, to discuss these things with me, the confinement officer. So this is the approach that he had taken up until this point. However, after his discussion with Christopher on Sunday, he decided he could no longer discuss these things. And if I'm not mistaken, quote unquote, he said, 'The things that Christopher and I have discussed today are sacramental.' And to me, based on the extent to which we had discussed previous conversations between he and prisoner Christopher, I felt that prisoner Christopher had related something of importance to him, and I did not inquire as to what it was, because it was in fact sacred."

On Sunday afternoon, Ames said, following the priest's visit, a guard informed Ames that Christopher asked to see him. Ames went to the cell and found Christopher sitting on his bunk. "He seemed to be disturbed or moved, emotionally," said Ames. "His eyes were kind of watery. I leaned over and said something like, 'What can I do for you?' He looked up at me and he said, 'You know that thing in Buffalo?' I said, 'Yes, I know what you're talking about.' And he said, 'I did it.' I looked at him in his eyes and I said, 'I believe you.' He looked at me and said, 'I know you do.'

"And I asked him, 'Well, why do you want to tell me this?' And the reason why I asked him that is because Friday, when he was in my office, we had discussed the fact that there was no trust. I didn't trust him and he didn't trust me, so I wanted to know why me. And he said, 'Well, I just want to do what's right. I want to do right,' something to that effect. Then he said, 'What do I do from here? Where do I go from here?' I kneeled down, close to his cell where I could be on eye level with him because he was sitting on his bunk. I said, 'My God, give me strength. I don't know what to tell you.' Because he pretty much took me by surprise.

"Then I said, 'Well, I guess the best thing to do would be, let's get those detectives and let you speak with them,' but he said, 'No. They're not really Buffalo detectives. I checked their shields and they weren't the real Buffalo shield.' I said we could contact the CID but he didn't want to talk to the CID either."

At that point, the guard suggested that Christopher make a written statement but he declined that as well. Ames continued, "He didn't want to fill out a statement, but he said he would talk to a detective or investigator named Zach DiFusco."

Ames asked Christopher how he knew DiFusco. Christopher wouldn't explain, except to say that Zach DiFusco was with the Buffalo police. He seemed very eager to speak to this person. Ames had written the name down phonetically. Lobbett and Rash, of course, were already familiar with both the name and the man.

After concluding the interview with Raiford Ames, Lobbett and Rash returned to the CID office and contacted Major Morgan, Christopher's military attorney. Morgan advised them that he still represented Christopher on the military charges, and further that he had received a call on April 26 from Buffalo attorney Kevin Dillon, who was representing Christopher on any civilian matters. Dillon had instructed Morgan that he did not want Joseph Christopher questioned. Rash told Morgan that Christopher asked to speak with Buffalo police officers and that he and Lobbett were going to see him at the confinement center. Major Morgan said he would meet them there.

Lobbett and Rash phoned the task force. Captain Henry Williams instructed them to make arrangements with the army to have nurses Bernard Burgess and Dorothy Anderson fly to Buffalo as soon as possible.

DA Edward Cosgrove had decided to present what they had to a grand jury. The pressure was on. Two Buffalo black leaders, Assemblyman Arthur Eve and Sheila Nickson of the Black Leadership Forum, were meeting with Governor Hugh Carey to request appointment of a special state investigator because, Arthur Eve told the press, the black community had lost confidence in Cosgrove's conduct of the probe.

Major Morgan had already visited Joseph Christopher by the time Lobbett and Rash returned to the stockade. As the men approached his cell, they heard Christopher say, "Who's Lobbett?" Those were the only words they'd hear him speak, despite their efforts.

Christopher sat on his cot. They showed him their identification. He made no comment. They asked him if he believed they were Buffalo police officers. Christopher shook his head no. He smiled, reclined on his cot, and pulled the blanket over his face.

The session was taped. It amounted to thirty minutes of Lobbett and Rash trying to convince Christopher that they really were officers from Buffalo. Christopher made no verbal responses. According to the report filed later, he just smiled or smirked and kept pulling the blanket over his face.

Major Eleanor Law had declined to speak with Lobbett and Rash on their first visit to Fort Benning. She had since consulted with her commanding officers and had been instructed to cooperate with investigators.

Major Law, chief psychiatrist at Martin Army Hospital, had met with Christopher on a few occasions throughout his time in the psychiatric ward. On the morning of April 28, she spoke with Mel Lobbett, Thomas Rash, and two detectives from New York City in the presence of CID Agent Tom Carr.

Asked about Joseph Christopher's current state of mind, Dr. Law told the investigators, "At the present time, I would have to say he is suffering from a major or significant psychopathology. He is—I would refrain from offering any comment as to a diagnostic opinion, but I think it would be safe to say that he is significantly psychiatrically impaired."

She had last seen Christopher on Friday. It was the first time she had spoken with him since learning of the statements he had made to nurses Burgess and Anderson. Of that Friday meeting, Major Law said,

"As we talked, my purpose I think was to try to establish in my own mind where he was in terms of this confession. Whether his confession to the nurses was real or not. I asked him if he could talk to me about the confession that he made to the nurses and initially, he was reluctant to do so. Finally, he said to me, 'If I talk to you about it, what will happen?' And my response to him was, if you tell me that you did do these things, you said nothing more to me than you said to Captain Burgess and Lieutenant Anderson. If you tell me that you did not do these things, then I think you've got significant problems that we're going to need to talk about.

"At that point, he paused and looked down at the floor and looked back up to me and said, 'Yep, I did it.' And I said, 'You did the things that you said you did?' And he said, 'Yes. It seems like a fantasy.' At that point he withdrew from me, as he very often does in talking with him. He sort of withdrew. He sat back in his chair. He closed his eyes. And my efforts to get him to elaborate further about the various incidents, even to get him to tell me about when they started, or, you know, if he could just give me some general details. He was unable to give me anything further. So that was essentially the nature of the conversation."

"Has Private Christopher been under any medication for his problems here?"

"None," Law answered. "He might say he refused all medications, but I'm not sure we would have given him anything anyway."

"Do you believe he has presence of mind and knows where he is, knows right from wrong?" Lobbett asked.

"I think he's level with orientation in terms of knowing who he is and where he is. He very often seemed preoccupied and unable to participate in the interview process. It's difficult to pin down exactly why, but both myself and Dr. Levine and others would be compelled to feel that a very significant factor in that was the underlying psychopathology."

"Do you think he's telling the truth now, major?"

"The truth about . . .?"

"The truth about what he told the nurses. Actually about anything, but specifically about the crimes?"

"Again, I would have to really refrain from offering you an opinion at this point," Law replied. "I just don't know. People often times do have significant psychiatric problems for which they may feel guilty and will confess to things that they have not done. And I just, at this point in time, I mean he's just not given us a great many details. It's very difficult to really offer a professional opinion about the truth or falseness of what he's saying. It would take a good bit more verbally from him before I would be able to offer you a professional opinion on it."

Lobbett asked, "Do you think he's the type of person that would tell the truth or try to avoid it by maybe standing mute?"

"Silence can mean many things," Law replied. "And this has been the difficulty we have had throughout this process with him, trying to interpret and understand his withdrawing behavior and his reluctance to speak. It can have meanings at all different levels. At one level, it can be a conscious attempt to avoid people. Another level, it can be an unconscious attempt to deny. At an even further level it can represent very significant disorganization in his thinking processes, such that he's really unable to tell you what's going on inside his head. So in my opinion, at this point, we're limited because we don't have a lot of objective psychiatric data from the patient himself, and that has made it very, very difficult to pin down the exact reason for his reluctance to speak."

"Do you think he's conniving to be sent to Buffalo or a veterans' hospital, to try to work himself back to Buffalo?"

"I'd be surprised if that were the underlying motivation," she replied. "I don't think so."

"Do you think he really has a problem trying to explain things?"

"Do I think he has difficulty in explaining himself? Yes, I do," Law answered. "I can't offer you the exact reason for that, but I think he does."

"Do you think he wants to tell the truth and confess, but doesn't know how?"

"Again, if you're asking me to read into this, beyond what I have stated, I'm hesitant to do that, okay? I can't really offer you a solid opinion on that."

"Do you think that we are wasting our time trying to interview him?" Lobbett asked.

"Well, I think you're going to have a difficult time if his behavior is consistent with what we've seen on the ward. And I think it is consistent.

There have been various people who've attempted to interact with him. I don't know of anyone in the period of time that we've had involvement with him, over six weeks, who has been able to establish good rapport with him."

Lobbett asked, "Do you find that anytime he did want to speak, that he initiated the action?"

"Very much the opposite," Dr. Law said. "Most often someone here on the staff initiated any interaction with him. Now, intermittently—and this seemed to be a reflection of the degree of stress he was under—intermittently he would offer something to us spontaneously. And that happened on several occasions while he was here. But usually that would start out with something spontaneous but then he would very quickly withdraw from us again."

"In your interviews with him in treatment, does he have any hang-ups about blacks? Black males?" Lobbett asked.

"Not that he's ever verbalized to me."

"Major, if we were to talk to Joseph Christopher, could you suggest any approach that would be of more help to us in initiating a conversation with him?"

"Well, I think you have to understand that you're dealing with an individual who doesn't think like you or I. I really can't offer you a great deal of advice because none of us have been terribly successful in getting him to trust us enough to speak with us and I think that that's the basic issue, that he has a difficult time establishing trust.

"From what I've seen and observed, I don't see anything in the immediate future that's going to change the way he interacts with the world. Again, I think what information has been gained has come about during periods of stress. I think that has been the factor that's given us the information that we've gotten thus far."

"Based on your experience and your knowledge of Joseph Christopher and the type of psychotic problem he has, is he capable of that much violence on other males by himself?"

"It's difficult for me to give you that kind of—to qualify in that way," Dr. Law answered. "I recognize a certain difficulty he has with impulses that would suggest to me that he does have potential for doing things impulsively. Now the degree to which he does those things, I couldn't tell you. But I can tell you that my observations have been that he has very poor impulse control.

"There was an incident at the very end of the interview that I had with him on Friday that I think speaks to this issue of impulsivity. Just after he told me of his being involved in this killing, I told you he sort of withdrew from me, like he sat back in the chair and closed his eyes and wouldn't respond any further to my questions. And after a few minutes of this, in my efforts to sort of get past that with him, kind of get him to talk to me, he sat up all of a sudden with sort of wide-eyed look on his face. He reached over and grabbed my breast and I reached up and grabbed his hand and pushed it down and told him that that was inappropriate. At the same time he made a statement that he would like to fuck me. And I said, 'That's not possible.' At that point I stood up to get away from him and he reached over and tried to grab me again and I told him to keep his hands to himself. Captain Allen was just outside the door and he came in at that point.

"But I think, again, he was quite stressed by the questioning and his way of dealing with that stress was to try to intimidate me with this kind of a statement and then the behavior that followed. I don't think that was the first time this kind of behavior had occurred with people trying to work with him. Apparently while I was away, there were several incidences here on the ward where this sort of thing had come up.

"Now this sort of behavior in someone who's seriously disturbed, who's never committed any offense, occurs also. I mean this is not uncommon behavior for someone who has significant psychopathology."

An investigator asked, "It's like impulsive behavior? Like he doesn't know the reason why he's doing it?"

"Well, I'm interpreting it. I'm giving you my interpretation of his behavior. I don't think he was saying to himself, 'I've got to intimidate this woman.' It happened on an unconscious level. I don't think it was by design. I think that it just happened."

"I find that with law enforcement officers that it seems to be a game that he wants to play with us," said Lobbett. "See who was smarter, or who's got more power than the other."

"Yeah, again, now I'm not sure at what level this operates," said Dr. Law. "I don't think he's consciously saying, 'I'm going to play a game with these people.' But I think there is a need on his part to feel powerful in a situation, and one way of feeling powerful is to manipulate other people. And I think that's what was going on there. He needed to feel powerful because he feels very, very weak underneath it all."

"Major, did he specifically tell you that he did the crimes in Buffalo or New York City or both places, or anywhere?"

"He gave me no further details than what I told you. The only thing he would acknowledge to me was that he had done things that he had said he had done and that it seemed like a fantasy to him now. Those were his words."

———————

Kevin Dillon and Mark Mahoney tried, unsuccessfully, to bar the testimony of the psychiatric nurses before the grand jury. Justice Samuel L. Green rejected their argument that statements Christopher had made to nurses while under treatment in a hospital were privileged communications. Dillon and Mahoney asked Judge Green to halt the grand jury proceedings until they could argue the point in a court hearing but Green refused, stating that if the nurses' testimony were later ruled illegal or improper, and that was the only evidence presented for an indictment, the indictment would not meet legal requirements.

In addition to testimony on ballistic comparisons of .22 caliber casings found during the searches and bullets or casings recovered from the first three homicides—Glenn Dunn, Harold Green, and Emanuel Thomas—the grand jury also heard from witnesses who affirmed that Joseph Christopher had owned a 10/22 Sturm-Ruger rifle and were shown the photograph of Christopher holding that model rifle at his cabin in Ellington. Indictments for the first three .22 caliber murders were handed up by late morning. The fourth shooting, of Joseph McCoy in Niagara Falls, had occurred in Niagara County. Evidence on the McCoy slaying would have to be presented to a grand jury in that county.

On the same evening that her son was indicted in Erie County, Therese Christopher boarded a plane to Columbus, Georgia, with Kevin Dillon and Mark Mahoney.

The detectives from New York City had departed Fort Benning on April 28. Lobbett and Rash remained. They reinterviewed Father Freeman and took a sworn statement from him in which the priest repeated his earlier accounts of his talks with Christopher and affirmed that he'd since had a "privileged conversation" with him. This could only mean the Catholic rite of confession. Whether Christopher had actually confessed to murder hardly mattered; the confidentiality in this instance worked in favor of investigators since the inference was clear, accurate or not.

Dillon and Mahoney met their already notorious new client for the first time on April 30. The two attorneys shielded Mrs. Christopher from reporters as they made their way to Fort Benning. After visiting with her son, a shaken Therese Christopher returned to her hotel and penned a letter addressed to Kevin Dillon and Mark Mahoney on Holiday Inn stationery. She wrote that she had determined that Joseph was incapable of managing his own affairs and unable to make legal decisions at the present time. As his mother, she would be solely responsible for such decisions. She authorized Dillon and Mahoney to do all things they considered necessary and proper in representing her son.

State Police Investigator Michael O'Rourke and Assistant District Attorney John DeFranks also arrived at Fort Benning that morning. They went immediately to the provost marshal's office and filed a detainer and felony warrant on Private Joseph Christopher. They conferred with the commanding officer of the Staff Judge Advocate office. The army agreed to defer the pending military charges against Christopher and release him to civilian authorities, paving the way for his extradition from Georgia to New York.

By early afternoon, Private Christopher was in the custody of the Muscogee County Sheriff's office and, with reporters in pursuit, was driven to the county jail. Officers covered his face with a newspaper to prevent TV or news media from taking his picture.

Joseph was confined to an isolation cell with a mattress on the floor, no bunk. The cell had a commode, wash basin, and slot in the door through which he would be given food. The sheriff advised the lawmen from Buffalo that the prisoner would wear just a T-shirt and slacks, no underwear, and that the only object he'd be given was a metal cup. A guard would be constantly watching him.

Dillon and Mahoney joined DeFranks at the courthouse along with the local DA and a Georgia defense attorney. Kevin Dillon addressed the court and refused to waive extradition to New York. The judge scheduled a hearing for May 8.

Back in Buffalo, the media was aflame with news of the indictment and Christopher's transfer to a civilian jail. Edward Cosgrove had held a press conference to announce the grand jury's return of a sealed indictment in the first three .22 caliber murders. Cosgrove refused to divulge the name of the indicted, though it hardly mattered, since Joseph Christopher's name had already been heralded by television and print media, including the *New York Times* and the Associated Press, on a daily basis for the past week.

Mark Mahoney would comment years later that one of the lessons he took from this case was that once the media has adopted a certain spin, it can never be undone. The assertion that Christopher became a suspect because he "bragged" and "boasted" about killing black men had already become the standard through line in the press before Dillon and Mahoney had even entered the case. Some accounts stated that the nurses had "overheard" Christopher bragging about the killings. While these claims of bragging and boasting about killing were in contrast with the facts, they did serve to bolster the motive, long ago established by authorities and the media, that the murders were pure and simple hate crimes. The presumption of a remorseless racist assassin became the wallpaper for the case, Mahoney recalled, and couldn't be undone—particularly with a client who, the defense attorneys would soon learn, was wholly incapable of assisting in his defense.

———

On April 30, the day after the indictment, newspapers in Buffalo were dominated by updates, recaps, and reactions. The *Courier-Express* printed a sizeable photo of Joseph Christopher, taken from a high school yearbook, on its front page. The photo was shown on TV and reprinted in other newspapers. Some of the coverage had a celebratory tone, and in certain instances read almost as if a conviction had been handed down rather than an indictment. Daniel Acker was quoted, "It's the best news we've had in seven months. Something we've been working for, praying for, looking forward to, and helps to relieve some of the tension, some of the frustrations in this community."

Accounts of the press conference expressed praise for the task force and for Cosgrove in particular. The *Buffalo Evening News* described it as "another media spectacular" with Cosgrove as the "star performer," though the headline described the DA as low-key in his big moment. "On a day that was clearly his triumph," the article read, Cosgrove thanked every police agency involved in the investigation and singled out Chief Leo Donovan and Captain Henry Williams for helping to bring the case to a "preliminary finality." Columnist Ray Hill wrote a reflective piece that brimmed with adulation for the district attorney, declaring "this, then, is Ed Cosgrove Day in Buffalo."

Following the press conference, Cosgrove spoke of the break that had led investigators to their suspect. He credited the dogged police work of the task force. "You always have to have good fortune but we worked to make ours," he said, noting that the task force had recently redistributed information on the crimes to law enforcement around the country.

Captain Henry Williams agreed. "You often make your breaks," Williams said, "and that's what happened here." Captain Williams and Leo Donovan cautioned that there was still much work to be done, particularly on the remaining cases.

The *Courier Express* interviewed family of some of the victims for their reactions to Christopher's indictment. Glenn Dunn's mother was quoted, "I know the Lord said 'vengeance is mine.' I know the Bible says we shouldn't hate. But Lord help me, I hate him! I hate him! I hate him!" The reporter described Mrs. Dunn's voice as suffused with "anger and grief, with a pungent overlay of bitterness." The reporter noted that though Christopher had not been convicted, Mrs. Dunn and other members of the family seemed to assume that he was the .22 Caliber Killer. Mrs. Dunn stated that she was grateful for the indictment but felt that it hadn't come soon enough. "It took them (investigators) seven months to get into this thing. Now that they've caught him, my son can rest in peace. I'm glad they caught him and I hope he gets what he deserves." She believed that "if seven white men had been killed, they would have been grabbing any black man off the street. Seven months . . . that really hurt me."

Mr. Dunn said, "I just hope to God the man does some time."

Emanuel Thomas's widow spoke of the grief she and her young daughters still suffered. The girls missed their father intensely. She dreaded the coming summer, the first for her daughters without their daddy. Of the indictment, "All I can say is that I'm glad. I had stopped reading the newspapers and looking at TV. My nerves are shot. Every time they said there was nothing new, I'd start to cry."

Joseph McCoy's mother said she found no comfort. Every day, she said, her son's death still hurt. "There were so many things I never got to say to Joe before he died. I'm just hurt."

Neighbors of Joseph Christopher expressed their own hurt and shock. Several spoke of Joe's generosity, how he had done home repairs for little or no money and helped so many people on the block. An elderly woman described Joe as "a good kid," saying he had tried so hard to get a job last summer. A woman who lived next door to the Christophers told a reporter that her own memories of Joe offered her no way "to connect him with that other business," meaning the murders. Speaking of the enormous media attention suddenly focused on her street, she added, "I feel involved in something I don't like being a part of."

One resident said of Joe, "To see a person who just helped everybody and to hear it's possible he could have committed crimes . . ." She shook her head. The neighbors, she said, especially the senior citizens, were heartbroken.

Another said, "It's like my own son going down the drain. I hope this isn't true. Honest to God, it kills me."

Among the day's coverage was an article listing the area's "8 Black Slaying Victims" with a paragraph on each individual. The list included the four .22 Caliber victims along with Roger Adams and Wendell Barnes, the two men stabbed to death in Buffalo and Rochester respectively, and cab drivers Parler Edwards and Ernest Jones. This was another obstacle that Christopher's defense attorneys would perpetually have to contend with, in the court of public opinion if not an actual courtroom. The remaining unsolved crimes were mentioned in story after story on the crimes for which he had been charged, particularly the grisly murders of the cab drivers. Though there was no indication, much less any evidence, that Christopher had any connection to the deaths of Parler Edwards and Ernest Jones, the so-called cabbie killings had already become almost inextricably tied in the public mind to the .22 Caliber Killer.

Despite the confidence expressed by key members of the task force and the positive reinforcement from the media, some felt it was a bit early to open the celebratory champagne. The *Buffalo Evening News* ran an article on May 3 with the headline "Case Against Christopher Is Weak, Experts Assert." The *News* had consulted three prominent defense attorneys who were all of the opinion that evidence revealed so far appeared insufficient to convince a jury beyond a reasonable doubt. Though Cosgrove had called the ballistics evidence presented to the grand jury "conclusive," one of the attorneys asserted that ballistics tests were "judgmental, not conclusive," particularly in the absence of a weapon. The Sturm-Ruger 10/22 owned by Christopher still had not been found. Investigators had been able to obtain a sales slip from a local gun center showing the purchase of such a rifle by Nicholas Christopher in 1974.

The legal experts described the grand jury testimony of the two nurses as legally vulnerable, based on past rulings in New York courts that had deemed statements of patients to medical personnel caring for them as privileged communication, as Dillon and Mahoney had argued before Judge Green. One of the attorneys interviewed said, "It looks like they're a long way from making this case. Under other circumstances I doubt there would have been an indictment at all."

The subject of the sealed indictment remained in county jail down in Georgia pending his extradition hearing. Military authorities refused to comment on the investigation or on Christopher's status, though the base's public information officer told a reporter, "I doubt very seriously if he even knows he's been indicted."

Kevin Dillon and Mark Mahoney were perhaps wondering the same thing. The defense attorneys were quickly finding out that the vigorous efforts of investigators and the massive publicity were not to be their only challenges—nor even their primary ones. Communicating with their client about anything, on any reasonable level, was proving difficult.

Christopher had shut down on Kevin Dillon. He would not talk to him. He would speak only to Mark Mahoney, and even then, not to great effect. With the amount of work to be done on the case, the legal research, and sheer number of persons to be interviewed at both Fort Benning and in Buffalo, Mahoney could not afford to spend all his time with Christopher.

Lobbett and Rash had remained at Fort Benning until May 3. They had interviewed witnesses to the Leonard Coles stabbing, reinterviewed the nurses and other personnel who had interacted with Christopher, and taken sworn statements from Raiford Ames, Father Freeman, Christopher Corwin, and the guard who had been present when Christopher had asked to speak with Zach DiFusco.

Zach had been informed that Joe wanted to see him. Zach was willing to go to Fort Benning, but Leo Donovan nixed the idea.

The army provided investigators with their records on Christopher, including the case file on the Coles stabbing and nursing notes right up to the time of Christopher's transfer to the local sheriff. Christopher had not said a lot during his waning days at Fort Benning, but he had spoken briefly of the self-inflicted injury to his penis, telling nurses that he had been drugged at the time and wasn't thinking straight. He claimed the drugs had been given to him against his will and without his knowledge. On a similar note, one thing that Christopher had communicated to his defense attorneys was his belief that he was being poisoned while in the stockade. That's why he had stopped eating, because of the poisoned food. He feared the jail food was tainted as well.

Kevin Dillon did not make things easy on Sam Slade at the extradition hearing. As an officer of the New York state police and senior task force member, Slade appeared in a Georgia courtroom on May 8 on behalf of authorities requesting Christopher's extradition to New York. Dillon challenged Slade on the fact that he had never met Joseph Christopher and therefore could not personally verify that the individual in the county jail cell was, in fact, the person named in the indictment. Slade conceded that he had only seen photographs of Christopher and not the man himself.

Though the judge ultimately ruled in favor of the lawmen who had come to escort Joseph back to Buffalo, Dillon's arguments at the hearing were a precursor and unsubtle message to prosecutors: he intended to give his client the vigorous defense he was constitutionally guaranteed.

Mark Mahoney was meanwhile in state supreme court in Buffalo requesting that the two search warrant applications should be sealed, arguing that disclosure of the documents, which contained the statements of the two army nurses, could impede his client's right to a fair trial. Mahoney argued that prosecution news leaks had already severely damaged Christopher's chances for an unprejudiced jury trial. Attorneys representing the city's major newspapers and television stations offered strenuous objection to the sealing of the search warrant applications. Justice Theodore Kasler requested the media to turn over transcripts of their reporting on Joseph Christopher, stating he was "distressed" and "bothered" about confidential prosecution leaks that had been reported on television prior to Christopher's indictment.

Therese Christopher had returned to Georgia for the extradition hearing. During her few days home following her first trip to see Joe with Dillon and Mahoney, Therese had taken steps to remortgage her house in order to pay for her son's legal fees. She stayed with Joe outside his cell during the hearing. Immediately after its conclusion, Joseph was turned over to Sam Slade, Leo Donovan, and Peter Scaccia of the Erie County Sheriff's Office for the trip to Buffalo. The Georgia judge instructed the New York lawmen not to speak with or question the suspect during the journey.

New York Governor Hugh Carey provided a twin-engine turboprop plane for the extradition. Christopher sat alone and silent during the four-hour flight.

The plane landed at the Niagara Falls Air Force base at 8:35 p.m., met by Ed Cosgrove, assistant DA Karl Keuker, and a contingent of task force members from the state police, along with the media. The question arose among the lawmen of how to conceal Christopher's face. They still did not want his image broadcast, though his picture had already appeared in the papers. Someone suggested putting a paper bag over his head. Trooper Amador Ortiz remembered that he had his son's gray knit ski mask in his car. Ortiz retrieved the mask, which was placed over Christopher's head before he was removed from the plane.

News photographers captured photos of Joseph Christopher, in handcuffs, waist chain, bulletproof vest, and the ski mask, standing outside the plane in the custody of Edward Cosgrove and state police. Before departing for the Erie County Holding Center, Cosgrove, Keuker, and the state troopers posed for a smiling group photograph.

Christopher was seated in a car between Donovan and Slade. Three cars headed in tandem to the holding center—two intended as decoys to throw the press off the scent of the prisoner. The ruse worked. Reporters chased one of the cars containing state troopers to the driveway of the holding center while the vehicle carrying the prize sped into the garage, doors slamming shut behind it.

In leg irons, manacles with a chain that passed beneath his groin and wound around his waist, a bulletproof vest, and the gray ski mask, Joseph was led into court for his arraignment on Monday, May 11. Deputies held his shackled arms on either side as Leo Donovan led the way with his hand grasping Christopher's waist chain.

The bulletproof vest had been ordered by Sheriff Kenneth Braun, who said, "I don't want another Dallas here," referencing the shooting of accused presidential assassin Lee Harvey Oswald. Security was extremely tight. Scores of law enforcement officers formed a human corridor through which Joseph passed on his walk to the courtroom as scores of reporters hung on stairs and any available space in the hallway to film and photograph the procession.

Inside the courtroom, Justice Samuel Green instructed officers to remove the ski mask. Assistant District Attorney Karl Keuker objected.

The mask was needed, he explained, because Christopher had not yet appeared in a lineup. Prosecutors did not want to take a chance on witnesses being influenced by seeing the suspect's face on television or in newspapers ahead of time (though his photo had already appeared on both). Judge Green was unmoved. "I will not arraign a defendant without knowing and seeing who he is. I don't know whether that is Joseph Christopher or someone else beneath that mask, and I want it removed. Otherwise, get him out of here."

Keuker had deputies and officers surround Christopher to shield his face from view of the spectators and press. The mask and handcuffs were removed.

The indictment was read. Christopher was informed of his right to an attorney.

"Do I need an attorney?" he asked the judge.

"You should have an attorney," Judge Green replied.

"I don't want an attorney," he said. "Do you have evidence against me?"

The judge explained that he had been indicted based on evidence presented to a grand jury. Christopher told the judge, "I don't feel they have anything against me." He entered a plea of not guilty and said he would represent himself.

Over his defense attorneys' objections, Christopher had an exchange with Judge Green.

"Do you feel you can represent yourself?" the judge asked.

"Yes, sir," Joseph responded. He conceded that he had no legal training.

"Don't you understand the law is very technical?" Green asked. "How will you be able to defend yourself?"

"I will represent myself," he insisted. "You ask me a question and I'll answer it."

Dillon and Mahoney tried to quiet Christopher but he persisted. "I don't feel I need a lawyer," he told the judge, further stating that he would not cooperate with any lawyers. The courtroom was stunned. Therese Christopher and Joe's sister Sophia sat silently among the spectators.

Mahoney spoke up. "Your Honor, I'd like a moment to speak with my client."

Dillon and Mahoney spoke to Joe in hushed tones. Judge Green then asked the defendant if he wanted to speak with his mother. "No, sir," Christopher replied. He still insisted he would defend himself.

Judge Green asked why he didn't want the attorneys hired by his family to represent him. Christopher responded, "I'll represent myself, sir. I don't want no lawyers."

Judge Green called a recess. When he resumed, the judge told Joseph that he could represent himself. However, Judge Green was appointing Kevin Dillon and Mark Mahoney "to advise him at all stages" of the trial. The judge further informed Christopher that he was ordering a psychiatric examination to determine if he was mentally competent to stand trial. This drew a fervent objection from the defendant: "I understand what the charges are, and I don't want to see any doctors. I'm not going to communicate with any doctors."

Judge Green ordered him to undergo a mental competency exam by a psychiatrist of his attorneys' choosing. Joseph persisted in saying he did not want to see a doctor and would not cooperate.

The arraignment lasted forty-five minutes. Judge Green ordered Joseph Christopher to be held without bail. The ski mask was again placed over Joseph's face and he was escorted back to the holding center.

For Kevin Dillon and Mark Mahoney, their client's behavior at the arraignment was only a minor preview of things to come.

Chapter 15

"**THERE IS A** firmly established right to self representation under the 6th amendment. The right can be exercised by an individual even when the exercise of the right is to his own detriment," Kevin Dillon wrote in a memo to Mark Mahoney. Their client's surprise announcement in court had forced Dillon to scrutinize legal rulings on the matter of self-representation. He prepared a detailed three-page memo with citations that ended with his conclusions on the issue.

"In sum, it appears to me that Christopher has an absolute right to represent himself . . . The court must conduct an examination to determine whether he understands the advantages and disadvantages and possible pitfalls of self representation. If he is possessed of at least average intelligence, then his legal knowledge or lack thereof apparently becomes irrelevant. In other words," Dillon wrote, "if he wants to screw himself, the constitution will provide the lubrication."

Their best option, of course, would be to persuade Christopher to change his mind and allow them to represent him. Whether this could be accomplished remained to be seen. If so, it seemed it would have to be Mahoney who did the persuading, since Christopher refused to speak to Kevin Dillon at all. He would not even acknowledge Dillon's presence when they were in the same room. He gave no explanation, except to say that he did not want to communicate with Kevin.

Not that his communication with Mark Mahoney was much better. In the couple of times Mahoney had visited him at the holding center, he had found Christopher lying on his bed with a towel over his face. When

Mahoney attempted to discuss incriminating statements Christopher had made in the army, he had merely responded with, "Don't worry about that. I'll take care of it."

Based on their own interaction with him and the limited information they had so far, Dillon and Mahoney had little doubt that Joseph Christopher had some mental instability, at the very least. Determining the extent of his apparent mental problems would be key, though this created another highly sensitive problem: Christopher balked at any suggestion that he might have mental issues. This may have accounted for why his attitude toward Dillon had suddenly gone from aloof silence to thinly veiled hostility. Christopher seemed to believe that Dillon was the sole source of instigation for Judge Green ordering a psychiatric exam.

Before the attorneys could delve further into the question of Joseph's mental competence or the prospect of him representing himself at trial, there were other pressing matters. Christopher had to appear in lineups at the district attorney's office on the afternoon of May 12.

Twenty-seven witnesses, including seven from New York City and one from the Rochester slaying, were brought in for the lineups, which were held in the grand jury room. Deputies walked Christopher over via an underground tunnel that connected the Erie County Holding Center to the district attorney's office, located directly across the street on Delaware Avenue. Christopher again wore the ski mask, along with leg irons and manacles, all of which were removed for the actual witness viewings, of course.

A total of six men were placed in the lineup. Along with Joseph Christopher were five decoys, which included two assistant DAs, two police academy recruits, and a recruit from the Coast Guard Academy named Edward Silvestrini. There were eighteen individual lineups. The process lasted more than five hours. Silvestrini, as a young cadet who had been told without explanation to immediately report to the district attorney's office, later said he felt that of all the men who participated in the lineups that day, Christopher appeared to be the least anxious. Over and over, they were instructed to change clothes and hats, don numbers, and parade in front of a closed room filled with dozens of law enforcement officers and revolving witnesses. "I was nervous," Silvestrini recalled. "You could feel the heavy atmosphere. It was definitely serious business. It went on and on. By the end I was feeling exhausted, both from the tension and the time we'd spent.

"Christopher really seemed unfazed by the whole thing, which I thought was kind of amazing. I mean, I was just there as a decoy and it had me on edge. I only remember him saying one thing the whole day. Lunch had been sent over from the holding center and I remember him asking if he could have more cookies. Very polite and real casual about it, just asked for more cookies, as if we were at a picnic."

Dennis Vacco would one day serve as New York State Attorney General. On the day of the lineups, he was a twenty-eight-year-old assistant DA, tasked with being a lineup decoy and reporting on the event to prosecutor Karl Keuker. Afterward, Vacco gave his impression that Christopher's demeanor was of a cool and calculated individual with an aura of cockiness about him. His report noted that Christopher spoke very little, but Vacco and fellow ADA Michael Stebick both related one particular exchange that stood out. About two hours in, Christopher and the stand-ins were instructed that during the next lineup they would each be required to say, "You fucking nigger." Christopher had raised his hand and said, "Excuse me, sir, but I don't swear." He then added, "But I do say fuck."

Five of the twenty-seven witnesses identified Joseph Christopher. Among the five were Albert Menefee and Calvin Crippen, the two men who had survived knife attacks in Buffalo on New Year's Eve and New Year's Day, respectively. Ivan Frazer, who had been slashed on the Long Island Railroad on December 22, also picked out Christopher immediately. "There's the son of a bitch," Frazer had muttered when he spotted Christopher. A woman who witnessed the fatal stabbing of Luis Rodriguez in Manhattan also identified Christopher.

The nurse who had interrupted the strangulation of Collin Cole in the hospital did not identify anyone, nor was anyone identified as the murderer of Wendell Barnes in Rochester.

Witnesses to the four .22 caliber shootings viewed the lineups. Of the Emanuel Thomas murder, Frenchy Cook was the only one to identify a suspect. He picked assistant DA Michael Stebick. A witness to the

Menefee stabbing also picked Stebick. Only one witness to the Harold Green murder identified a suspect from the lineups; he picked one of the police recruits. On the murder of Joseph McCoy in Niagara Falls, none of the observers made an identification.

Three witnesses to the Glenn Dunn homicide were present—Madona Gorney, Larry Robinson, and Kenny Paulson. Initially, only Madona Gorney identified a suspect. She picked Joseph Christopher as the man she had seen sitting outside the Tops market just prior to the shooting. Kenny Paulson, who had actually seen the shooter, did not identify anyone. Not at first.

John Regan had made two more follow-up visits to Paulson since reinterviewing him on April 20. He had asked him again if he knew Joseph Christopher. Paulson said no. Two of Paulson's older sisters had been present and said that they did know the Christophers. Kenny did offer some new information, however. He now remembered seeing a white man sitting outside Tops that night, before the shooting. He described him as a white male wearing wire-rimmed glasses and a dark hooded jacket. This sounded very much like the description given by Madona Gorney of the man she had seen.

Regan visited Kenny again five days later, and this time Kenny remembered that the person he'd seen sitting outside Tops had been dressed exactly like the shooter. He now gave a much more specific description: white male, seventeen to twenty-five years of age, light brown hair, clean shaven, wearing silver wire-rimmed glasses, a blue hooded sweatshirt, and jeans. The man's height was between five feet seven and five feet nine and his weight about 160 pounds. Kenny said the man had been sitting on the railroad ties with his hands in his pockets, staring straight ahead. When he'd first seen the man, Kenny said, the hood on the man's jacket had been down. When the man fled from Glenn Dunn's car, the jacket hood had been up.

Kenny's memory seemed to have improved markedly. Regan asked him if he'd be able to identify this person and Kenny had replied that he could if he saw him in person. At the lineup, Kenny hadn't identified anyone. As Kenny exited, John Regan met him in the hallway.

"Kenny, what happened?" Regan asked.

Paulson hemmed and hawed. Regan didn't push. Paulson left. He came back a few minutes later and told Regan that after thinking a little more, he could identify someone after all. He gave Regan the numbers that the man had been wearing in the two lineups he had viewed. They were the numbers worn by Joseph Christopher.

———————

A second grand jury was convened in an effort to secure additional indictments against Christopher. This time the jurors heard from a variety of witnesses, including Raiford Ames, Christopher Corwin, Albert Menefee, Calvin Crippen, and Madona Gorney. Kenny Paulson also testified, but now he said the shooter had blond hair.

The ballistics evidence presented this time was stronger. Michael Dujanovich, ballistics technician at the Central Police Lab, had conducted a meticulous analytical comparison of evidence from the four crime scenes against items seized in the search warrants. Among those items were a .22 caliber cartridge and two fired cartridge cases, all exhibiting a wedge-shaped firing pin impression. One of the cartridges held a misfire. It had a firing impression on it but the bullet was still seated in the cartridge case. A positive comparison was established between these three items and the fired cartridge cases recovered from the Dunn, Green, and Thomas homicides. Bullet fragments from the McCoy murder had already been linked to the first three shootings. Dujanovich testified that this indicated the same firearm was used to fire, or attempt to fire, all of these components. Based on the examination of the markings on the recovered evidence, the most probable weapon was a Ruger model 10/22 rifle. Dujanovich had researched the firearm question extensively. He knew of no other weapon that would leave the combination of markings found. The rotary magazine recovered at the Weber Street home had a Ruger logo. Dujanovich testified that he was not aware of any other firearm with a rotary-type magazine of those specific dimensions.

A superseding indictment was handed up on May 28, recharging Christopher with the murders of Dunn, Green, and Thomas, and attempted murder of Albert Menefee and Calvin Crippen. Two days earlier, a Manhattan grand jury had indicted him for the murder of Luis

Rodriguez and the slashing of Ivan Frazer. New York City delayed setting an arraignment date, as the grand jury there was still investigating any involvement Christopher may have had in the remaining Midtown Slasher cases.

No indictment came from Rochester. Nothing had even been presented to a grand jury in that jurisdiction, as they had nothing to present. Christopher had not mentioned Rochester in his confessions, a detective told reporters, and they had reached a dead end in linking him to the murder of Wendell Barnes. The lineup witness had failed to identify him, and two Canadians who witnessed the stabbing had informed Rochester authorities that they were unable to identify Christopher from photos sent to them.

Erie County wasted no time in scheduling an arraignment on the superseding indictment. Mark Mahoney accompanied Christopher to the downtown Buffalo courthouse on May 29. As opposed to the arraignment two weeks prior, this second appearance was a routine proceeding that lasted ten minutes with no surprise announcements from the accused. Mahoney entered pleas of not guilty to all charges. Judge William Flynn asked the defendant if he wished to have Kevin Dillon and Mark Mahoney represent him and Christopher replied, "Yes, sir."

It was Christopher's first court appearance without the ski mask. Reporters noted how little resemblance there was between Christopher and the composite sketches that had been circulated during the manhunt. Ed Cosgrove refused to comment on the matter. Some task force members pointed out to the press that Christopher had lost a great deal of weight since the killings last fall. The weight loss, however, did not explain the wide disparity between the facial features depicted in the .22 Caliber Killer composites and those of Joseph Christopher. Political cartoonist Tom Toles drew renderings of the composite and the suspect placed side by side with the caption, "Helpful Clue of the Year Award, presented to the multimillion dollar Federal Suspect Sketch Program." A follow-up cartoon by Toles titled "The prosecution defends the .22 caliber sketch" listed the various differences between "sought" and "arrested" and ended with the observation, "Same sketch can be used equally well in any case for any suspect."

Though few of the investigators commented publicly on it, the lack of resemblance between the sketches and Christopher were not lost on them. Some felt dismayed that the composites had turned out to be more hindrance than help. As Joe Cooley quipped years afterward, "We were looking for a guy who looked like Jack Armstrong and instead he looked like Al Pacino."

Investigators meanwhile scoured the land around the Ellington cabin with metal detectors in search of the gun, to no avail. They continued interviewing Christopher's friends and acquaintances in an effort to further build their case, and either find the Ruger or, in the absence of that, find out what became of it.

There was also the prickly matter of whether Christopher had an accomplice. The GI from the stockade who had told police what Joe had said about having "wasted" blacks with a friend could not remember the name Joe had mentioned. Investigators asked him to undergo hypnosis in the hope of enhancing his memory, but he refused.

Questioning of Christopher's known friends and associates had so far not produced any viable candidates. According to everyone police spoke to, in fact, Joe didn't appear to have been spending time with anyone around the time of the murders, despite what he had reportedly said to the soldier in the stockade about hanging out at a buddy's apartment talking about survival training and nutrition, presumably in between killings. The prospect of an accomplice was all the more intriguing because of the wide discrepancy between certain witness descriptions of the gunman and the failure of some observers at the lineup—witnesses to the Niagara Falls shooting, for instance—to identify Christopher (or any of the decoys who looked similar to him) as the shooter. If Christopher had indeed had an accomplice—perhaps a blond man—that could explain why bystanders at the different murders, committed with one gun, had described such different-looking men. It could also explain where the sawed-off Ruger could be found: perhaps in the possession of the accomplice.

Determining whether a friend had aided Christopher—or even whether such a person actually existed—was problematic. The deeper they dug into the history of Joseph Christopher, particularly his recent past, the more contradictions, oddities of behavior, and outright lies—or fantasies—of

Christopher they uncovered. If the accomplice did not exist, it wouldn't be the only relationship that was a figment of Joseph's imagination.

Darryl Smith and John Sullivan had met Joseph Christopher on the day they entered the army. Darryl and John, who were both from Cheektowaga, were friends who had enlisted together. An army sergeant had introduced them to Christopher on the morning they were sworn in. The sergeant said that Joe needed a ride to the airport and Darryl was glad to help. When they got to his car, Darryl asked Joe if he wanted to go home first, since they had five hours before they had to catch the plane. Joe said no. Darryl introduced Joe to his family and invited him over to his house. Darryl's parents and sister had come for the swearing-in. Joe seemed to be the only guy who didn't have any family or friends there.

Joe spent the afternoon at the home of the Smith family. Darryl recalled that Joe wasn't much of a talker. He didn't initiate any of the conversations. To Darryl, it seemed like he was in a trance most of the time. About the only time Joe would say anything was if Darryl or his dad asked him something. Joe said he was a carpenter and a mechanic. Darryl asked about his family and Joe told him he had a wife and four-year-old daughter.

Darryl, John Sullivan, and Joe were housed in the same barracks at Fort Jackson, where they remained for seven days. Neither of them spoke with him much. Joe brushed aside questions about his family and became evasive when he was asked about them. He mainly kept to himself and either read the Bible, which he would even read by flashlight after lights out, or *Guns & Ammo* magazine.

Neither of them ever heard Christopher utter any racial remarks. They did recall one little hassle where a black soldier had grabbed a magazine out of Joe's hand while he was reading. Joe jumped up and looked like he was going to punch the guy but he didn't; he just told him not to mess around with his stuff.

Joe had an old beat-up blue gym bag that he carried everywhere; he would never let go of it. He had it from the time they met him until they got to Fort Benning. Neither of them knew what Joe kept in the bag. He never put it down or opened it in their presence. Joe was even carrying the bag when they left Fort Jackson en route to Fort Benning. All the guys' duffel bags were piled on the ground but Joe held his blue gym bag and kept walking continuously up and down among the duffel bags, smiling to himself.

At Fort Benning, they had been in the same barracks, but Joe was in a different building. They pretty much only saw him in the mess hall, where Joe worked as a server, and just said hello. Darryl said he didn't talk to Joe much after Christmas leave because Joe always appeared to ignore him when he did try to talk to him.

Darryl and John had both traveled to Buffalo for the Christmas holidays but neither had seen Joe on the trips to or from. Two weeks before leave, Darryl said Joe had told him he wasn't going home for Christmas. A couple days later, Joe said he was going to visit friends in New Jersey at Christmas.

As for the stabbing at Fort Benning, neither Darryl nor John had witnessed it. They only saw Joe being put into the MP car. They'd heard that on the day before the stabbing, Joe had "flipped out" and started taking his clothes off in the mess hall line.

Investigators showed Darryl and John all of the composite sketches. They both said that Joe didn't look like any of them, especially not the one depicting the perpetrator in the Niagara Falls homicide.

———

John Regan interviewed a young lady named Grace who was a friend of Joe's sister, Lorraine. Grace was the same age as Joe and had known him since they were both fifteen. Grace had dated Joe casually in the year prior to him joining the service. At least Grace had considered it casual. She had therefore been taken completely by surprise when Joe had proposed to her the previous summer.

She and Joe had been going to the movies a lot, she said, mainly at the Como Mall. This prompted Regan to ask if they had ever eaten at the Burger King across the street—that was where the Harold Green murder had occurred—but Grace said no. She described Joe as all of his other friends had: a quiet man who was never hostile to anybody and liked hunting and working on cars. Very close to his father, had taken his death very hard, and visited the grave almost daily. As for what Joe wanted out of life—he had told her he wanted to get a good job, settle down, and live in the country. One day the previous August, he had asked her to go for a ride. He drove to a park and asked her to get out and walk, which she did. They sat down under a tree and he asked her to marry him. She told him no.

Grace emphasized what a total surprise this had been. She had always considered their relationship more brother-sister than anything else, nothing serious at all. She'd been dating someone else at the time too. Asked about Christopher's reaction, she said she didn't think he took it badly. He'd asked if they could still be friends.

The last time she saw Joe was in October. They'd gone to see the movie *Kramer vs. Kramer*. Grace had heard that Joe was coming home for Christmas, and she had told his sister Lorraine that she'd like to see him, but Lorraine said he didn't want to see her.

Grace and Joe had exchanged a couple of letters while he was in the army.

———

Joe never told his family that he proposed to Grace. In his waning days in the army, however, he had written a letter on the subject of marriage to the elderly Bianchis. After his legal troubles were straightened out, he wrote, he would like to be married. He wrote that he had asked Grace to marry him, that she was the best he knew and she'd always been special with him, but claimed there was another girl who had his child. He gave her name. He thought the Bianchis might be related to her. He wanted their help, because in Italian families, he knew, marriages are sometimes arranged. He promised to give love and respect if somebody would marry him. Kindness was easy for him to give, he wrote. He wanted to take care of his child.

As far as anyone knew, the girl did not exist.

———

Therese Christopher and her daughters had been subpoenaed to appear before the second grand jury. The *Buffalo Evening News* quoted a source as saying that the family would be questioned as part of a "mechanical and methodical" probe into Joseph's background. This raised some unsettled legal questions on state laws concerning family confidentiality privileges.

Prosecutors, sources told the *News*, would have to be careful in eliciting information from Christopher's relatives.

Karl Keuker handled the questioning of Joseph's mother and sisters. Legal matters aside, the family had no knowledge of Joe being involved in any of the crimes and found it impossible to believe that he could be.

They had little to offer about Joe's activities while he was home on Christmas leave. Therese and her son-in-law had picked him up at the bus station on Christmas Day. The week in between had been ordinary. Therese said that Joe had mostly just stayed around the house and slept on the couch a good portion of the time. He'd soaked his feet a lot because they had blisters that were hurting him badly.

The only day during the Christmas holidays that stood out in memory for Therese and her daughters was New Year's Eve. Therese and Sophia had spent the afternoon shopping at various stores and Joe had driven them around. After dropping Sophia off at her home around 3:30 p.m., Therese and Joe had returned home themselves. Joe had stayed at the house until around 9:00 p.m., when one of Therese's sisters had picked them up for a family gathering. Asked what Joe had been wearing that evening, Therese recalled that he wore a beret, jeans, and a sweater with a light jacket.

Karl Keuker questioned Therese about the letter she had written to Joe's commanding officer in the army. "You indicated that based on your experience in a psychiatric hospital, at Gowanda State, that you had an opinion that perhaps Joseph has become a manic-depressive schizophrenic. Is that correct?"

"Yes."

"Could you perhaps maybe just enlighten this Grand Jury as to what you meant by that?"

"Schizophrenic is a person with two different personalities," Therese said. "Manic-depressive, he is temperamental at times and depressed at times."

"When you say temperamental, would you say he had a temper?"

"Not a severe temper, no."

"When you indicated that he was schizophrenic, which you defined as having a split personality—I'm trying to find out what you meant.

What two personalities you observed in him during this time period of 1980 before he went into the service?"

"I didn't think he was that way before he went into the service, I thought he was depressed," Therese answered. "But, until this incident happened down there, I thought he's not thinking right anymore. I knew he was depressed at home but I believed it was because he wasn't able to get a good-paying job. And he—he tried several different jobs. He would give me money that he earned just doing extra work for people whenever he could. But, after he started this starvation diet business, he said that after a few days he felt really good and that his thinking was clearer.

"And army food, he thought there was something in it that, you know, it would just cause him to feel uncomfortable and bloated. And he would go off jogging by himself and he'd go for sometimes six days without eating, just drinking fluids. And I told him that this was a dangerous thing to do, that it changed the blood chemistry and sometimes his reactions and even his thinking would be—wouldn't be normal, if he insisted on starving like that. He had lost quite a considerable amount of weight in the first month or so. He had gone from a hundred and fifty-two to a hundred and ten pounds, which was to me too severe. And I thought if he wasn't eating right, he wasn't thinking right."

Keuker inquired if Therese had told Joseph about what had transpired in Buffalo when she went to see him Georgia. "No, I didn't say what happened. I just told him that we all loved him and he was worried about—he was very—he had been in the hospital. He told me he felt that he was being drugged, that he felt dopey. He couldn't put two sentences together. He was given a letter, it took him almost ten minutes to get it opened and read it. Very catatonic. The second time I visited him he was in a different jail and he was much brighter, much more responsive."

"You never discussed with him the events that occurred in Buffalo, which he was being accused of or charged with?"

"No," Therese answered. "He apologized for all the trouble that was going on."

The family had visited Joe at the holding center since his return to Buffalo. The grand jury could not explore the nature of their conversations because of family confidentiality privileges. Their visits with Joe, however, had not included any talk about the charges against him and were revealing only of his distraught state of mind.

Joe was terribly worried about the effect that all of this was having on his family. They assured him of their love and support. His sister Lorraine had tried her best to comfort and cheer him during her visit to the jail. They talked mostly of family matters. Lorraine tried to make him laugh. Joe cried for much of the time. They said the rosary together.

Donna Vanalden had accompanied Mrs. Christopher on a visit to the holding center. Joe had not said much. Donna didn't know what to say beyond the customary, "How are you doing?" She blurted something about how she never thought in a million years she'd ever see him in jail. He gave her a sad little smile through the mesh wire that separated them.

Therese had accepted the painfully obvious fact that her son was seriously mentally ill. She still could not conceive of him being a murderer, particularly not the racist assassin who was being portrayed in the press. Everyone who knew Joe found this absolutely impossible to believe, none more so than his black friends and coworkers, none of whom were called to testify. Grand jury proceedings are the domain of prosecutors. The accused is not permitted to call witnesses, nor are their attorneys allowed to be present during testimony.

Charles Walker had worked with Joe and Ernie Smith on the maintenance crew at Canisius. Charles and Ernie had grown up in the section of the east side known as the Fruit Belt. Charles still lived on Grape Street and was also a good friend of one of Parler Edwards's sons. Like everyone else in the city, Charles had been well aware of the attacks on black men that had paralyzed the community the previous fall and winter. He had been one of a group of African American men who had helped form a neighborhood watch to assure that people traveled in pairs and stayed safe during the killing spree. And, of course, he heard the news of the arrest and indictment of a suspect. Hearing the name, Joseph Christopher, had not rung a bell with Charles. It had not registered with him at all, in fact, until he happened to see a photo in the newspaper of the unmasked suspect, a photograph in which the man was pictured wearing glasses. He had looked closer, and finally said to himself, *Oh my God . . . that's Joey!*

As Charles Walker would later recall, "I ran down to the bus stop and waited for Ernie. He got off the bus and as soon as he saw me, we pointed at each other and we both said, '*Joey*?!' We just couldn't believe it. We could not believe that was our Joey."

The three of them had been good friends at Canisius. Ernie and Joe had been particularly tight. In addition to Ernie and Charles, there were several black men on the maintenance crew. As Charles recalled, "Everybody liked Joey. He was crazy, but I mean in a fun way. A real jokester, witty, always laughing. Just a crazy white boy.

"He was always cool with us. He was a lot of fun and we had a good time. We would have to clear the parking lot during snow storms and Joey drove the big plow. We'd go out there and throw snowballs at each other. Just doing what guys do.

"Joey popped pills all the time. I don't know what they were, but he'd be flying, acting silly. Me, him, and Ernie would go grab something for lunch. We'd go out to his pickup truck and he'd pop a pill. He offered some to us but we said no thanks. We were like, 'You're crazy, Joe.' He'd just laugh.

"He took us out to his cabin a couple times. It'd be the three of us and we'd hang out, talk, have a few beers. He showed us his guns and his hunting gear. He invited us to go hunting but it wasn't my thing. I told him I'd take some venison, though. I bought a house during the time we worked together and I remember him helping me out, giving me a lot of tips on some plumbing and home improvement work I had to do. He knew his stuff.

"I never detected a prejudiced bone in his body. The three of us were like brothers. We could never wrap our heads around what they were saying about him being this racist killer. It was like they must be talking about some other guy."

Charles thought about his friend in later years but still had no answer for how he could've become the infamous killer. "The only thing I could ever come up with was that it must've been a combination of the drugs he was taking and possibly being bullied. I could see him being bullied because Joey wasn't a tough guy. Ernie and I would tell him stories about

growing up in the Fruit Belt, the school of hard knocks, and he was mes-
merized. Joey was a really nice guy, and like I said, not a real tough guy,
and sometimes nice guys bear the brunt of being ridiculed and bullied.
Unfortunately, some people take kindness as a sign of weakness. In spite
of what went on with him, I remember him as a nice guy."

Police spoke with Louis, Joe's fishing buddy, who told them that he
and Joe used to meet for coffee all the time at Costanzo's Bakery. Leonard
Holmes had been Joe's boss at an auto repair shop in 1979. Both Louis
and Leonard were African American. Both said Joe had never shown any
signs of racism.

They spoke with his supervisors at Canisius, in addition to guys, both
black and white, who had either worked with or dealt with him. They
heard the same thing over and over: Joe was not a racist. Joe was not
hostile. The maintenance supervisor at Canisius who had fired Joe told
investigators that Joe hadn't even raised a fuss when he was let go. Other
than the instances of sleeping on the night shift, the offense that led to his
dismissal, Joe had been a great employee.

Reporters had the same experience. Joe's friends and acquaintances,
black and white, defended him. Donna Vanalden spoke with a reporter
on the condition of anonymity. "He was a sensitive, compassionate individual. I didn't consider him to be a loner because he had an outgoing
personality and was easy to get along with." She mentioned how she had
laughed at the idea of Joe being a suspect when the police had first come
to question her. "The whole thing is ridiculous, and I'm apprehensive
because mistakes have been made in the past where the wrong person has
been accused of something."

Members of the Bisonite Pistol and Rifle Club echoed the disbelief of Joe as a murderer. One of the club founders said, "He was a good
instructor, he was good on the range, and he was very safety conscious. He
wasn't a troublemaker and he was a good worker."

The only account of questionable behavior from Joe came from
gun club member John Hemphill, a black man, who told Bob Keeler of
Newsday, "When I first met him, he seemed like the typical timid kid. He
was a nice kid, and he was trying to learn [to shoot well]." Hemphill had
spent time on the range with Joe helping him perfect his skills. According

to Hemphill, Joe had even brought in a Ruger .22 caliber rifle and asked him to help zero it in, to make it more accurate. As time went on, he noted that Joe had a temper. "He had a short fuse. When he couldn't get it [shooting] like he wanted it, he would slam the gun down. I used to try to calm him down." Hemphill referred to Joe as "just gun-happy" and said he had a phobia about someone in his family taking his father's guns. Joe had wanted to be gun club president, he said, and was a little upset when Hemphill got the position instead.

Ernie Smith spoke of his friendship with Joe to a *New York Times* reporter. The only thing Ernie could recall Joe ever saying that even touched on race was that he had once "been ripped off by some blacks when he was a boy." Ernie said, "He never seemed to have any strong feelings about race. If he did these killings, something has to have come over him lately."

Unknown to police or press were two individuals who'd had encounters with Joe during the time of the killings that left them easily believing he was the murderer. Bobby Grot, the young boy who sat on a bench next to the stranger who told him his name was "JC, like Jesus Christ," recognized Joe Christopher instantly when he saw him on the TV news. Bobby told his parents about the incident, that the guy they kept showing on TV was the stranger who'd told him that bricks were for throwing "at niggers."

Kim Edmiston also recognized Christopher as the crazy man who had chased and assaulted her in the predawn hours of New Year's Day, 1981. As she later said, "I was dumbfounded when I saw him on TV. I said right away, 'Oh my God, that's him!' I had gotten a long and very close look at his face when he held me against the door and there was no doubt in my mind it was the same guy. That was the moment I realized who I was dealing with that night and I felt more lucky to be alive than I ever had at that particular time in my life.

"I thought about calling the police, but then I thought better of it. No way did I want to be involved in that media and legal circus that was playing out on TV and in the newspapers. I was just so relieved that my attacker was caught, I didn't really care who he was or exactly how he would be dealt with, just that he would be. And for far worse crimes than his assault on me." Decades afterward, Kim was able to describe what Christopher had been wearing that night, details that had only been divulged in sealed testimony.

Memory of the encounter remained with her in vivid detail. "Seeing those rapid frozen breaths in the air when I was walking to my apartment was one of the most terror-filled moments of my life. I felt foolish and overconfident for going back there and I knew no matter which way I went, either back to the car or to the house, that he was close enough to catch me. I didn't know if I was going to be robbed or raped or what, but I knew at that moment that he had waited there for me to come back, which was very horror-movie style horrific and terrifying to me. I also felt foolish for underestimating him based on his physical size. When I first saw him jogging down the street, I assumed he was a young teen because of his slight size and I didn't perceive him as being a big threat, just an oddity at 4:00 a.m. in the freezing cold. But once he charged me and slammed me against the front door I realized he had a lot of physical power and a ton of grown up bad intent.

"I always felt like him coming after me was impulsive, like I wasn't really what he was looking for but I was this opportunity that came along and he just reacted. The cops thought I was nuts when I told them he was marching and doing all these military-type moves. It made a little more sense when I heard he was in the army. I mean, as much as any of it could make sense. The way he acted through the whole thing was just beyond strange. Like he was playing this weird game that only he knew about."

Per the order of the court, two psychiatrists examined Joe at the Erie County Holding Center to assess his competency for trial.

Dr. John Wadsworth met Joseph for an hour in the presence of another physician and Kevin Dillon. In his report to Judge Green, Dr. Wadsworth wrote that Christopher was unwilling to discuss his recent hospitalizations in the army or the laceration of his penis, although in regard to his injury, he implied that he just wanted to get away from the jail. After his arrest, he believed his food was poisoned. Regarding Christopher's army hospitalizations, he wrote, "It was questioned at the time as to the existence of schizophrenic illness. It is apparently possible that such an illness did exist at that time."

Wadsworth noted that Christopher was aware of the charges against him and had a basic understanding of the roles of judge, jury, and attorneys.

"Mental status evaluation revealed a suspicious, distant individual who expressed hostility initially but who eventually seemed to relax enough to answer questions reasonably and even volunteer certain material towards the end," Wadsworth wrote. "He has a sensitive understanding of what questions to answer and what not to answer and was reluctant to approach any material even vaguely related to criminal activity.

"At times, he stared very suspiciously and hostilely at the examiner. His behavior in the interview situation was generally appropriate, although at other times he was noticed to be spending long periods of time in the cell alone, refusing TV, radio, or books. Occasionally he seemed overly suspicious, and at times he didn't seem to understand the questions well and accused me once of attempting to confuse him. There was a certain blandness of affect, and in some areas he seemed to deny the seriousness of the crimes of which he is accused.

"There is a definite paranoid quality. Some of this is a litigious quality and some may be a possible psychotic process that exists. His judgment has been fairly good in most situations although it's difficult to evaluate it completely. There are evidences of extremely poor judgment in a number of situations.

"At the present time, I find Mr. Christopher to be competent. I do believe that he understands the charges against him and can assist in his own defense. It is possible that his psychological state may prevent him from assisting in his defense in the future, but at the present time he seems more and more able to do so." Dr. Wadsworth gave a diagnosis of schizoid personality.

The second psychiatrist, Dr. George Molnar, did not offer a diagnosis. In a two-page report to the judge, Molnar described Joseph as a "slight young man of scant physical vigor" and wrote that he "was controlled and guarded and selective in his replies," but was otherwise quite cooperative and showed no evident hostility. "His answers were deliberate and carefully thought out, giving the impression that the appearance of logic and coherence was maintained with considerable effort."

Dr. Molnar found no evidence of delusional thinking, hallucinations, or clinical depression. Joseph was correctly oriented to time, person, and place. Molnar estimated his intelligence as within the normal to dull-normal range. "Judgment and insight appeared superficially intact, but it was my impression that his defenses were brittle and that aggressive probing into certain areas would have elicited some pathological material." Noting that Joseph was on no medication and had resumed eating, Dr. Molnar had noticed that the pupils of his eyes were unequal. "While this finding may be of little consequence, I think it is essential to conduct a neurological examination including an EEG and CAT scan."

Molnar questioned Joseph about the purpose of a trial and the roles of judge, jury, and attorneys, and felt his answers indicated an adequate grasp. "In conclusion, Joseph Christopher's behavior and mental and emotional processes are now much better organized and under better control than when he was examined in Georgia. It is my opinion that he is competent to stand trial, capable of instructing counsel and assisting in his defense."

On June 3, the court thus ruled Christopher competent. Justice William Flynn sealed the psychiatric exams.

Dillon and Mahoney were not pleased with either the examinations or the competency ruling, the latter of which could effectively mean that Joseph would be allowed to represent himself at trial. There was no telling when he might change his mind and decide once again that he didn't want any lawyers.

Mahoney complained that the psychiatrists had spent very little time with Christopher. And, as Mahoney knew well by this time, Joseph's behavior often changed from day to day, if not moment to moment. Despite what Joe had told Dr. Wadsworth about his willingness to work with his attorneys, he was back to refusing all contact with Kevin Dillon. Mahoney's visits with Joe were an exercise in futility. Rather than discussing his case, what Joe mostly wanted to talk about was his persistent belief that his food was being poisoned. On one occasion, he handed Mahoney a sample of his meal and insisted that he have it tested for the presence of poison. The only remotely relevant thing he would say concerning his case ran along the same lines; he had made those incriminating statements, he said, because the army had drugged him.

Joseph remained in isolation at the holding center under twenty-four-hour suicide watch. According to deputies who supervised him night and day, he did nothing but sleep or sit still on his bunk. He often kept the towel over his face and sometimes stuffed toilet paper in his ears. He wanted the TV removed from his cell.

He refused to submit to any medical tests, including the EEG and CAT scan that Dr. Molnar had advised as "essential." Joe would not explain his refusal to undergo testing, but it was his right to decline. His adamancy on the point could be traced back to his army days, and may have indicated wariness—or possibly a deep-rooted fear—of medical equipment. Twice during his brief time in the military, he had complained of a toothache. He had been sent to the dentist but balked when they wanted to take an X-ray. The dentist had refused to treat him without benefit of X-rays and Joseph had withdrawn from treatment rather than comply. His sudden aversion to X-rays seemed odd; a full set of dental X-rays had been taken during his military processing at Fort Jackson back in November.

As for Joseph's military records, the defense attorneys were not finding the army nearly as helpful to their cause as it had been to the task force. The provost marshal had testified before the second grand jury and remained in Buffalo for a time afterward in order to assist investigators, according to a newspaper account. For Dillon and Mahoney, information they requested from the army was trickling in at a slow pace, when it came at all.

There was plenty to do in the meantime. Dillon and Mahoney appeared in court in June to further argue against public disclosure of the search warrant applications. Justice Kasler had reserved decision on the matter. The defense team faced fervent opposition from attorneys representing the media. Dillon and Mahoney maintained that release of the documents would impair Christopher's right to a fair trial and make the news media "arbiters of guilt and innocence" rather than the courts.

Dillon and Mahoney were not alone in their feelings about harm being done to their client by biased pretrial publicity. The *Buffalo Evening News* printed a letter from a reader who complained that the press had already convicted Christopher. Councilman James Pitts had early on voiced his concern that publicity found to be prejudicial could inhibit a conviction. The *Columbus Ledger* had written critically of all the information that "seemed to be leaking from the Buffalo task force." The *Ledger* asked a New York television reporter, who in Buffalo is talking? "Who's not?" was the reply.

Negative portrayals of Christopher ranged from overt to subtle. The press persisted in claiming that Christopher had bragged of being a killer. (One black leader had publicly asked, rhetorically but with apparent sincerity, why there was a need for a trial at all, since Christopher was an admitted killer.) A local reporter who wrote of the case on a near daily basis consistently referred to Christopher as a high school dropout and repeatedly reminded readers that Christopher's defense was being paid by taxpayers, since his widowed mother's resources had run out.

There were also the inevitable instances of erroneous reporting, such as the allegations that Albert Menefee and Roger Adams had been bitten by their attacker and that officials had taken Christopher's dental impressions to compare with the bite marks. While impressions of Joseph's teeth had been made via court order, this material had been gathered, along with his blood and hair samples, so that investigators would have a complete profile, according to Edward Cosgrove. Medical records for Menefee and the autopsy report of Roger Adams indicated no bite marks on either victim, nor had witnesses to either attack—including Albert Menefee himself—reported any biting by the assailant.

Larry Little, the man who reported an attack by a knife-wielding white man on January 2, claimed he had bitten his assailant on the leg. Investigators had discounted Christopher as a suspect.

Occasional news accounts would bring up problems with the prosecution's case. Chief among these were the composite drawings. Much-touted during the investigation, they had now become lingering specters that haunted the district attorney. Dan Herbeck wrote a lengthy article in which he posed the question, "Could a man who looks so strikingly different from all the composite sketches issued of the killer be that killer?"

Cosgrove responded that the composite was a "tool—one of hundreds we employed during this lengthy investigation. It was never intended to be a picture of the person responsible." While he refused to comment directly on the discrepancy regarding Christopher, he said he was "very pleased and satisfied with Mr. Haefner's [sic] work."

Mark Mahoney assured the reporter that the composites "definitely will be playing a role" in the trial and took the opportunity to point out that eyewitness identification "is generally the least reliable form of testimony," adding that such discrepancies could also show "the capability of witnesses to pick somebody out of a lineup who looks nothing like the suspect they saw."

Horace Heafner also refused to comment directly on the sketches he'd drawn but said he'd much prefer to work with one good witness rather than a group of them. Leo Donovan said it wasn't unusual for sketches to bear little or no resemblance to a suspect. Others in the police department believed that Cosgrove had placed too much stock in the sketches and would pay for it in court. One source commented, "The defense is going to cream them on that one."

———————

"Officials Favor Insanity Plea by Christopher." On June 9, the *Buffalo Evening News* reported that prosecutors wanted Joseph Christopher "to enter a mental illness plea that would send him to a psychiatric institution rather than a prison for Buffalo's so-called .22-caliber killings and possibly related attacks on blacks." According to the article, unnamed senior law enforcement officials on the case viewed such a plea as "the best way to resolve the escalating legal proceedings," and wanted to convince Christopher's lawyers of the need for it. "The hoped-for prosecution scenario, sources said, would see the 25-year-old army private admit the crimes but plead 'not responsible' by reason of mental disease."

The article noted that the plea would have to be approved by Edward Cosgrove and Manhattan District Attorney Robert Morgenthau. Both declined comment on either the prospects or their hopes for an insanity plea.

Stating that they had not been approached on the matter by prosecutors, Kevin Dillon told the *News*, "We don't want a plea. We have not even considered the possibility of a plea. Our intention is to proceed through trial and acquittal."

A follow-up story in the next day's paper had Dillon clarifying that they did not intend to file an insanity defense "under the present circumstances." Without elaborating, he said, "As you know, this case changes from day to day."

News of a plea had provoked an immediate reaction from black leaders. The Reverend Walter L. Bryan of the Black Leadership Forum said that any willingness from prosecutors to accept a mental illness plea would be "upsetting." Others stated their position in stronger terms. "I think it would be just a further indication of the insensitivity on the part of the district attorney and his staff to the black community," the Reverend Will Brown was quoted, while another called an insanity course a "blatant betrayal of the confidence that the district attorney has requested from our community."

Ed Cosgrove stated that he would be the sole judge of any plea negotiation and said, "There has been no consideration of any plea of any kind relating to mental disease." He assured that Christopher would be "fully and firmly prosecuted under the law."

A Niagara County grand jury returned an indictment against Christopher on June 29 for the murder of Joseph McCoy. He was arraigned four hours later, transported under heavy guard to appear in court alongside Kevin Dillon, whom he ignored.

Joseph entered a plea of not guilty and said he would represent himself.

"GET THE HELL OUT OF HERE!"

Bob Schmitt ran to his front window and looked across Weber Avenue. His wife's uncle, Laverne Becker, stalked toward Mrs. Christopher's front porch, where a reporter stood with microphone in hand, cameraman standing by. "You have no business bothering these people!" Laverne screamed. "Leave these people alone!"

Laverne picked up a rock. Bob Schmitt flew out his front door and across the street. Bob managed to grab Laverne's arm as he wound up to hurl the rock at the news crew. "Get out!" Laverne shouted as they scrambled off the porch. "Stay away! You have no damn business being here!"

Bob managed to hold Laverne's arm so he couldn't throw the rock. It didn't stop his uncle's mouth, though. He raged at the reporters as they ran to their car.

"Red! What are you doing?" Bob pleaded.

"These people have no reason to come here!"

The news folks sped away. Bob's wife, Cheryl, came outside. It took them a while to calm him down. They understood. Laverne felt very protective of Mrs. Christopher and the girls. And the reporters could be relentless, that was for sure. One had barged into the Christopher home through the back door. Others would pound on the front door for minutes. Sometimes they were almost as intimidating as the vandals. For the past two and a half months, life hadn't been the same for anyone in Joe's circle.

Zach DiFusco endured his share of harassment. As a police officer and cousin of the accused killer, he was a prime target for reporters. When he declined to comment, a writer for the *Courier-Express* warned him, "It's not wise to refuse to cooperate with the press." Zach could handle the hassle. He was far more concerned about his Aunt Therese. He spoke with his superiors in the police department about the firecrackers thrown at her house and threatening phone calls she'd received before changing her number. Officials promised to look into it.

Angela Christopher graduated from high school that month. As she sat on stage with her class, the guest speaker went off about Joseph Christopher, referring to him as a monster.

After the ceremony, Angela approached the commencement speaker in a hallway. She told him her name and said, "Joe Christopher is my brother. I just wanted to thank you for a memorable graduation."

Angela turned, walked out of the building, and never looked back.

———

Not everyone in town thought of Joseph Christopher as a monster, even if he was guilty. Or especially not if he was guilty. A guard at the holding center looked in on the forlorn prisoner one day. "Joe," he said, "they should've given you a medal." Joe glanced up, gave a wan smile, and looked back down at the floor.

———

Joseph was arraigned in a Manhattan courtroom on July 20. Mark Mahoney and Frank Bress, the New York City defense attorney appointed to represent him, were present as Joseph pleaded not guilty to charges of murder, attempted murder, and assault in the first degree. The proceeding lasted only six minutes.

The arraignment had originally been scheduled for July 13 but had to be postponed when commercial airline US Airways refused to fly him, citing their policy of not carrying "people who are known to be dangerous." A charter plane service flew Christopher and Mahoney to and from New York City.

Pretrial hearings began in Buffalo two days later. The week prior, reinforced wire barricades had been erected outside the third-floor courtroom where the accused .22 Caliber Killer would have his days in court.

A trial date of September 8 had been set. Wade and Huntley hearings would come first. A Wade hearing addresses identification evidence, such as police lineups and issues related to witness IDs of a suspect. A Huntley hearing deals with the admissibility of statements that the prosecution contends were made by a defendant. Following closed-door conferences with prosecutors and defense attorneys, Justice William Flynn ruled that the pretrial hearings would be closed to press and public.

This decision did not sit well at all with the local media, who employed a battery of attorneys to argue that the hearings should be open to them. As Judge Flynn explained of his ruling, the hearings would disclose testimony of principal witnesses and much of the evidence to be presented at trial; however, "These hearings also will disclose evidence which might never be heard later at trial if the court grants the motion to suppress such evidence." Flynn's decision came as yet another blow to zealous reporters and journalists. Judge Kasler had earlier upheld his own ruling that the search warrant application should remain sealed, calling the document "highly prejudicial" to Christopher's fair trial rights.

Attorneys for the media argued that much of the information that would presumably be presented at the pretrial hearings had already been broadcast or published. Judge Flynn countered by stating that a lot of what had been disseminated thus far had come "from improper leaks to news media in violation of fair trial and free press principles," adding that the court did not wish "to add its own approval to the impropriety." Judge Flynn also issued a gag order on all those involved in the case.

Media attorneys made ongoing legal challenges to the closing of the hearing throughout the summer of 1981, twice delaying the proceedings. Judge Flynn met with the attorneys to hear their arguments. Following the meeting, the judge held firm with his decision. He further issued a gag order on them as well. The media took their arguments all the way to the Appellate Division of State Supreme Court in Rochester and US Supreme Court Justice Thurgood Marshall, to no avail. The hearings remained closed.

Kevin Dillon and Mark Mahoney spent the months of July, August, and early September waging battle on three major fronts. There was the examination of witnesses and arguments for suppression at the pretrial hearings. They also had to deal with the reluctance or refusal of prosecutors to turn over investigative material to them without court orders. There were ongoing arguments over what and how much of the mountain of material amassed by the task force investigation should be turned over to the defense. And then there was their client.

Joseph Christopher's dislike—or aversion, or distrust, or whatever it was—of Kevin Dillon had transformed into open hostility and vocal opposition to Dillon that bordered on verbal abuse.

As usual, Christopher's behavior could vary from day to day. The only aspect that remained constant was his apparent abhorrence of Dillon. He had also stopped speaking to his mother and would no longer see her when she came to the holding center to visit him. Though Therese felt reluctant about putting anything to her son in writing, she wrote to him the weekend before the hearings began.

Dear Joe,

Because you refuse to see me even if only to be in the same room with me I have decided to write this letter to you. I pray that you won't refuse to read it.

You know Joe that I am heartsick over your situation and I wish I could take some of the pain of it for you but it seems I can do nothing.

I know that you don't want me to talk to you about Kevin

Dillon but I implore you to be civil with him and allow him the courtesy of your cooperation. You do remember that you made a vow before God that you would allow them to defend you. They both believe that they can successfully defend you but you do yourself a great disservice by your attitude toward Mr. D.

I worry so much about this problem that I am having trouble sleeping and feel like crying all the time. Please Joe, for the love of God and for my sake try to resolve this problem.

Yesterday Mark & Kevin sent me a seventy seven page copy of the motions they are making in the pretrial hearing & that was a shortened version of the full package. They have a very good case to present if you will help them.

Finally Joe - I have to tell you although it hurts me to do so - that when I said I was heartsick I meant that literally. I have been having chest pains lately. I don't know whether it is from fatigue from not sleeping or just from the anxiety over you.

Mr. Dillon['s] presence the day you talked with the psychiatrist did not indicate that he thought you were mentally ill. He was there because the judge ordered him to be there. The reason the psychiatrist exam was ordered in the first place was that it is required by law that every defendent be proved competent to stand trial. You have apparently been judged fully competant.

I am sorry to have you spend all this time in custody but hopefully with the help of the Blessed Mother and the good Lord we will all see better days.

I feel responsible in a way for all the notoriety brought down on you because in trying to help you I wrote letters to people whom I thought would help you and those letters apparently only made them suspicious of you. For this I am deeply sorry. I thought I was doing all I could do to help you.

Please forgive me?

All my love

Mom

———

"Your Honor," Kevin Dillon addressed the court on the afternoon the hearings began, "prior to commencement of today's proceedings I have some information that I must impart to the Court and I feel an obligation to do so at this point.

"In previous discussions with the Court I have indicated Mr. Christopher at various times was reluctant to speak with me and I have attempted to convey his sentiments to the Court on that issue.

"Now at the commencement of yesterday's proceedings, I approached Mr. Christopher in an attempt to talk to him and he again indicated to me in a quite agitated state that he did not want me present and he repeated on three or four occasions, he requested that I 'Get out of here.' After yesterday's proceedings, I informed the Court that I was very, very concerned about Mr. Christopher having adequate, competent, full representation in this matter. I had discussed the problem with Mr. Mahoney, and due to the fact that Mr. Christopher was facing a large number of charges in this particular county and the labors involved in his defense, I felt that it would be very, very difficult for one attorney to assume full responsibility for representation at this particular time.

"Today, just immediately prior to us entering the courtroom, Mr. Christopher again conveyed to me his sentiments that I 'Get out of here.' I now am in a position where, due to the length of our involvement in this case, I have a large amount of material that I have prepared, some of which Mr. Mahoney has only a brief general knowledge due to the division of labor. But this is a problem that has arisen and I assured Mr. Christopher today that I would bring it to the Court's attention."

Mark Mahoney told the judge, "I do feel, given the nature of the case, that it's in Mr. Christopher's best interests to have two attorneys involved. I have conveyed that to him and also told him that I would see to it that his position was noted on the record. I don't know if Mr. Christopher has anything to add?"

"I don't want to see Mr. Dillon again. Out," Joseph said.

"Well," said Judge Flynn, "the Court has seen all the work both attorneys have done. There's been an enormous amount of paperwork and a great number of court appearances. It's more work than Mr. Mahoney alone could do and I think we will have to ask Mr. Mahoney to call on Mr. Dillon for assistance. Do you understand the situation, Mr. Christopher?"

"No sir," Joseph answered.

"Do you want to tell us what your own wishes are with respect to Mr. Dillon?" the judge asked.

"Have Mr. Mahoney represent me as my full counsel."

"Your Honor," Dillon interjected, "perhaps I could suggest, for today's proceedings I would be willing, in order to satisfy Mr. Christopher and protect his rights under the Sixth Amendment and his rights to have counsel of his own choosing, that I will simply remain in the background and if Mr. Mahoney does need anything that I do have, I will simply give it to him and I will not participate in the proceedings or in Mr. Christopher's representation."

"All right," Judge Flynn said. "Suppose you step away from the counsel table and let Mr. Mahoney handle the matter entirely and if you have materials Mr. Mahoney needs, you will furnish them to him."

"Your Honor," Joseph said. "I don't wish to have Mr. Dillon in the courtroom at all."

"We indicated Mr. Mahoney is your attorney," said Judge Flynn. "As far as Mr. Dillon, the Court can determine who is present in the courtroom. You can determine what attorney is to represent you."

"I want him to have nothing to do with it."

"You have stated your position and we have honored your position," the judge told him. "Call the first witness."

———

The hearings were laced with contention between Mark Mahoney, who had the burden of presenting the defense case himself, and prosecutors Duane Stamp and William Knapp. Despite Joseph's objections, Dillon remained in court throughout the hearings and assisted Mahoney with arguments and motions. Dillon also continued working on Joseph's behalf out of court, preparing for what would surely be a daunting and protracted trial.

Mahoney, of course, had to be the one who communicated with Joseph, visiting him at the holding center between court appearances.

Joseph was no longer starving himself. He now went in the opposite direction, gorging himself and asking for more and more food. He was also caught eating paint chips off the jail floor.

————————

Raiford Ames, commanding officer of the Fort Benning stockade, was one of the army witnesses who testified at the hearing. Mark Mahoney elicited information about his interaction with Christopher that, even without benefit of a court ruling, effectively eliminated Ames as a prosecution trial witness.

Mahoney confronted Ames with additional details of the lengthy conversation he'd had with Christopher in his office that hadn't come up in his interview with the investigators or in his direct testimony by the prosecution. Under questioning, Ames acknowledged that he had asked Christopher, "Did you come to my office to kill me?" Joseph had answered no. "It was your hope that Mr. Christopher was going to make statements to you regarding the offenses in Buffalo. Isn't that true?" Mahoney asked.

"In a sense, yes, sir."

"And you were hoping that those statements would be seen to be voluntary?"

"Yes." Ames acknowledged that he wanted to gain Christopher's confidence so that he would feel free to talk.

"At the time that you engaged in this conversation with Mr. Christopher, you went further into the question of race, did you not?" Mahoney asked. Ames replied affirmatively. "Didn't you talk with him about the word 'nigger'?"

"Repeat?"

"Did you talk to him about the word 'nigger'?"

"Yes, sir, I did."

"What did you say to him?"

"I asked him to say the word nigger," Ames answered. "I guess just to see his reaction."

"Did you want to make him feel comfortable in saying the word 'nigger' to you? Make him feel comfortable in any feelings he may have about race?"

"That may have been the case, sir."

"Did you tell him that he was in trouble because he had been running off at his mouth and if he hadn't done that, then he would be let free to go and kill fifty or sixty other blacks?" Mahoney asked.

"That's true, sir," Ames said.

"You told him that the attention that he was receiving, with all that attention he was becoming a celebrity, perhaps, like a hero?"

"Yes."

"These were things again to try and develop this rapport with Mr. Christopher, weren't they?"

"I don't know, sir."

"Why did you say it?" Mahoney asked.

"I thought it was a true statement."

"Did you say that," Mahoney inquired "to play upon his ego? To make him feel good about the fact that he was a hero?"

"That could possibly be true."

"You were trying to make him feel good about himself, weren't you?"

"Perhaps, sir, yes, sir."

"At the time you were talking to him your conversation was interrupted by this lady friend of yours who had appeared. Is that true?"

Ames said this was true and that the woman was not a military person, but his dinner date for the evening. He acknowledged that the woman participated in the conversation between himself and Christopher.

"You did nothing to prevent that, did you, sir?" Mahoney asked.

"No, sir, I did not."

"And she very pointedly asked him about the events in Buffalo?"

"Yes, sir, she did."

"You were very interested to know what his answer would be to that question, weren't you?"

"Yes, sir," the witness answered. Ames had stated on direct questioning by William Knapp that Joseph's answer to whether he'd killed people had been, as Captain Ames had previously told police, "People say I did."

Mahoney asked if Ames had told Christopher that a woman was coming to his office. Ames replied that he had. He told him he had a female companion coming.

"What else did you tell Mr. Christopher about her?" Mahoney probed.

"That was basically it."

"Wasn't there something else that you recall?"

"That if he wanted to talk to her, he could," Ames answered.

"That is all, sir? Wasn't there something else you told him?"

"Sir, you need to be more specific."

"All right, I will be more specific," said Mahoney. "Did you tell him that you would ask her if she was willing to engage in sexual activity with him?"

"I told him if he wanted to ask her, he could. I wouldn't ask her that."

"You didn't feel it would be proper for you to ask her?" Mahoney inquired.

"Objection," prosecutor William Knapp said. "Question argumentative."

Mahoney forged ahead. "When she came in, the topic of her having sexual activity with Mr. Christopher was mentioned, wasn't it?"

"Yes, sir, it was," Ames replied.

"Didn't you ask her if she was willing to do that?"

"I don't recall asking her," said Ames. "I recall prisoner Christopher asking her that."

"And she said that there was no place to go at that time, didn't she?" Mahoney asked.

"I don't recall what her specific answer was but I do know she declined his offer."

"You told him that she was coming and that's when you told him that he could ask her if he wanted to have some sex with her?"

"Yes, sir."

"Objection," Knapp interjected. Judge Flynn overruled.

Mahoney questioned Captain Ames about Father Freeman's visits with Joseph. Ames acknowledged that Freeman had discussed their conversations with Ames, and further that Father Freeman had called Ames to alert him to the fact that he'd had a sacramental conversation with Christopher. In response to a question by Mahoney, Ames agreed that this had caused him to think that Christopher must've said something of importance to the priest.

When court resumed after the lunch recess, Mahoney asked Captain Ames if he'd had a conversation with the prosecutors during the noon hour. The witness replied yes and Mahoney asked him what was discussed. Judge Flynn overruled Knapp's objection and the witness answered, "We discussed the case surrounding the prisoner Christopher and myself, incidents that took place, clarification of some of those incidents, refreshing myself and trying to get things straight as to the sequence in which things happened."

Mahoney asked if his recollection had been refreshed in regard to his lady friend and the witness replied, "We discussed her, yes, sir."

"Did you have occasion to call her over the noon hour, as did Mr. Dillon?" Mahoney asked.

"No, sir, I did not."

"Having thought the matter over, do you agree that she was in the room with you and Mr. Christopher for over a half hour, approximately forty-five minutes?"

"She may have been, sir."

"Do you recall that you said to Mr. Christopher that she is a pretty nice black girl?"

"No, sir, I don't recall."

"Do you recall telling Mr. Christopher, wouldn't you like to get to know her?"

"No, I don't recall."

"Are you denying that you said such a thing?" Mahoney asked.

"No, sir, I am not."

"Did you tell Mr. Christopher then, would you like to have sex with her? And did Mr. Christopher indicate that he would like to have sex with her since he had been locked up for months?"

Ames said he didn't recall either statement but made no denials. He recalled the woman saying she wasn't interested. "Did you ask her," Mahoney inquired, "is that because he is white?"

"I don't recall, sir."

"Do you recall that after this conversation she stayed in the room while you talked with Mr. Christopher about his family, his beliefs, and plans for the future?"

"That may be the case, sir. I am not sure."

"Are there other things that you recall about that incident with Mr. Christopher that you care to tell us?" Mahoney asked.

"No, sir."

Eighteen-year-old Kenny Paulson had been interviewed by prosecutors in the wake of the lineups and his grand jury testimony. Kenny's memory was improving all the time. He remembered that he used to date Angela Christopher.

He said he didn't know her brother Joe, though. Kenny claimed he didn't know that Joe and Angela were related until one of Kenny's own sisters, who had been present when police asked him whether he knew Joe Christopher, told him a day or so later that Joe was Angela's brother.

John Regan didn't buy it. In Regan's opinion, Kenny had known from the start who shot Glenn Dunn that night. There was no way to prove this, however, and Kenny further had to be handled with some delicacy, as he was potentially a key prosecution witness, providing they could get him to testify truthfully and navigate his credibility issues.

Under questioning by Mark Mahoney, Kenny said he had initially misled police and declined to make an ID at the lineup because he didn't want to be involved, but had changed his mind because he didn't want to have it on his conscience.

Regan wondered if Kenny's improved memory had less to do with conscience and more with seeing stories in the news about the substantial reward money the psychiatric nurses might be receiving as a result of their testimony. Either way, Kenny Paulson was no longer John Regan's problem. It was probably a good thing for both of them that they wouldn't be spending any more time together.

Pretrial hearings concluded on September 8. The start of the trial was delayed four times, twice as a result of arguments by Dillon and Mahoney that the prosecution was holding back material to which they were entitled, including potentially exculpatory information, such as confessions to the crimes made by other suspects. The delays irritated prosecutors, who were eager to proceed to trial. Judge Flynn told the media that he granted the defense requests "to eliminate the possibility that prosecutors may have inadvertently overlooked material in their files that they should have given to the defense."

As the trial approached, the defense attorneys had made no progress with their client in terms of rational participation in his defense. Mahoney continued hitting a brick wall when he tried to discuss trial strategy or how to respond to evidence expected from the prosecution. Joe's answers to anything related to witnesses, evidence, or possible defenses were always the same: "I'll take care of that" or "Leave that up to me." He never explained or elaborated. He flatly refused to discuss the charges against him. He insisted he was going to make his own decisions. At the conclusion of the pretrial hearings, he had asked Mahoney what they were all about.

Jury selection began on October 20, 1981. Dillon and Mahoney had an in-chambers conference with their client and Judge Flynn before the proceedings. "Your Honor," said Mark Mahoney, "the subject I wish to bring up is the fact that because of the nature of the accusation in this case and because of some public comments made by the district attorney during the investigation of these cases regarding the possible sanity or not of the person who may have committed these offenses, and because of the fact that at the time suspicion fell on Mr. Christopher, he was in a psychiatric ward receiving treatment at Fort Benning, we have explored the possibility of raising the defense of insanity with Mr. Christopher throughout.

"We have offered him the possibility of discussing this matter with us and with a psychiatrist appointed by the defense, and Mr. Christopher has to this point declined the opportunity to pursue that avenue of defense. I add that we are not in disagreement with him, but I think that it's important for us to establish on the record that this avenue of defense has been explored. We have discussed with Mr. Christopher all the strategic implications of both the defense of not criminally responsible by reason of insanity and the more or less factual defense to which we are committed at present. And, I think he has had the opportunity to evaluate those choices, and as I say, he has made a decision. I want to bring it to the attention of the Court at this time so that we can establish that it is his decision as well as something that we have done on his behalf."

Kevin Dillon spoke. "Your Honor, two brief things I would like to add to what Mr. Mahoney just said. The statements he was referring to by the district attorney were made in the spring by District Attorney Cosgrove to a press conference of some sort, that were to the effect that any attorneys who represent the person who will be ultimately charged with the commission of these crimes that does not raise an insanity defense is insane themselves. Secondly, we had had direct contact with Dr. Lynch, have met with him personally about the possibility of interposing an insanity defense on Mr. Christopher's behalf."

"All right," Judge Flynn responded. "Is that it?"

Mark Mahoney turned to his client. "I'm wondering, Joe, is there anything you would like to say in this regard? Are you satisfied that we have explored that possibility and intelligently rejected it?"

"I don't know what the hell you're talking about, man," Christopher said.

"Anything else?" Judge Flynn asked.

"Well," said Mahoney, "I really don't necessarily want to leave it at that, your Honor. Does your Honor wish to examine Mr. Christopher at this point?"

"No," said Flynn. "That's something I don't enter into. That's a matter between defendant and counsel. I think you made it clear on the record what the position is."

"Joe, is there anything you would like to ask me to clarify at this point?" Mahoney asked.

"No."

"Is there anything that you don't understand about what I just told the judge?"

"You asked me before if we wanted to enter an insanity please and I told you no," said Joseph.

"You still agree with that?" Mahoney asked.

"Yes," he answered.

"All right, thank you," said Judge Flynn.

Jury selection was under way when the defendant suddenly stood up.

"I don't want a jury."

Kevin Dillon and Mark Mahoney were floored, as was everyone else in the packed courtroom. For a moment, no one spoke.

"You don't wish to have a jury hear your case?" Judge Flynn asked.

Christopher said he didn't. Judge Flynn asked him why.

"I feel you are an educated man. You know the law and you are the judge," Christopher said.

"And you wish to waive a jury trial?" the judge asked.

"That's right."

"I don't approve of this," Mark Mahoney interjected.

Dillon and Mahoney leaned in and spoke to Joseph. Or tried to. He ignored them and told the judge, "No jury."

Judge Flynn advised Christopher that he had a constitutional right to a jury trial. While he had a right to waive it, the judge told him, there were many advantages to a jury trial. The defendant replied, "Constitution says it's my right to waive the jury. Is there some reason you don't want to handle the case?"

Judge Flynn told Joseph that he would have to sign a jury waiver before the court.

"I'm not signing anything. Just put on the record I'm waiving a jury."

Mahoney interrupted. "Your Honor, it is our position that he's not doing this knowingly. We do not approve of this." Mahoney and Dillon protested. Christopher did not understand the ramifications of waiving a jury, they said.

"Am I on trial against my attorneys or am I on trial against an indictment?" said Christopher.

Judge Flynn pointed out that Christopher had been found competent to stand trial. He therefore had no discretion to refuse his jury waiver request. The attorneys continued objecting. They asked for a hearing to determine if Christopher was knowingly and intelligently waiving his right to a jury trial.

The court presented Christopher with a jury waiver form. He refused to sign.

Judge Flynn told him he'd have to proceed with a jury trial unless he signed. Christopher looked at the waiver. He didn't believe it was a real court form. He argued with the judge, saying that it wasn't an official court form because it "don't have any numbers on it." Judge Flynn told him again that the law required him to sign the waiver and Joseph complained, "So it doesn't matter what I want, you're just going to do what you want?"

Dillon and Mahoney sat back and let Joseph Christopher speak, perhaps hoping the judge would realize that the emperor had no clothes.

Judge Flynn ordered the prospective jurors brought in. Christopher stared intently at the jury box. He then told Judge Flynn he'd sign the form and did so amid renewed protests from his attorneys.

"I don't approve of this," Mahoney told the judge. He pressed for a hearing. "The record is insufficient to support the supposition that the defendant knowingly and intelligently waived his right to trial by jury." Arguing his point, Mahoney said that "at the time suspicion fell on Mr. Christopher, he was diagnosed as psychotic."

"I'd rather Mr. Mahoney not finish," Christopher said. "Can I approach the bench?"

"You have made it clear you want to waive a jury, despite Mr. Mahoney's arguments," said Judge Flynn. "It would be intolerable to force the defendant into a jury trial when he said he doesn't want it." Judge Flynn approved the waiver.

An intense exchange followed between Flynn and Mahoney.

"Your Honor, the court did not inquire at the time of the plea . . ."

"It was not a plea," the judge interjected.

"Excuse me, your Honor," said Mahoney. "I tend to equate the two. The waiver is as important as a plea and should be dealt with as seriously."

Flynn ruled the waiver was acceptable.

Dillon and Mahoney pressed their arguments in a closed-door session with the judge the following day. Judge Flynn agreed to have Christopher reexamined by the psychiatrists who had declared him competent in May.

Drs. Molnar and Wadsworth reexamined Christopher the following week with an eye toward determining if he had sufficient competence to waive a jury. This time, there was no consensus; Dr. Molnar maintained he was competent, while Dr. Wadsworth revised his diagnosis to paranoid schizophrenia and declared him incompetent.

The court ordered two more psychiatrists, Dr. Brian Joseph and Dr. Harry Rubenstein, to examine Christopher. Dr. Joseph diagnosed Christopher as suffering from paranoid schizophrenia and deemed him incompetent. Dr. Rubenstein gave no diagnosis but judged him competent.

A fifth psychiatrist was brought in as a tiebreaker. Dr. S. K. Park diagnosed Joseph as a paranoid schizophrenic and gave the opinion he was incompetent to stand trial.

Edward Cosgrove expressed anger over the trial delay and requested that the competency hearings be open to the public. Judge Flynn granted the request. The five psychiatrists presented their findings in open court and underwent questioning and cross-examination by attorneys for the prosecution and the defense.

Prosecutors Stamp and Knapp argued vigorously for a finding of competency. Stamp complained to the judge that Mark Mahoney, who had been present as an observer during the psychiatric exams, had attempted to influence the findings by telling the doctors about his own interactions with Christopher. Mahoney countered that it was reasonable and appropriate to provide examiners with the background, and further that the pre exam discussions with the psychiatrists had been permitted by the supervisor of the Forensic Mental Health Service. Mahoney spoke in open court about the numerous difficulties he'd personally experienced with Christopher and argued for a finding of incompetency to stand trial, much to his client's objection and displeasure.

Christopher interrupted the proceedings throughout the competency hearings, calling out questions and comments to doctors as they testified. When psychiatrists cited examples of Joe's behavior that they interpreted as signs of mental illness, he would cry out, "That's an irrelevance," and otherwise argue as judge and defense attorneys urged him not to speak out of turn.

Judge Flynn gave his ruling on December 16. The law defines an incapacitated person as a defendant who, as a result of mental disease or defect, lacks capacity to understand the proceedings against him or to assist in his own defense. Flynn's decision had been difficult due to the conflicting psychiatric opinions. Even the psychiatrists who had deemed Christopher competent had nevertheless found him suffering from serious mental disturbance.

The judge adjudicated Joseph Christopher an incapacitated person. He ordered Christopher committed to Mid-Hudson Psychiatric Center for treatment until such time that he was deemed mentally fit for trial.

"I am not an incapacitated person!" Christopher protested.

He was led from court. The following day, he was transported under heavy guard to New Hampton, New York, and admitted to Mid-Hudson.

There was an outcry from black leaders, who voiced strong opposition to Judge Flynn's ruling, convinced it meant that Joseph Christopher would never stand trial. Councilman James Pitts was quoted, "Something has to be done to make judges more accountable. This is a slap in the face, particularly to the black community and the City of Buffalo." Pitts continued, "If someone is not brought to justice for the killings, you are going to have a violent reaction from some sectors of the community."

Daniel Acker of the NAACP said of Flynn's ruling, "This is the kind of decision that causes more violence in our cities."

Their acrimony was not limited to, nor even solely based upon, Judge Flynn's decision; DA Edward Cosgrove was the main target of dissatisfaction.

Cosgrove's term was coming to an end on December 31. He had decided not to seek reelection. He had also decided to disband the task force.

Learning that the Buffalo Common Council had scheduled a ceremony during which they intended to cite the outgoing district attorney for his accomplishments over the past eight years in office, members of the Black Leadership Forum announced they would attend for the purpose of delivering a "citation of infamy" for what they viewed as Cosgrove's poor handling of the investigation. There was widespread belief in the black community that more than one person had been involved in the murders. The forum wanted the task force to remain in operation to investigate the slayings of Parler Edwards, Ernest Jones, Roger Adams, and Wendell Barnes. Incoming district attorney Richard Arcara promised to take their concerns under consideration.

As for the commitment of Joseph Christopher to a psychiatric facility, Cosgrove called it a disappointment and black leaders referred to it as a "miscarriage of justice." They wanted Christopher to stand trial. Their greatest ally on these points was the subject himself.

Joseph refused to cooperate with the mental health staff. He would not answer questions or undergo any tests. In January, his mother had to fill out his personal and medical history forms.

Among the detailed information she provided, Therese informed them of a head injury Joseph had suffered in 1979. While making repairs underneath a pickup truck, the jack had slipped and the truck fell. Joe was hit in the head by the axle and was semiconscious for about five minutes. His forehead bled profusely and was swollen. He received stitches but he had refused to submit to a CAT scan because he was afraid it would cause brain damage.

Joseph believed that army personnel at Fort Benning had told him that he had sexually attacked his mother. He also believed that the army was attempting to make him give up his religious faith.

On January 26, 1982, the director of Mid-Hudson Psychiatric Center, Dr. Erdogan Tekben, wrote a letter to Judge William Flynn that read, "Our efforts to reach an appropriate psychiatric diagnosis by utilizing available diagnostic tools have been hampered by the unwillingness of the defendant." Christopher had refused a brain scan, which they felt was necessary because his unequal pupils warranted further exploration. He also declined to participate in all psychological testing, which would be, Tekben wrote, "a significant aid toward establishing an accurate psychiatric diagnosis, especially because he is not informative." Christopher would not even submit to routine blood and urine work. "We have utilized every clinical approach to persuade him to accept the administration of these tests but we failed, as others did in the past. I would be most grateful if you would advise me whether the Court can and is willing to compel him to submit to these tests, which may prove to be essential in reaching an accurate diagnosis and opinion of his fitness to proceed."

There was little time for Judge Flynn to consider such a measure. In addition to not cooperating with the center, Joseph made continuous and concerted efforts to gain his release, filing a writ of habeas corpus on

January 18 with an Orange County court, which ordered a hearing on January 20 and then the appointment of an independent psychiatrist. Two weeks later, Dr. Richard Weidenbacher examined Joe at Mid-Hudson and found him fit to proceed with a diagnosis of paranoid schizophrenia in remission. Joe told Dr. Weidenbacher that he was eager to go to trial and thought he'd be acquitted.

> Your Honner
> I have been interviewed by five Doctors, two of witch found me competent, two incompetent and one was undecided, opt to futheir test in a theiaputic enviorment. In that they only spent short minutes of time with me. Hence I was adjuidicated to Mid Hudson P.C. I was found competent, by five doctor and also an indepennend doctor. In New York States number one ranked theiaputic center. I, their now being a preponderence of evidence, nine Doctors supporting my position and two not, will not be a party to another test or feel a need for a hearing, because the result of the pervious did not support the preference of someone else
> I coralate my position to a man that wins a trip in Las Vegas, was sent their takes the house and comes back. An acquaintance possiably having interest in say's Hay how bout me and you go to Atlantic City I'll provide the tranportation, how is that! how about! how about!
> Sincerely
> Joseph Christopher

On February 24, Joseph was discharged from Mid-Hudson and returned to Buffalo to stand trial.

PART FOUR
THE GAUNTLET

"I could tell you my adventures—beginning from this morning, but it's no use going back to yesterday, because I was a different person then."

—Lewis Carroll, *Alice in Wonderland*

Chapter 16

"WELCOME HOME."

A deputy smiled and greeted a shackled Joe Christopher as he entered the Erie County Holding Center. Joe smiled back. "What's for dinner?"

Christopher's comings and goings were still big news. Officials who were part of his travel entourage told reporters that Joseph Christopher seemed like an entirely different person upon return from his ten-week stay at Mid-Hudson. He was much more outgoing, they said, even laughing and joking around with his captors on the ride back. He had also taken up smoking. He brought cartons of cigarettes back with him, along with the books *The Way* and *Shogun*.

Salvatore Castiglione was an Erie County sheriff's deputy who worked at the holding center. Unlike the men who accompanied Christopher on his trips in and out of town, Sal spent time with him on a daily and hour-to-hour basis. Sal had been assigned to the 24/7 watch of the holding center's most notorious prisoner since his arrival the previous spring and resumed the duty when Joe returned in February.

Sal had been working at the county jail for a decade but rarely had as much interaction with an inmate as he had with Joseph Christopher. The immensely high-profile nature of the case, combined with Christopher's tenuous mental condition and the widespread hatred of him by black inmates (who made up the vast majority of the holding center population), necessitated a very strict and thoroughly literal adherence to the round-the-clock watch policy. The two principal concerns were that Christopher would kill himself or be killed by someone else, either of which would have resulted in some very bad publicity for the sheriff's department. Thus, there was not a single moment when he was left alone or unobserved.

Christopher had been kept in the hole, a segregation cell, when he had first arrived in May of 1981 but was soon moved to special housing on the main floor in the infirmary, a four-cell block that he alone occupied, and it was to this special confinement area that he returned in February 1982.

A sheriff's deputy—most often Sal, who worked this assignment five to six days per week, plus overtime—had to sit right outside the cell at all times, eyes on the prisoner. Christopher's every movement had to be written down in tedious detail. Time gaps would trigger questions from superiors. Deputies were required to not only maintain the log during their shift, but also to review the log of the deputy from the prior shift. With all this insistence on detail, the day-and-night "Joe Christopher" reports typically read something like: 3:02 p.m. Picked up pencil, was drawing picture. 3:06 p.m. Dropped pencil, bent over to pick it up. 3:22 p.m. Used commode, went and sat on his bunk at 3:25.

A light remained on in the cell at all times. There was no curtain or any type of obstruction blocking the deputy's view of the commode or the shower. Standing or sitting just outside the cell at no more than a few feet away, the deputy was required to observe and record all hygienic activities as well.

"You like watching men shower?" Christopher would taunt.

"Nah," Sal would answer, "you don't have anything that interests me," and they'd both laugh. They'd toss little jabs at each other, making the best of a set up that was odd and uncomfortable for both of them.

It was a very unique assignment, in more ways than one.

Sal would outfit Joe in the bulletproof vest and shackles and escort him through the jail to his many court appearances. Christopher had been an object of derision from the start. He eventually started striking back, wearing his serial killer persona like a glove. As Sal recalled, "In the mornings, all the court cases are being set so all the prisoners come down to the bullpens on the main floor. So you've got probably one hundred fifty inmates in these different bullpens, usually about fifty in each. They'd see me coming out with Christopher and all of a sudden they'd be screaming and throwing things. 'There he is! There he is! There's that mother!'

"I got peppered by all kinds of stuff because I had to try to drag him through the hall. And he didn't want to go fast. He would smile at them and say, 'I should've killed more of you fucking niggers.' And I'd be saying to him, 'Shut up, shut up!' Yeah, he didn't make my job too easy.

"We had him locked in and he'd keep saying it, real loud, down the hall, 'I shoulda killed more of those fucking niggers!' while I'm telling him to be quiet. And they're all screaming my name, because they knew me from working in the jail for eleven years, they're yelling, 'Sal! Bring him over to the bars, we'll take care of him for you!' And I'm going, 'I can't.' They wanted a piece of him real bad. Some of the inmates would tell me, 'Sal, you want a Cadillac? We'll get you a brand new Cadillac for five minutes alone with him.' And Joe used to just laugh. I'm looking at him thinking, oh my God, this kid is sick."

Protesters would show up outside the jail and in the courthouse. "We'd have people with signs demonstrating in the hallway, throwing their signs, saying, 'Give him to us! We'll take care of him!' And I'm saying to myself, 'Oh no, they're gonna take care of him and I'm gonna get killed trying to protect this lunatic.'

"There'd be a wall of deputies on both sides of him and me. If somebody tried to come through the line we used to grab them and pound the piss out of them, you know, because they were trying to get to him. You never knew who was going to break through the line with a knife or a gun or whatever. It was like going through a gauntlet. And Christopher would be saying to them, 'Why don't you shove those signs up your ass?'"

Christopher's change in attitude might've been influenced by feedback he was getting from some of the deputies. "They'd pass by his cell and tell him, 'Joe, we're raising bail money for you so you can get out there and finish the job.' Joe would tell them, 'Keep up the good work,' and they'd laugh and say, 'Yeah, you too!'

"Joe ate it up. He liked feeling like one of us. One guy told him, 'Joe, they caught you too soon. We had a list for you to take care of.' Joe said, 'I'd have gotten the job done.' Crime had gone way down when he was out there doing these killings. Blacks were afraid to go out on the street.

There were people back then saying, 'Keep it up, man. Keep it up,' before anybody knew his name."

Back in his cell, Joe didn't have much to occupy his time. He drew pictures of the deputies or shined shoes. He still refused to have a TV or radio in his cell, which Sal found odd. Authorities at the jail wanted to keep the peace with Christopher and they would've given him anything he wanted, within reason, to keep him busy. All he ever asked for was food. Quite a lot of it, in fact, though he insisted it was poisoned.

"Here, you try some," he'd say to Sal.

"No, you just got done eating. I'm not gonna try any of your food."

"Because it's poisoned, isn't it?"

"No, it's not," Sal would tell him.

Joe was also convinced they put saltpeter in his food. He ate it anyway. He didn't exercise and started gaining a lot of weight.

Joe could be very talkative during the long hours when it was just the two of them, though he tended to go "on and off like a lightbulb," as Sal described it. "He'd be real quiet for long periods of time. He'd sit there writing and writing and writing. And I'd be saying to myself, 'What the hell is he writing about?' Then he'd put the pencil down and start talking, as if he just woke up."

He often asked Sal about his time in the service. Sal had spent four years in the Marines, where he had set a marksmanship record and once captured a spy taking photos around the Marine Corps Air Station at Miramar. Joe was impressed. He told Sal about his own experience in the military. "He said he liked the army. He wished he was still in the army. He said that some of the best friends he ever made were in the army.

"The only thing he didn't like about it was the blacks. He said to me, 'I knew I couldn't do anything about the blacks around me. I could only do it away from my base so nobody would suspect me.' He'd wait till he came home on leave."

Joe would suddenly turn the conversation to more pointed topics.

"Sal, did I ever tell you about the one I shot when he was coming out of the store?"

"Coming out of the store?"

"Yeah. I walked up behind him, BOOM, just like that."

"Huh. Did he die right away?"

"Yeah, I think so. I shot him right in the back of the head."

That type of talk wasn't unique at the holding center. "A lot of prisoners liked to boast about what they did," Sal recalled. "Now with Joe Christopher, this is a guy who lived in some kind of fantasy world so he probably made a lot of stories up. I knew he was fighting his own, you know, thoughts and mind. I worked with enough crazy people in the jail that I knew when a guy wasn't all there.

"I asked him, 'Why'd you pick on the blacks?' He said it was because a black guy raped his sister. I don't know, but that's what he told me. I took everything he said with a grain of salt. I said to him, 'Well, you can't blame all people for one person doing something.' And he goes, 'They're all no good. They all deserve to die.'

"He used to talk about these guys he killed and tell me he enjoyed it. I'm going, 'You enjoyed it?' He said, 'Yeah. I only regret I didn't kill more.' He'd be smiling when he was telling me about it. No guilty conscience. But then at one time, he thought he was going to make it right by confessing. He would switch, you know? Light on, light off."

Because Sal had to remain with Joe at all times, including during visits from attorneys, there was a confidentiality imposed. "His lawyers would tell me, 'Now remember, Sal, anything you hear . . .' and I'd tell them, 'Yeah, I know, I know.' I also told them, 'Your client is telling me everything, you know.'"

Joe seemed to constantly be at odds with his lawyers. "I think they were nervous being locked in with him because he was a crazy person and you never know what a crazy person is going to do."

Joe also claimed to have committed more crimes than anyone knew. "He said to me, 'I've done more than what they think I've done.' And I said, 'How many more?' I said, 'Don't you want to be known in the books as the best mass murderer going? You got a certain number, you'll probably break a record.' But he wouldn't fall for that. He'd just say, 'Nah. There's a lot they don't know I did.'

"I asked him once, 'Why'd you pick on poor working guys just trying to make a living, like the cab drivers?' He said to me, 'What makes you think I did that?' I asked him, 'Well, did you?' He just smiled and didn't say anything."

A thin metal wall separated Joe's area from a cell block. The door was kept shut but sound traveled, bouncing off the concrete and metal. If things were too quiet, Joe would tell Sal, "Let's get things going." And he would start shouting toward the door, "You fucking niggers! Hey! Can any of you fucking jungle bunnies read and write?"

A pounding cacophony would fill the floor as scores of prisoners screamed back and hurled objects against the bars. "You honky piece of shit! You coward! If you didn't have your gun, a two-year-old could kick your ass!"

"Fuck you, niggers!" Joe would yell back. "If it weren't for the white man, none of you would even be eating!"

Sal would try to get him to shut up. "Joe, come on, you're making the deputy's job miserable over there."

The deputies would have to threaten a lockdown to get things quiet, which, of course, was no threat at all to Joe. They'd have to bribe him to stop cutting up. "If you give me some ice cream, I won't start anything tonight," and they'd do it, since there was little else they could do to control him. Joe Christopher had celebrity status and couldn't be touched.

"Joe was actually a wimp," Sal said. "If he'd been in the general prisoner population, he'd have been eaten alive. He could be a nice guy at times, believe it or not, but he'd let his temper get the best of him. Many times I thought I was going to have to fight with him because he would get frustrated. I could see him clenching his fist and his body would be tensing up." Sal recalled this happening mainly during the competency hearings. "He hated the psychiatrists. Absolutely hated them. He would've killed them if he could have. He'd say to me, 'They think they're so smart! They don't know anything!'

"He couldn't stand hearing what they had to say about him in court. He would stand up and tell the judge, 'I'm out of here.' The judge would say, 'No, you're not. Sit down.' And he'd say, 'I don't want to listen to any more of this fucking shit,' you know. The judge would look at me and say, 'Sal?' And I'd grab him, put him down. Joe would turn to me and say, 'I thought you were my friend.' I'd tell him, 'Christopher, I am your friend but I have to listen to the judge. This is painful for me too but we've both got to sit here and listen.' And he'd go, 'Oh okay, I understand.' That was when he got the most agitated, listening to the psychiatrists. He didn't think there was anything wrong with him."

Kevin Dillon received a call from assistant DA Duane Stamp, who had received a call from the Buffalo Psychiatric Hospital. In cleaning out some records, the hospital director learned that on September 8, 1980, Joseph G. Christopher of Weber Avenue had come to the psych center seeking help for mental problems he said he was experiencing. The director thought the district attorney might want to know about this.

On that date in September, Christopher had met with a social worker and a staff psychiatrist. Joseph asked to be admitted to the psychiatric center. Based on the interview, which lasted about thirty minutes, they didn't feel he was a threat to himself or others. They had turned him away. They'd suggested he get some counseling and told him they'd have an outpatient clinic give him a call. When the clinic called him a week or so later, he told them that he had joined the army.

Newspapers got a hold of the story. "Christopher Sought Psychiatric Care Two Weeks Before Killing Started."

Joe was furious. He placed a call to the *Courier-Express* and told them to send a reporter to the holding center. He had a statement to make.

Mark Mahoney rushed over to see Joe and pleaded with him not to talk to reporters. Joe would not be dissuaded. Mahoney finally left in frustration as an editor and staff reporter arrived at the holding center for the scheduled interview.

"I'm not really going to answer any direct question to me," Christopher told them. "I'm just going to show you a little comment I wrote." He slid a handwritten note across the table.

In reguards to Wednesdays sensationalism, As for being sent to the hospital at Fort Benning, I was sent to the hospital as a result of my not eating in the stockaid. I was being sliped some kind of drug every time I ate. I went from 152 to 116. In the hospital I gained weight and was sent back to the stockaid. Again I was druged, I made a small slice in the skin on my penis and asked to go back to the hospital. At prior stay in the hospital the main topic of conversation was The Atlanta Case. I have just this comment for know. Joseph Christopher

---

"I thought he was already in the military."

Sergeant Pauline Ratcliff was an army recruiter. She was telling Kevin Dillon and Mark Mahoney about the day in September when Joe Christopher had shown up at her office, looking to enlist. She had initially mistaken him as already being enlisted in the army, a serviceman perhaps looking for guidance on some matter. "His hair was extremely short," Ratcliff said. She remembered this quite clearly because she had been struck by the fact he wore his hair in a military-style cut.

Ratcliff pulled out her records on Joseph Christopher. He had come to see her on September 16, 1980. She'd considered him a great prospect, since he had already passed military aptitude tests the year before. He had scored quite high, too.

He wanted infantry. She'd also noted on his card that he wanted to leave for the army as soon as possible.

Judge Flynn was not keen on further competency hearings. He felt there had already been enough. Mid-Hudson had certified Joe as competent to stand trial and both judge and prosecutors wanted to get on with it.

In New York City, however, Judge Benjamin Altman had ruled Christopher incompetent to stand trial on the Manhattan murder and attempted murder charges. Altman had agreed with Buffalo psychiatrists who deemed Christopher unfit, issuing his ruling on February 10 while Christopher was still at Mid-Hudson.

Kevin Dillon and Mark Mahoney were stunned by Christopher's quick return from the psychiatric facility and highly skeptical that he could have been successfully treated in such a short period of time.

Christopher had filed his writ seeking release without the knowledge or consent of his attorneys.

Dillon and Mahoney wanted their client reexamined by the Buffalo psychiatrists who had testified at the competency hearing to determine if any progress had been realized in his mental status with the goal of determining if Christopher was truly any better able to assist in his defense. At a conference with Judge Flynn and prosecutors on March 9, they asked the court to grant their request for reexaminations and allow funds for such. Prosecutors were vigorously opposed to hiring psychiatrists whose testimony had previously led to Judge Flynn's incompetency determination and urged Judge Flynn to refuse the request. Mahoney cautioned that the prosecution's argument was "a clear demonstration of the People's willingness to urge the Court into errors that could result in a reversal of this case later on." Judge Flynn made it clear, however, that he favored the prosecution's position on the matter.

Two days later, Mahoney filed an affidavit in support of their application for psychiatric services. "In the clinical summary, dated February 18, 1982, authored by Dr. P. Chellappa, psychiatrist at the Mid-Hudson Psychiatric Center, and submitted in connection with the notification of fitness to proceed, it is described that Mr. Christopher 'continued to maintain the same mental status' in response to the program for him at that center. Nevertheless, the defendant was certified as 'ready for trial.'

"If the defendant's mental status has indeed remained the same," Mahoney wrote, "and if that mental status continues to cause him to be unable to participate effectively with his defense counsel, then this Court could hardly reach a different conclusion on the issue of the defendant's fitness to proceed than it did on December 16, 1981."

Mahoney had spent in excess of four hours with Christopher since his return to Buffalo. He still could not get his client to speak with him about the case in any rational way. When Mahoney had broached the subject of finding expert witnesses for ballistics testimony, Christopher had told him that he had an expert witness but wouldn't tell Mahoney who that might be. On dealing with incriminatory statements the prosecution was alleging he had made, Christopher still kept insisting, "Leave all that to me."

"I conclude that Mr. Christopher is no more able to assist in his defense than at any previous time," Mahoney wrote. "To the contrary, he exhibits an even greater tendency to make unreasoned and precipitous decisions about his case which introduce additional barriers to effective assistance in his defense."

Referring to the competency hearing that had concluded only three months before, Mahoney wrote, "Three psychiatrists examined Mr. Christopher solely on the question of his fitness to proceed. Drs. Park and Joseph concluded that the defendant was an incapacitated person, while Dr. Rubenstein believed the defendant was competent to stand trial. At the hearing, these psychiatrists testified at length. The doctors largely testified according to the conclusions contained in their previously submitted reports. However, Dr. Molnar, on cross examination, conceded that the defendant did indeed suffer from a mental disease and that, as a result of same, he was 'inflexible' in his ability to cooperate with defense counsel. This particular testimony, of course, is not consistent with a finding of fitness to proceed. Only Dr. Rubenstein, who found himself unable to reach a diagnosis of Mr. Christopher after a thirty-five-minute interview (at which only 10 percent of his questions received responses), the only non-certified examiner, remained unambiguously on the side of a finding of fitness to proceed.

"I am not unmindful of the indication made by this Court, in the conference of March 9, 1982, that the Court would not allow any psychiatrist to testify who did not file reports on behalf of the Mid-Hudson Psychiatric Center. I am confident that, on reconsideration, the Court will agree that the scope of a competency hearing cannot be limited to the psychiatrists who examined pursuant to an order of examination without serious violation of the rights of the defendant to compulsory process, effective assistance of counsel, due process and equal protection of the law, and the right not to be placed in jeopardy without a full and fair opportunity to litigate his capacity to stand trial.

"The defendant's indigency should have no bearing on his ability to obtain such reexaminations and have access to such testimony. As it is necessary to have as many as four psychiatrists appointed, it is requested that any authorization herein not be limited to compensation of $300."

Judge Flynn denied the request. Dillon and Mahoney offered to pay for the psychiatric exams out of their own pockets. Judge Flynn was still unmoved. He maintained that there would be a hearing at which only one psychiatrist would give testimony: Dr. Paul Chellappa of Mid-Hudson, who had deemed Christopher competent.

Dr. Chellappa was examined and cross-examined for three days in March. The judge allowed Christopher to skip the proceeding and remain in his cell. Joseph had voiced very strong objections to the judge allowing any hearing whatsoever on the question of his competence. He swore he would not come to court if one were held. This time, the judge didn't fight him.

Following the testimony of Dr. Chellappa, Judge Flynn heard closing arguments from prosecutor Duane Stamp and the defense attorneys. An observer might've mistaken Stamp for Christopher's attorney. The prosecutor defended the competency ruling along with Joseph's resistance to further tests and his request for a nonjury trial. Stamp characterized Joseph as stubborn rather than mentally disturbed, telling the judge that his stubbornness "is rivaled only by the stubbornness of his appointed counsel, who insist things be done the way they want things done" in opposition to their client's choices. Responding to nursing reports that stated that Christopher stayed reclusive while at the hospital, Stamp said that this demonstrated his sanity. "Mr. Christopher's interaction with inmates and his social inability at the institution was entirely appropriate, given the fact that he was not psychotic and the others were. If you were sent there," he asked the judge, "would you keep to yourself or talk to every passerby?"

Mahoney pounced on both the testimony and credentials of Dr. Chellappa. He brought out that Chellappa, having failed the required examinations on multiple occasions, did not have certification from the American Board of Psychiatry. "I think it takes quite a lot of gall for a person who's tried for ten years to become certified as a psychiatrist to lay blame for Mr. Christopher's unwillingness to communicate on attorneys and the other psychiatrists who have found him incapacitated," Mahoney told the judge. Chellappa had said he made his decision to certify Joseph as competent within twenty minutes of meeting him and without benefit of the physical, psychological, and psychiatric tests that the director of Mid-Hudson had said were required. When Mahoney confronted him with the January 26 letter to Judge Flynn from the director stating that they could not make an accurate diagnosis without having Christopher undergo the tests, Chellappa had responded angrily that his superiors never should have sent that letter, that he had the situation under control (he had already determined that Christopher was competent on January 18) and his superiors had not consulted him before sending it.

"He told the court he could see it [Christopher's competence] immediately, after just twenty minutes with the man," Mahoney continued, "even though the court and the others couldn't see it with all the time they had. And he said it was only out of 'courtesy' to the court that he decided to keep Mr. Christopher at Mid-Hudson for two months."

Chellappa had claimed to have found "the real Joe Christopher" because he did not "bully" him, as he asserted others had. "He concludes he's better than the other psychiatrists," Mahoney said. "He apparently believes he's done something no other psychiatrist did. He's proud of the fact that he was able to establish the competence of Mr. Christopher.

"Dr. Chellappa is one who pretends to more knowledge than he possesses and is apparently a quack," said Mahoney, referring to Chellappa also as "a charlatan."

Duane Stamp argued that Dr. Chellappa's findings were "common sense" and asserted that Joseph had come out of his shell because this doctor was the first person to treat him as a human being. "Mr. Christopher is able to understand and to cooperate if he's treated with respect, not bullied," Stamp said, accusing Dillon and Mahoney of bullying their client, disregarding his wishes and thus not providing him with proper representation.

"The client of the DA is not so enamored with his representation," Dillon shot back, the DA's client being the people of Erie County. "If the client had its way, believe you me, you would have a special prosecutor in here right now."

Judge Flynn ruled Christopher fit to proceed. He encouraged him to opt for a jury trial. Christopher insisted he was sticking to his decision for trial by judge. He still refused to say why. Judge Flynn approved his request for a nonjury trial, to begin without further delay.

The only victory for defense attorneys was the granting of their motion that Justice Flynn recuse himself as trial judge. Since Flynn had been privy to evidence and private conferences concerning the case over the past ten months, Dillon and Mahoney felt he should not be the one to sit in judgment of Christopher. Judge Flynn agreed, stating "the appearance of impartiality would best be served if the trial now proceeded before another trial justice."

Chapter 17

JOE AGREED TO get a haircut. But that was the only piece of advice he'd take from his attorneys. He entered the courtroom on April 12, 1982, for his first day of trial, with short hair. He wore the same old dark-blue corduroy jacket, white shirt open at the collar, and army boots. He sat down at the defense table, nodded to Mark Mahoney, and ignored Kevin Dillon.

State Supreme Court Justice Frederick M. Marshall had replaced Judge William Flynn. Marshall, age sixty-two, had been chief of the trial bureau for the Erie County District Attorney's office from 1959 to 1961. He had served as a State Supreme Court judge for the past fourteen years. Now he sat as judge and jury in the trial of the *People v. Joseph G. Christopher*.

Duane Stamp and William Knapp sat at the prosecution table with Al Ranni, the lead prosecutor. Ranni had joined the district attorney's office in 1968 under former DA Michael F. Dillon, father of defense attorney Kevin Dillon. Ranni was appointed deputy DA in charge of prosecutions by District Attorney Richard Arcara, who had replaced Edward Cosgrove on January 1. Ranni was known as a ferocious prosecutor with a very physical and bombastic style in the courtroom. He was a rather controversial figure, described by a friend as someone who thought "judges were to be ignored."

In his opening before Judge Marshall, Ranni addressed the fact that the prosecution did not have the murder weapon of the alleged .22 Caliber Killer. He assured the judge, however, "We expect your Honor not to be disappointed. This is not a no-gun case. We only want the gun to see if it put marks—We only need a gun in order to test fire it. The only thing it's good for is discharging a test cartridge in order to thereafter compare the crime evidence to the bullet that was discharged, bullet and shell.

"The People will show through extensive scientific proof that no two firearms in the entire world are exactly the same," Ranni said, "even though produced by the same manufacturer, same model and produced consecutively. Moreover, the People will prove no individual part of one weapon is exactly the same as the part on a corresponding part on another weapon. Firing pins, barrels, bolts, chambers, they're all different. They may appear the same to the naked eye, but in the microscopic world of the forensic scientist, they're grossly dissimilar."

Ranni spoke of the many prosecution witnesses to come. He mentioned Kenny Paulson, who he said would positively identify the defendant as the man he'd seen shoot Glenn Dunn. He touched on the fact that Paulson had not immediately identified Joseph Christopher at the lineup because Paulson "had some fear when he faced him, confronted him face to face," though he did not explain why Kenny would have such fear at a lineup in a room packed with law enforcement officers and in which Christopher could not even see him.

Speaking of the defendant, Ranni said that when he was in the army down in Georgia, "He began bragging how he hates blacks, how he hates niggers. While he was being treated in a hospital down there he smugly bragged about how he committed some despicable acts in Buffalo.

"He told these black nurses, these black people, he taunted them and told them, 'I'm a mass murderer. I killed those people in Buffalo, New York. I killed them because I—just something I had to do. I felt I had to do it.'"

Ranni told the judge of the search warrants that had been executed and said, "They found the gun collection that the defendant treasured so well. It was locked up. It was intact. One gun was missing—the Ruger."

Mark Mahoney kept his opening remarks short. He said the prosecution's case had two separate stages. The first he called the objective phase, when police gathered facts. The second he called the bias stage, which occurred after suspicion had fallen on Joseph Christopher. "I think you'll see from the evidence there occurred a point in time where rather than the investigation being guided by known facts and the theory that had been developed, the facts and theories are accommodated to deal with the defendant as a suspect, where the theory is molded to fit him and facts are rejected and portions of the theory are likewise rejected.

"I think you'll see that in the first stage there are suspects and theories rejected because they were not consistent with the theory, and in the second stage, I think you'll see a rejection of facts and theories which aren't reconcilable with the defendant as a suspect."

––––––––––

In the year that had passed between the time Joe had become a suspect and his trial, Donna Vanalden and Peter Tramontina were in turmoil. Because they were the two people who had been closest to Joe, and who could not invoke any privacy privileges afforded to relatives, investigators had focused on them and interviewed each on multiple occasions over a period of months. Both were on the prosecution list of witnesses.

Donna found the entire situation wrenching. She had spoken with Kevin Dillon and Mark Mahoney at length, but realistically she had little to offer the defense. She didn't feel she had much to offer the prosecution either, though they insisted she keep in close contact with them and be ready to testify.

In the fall, she'd had a long interview with Knapp at the district attorney's office that had left her very upset. She felt that he was trying to get her to answer questions a certain way and if she gave an answer that he didn't like, he would say to her, "That's not what I'm looking for," and reword the question. He appeared to get frustrated when she would not classify Joe as a marksman. He advised her that he did not want her to come across as a hostile witness in court, because the situation could become "very uncomfortable for her" if she did. He told her she had been very cooperative with them so far, and he would not expect her to call Kevin Dillon when she left and repeat to him what they had discussed.

She had been asked repeatedly if Joe looked any different from when she had known him. She said his nose looked different (likely because it had been broken when he was in the stockade), but otherwise no. She told them that his hair had always been tight, curly, and brown. It had never been long, stringy, or blond. Donna felt like they were trying to make him look like the composites.

Investigators asked her over and over again about Joe as a hunter and his knowledge of anatomy, whether he butchered animals. Did he know a lot about anatomy? Would she say he had a very good knowledge of butchering and anatomy? Until she had finally snapped back, "You mean like how to cut out a heart? No!"

————

Weber Avenue was once again a hot spot. Every new stage in the case brought renewed attention and unwanted visits.

There had been some bad moments last fall. A deer carcass had been left in the Christophers' driveway. On Halloween, some black kids had thrown a pumpkin through the front window of the house and vandalized a neighbor's car before being chased off by Bob Schmitt.

As Joe's murder trial opened, Laverne Becker was distraught. He went to his niece Cheryl's house across the street to commiserate. Laverne felt so terrible about Joe, so very bad about what was happening to him.

Cheryl listened to her uncle. She knew he was sincere, that he was truly suffering. She comforted him as best she could. Though she didn't say so—and hated to even think it—it occurred to Cheryl that perhaps her uncle had cause to feel very bad about what was happening to Joe.

————

The prosecution rested their case after eight days of testimony and thirty-eight witnesses. Kenny Paulson identified Joseph Christopher as the shooter of Glenn Dunn. He admitted giving police false statements. Kenny claimed his conscience had finally compelled him to tell the truth. Al Ranni downplayed the fact that Kenny had told the grand jury that the shooter had blond hair. Under cross-examination, Kenny testified that he had lied to police and the grand jury. He admitted he was aware of the more than $100,000 in reward money.

Madona Gorney, by contrast, was a strong witness. She was articulate, straightforward, and her account had never varied. Though it was never brought out publicly, Madona had withstood some opposition to her involvement in the case, from some of her own friends and family. A relative with the state police had pointedly told her not to get involved. Another told Madona that her father would "roll over in his grave" if he knew she was testifying against a white man accused of shooting a black. Some neighbors stopped speaking to her and her husband.

Looking back on it decades later, Madona Gorney would say, "I feel like I did the right thing. My father was a very prejudiced person, and so were a lot of people we knew, but that didn't mean I had to be. I've always felt like I did the right thing. I never regretted it."

Pretrial motions to exclude testimony of the army psychiatric nurses and Father Freeman had been rejected. All three took the stand for the prosecution, as did stockade guards Christopher Corwin and Richard Morganstern, the latter of whom had been present when Joseph told Captain Ames that he had done the things he said he did in Buffalo. Ames did not testify.

Father Freeman told of Christopher confiding in him that he had been bullied by blacks in his unit. "They called him faggot and wimp," the priest said. Freeman testified that Christopher had also been bullied by blacks in high school. Stating that he was bound by the priest-penitent privilege on other talks they'd had, Freeman said that Christopher had released him to disclose this particular conversation in order to help him get psychiatric treatment. "He said he was depressed and wanted to see a psychiatrist." Father Freeman described Christopher as "angered and depressed" because he felt he was being harassed in the training brigade. "He said he felt persecuted and could not find peace of mind." The priest said he had given no indication that he had acted on his anger.

Peter Tramontina testified that a Ruger .22 rifle had been among the Christopher gun collection. Peter had not seen the gun since late 1978 or early 1979. Donna Vanalden was not called to testify.

The prosecution's final witnesses were ballistics technicians Michael Dujanovich and Robert Perrigo, director of the Central Police Services crime lab. Perrigo generally confirmed the earlier ballistics-related testimony about matches between shell casings at the crime scenes and those found at the defendant's home and cabin. Cross-examined by Mahoney, the prosecution's firearms experts conceded that not all of the crime scene shells matched exactly with those found at the Christopher properties.

Arguing for dismissal on the grounds that the prosecution had not proved its case, Dillon noted the prosecution's failure to call Frenchy Cook, the man who had been walking with Emanuel Thomas the night of the murder. Cook had gotten a clear and close-up view of the killer and had said, "I will never forget his face." He had not identified Christopher nor anyone else at the lineup. Dillon found it telling that the prosecution had chosen not to put him on the stand. He argued that the murder of Harold Green was the weakest case. "There is a paucity of evidence that connects Mr. Christopher to that shooting. The best the people have been able to offer are witnesses who saw the back of someone running away from the scene, someone they believe was a male because of the way he ran." Concerning the Glenn Dunn shooting, Dillon said, "I can't conceive the court considering the testimony" of Kenny Paulson. Judge Marshall denied the motion for dismissal.

The defense case lasted three days. They called eleven witnesses that included one brought to counter the ballistics evidence. Peter Vito was a private investigator in Buffalo. Vito would say years later that he was not the ideal choice as a ballistics expert. He was, however, the best the defense could do within their resources. Therese Christopher, who earned $150.00 per week, had paid more than $6,700 for her son's defense by the previous May, using all her savings and borrowing money from friends and family, after which she remortgaged her home and put the Ellington property up for sale. Her funds having long since been exhausted, the defense was being paid from the public fund for indigent defendants.

The defense called army recruiter Pauline Ratcliff and one of Joe's aunts to testify that his hair had been short and dark brown in the fall of 1980. Army psychiatrist Major Eleanor Law took the stand to tell the court of her conversations with Christopher. She gave her opinion that Christopher may have been "delusional" when he had talked of the killings. In the absence of an insanity defense, it was the closest Dillon and Mahoney could come to introducing testimony about the defendant's mental state.

A witness to the shooting of Emanuel Thomas testified that the shooter had shoulder-length blond hair and a bald spot on the back of his head. His testimony was consistent with the statement he had given police in October 1980. The witness, a young man of mixed black and white race, conceded that he had waited a month after the murder before giving police a statement because he had not wanted to be involved in the case. He said his mother had also told him to lie. The young man claimed, as he had in the month after the murder, that two other young men had been with him and had also witnessed the shooting. Police had questioned the two men at the time but both denied being around or seeing anything.

Closing arguments were heard on April 26. Paulson and Gorney were the only witnesses who could place Christopher at any of the murder scenes. The prosecution argued that whoever had killed one victim must have killed all three, since the bullets had all been fired from the same gun.

In his closing, Mark Mahoney noted that at best, the prosecution had only proven that Christopher may have had access to the gun at one time, since all that had ever been found were a misfire and shell casings at his family homes. That did not prove he was the shooter. Further, the prosecution could not produce anyone who had seen the Sturm-Ruger 10/22 owned by Nicholas Christopher at any time within the past two years. He pointed out the wide variance between the defendant's appearance and witness descriptions of the shooter or shooters.

Reporters interviewed spectators of the trial for their thoughts. One black man explained why he had attended the trial, "My main reason was to find out if he really committed the crimes and also to find out why anybody would kill people of a particular race." He commented on the detached look of the defendant and wondered what had been going through his mind. "I can't say whether he did it or not. I'll leave that up to the judge."

Several people mentioned Christopher's disconnected look. One commented, "He seems like he's in another world."

On April 27, the morning after closing arguments, Judge Marshall found Joseph Christopher guilty of three counts of second-degree murder. The defendant showed no reaction. Therese Christopher, rosary beads clutched in her hand, took the verdict calmly.

Outside there were celebratory screams and cheers of delight from a large crowd who had assembled for the verdict. "He's guilty! He's guilty!" As the *Buffalo Evening News* described the scene, "It was a collective sigh of relief, a release of the doubts that had entered the minds of spectators, officials and reporters alike."

The Reverend Bennett Smith said he doubted the evidence presented at trial "was strong enough to convince twelve men and women beyond the shadow of a doubt," adding, "I think the black community can be proud that we have sitting on the bench in this city some of the best legal minds in the country."

Former DA Edward Cosgrove said, "I feel relief and satisfaction now that the investigation, prosecution and public anxiety have come to an end." He expressed sadness at the sorrow of the victims' families and the anguish of Mrs. Christopher, whom he called a "fine Christian person. Her family and all of the families harmed need our support and prayers."

Black leaders expressed satisfaction with the verdict but called on the current district attorney, Richard Arcara, to pursue investigation of the unsolved cases. Councilman George Arthur told reporters that he didn't believe Christopher was involved in the other murders that had taken place around the same time period. Councilman James Pitts echoed this sentiment, saying "I think there should be a redoubling of the efforts to solve the unsolved murders of two cab drivers," Parler Edwards and Ernest Jones. "Hopefully, Joseph Christopher will not be made a scapegoat."

––––––––––

In his last couple weeks at the holding center, Joe turned on Deputy Sal. He got hostile toward him and wanted to fight.

"Don't even think about it, Joe. I'll do ya," Sal told him.

"Call me Mr. Christopher!"

"How about if I call you Mr. Shithead?"

"That's it!" Joe yelled. "You and I are done!"

The argument was overheard and Sal was taken off the detail. The sheriff's department didn't want any problems with Christopher, especially now, when they were so close to getting rid of him.

———

On May 24, Judge Marshall sentenced Joe Christopher to sixty years in prison: twenty-five years to life for the murder of Glenn Dunn, twenty years to life for the murder of Harold Green, and fifteen years to life for the murder of Emanuel Thomas. The sentences were to be served consecutively. He would not be eligible for parole until the age of eighty-five. By 2:00 p.m. the same day, he was delivered to Attica Correctional Facility. The following day, he was transferred to Auburn Prison, over one hundred miles further east. For security reasons, authorities felt it best to place him far away from Western New York.

PART FIVE
THE BOX

I have seen mad people, and I have known some who were quite intelligent, lucid, even clear-sighted in every concern of life, except on one point. They could speak clearly, readily, profoundly on everything; till their thoughts were caught in the breakers of their delusions and went to pieces there, were dispersed and swamped in that furious and terrible sea of fogs and squalls which is called MADNESS.

—Guy de Maupassant, "The Horla"

Chapter 18

"**I AGREE WITH** the psychiatrists who diagnosed this man as a Paranoid Schizophrenic," the staff psychiatrist at Auburn wrote on May 25, 1982. "Joseph Christopher is a 26 year old, single, white male who just arrived in the correctional system. A request was made to see if he was a suicidal risk. Mr. Christopher is a notorious case; there was much about him in the newspapers.

"Mr. Christopher has been seen by a number of psychiatrists during the past few months who examined him to see if he was competent to stand trial. He was in Mid-Hudson to rule out malingering or a psychotic process. He refused to have psychological testing performed; they diagnosed him as an Atypical Personality Disorder.

"While in the stockade there is a history of alleged self-mutilation of the skin of the penis requiring sutures. We questioned Mr. Christopher directly about this. He said that someone had slipped him drugs and he was out of control at the time. When examined today in the Special Housing Unit, Mr. Christopher was guarded. He did not want to give any information; he felt it better not to. When asked if he was upset about what had happened, about the long sentence that he was recently given and particularly the fact that he says he is innocent, Mr. Christopher said he is able to keep cool. During the interview, he had a certain smile on his face—almost fixed. He denied any suicidal intent.

"Right now, the number one risk is that another inmate will kill him and so he will have to be watched very closely. Although possibly not acutely psychotic at present, he is a person who is very fragile and could decompensate very quickly. When he does decompensate, he will be a suicidal risk."

The Department of Corrections decided to keep Joseph Christopher in permanent protective custody to prevent him being harmed by other inmates. He would be kept in solitary confinement, known as "the Box," at Auburn.

Prison psychiatrists checked on Joe daily. He refused to speak to them. He sat quietly in his cell. He wrote a letter to his sister:

> I love you
> I still want the Tupperware
> also I can receive 40 lbs of food a month. I want 30 lbs of eggplant
> I don't want to have to eat to much state food they put stuff in it
> make me hurt inside and the base of my spine and sometimes your
> sholder joints unless they switched that jar of pickels I set out
> it will give pain and sorness in intestine & testicals.
> I hope to hear from the lawyer
> Take Care Love You
> Joseph Christopher

In early June, he was shipped to Rikers Island pending a court appearance on the New York City indictments. The district attorney in Manhattan asked Judge Benjamin Altman to vacate his prior ruling of incompetence for Joseph Christopher, based upon the determination by Justice William Flynn in Buffalo that Christopher was competent. Judge Altman declined to do so, stating that he was inclined to proceed with caution where there was a finding of incompetence made and reversed in such a short period of time.

Frank Bress, a defense attorney in New York City, and Mark Mahoney were court-appointed counsel for the Manhattan cases. Given Christopher's animosity toward Kevin Dillon, it made sense for Mahoney to work with counsel in New York City.

Frank Bress chaired the 18B Central Screening Committee, which assigned legal services to indigent defendants. He had formerly worked in the criminal defense division for the Legal Aid Society of New York and currently taught a criminal defense clinic law at New York University School of Law.

Bress had so far only met Christopher once, during the arraignment in a Manhattan courtroom in July 1981. He had been alarmed at Christopher's demeanor at the time. He'd found him catatonic. He had his first real meeting with his client in June of 1982. As Frank Bress would later recall, "It was very clear to me that he had very serious psychiatric difficulties. It was hard to have a conversation with him where he stayed on track. He spun off into delusional topics. I couldn't get him to focus on anything substantive about his case. He kept talking about a conspiracy.

"At the time, I was doing a lot of homicide defense work dealing with psychiatric defense. I had represented people who were malingerers and I had represented people who were seriously mentally ill, and he was seriously mentally ill. It was clear to me that he was not competent, and it was also clear to me that the best defense, if not the only defense, he had on the New York City charges was psychiatric. He refused to allow me to interpose the mental disease or defect defense. And that becomes a catch-22. If he's not competent, how can he make the decision? Contrary to his wishes, I made the motion for a competency hearing."

Joe was taken to a clinic in the Manhattan courthouse but refused to speak to the psychiatrist. He was then scheduled for a psychiatric examination at Rikers Island on June 9. He refused to come out of his cell. He wanted to talk to his attorney.

He called Frank Bress and asked him to come out to Rikers as soon as possible. His food was being poisoned, he said. He had managed to save a sample of it in a plastic bag and he wanted his attorney to have it tested.

Bress met with Joe prior to another court appearance in June. Once again, Bress attempted to discuss his case and the charges against him. "He had his moments of lucidity," the attorney recalled. "He could be helpful in talking about historical things, his family, his time in the army. But then he'd get caught in these little loops, where things were tangentially related to one another but had nothing to do with the case. It was impossible to get him to focus." Bress asked him if and when he had been in New York City in December 1980. "The West Village is full of fags," Joe told him. "Christopher Street is in the West Village. It's named after me, but I'm not gay." As Bress recalled, "I had many, many conversations with him like that, where he'd spin off into things that made no sense at all."

The client was adamant that he would not submit to mental examinations.

Frank Bress inquired about the possibility of having Christopher committed to the psychiatric ward at New York's Bellevue Hospital if he continued to be uncooperative with the state psychiatrists. Hillel Bodek, an administrator at Bellevue, expressed concern over security at the institution. Bellevue was overcrowded, which would make it difficult to isolate Christopher. As the majority of the facility's population was black, Bodek feared for both the safety of Christopher and the hospital's patients and support staff.

Bress spoke with Joe and told him that the psychiatric exams had been ordered by the judge and that they had to take place. Joe insisted he was eager to get to trial. "Then cooperate with the psychiatrists," his attorney told him, and further advised that if he didn't speak with the state doctors, he might be sent to Bellevue.

Christopher was delivered to court for an appearance the following day. He had refused to leave Rikers, but guards had told him "one way or another" he was going. Christopher was brought into the courtroom briefly and then sent to the holding pen while another case was heard. When he reentered the court about twenty minutes later, Frank Bress noticed that he was wearing different clothes.

Judge Altman asked Christopher why he refused to cooperate with psychiatrists. Christopher gave a rambling answer, disjointed and without a logical sequence, basically stating that he'd been found competent by Mid-Hudson and he just didn't want to see any more doctors. The judge explained that he was aware of the prior examinations but he was not going to accept these dated findings. He explained that it would be in Christopher's best interest to talk to the psychiatrists for an hour rather than be committed to a mental institution for a month. Joseph replied, "I won't talk to any psychiatrists." Judge Altman ordered him directly to Bellevue for a period of thirty days. He was taken back upstairs to the holding pen until arrangements could be made for his transport to the institution.

When Frank Bress emerged from court, reporters asked him about the "incident" that had happened upstairs with Christopher. He didn't know of any incident. Bress went and spoke to one of the court officers who told him that Christopher had been assailed by garbage and excrement thrown by inmates. Guards and officers had formed a circle around Christopher to shield him from further assault. Christopher had been hit by the refuse, and that's why he had changed clothes.

Bress went to the correction office at the courthouse to inform a supervisor about the assault. The supervisor was unaware of the holding pen incident and was furious that a court officer had informed the attorney and the press. He called the correction desk and told the officer, "You'd better tell those guys to mind their own business and learn to keep their mouths shut!" The officer claimed that only water was thrown at Christopher. The supervisor didn't buy it.

Bress remained in the office while the supervisor called Bellevue to see what arrangements were being made for Christopher to ensure his safety. Discussing the situation over the phone with Bellevue, the corrections supervisor said, "There are inmates, and there are inmates. But inmate Joseph Christopher is like Adolf Hitler."

The supervisor hung up and explained to Bress that his client couldn't be sent to Bellevue until early July. To house Christopher in a cell by himself, four inmates would have to be moved. They'd also have to arrange for a twenty-four-hour, one-on-one guard. Bress said that he hoped this would be adequate, to which the corrections supervisor replied, "Why don't he just attempt an escape—others have—and make it all easier on everyone."

———

Therese Christopher went to Rikers Island to visit her son. She and her daughters kept largely within their own tight circle. According to friends and neighbors, they did not mention or discuss Joe with anyone outside the family.

Weber Avenue, at least outwardly, had returned to normal after Joe's sentence and transfer out of the city. The reporters no longer knocked on doors or showed up with cameras. There remained, however, a perceptible change; a lingering awareness about what had happened, and a sense of discretion. No one wanted to make things any worse for Therese and the girls by bringing up what felt like an unmentionable subject.

"We all felt bad for the Christophers," Cheryl Schmitt recalled. "We wanted them to know we cared. But nobody knew what to say. I ran into Mrs. Christopher at a grocery store that summer and I said, 'Hello, Mrs. Christopher!' She just kind of ducked her head. I think she was afraid of anyone recognizing her. I went to school with Joe's oldest sister and I'd see her once in a while. There were many times I wanted to ask how Joe was doing but I just didn't know if I should, so I didn't."

Following his conviction, most people who knew Joe came to accept that he was guilty of being the .22 Caliber Killer. The big question was why.

Laverne Becker still mentioned Joe to his niece. He missed him. It was quite the loss for Laverne. He lamented that he'd never see him again because Joe would spend the rest of his life in prison.

Everyone seemed to agree that Joe must have snapped. That much seemed clear. As for the victims he'd targeted, people who had known Joe for a long time had their theories.

"I hate to say this," Cheryl Schmitt would say years later, "but my uncle Laverne was a very prejudiced person. He constantly ranted about blacks, but he didn't say 'blacks.' He hated them and he was very vocal about it. Joe spent a lot of time with Laverne, especially after Joe's dad died. I felt like my uncle had a big influence on Joe, and not a good one, at least when it came to that.

"Laverne was all about 'protecting' the area from blacks. He had lived in that neighborhood forever and he absolutely did not want any blacks living there, or even passing by, really. The neighborhood had started changing in the late '60s and some black people had started to move in. He didn't want them here. He wanted them to stay out, stay away."

According to neighbors, Mr. Becker found a kindred spirit in Nicholas Christopher. "The two of them were pretty tight friends and they'd just go off about it all the time, constantly using the n-word," said another resident. "The city put in a basketball court in the Lang-Weber playground at the end of our street. One night somebody cut off all the basketball hoops, and everybody in the neighborhood believed it was Red Becker and Mr. Christopher.

"Joe and I were friends when we were kids, pretty good pals up until about the age of twelve or thirteen. I used to hang out at his house and we'd camp in a tent in his backyard in the summer. We went our separate ways as teenagers, when he got into cars and hunting and I was all about playing sports, and just saw each other occasionally. I wasn't in Buffalo at the time the killings were happening or when he was on trial. My mother sent me clippings from the newspaper.

"The guy they were describing didn't sound anything like the guy I knew. My memories of Joe were all good. He was a couple years older than me and I remember him looking out for the younger kids. I came home crying one Halloween because a bully took all my candy and Joe went and found him and got it back for me.

"The one thing that struck me when all this came out was thinking back about his dad and Red Becker, their attitude and the way they always talked about blacks. Even for that time, they were extreme. I only heard that kind of talk when I was over at Joe's house but Joe heard it all the time. I'm not saying that it was anybody else's fault that Joe did what he did. I wondered, though, when his mind went, if all that stuff he heard all the time about blacks when he was growing up had something to do with why he turned in that direction."

The family of Laverne Becker confirmed that he and Nicholas were responsible for destroying the basketball hoops in an effort to keep black kids out of the playground.

Domenic Cortese had been in elementary school and Cub Scouts with Joe. By the time his childhood friend made headlines, Domenic had long since moved away from the east side and owned a large and successful construction company. He kept in touch with guys from the old neighborhood and naturally enough they discussed the news about Joe Christopher. "Everybody was stunned when they first announced who the killer was. Frankly, we thought it had to be a mistake. The most remarkable thing about Joe was how unremarkable he was. He was a nice kid, never a troublemaker, but very reserved and passive. He was hard to get to know. We more or less co-existed throughout elementary school and scouting but never really became friends. My mom was the den mother for our Cub Scout pack and I remember her feeling a little sorry for him, you know, poor kid, he had to be cajoled into doing anything.

"A lot of us talked afterwards and we tried to think back to who his good friends were and we really couldn't come up with anybody. He never seemed to have any close connections."

Another friend from those days remembered Joe much the same way, and recalled Mr. Christopher, who volunteered with their Cub Scout pack, as a nice man. While most acquaintances from Joe's early childhood remembered Nicholas Christopher as just a strict Italian father, not terribly different from many others of that era, the dynamic seemed to change when Joe entered his teens. Joe's friends from adolescence and young adulthood described the same personality traits in Nicholas that others had observed—the racism, the criticism of his son—as intensified, or perhaps just more readily on display.

Speaking of Nicholas, another friend and neighbor of Joe's said, "He was the most racist guy I ever met in my life. If a black person walked by his house, he'd take potshots at them with a pellet gun and yell out, 'You niggers don't come by my house. Get away from here. You don't belong here.' Stuff like that.

"He was nuts. And he had a ton of guns. He was a small man in stature but everybody knew that he had a million guns so nobody messed with him. I was scared to death of him. So was Joey, actually. I was just glad I was the right color, so to speak. My dad couldn't stand Mr. Christopher. And my dad had his own prejudices, but Joey's dad was something else.

"Now Joey, he wasn't like that," his friend continued. "Joey was the nicest guy ever. He liked everybody. Joey had black friends but he had to be secretive about it. His dad didn't allow it and he used to get his ass beat if he talked to anybody that wasn't white. Joey was friends with this one black kid named Greg. Well, one day his dad caught him walking home from school with Greg. Joey got in a shitload of trouble for that.

"We could always tell when his old man had worked him over because the next day he didn't say much, was very quiet and to himself. Kind of closed in. He'd have a big shiner and we'd ask, 'What happened to you?' He'd say, 'Oh, I got in a fight with a bunch of niggers,' or something like that. That's what he would tell everybody. And it wasn't that. Because Joe had black friends. One day I said to him flat out, 'Joey, why don't you hit your old man back?' He was in his late teens by then and he was a couple inches taller than his dad. He said to me, 'I can't. He'll kill me.' He just cowered in front of his father. The guy was such a bully.

"We'd hang out at the garage near Joey's house, working on cars," the friend said. "Joey was real proud of that '67 Camaro he had, the way he'd gotten it all fixed up. One day his dad walks in. Joey had the car all polished. Mr. Christopher looks and tells him there's a dent on the fender. Joey's saying, 'Where? Where?' His dad keeps pointing and Joey tells him he doesn't see the dent. Mr. Christopher picks up a ballpeen hammer, smashes it down on the fender and says to him, 'You see it now?' Joey just hung his head and walked away.

"He never stood up to his dad and he never said a bad word about him, either. His dad would call him names right in front of us, tell Joey he was like a queer. I never got why Joey kept taking it, why he never lashed back. I don't know. Maybe if you don't know anything else, it seems normal."

Even those who didn't hang out at the garage sensed Joe's trouble at home. Marilyn Chamberlain was the mother of Joe's high school friends, Leigh and Scott. Joe stayed at their home so often that Marilyn began to wonder. "He'd be with us for days. I'd ask him, 'Do your parents know where you are?' He'd tell me, 'Oh yeah, they know where I am.' I didn't know his parents so I didn't know what the situation was. I said, 'You sure I shouldn't be calling your mom or dad and finding out if it's okay for you to stay over like you do?' Because it was getting to be every night, you know.

"I finally took him aside one day and said to him, 'Honey, what's going on? Is everything okay? Did you get kicked out of your house?' He said no, he hadn't been kicked out. I asked if he was having problems at home and he told me, 'Well, I like my dad.' He said he didn't get along with his mother or his sisters. One of his sisters was dating a black guy and he didn't like that. I guess it caused problems with his dad.

"Joe was fine with us. He was always very courteous and nice to me, really sweet. One Christmas he gave me a beautiful crucifix. We had a lot of kids stay with us but he was the only one who ever brought me a gift. He was a very nice kid but there was something different about him, a little strange. He was very quiet. It was like pulling teeth to get him to talk, to carry on a conversation.

"He took to my kids and didn't want to leave. He liked being around our house. I think he just wanted to be in a quiet place, you know? Someplace where there wasn't a lot of yelling all the time."

Scott Chamberlain was close friends with Joe for a period of five or six years but had few memories of being at the Christopher home. "When we'd stop by his house, we never stuck around. Joe always wanted to get the hell out of there as fast as he could. They used to keep these beagles, hunting dogs, in a kennel in the backyard and it was up to Joe to clean out the kennels. We'd swing by so he could do what he had to do. His dad would come out and start yelling at him if the kennels weren't clean enough or whatever, just start these fights in the driveway. A couple times his dad ordered us to leave, or we just left on our own when the fighting started. One of Joey's sisters, one of the older ones, he didn't get along with at all. They would always have words.

"We spent a lot more time out at the cabin. The four of us would go out there, Joey, my brother Leigh, Peter Tramontina and me. We'd go out on weekends to camp and do a lot of shooting. That's where Joey seemed to be the most relaxed, when it was just the four of us hanging out at the cabin. He'd worry, though, about anything breaking or getting messed up. He was deathly afraid of screwing anything up because of his father. We had to be really careful to leave everything exactly the way it was when we got there."

The cabin seemed to be the place where Joe could escape the tensions of the city and his own home. As Scott recalled, "Joey told us about his sister dating a black guy and he wasn't too happy about that. Actually, it was the dad that was unhappy. His dad had found out about it. That might've been what one of the fights was about when we were over at the house once but it's hard to remember exactly because there was always something. I don't ever remember Joey saying anything else about blacks other than that whole thing over his sister. Joey was the only son and his dad expected him to do something about it."

Marilyn Chamberlain recalled, "We used to have this little dog that barked like mad whenever a black person walked by our house. I don't know why, because we always had black kids around. But he'd bark and chase them away. It was embarrassing. Once when Joe was over I said, 'I don't know what's wrong with this dog that he doesn't like black people.' Joe said, 'My father's like him.' I told him, 'Joe, don't talk about your father like that,' and he said, 'I'm not kidding you.'

"I was very surprised when Joe joined the army," Marilyn said. "It really surprised me that he'd get into something where he was bound to be yelled at a lot, because that's how things are in the service, and I thought, he went through all that at home and now he's putting himself in the same position again."

Like everyone else, the Chamberlains were stunned by Joe's arrest in Buffalo. They wanted to go and visit him at the holding center but were told that Joe didn't want to see anybody. "I thought for sure he'd see me," Scott said, "but no." The Chamberlains were equally baffled by the sketches that had appeared in the newspaper. "I looked at those pictures and I said, 'That's not Jocy.'

"At first I didn't believe any of it. After a while I thought, okay, the shootings with the .22, that could be true, because I knew Joey could shoot and it was the [his] neighborhood, and I knew he was upset about that stuff that had gone on with his sister and his dad. Not that it made any sense for him to go out shooting people. I guessed that he had just flipped out.

"I figured it had to be something his dad had said to him that set him off. When Joe's dad told him something—he was afraid of his father. And I'm sure his father said something to him and it just set him off. I thought maybe Joey did it to get back in his good graces or prove himself after the fact, even though his dad was gone, something like that. I mean, what else would set him off?

"I didn't think it had anything to do with being bullied in school. Burgard was rough, but I don't remember Joey getting bullied any worse than anyone else. He never got beat up that I know of. I'm sure he would have said something, because he knew damn well that the four of us, or the other three of us, we would've done something. And we got along pretty much with everybody around there."

Joe's friends from the neighborhood had the same theory. As one put it, "His dad was the ruler, you know. I mean he ruled the whole house. And when he died, Joey took it real hard and kind of took over the man-of-the-family thing, or tried to. He just snapped at some point, I guess. I can't give a reason for why Joey killed, because I mean he wasn't that type of a guy. He really wasn't. For whatever reason, he just lost it. I'm not sure he did all those shootings, though. I think there was somebody else out there too.

"The papers kept saying that Joe was a racist and that's why he killed people. None of the explanations made any sense. There was a story about a black guy stealing a gun from him and that's why he did it. Come on, who does that? Who wakes up one morning and says to himself, a black man stole my gun so I think I'll go on a killing spree?"

As it turned out, the missing Beretta handgun that Joe reportedly thought had been stolen from a backpack in his basement—and which had led to the suspension of his pistol permit—had not been taken at all. According to Zach DiFusco, the gun was found in the basement months later by Therese. It had fallen behind a sink.

The friend continued, "I'm not saying that Joey didn't do what they said he did, or at least some of it, but there had to be something else going on, something more than a stolen gun or being pissed off about high school. None of the stuff they were saying in the papers made any sense if you knew Joe."

There was another point on which most seemed to agree. Few were convinced that Joe had murdered Parler Edwards or Ernest Jones. As Scott Chamberlain said, "I never believed Joe had anything to do with cutting the hearts out of the cab drivers. The shootings, yeah, I can see that. But the thing with the hearts, that part I just said, no friggin way. That's not Joey. I never believed he would go that far. I think they just tacked those on to him. There's no friggin way Joey was that ruthless."

———

Frank Bress had become a part of the conspiracy.

He refused to have Joe's food tested for poison and drugs. He explained to Joe that he had discussed the matter with people he knew and trusted at Rikers and was assured that Joe's food had not been tainted. Joe clammed up and would have nothing further to do with him. In court, Joe raved to the judge, "It's a fucking conspiracy!"

Joe spent two weeks in Bellevue. He was discharged on July 26, his twenty-seventh birthday, and returned to Rikers Island. He wrote home.

A poor fool in rags is all I care to be
I don't need the once removed conversaded form of programing
I don't want the drugs
I am not a raceist everyone should socialize under one good
Ignorence is happiness: He who keeps closest to the earth
with the wind is best off
Jesus I Ask!
You!
are the wind?

Bellevue informed Frank Bress that they were awaiting receipt of Christopher's military documents before completing their report. Social worker Hillel Bodek told the attorney that he hoped the material would be available soon because Christopher was eager to go to trial. Bodek was of the opinion that Christopher was capable of cooperating with his attorney when he wanted to. As for the military records, Bodek said he didn't expect to glean much additional information. Major Law's report, he said, was sufficient for him to form a background opinion. He felt that Christopher was crazy at the time he cut his penis in the stockade. "Acute psychosis with remission." Of his own interview with Christopher, the social worker said, "I certainly think he's given me enough to go on. I'm waiting, officially, for the military reports, but my suspicion is that he'll be found fit. There's no evidence of either delusional thinking or behavior, at this point."

Asked if his meeting with Christopher had shed any light on his refusal to talk about his decisions, Bodek said, "My feeling is that they gave him sixty years to life, so what more can they do to him? He's not going to participate in this shit. He's had it with shrinks. He's had it with the whole thing.

"He's competent. He's fit. I think he should go to trial. Unless there's something super spectacular or surprising in the military stuff, which I don't expect there will be, then I know how I would find him. It's like I said all along. If he doesn't give us any indication to show he's unfit, he's fit."

Frank Bress had been cautious with Joe on the issue of the competency exam. He was afraid that if Joe knew he had requested it, the attorney-client relationship would be further damaged. Bodek told Joe it was Bress who had asked for the examination.

At a hearing before Judge Altman on July 27, Joe asked the judge if this was true. The judge hesitated, telling him that having the exam was in everyone's best interest, especially his own. Joe argued that he was competent, "by a preponderance of the evidence."

The case was adjourned until September 21 pending receipt of the report from Bellevue and completion of the competency phase, which Frank Bress felt should also include an examination by an independent psychiatrist. Joe asked if he could be sent to Auburn Prison instead of Rikers Island in the meantime. Bress told Joe that going back to Auburn would make it impossible for him to be examined by an independent psychiatrist Bress had contacted in Manhattan. Joe said it didn't matter, since he wasn't going to talk to the doctor anyway.

His request was granted and he was returned to Auburn.

Why, Why do people want to
be mean I don't want to be mean
and I am not So then I am locked
up and Every movement I make in
even just breathing, sitting, and
sleeping is visious or has sub
vertive underlain or hidden intent
to some averted eye
How did I get here I use to play

with children and walk old ladys
to the store and shovle snow
from walks at four in the morning
before I went to work

In September, Joe wrote a letter to Judge Frederick Marshall, who had convicted him in the Buffalo trial. He asked if Judge Marshall would consider representing him on his appeal. He also wrote that he'd like to return to Mid-Hudson Psychiatric Center, because he'd been unable to explain his feelings and reasoning when he was there before.

Therese visited Joe at Auburn. He told her he had decided to plead insanity in the New York cases. He said he'd had what he since had figured out were delusions. He asked her to write to Kevin Dillon and send him a note that he wrote. The note read:

Hello it is me
Who am I
I am an entity in a hypethectical
I tried to go to the bughouse but they would not let me in
so I was [unreadable]
the voice told me every wear I went the voice were
now I don't listen to the vocice I am in prison and
don't Belong hear because I am good Do you understand me
What voices?
delution
if the TV is talking and you think it is talking to you - delution
or people are talking and you think they are programing you

Therese asked Joe why he hadn't told Kevin about this before. He said he couldn't talk about it then. He thought he should go back to Mid-Hudson. He said he thought that if he pleaded insanity, he could get the previous sentence overturned and might get out of jail or a mental institution someday. His mother told him it was very unlikely that would ever happen.

In late October, Joe was sent to Mid-Hudson from Auburn. It was not by his own request, however, but at the request of prison psychiatrists, who advised that he was noncommunicative and a suicide risk. He also had to be examined for competency. Bellevue still had not submitted their report.

Dr. Paul Chellappa, who had deemed Joe competent earlier that year before Judge Flynn in Buffalo, met with him once again. "I came back because the last time I was unable to discuss the crime I was charged with, in detail," Joe told him. According to the report filed by Chellappa on October 31, Joe said he was in Manhattan in December 1980. He bought a knife and stabbed a man. He could not account further for the crime except to say he "had to kill this man." He wouldn't elaborate except to say, "I tell you I did it. I did it with my hands. I killed a man. This was in New York." When he was asked if he was confessing to a crime, he replied, "No, I'm just telling you what I did because I was unable to tell you the last time. I hope you can understand. I wanted to discuss this with my attorney and then go back to stand trial."

Dr. Chellappa wrote, "Having known this patient in the past, he continues to be stubborn with a teasing trait. No psychopathology indicative of any mental disorder noted."

On November 4, Joseph was examined by Dr. Ting, another psychiatrist at Mid-Hudson. Joseph related that the charges against him stemmed from around July 1979, in Erie County. Dr. Ting quoted Joe's statement: "I was at my parents' house. I was working, sweeping streets and shoveling snow for my neighbors. I joined the U.S. Army. I don't remember the dates, but I started shooting people on the street with a .22 caliber rifle left to me by my father. I sawed off the tip, hiding it in a paper bag. I shot without knowing who the person was, only I know they were of dark skin at close range. I can remember thinking I had nothing to lose. I shot three people, but actually four and left them there. I shot them in the head. It was broad daylight and at night too. There were some people around. I think somebody saw me, a lady saw me sitting, then I left. I shot four people in a couple of days. I left and went to a nearby shopping center and went home. I got rid of the rifle by melting it with a torch."

Regarding the New York City crimes, Dr. Ting noted that Joe was not sure of the date. It may have been September 17, 1979, or Christmas. "I went to New York City by bus because I thought I had to kill people. I purchased a kitchen knife, ten inches, at Macy Department Store, went to the street. I don't remember how many I stabbed in the chest. One person fights with me and he ran away later. I threw away the knife. I don't know where. I was supposed to have explained this to my lawyer."

Dr. Ting stated that Joseph grasped his charges of second-degree murder. "I killed someone. I shot and stabbed people." The psychiatrist had him explain the roles of judge, jury, and attorneys. When asked how he would plead, Joe answered, "I will talk to my lawyer about this." What happens if you are convicted? "I go to prison." If found not guilty? "My lawyer defends me. I go to some places so I wouldn't be stabbing or shooting people."

Dr. Ting concluded that Joseph had a schizoid personality disorder that did not interfere with his ability to cooperate with his lawyer or assist in his own defense. He declared him "at present competent to stand trial." He was sent back to Rikers Island.

On December 15, 1982, Mark Mahoney sent a letter to Erie County District Attorney Richard Arcara.

> Dear Mr. Arcara:
> On or about November 22 of this year, Tony Farina, investigative reporter with WGR-TV channel 2, reported on television that Mr. Christopher had confessed to psychiatrists that he was responsible for four .22 caliber killings in the Buffalo area in addition to killings in New York City and represented that this had been confirmed with law enforcement officers in Erie County.
> Frank Bress, co-counsel for Mr. Christopher, checked with James Vogel, in charge of the New York prosecution, who confirmed that information concerning the results of psychiatric examinations was only provided to members of your office and not to any other officials such as police, sheriff, state police, etc.

Therefore, it is reasonable to conclude that your office is directly responsible for the leaking of this information.

Obviously, this is an ethical problem for whichever assistant district attorney may have revealed this information, but it may be the subject of future applications to the court since there are pending indictments against Mr. Christopher in Erie County and unresolved appeals. I am providing the information to you at present so that you can cause the matter to be investigated and take whatever action you deem appropriate.

Joe was back to insisting that he was not mentally ill. He wanted a non-jury trial, immediately. He was also insisting, once again, that his food at Rikers was being poisoned and refused to eat.

He protested vociferously when they shipped him to Bellevue again on November 29. Once there, he would not cooperate with doctors and staff who tried to speak with him. He refused all medical tests. The only thing he had to say was that he had no mental illness.

Bellevue submitted their report to the court on December 1. Their diagnosis was borderline personality disorder, which they claimed did not interfere with his ability to understand the charges or effectively cooperate with counsel, if he chose to do so. "Although the patient may have a defense of lack of criminal responsibility or of extreme emotional disturbance in which he refuses to cooperate, and although he may wish to have a judge trial and waive a jury, he is correct in his view that such decisions are his to make. He certainly understands the consequences of such decisions, as has [sic] been explained to him by counsel. Such decisions are knowing and volitional.

"Psychodynamically, this case presents a young man with a history of learning disabilities, who had a stormy relationship with his father and who has been frustrated in his attempts to succeed in school. Often, learning disabled persons grow up quite frustrated at their limitations, which they cannot understand. Family dynamics often exacerbate such feelings and, as in this case, lead to the person's developing diminished self-esteem, lessened self-confidence, and depression. The patient developed significant and appropriate anger at his predicament, which he feared and attempted to control. Yet, eventually, it built up and surfaced, under the pressure of having to prove himself and under the added strain of his father's death.

"He is a lonely and depressed individual who fears being taken advantage of by others and fears losing control of his own emotions, which threaten to overwhelm him. He struggles to maintain his limited sense of self and sense of independence. Were he to lose this sense of some control over his life, he might well decompensate into a depressive psychosis once again, something he defends against.

"Although competent and not presently psychotic, this patient suffers from significant chronic mental illness. He is somewhat fragile emotionally, and has erected significant defenses to protect himself. Under pressure, he might once again decompensate and/or become actively suicidal."

In other words, he was significantly mentally ill and could have another psychotic breakdown under stress, but okay to stand trial.

Bellevue certified him as competent and shipped him back to Rikers Island.

Judge Altman was not so content to accept findings of competency from two overcrowded state institutions with an interest in cycling patients through their doors as expediently as possible. He granted Frank Bress's request for an examination of Joseph Christopher by an independent, board-certified psychiatrist.

Dr. John Baer Train was a Manhattan psychiatrist, a diplomate of the American boards of psychiatry and neurology. He met with Joseph for five hours in December and again in January 1983 at the Supreme Court Psychiatric Clinic.

Dr. Train reviewed the voluminous file. In preparing his own report, Dr. Train noted that Joseph's background was well documented elsewhere and need not be repeated, except for two points: "He was raised by a domineering, authoritative father who had a repressive influence on the defendant," and "After the father died, he became socially withdrawn and broke his relationship with his girlfriend. He appeared to pathologically mourn for his father, making daily visits to the grave."

Dr. Train asked Joseph pointed questions about the crimes and pending trial and recorded his answers. Joseph acknowledged that he had considered making a plea of "not guilty because of insanity at the time—being disturbed." He said he knew the purpose of this examination: "To give your opinion as to my mental condition in 1980 when these things occurred . . . because at the time it happened I was not in my control. Difficult things I heard and saw, listening to TV and radio and thinking they were talking to me, what the announcers say."

When asked if he would testify, Joe became confused. "To say what? Seeing what I've seen, it would be better for me to really not say." He shook his head, perplexed. "I don't think it would be—if I say something, they are going to try to—I've seen lawyers and they try to twist."

Asked why he did not attempt an insanity defense in Buffalo, Joseph said because he "didn't trust anyone" and made an irrelevant reference to not wanting a TV in his cell. He would give no reason for his adamant stand about refusing a jury trial. Dr. Train discussed this with him at length. Joe insisted he must have nonjury trials and would not consider an opposing opinion on this point from his attorney.

As to the offenses, Joseph said, "I know I shot a guy in the head and thinking before I pulled the trigger you have nothing to lose, like do or die. That is what I was feeling and I can't explain it. I thought people . . ." Pause. "Things happening to me . . ." Pause. "Like I was walking and this black guy hit me in the stomach and he said after work to come to this place. A few weeks later I hear the black man who I worked with said crazy shit to me." Pause. "I didn't understand what he said. Also on radio and TV, the announcers say things."

"Like what?" the doctor asked.

"I don't remember. Things you see—no specific thing. It was a collection. I remember one thing when I saw the black guy, I saw a dead animal." At that point in time, Joseph said, he "felt something was wrong" and went to a psychiatric clinic where he was told, "nothing was wrong with me" and he was sent home. He said that before enlisting in the army, "all kinds of things broke loose. I started shooting people." Asked why, he paused and said, "A combination of things I heard and seen telling me to do these things."

"Why?" Dr. Train asked.

"I don't know."

"Why only blacks?"

"I don't know." He made a gesture of futility and became confused. "I can't explain—like I said, I thought do or die."

"Were you told to shoot or kill?"

"Not in those words. It is what I concluded from what I believed was happening."

"If not told to, why do it?"

"It all meant do it or die. The kids on the street used to say there is my friend Joe." He vaguely tried to explain that his masculinity was in doubt if he "did not do such things as drink at a bar. If you can't do this or that"—he paused—"you aren't a man." If not a man? "A child." He explained, "These people were closing in on me. I heard different things like people in a restaurant. I hear them talk under their breath, like talking to me."

"Saying what?"

"I don't remember." He made an exasperated gesture of perplexity. He "heard things to come to New York and stick people." He related the same details as he had to Dr. Ting but he was now clear that this had happened while he was on Christmas leave from the army. He didn't know how many people he stabbed in the chest. During this period, he walked the streets singing "Silent Night" and visiting churches to pray and be warm. He mentioned a list of the churches he visited.

He returned to Fort Benning where he stabbed a black soldier. He refused to eat in the stockade and later cut his penis. Of the self-mutilation, Dr. Train wrote, "He can't or won't explain this bizarre action. Again, he believes he was drugged and because of it, spontaneously and voluntarily confessed to the murders." Dr. Train noted that Joe now believed his food was drugged at Rikers and he had given his attorney a plastic bag with food in it to be analyzed.

"He receives no medication and indicated he would refuse it if it were prescribed," Dr. Train wrote. "He would frequently make a gesture of exasperated futility when he could not explain his behavior or lose his trend of thought. He was ill at ease and guarded. His speech was frequently rambling and irrelevant with inappropriate pauses in the middle of and between sentences as he had difficulty in expressing himself. His mood and affect were inappropriate smiling and intransigence. It appeared necessary that he be in control of the situation and avoid being influenced. As a result, he assumed a posture of resistance, in a power struggle to protect his autonomy.

"There was a severe thought disorder with loose associations, tangential thinking, blocking, and loss of goal idea. As a result, he frequently surrendered to perplexity with a gesture of futility in trying to express himself when he couldn't maintain a trend of thought. When asked why he insisted on a non-jury trial, he irrelevantly stated: 'From what I understand as to what happened to me seems like bullshit. Like you go for a walk and go into a restaurant and hear people talk and think they are talking about me.' What has this to do with your decision to have a non-jury trial? 'None. I don't know why I said it.' When asked about his vague reference to masculinity, he stated: 'If you didn't do this or that you weren't a man.' Explain? 'An older person doesn't manipulate children with their hands. They just—I don't know how to explain it.'"

Dr. Train gave further examples of what he termed a severe thinking disorder with loss of goal idea. He asked Joseph if the offenses were wrong.

"I don't know," he answered. Pause. "I feel," pause, "this is what I got to do or die."

"Is it against the law?"

"I had no reason for the law. I never did anything with the law, I played with kids. I had no reason to steal, I had no need for money, a couple of dollars a week. I ate good, worked hard, and stayed in the country when I wanted to."

"What are you trying to say?" the doctor asked.

"I don't know."

"What was the question?"

"I don't know."

"Wasn't it if your acts were against the law?"

"Was Vietnam, World War II, World War I against the law," Joseph answered. "It is what I felt. It was what I had to do."

Joseph made vague references to delusions of influence but couldn't explain other than to say he heard people talk over TV, radio, and in bars.

He denied auditory hallucinations and denied motivation by a mission to get rid of evil or black people. All he could say was that in some nebulous way, his victims were his enemies and that from what he heard and the way people acted, he inferred that he was to join the army and kill. He was unable to say why other than "things you hear." He refused to discuss the self-mutilation of his penis other than to make a vague reference to something he heard someone say, not in relation to him; something he heard when he was young.

Dr. Train wrote: "He has only superficial insight in that he believes he was not 'mentally normal' at the time of the offenses and was not in his 'control.' After conviction and imprisonment, he began to believe he wasn't responsible and asked to be returned to Mid-Hudson to speak to Dr. Chellappa.

"He knew the nature of the weapons and that he used them to kill. He stated that he ran from the offenses 'to get out of the immediate area.' When asked why, he stated: 'Ever see a nature animal program on TV? You see a bear kill an animal and instinctively run away and then come back.' He believes that by having a no jury trial, Jesus Christ will convince the judge to free him."

Dr. Train gave a diagnosis of schizophrenia, paranoid type, chronic. He concluded: "This man is suffering from schizophrenia, a psychosis with a severe thinking disorder which renders him incapable of conferring rationally without loose associations, tangentiality, blocking, and loss of goal ideas. Although guarded and self-serving, the presence of this thinking disorder rules out malingering.

"Although he has a sophisticated understanding of legal procedures, the thinking disorder impairs his ability to relate, recall, and appreciate his condition. It makes him unable to confer meaningfully with his attorney. He overcompensates for his faulty self-image by a need to maintain his integrity of self through an exaggerated insistence on his own autonomy to make decisions and be in full control of his situation. At present, he does, as a result of mental disease, lack the capacity to assist in his defense."

"KILLED 13, CHRISTOPHER SAYS. 'Was Ordered' to Commit .22-Caliber Murders." The headline appeared in the *Buffalo News* on Sunday, September 18, 1983. It was the first installment of a two-part interview, the second half of which ran in the following day's newspaper. An announcement had appeared in the paper on Friday. "As the third anniversary of the nightmare that became known as the .22 caliber killings nears, convicted murderer Joseph G. Christopher has decided to speak out." During an interview at Rikers Island with Gene Warner, Christopher "tried to explain the mysterious forces that led him to kill."

Gene Warner was a reporter for the *News*. Warner had spent three years as a teacher at Kensington High School on Buffalo's east side before turning to the newspaper business. He had joined the staff of the *Buffalo News* in June 1980, three months before the killings had begun, mainly covering the weekend police beat. In 1983, Warner was not yet one of the paper's star crime reporters. He had landed this plum assignment when editors at the *News* had asked him to check into the authenticity of two strange, rambling letter-essays they'd received from Joseph Christopher with a request that the newspaper print them. They asked Warner to find out if Christopher had actually written letters.

The reporter verified with Rikers Island that the letters had indeed come from Joseph Christopher. Warner then wrote to Christopher and asked for an interview. Christopher agreed. Warner went to New York City. For three hours, he and Christopher sat alone in a visiting room at Rikers with a guard standing outside the door.

"It was like talking to a picture on the wall," Gene Warner recalled years later. "His affect was very flat. His answers were cold, staccato, unemotional, like he was talking about someone else, not himself. Impersonal to the nth degree. He didn't have much interest in one point over another. He seemed soulless."

Warner likened it to a *Dragnet* interview "but without the wisecracks at the end," referring to the TV show known for the clipped, monotone, just-the-facts dialogue of its principal characters. Christopher would not engage in small talk or pleasantries. He didn't smile once. After establishing that Warner should call him Joseph and not Joe, the subject spoke of the conspiracy.

"I was ordered to kill."

Warner naturally asked by whom. Christopher tried to explain that there had been a conspiracy consisting of two separate groups that had conspired against him as a test of his strength. "Do you believe that what you see in a courtroom is a trial? It's a dramatization," Christopher said. "Where's a need for a trial when the people conspire? They ordered me to do this, the ability to kill, as a test of me. They knew whether I had done it or I hadn't done it. So they were questioning my personal stature as a man. I judge myself as far as my stature as a man."

He further explained, "I wasn't supposed to be able to cope with having to kill someone after I had been degradated [sic] for such a long period of time. After I had been able to do what they said I couldn't do, they put me in a system [prison] and tried to grind me down, but I just got stronger."

Warner asked him more about the nature of the conspiracy. "I was ordered to kill," Christopher repeated. "Who ordered me to kill? Who set up the conspiracy? I don't know."

The essays he'd written to the newspaper contained the statement, "So it was a baseball game. 17 hits and 13 dead if they are dead." Asked about this, he explained, "I supposedly attacked 17 people and 13 of them are dead."

Warner attempted to ask him about specific crimes and victims but Christopher refused to give him direct answers. "I don't believe that discussing each individual incident would serve any purpose." He rebuffed several questions as being "sensational" and kept repeating, "Again, I was ordered to kill. That's all I'm going to say."

He did, however, pointedly deny the thwarted knife attack on Calvin Crippen that had occurred on New Year's Day 1981. "That's a degradation against Calvin Crippen," he told Warner. "I don't want to degradate [sic] him. I ask you not to put that in."

He didn't deny the New Year's Eve stabbing of Albert Menefee. When Warner asked if he had tried to kill him, Christopher replied, "That was my objective."

Christopher also claimed that Glenn Dunn had not been his first victim. A day or two prior to the shooting of Dunn, he said, he had attacked someone else. "It was downtown and I put a knife in somebody's throat. I don't believe he was hurt badly." He didn't know for sure "because there was never anything in the news about it."

Warner asked him about the killings of cab drivers Parler Edwards and Ernest Jones. Christopher replied, "I'm not denying anything. I don't want sensationalism." That struck Warner as odd, since he had denied the attack on Calvin Crippen, a crime for which he'd actually been charged. Then again, the entire interview was bizarre. Christopher went off on tangents in which he made oblique references to things like the movie *A Clockwork Orange* and a story about a boxer that his seventh grade class had been reading when Martin Luther King Jr. was assassinated, all of which he seemed to connect to the conspiracy against him. Gene Warner recalled, "I began to wonder why he had me come down. Often when people want to be interviewed, there's a basic point they want to make. With him, there didn't seem to be any purpose, nor even any interest in what I was going to write."

Warner had not known what to expect of Joseph Christopher, either in terms of the content of the interview or of the man himself. As for Warner's impression of Christopher, "He looked like the kid who sat in back of the class. A little weasel who nobody liked. An unremarkable physical specimen. He looked very young. I remember thinking he would've gotten eaten up at Kensington High School, which is close to Burgard [High School], where he went. I guessed he had probably gotten beaten up and picked on. He had developed a bit of a tough shell and I felt like he was trying to act like a tough guy, someone who could hack it in prison, but it just made him this unemotional, unappealing, unlikable character. His inner demons and lack of self-confidence were obvious."

They broke for lunch. Warner tried to gather his thoughts and come up with a way to salvage what seemed like a pointless and unproductive interview. He was at a loss at how to ask Christopher questions that might produce a worthwhile answer. Despite how things were going, the reporter didn't get the feeling that Christopher was lying or toying with him. "I didn't sense a hidden agenda. He didn't care about the interview but he was trying to be honest. I'd ask a question and it was like his mind would try to go there but then he'd hit a brick wall. Overall, I got the feeling that this was a guy who was just trying to survive from one moment to the next."

What Warner had really hoped to get from him was information about the cab drivers. Had he killed them or not? That seemed to be the question on most people's minds in Buffalo. Warner tried again, but no matter how he broached the subject or rephrased the question, Christopher just gave him the same preprogrammed answer, saying he wasn't denying anything; he didn't want sensationalism—whatever that meant.

Christopher kept insisting he was a soldier ("one tin soldier, you know") who'd been drafted and ordered to kill. He said he did not hate black people ("To hate is to lie. I deal with people for themselves.") and that all his victims were dark-skinned because "that was the directive."

His response to Mark Mahoney's courtroom claim that he was psychotic: "A psychotic act is sometimes an aggravated rational act." He explained, "If you take an animal and put him in a cage, and you keep sticking him and sticking him, and if you take him out of the cage and he bites you, that animal is [considered] psychotic. That, in a way, is what they did to me."

Christopher wouldn't discuss his father, beyond saying that he had taught him a lot. Warner was curious; the relationship with his father had been cited by psychiatrists, and Christopher had also mentioned him in the essays he'd sent to the *Buffalo News*. "My father told me a long time ago what they were going to do to me," Christopher had written. "Except I had no idea what his stories meant. So I have the voice in my head. I remember all the stories." The only reference he made to his father, in answer to a question about whether, in view of his long prison sentence, he had considered suicide, was, "The only movie I ever went to see with my father was *M*A*S*H*. The opening song was, 'Suicide is painless. It brings on many changes.' I would never try to kill myself. You don't die. They just change you."

He told Gene Warner that he would walk free, as soon as his army enlistment was up. "As far as I'm concerned, as of the 3rd of November— I think that is the date—my three-year contract with the army is up. They don't have any rightful cause to hold me, because I didn't do anything that I wasn't ordered to do."

———

The competency matter dragged on in Manhattan courtrooms. Dr. John Train had deemed Christopher incompetent while the staff at Bellevue, to which Joseph had been committed once again in the summer of 1983, continued to insist they saw no signs of mental illness in him. More exams with more doctors would be scheduled. A competency hearing would be held. Frank Bress would persevere—until he was removed from the case.

Decades afterward, Bress said, "I've never understood the resistance most prosecutors and judges have to a defense of mental disease or defect. I don't know if they're afraid that all defendants are going to try to use it or what, but there's such a small percentage of cases where there's a viable psychiatric defense, less than one percent of criminal cases in which it's applicable. Christopher was in the less than one percent." Bress was already well acquainted with Bellevue's director, social worker Hillel Bodek, who was regularly called in by prosecutors. "I had recognized the sensitivity of dealing with Christopher from the start, that I had to be careful about not letting on to him that I felt he was mentally ill. Judge Altman was sensitive to this as well. I was afraid Christopher would shut down on me completely if he knew I had a hand in requesting psychiatric exams. He'd refuse to work with me and ask for a new attorney. And that's exactly what happened. Bodek told him it was me who was pushing for a competency hearing.

"By this time, the case had been assigned to another judge, George Bundy Smith. Christopher went into court and started ranting again about a conspiracy against him that I was a part of. The judge removed me, thinking the problem was that Christopher just didn't like me and that if he had another defense attorney, things would be fine. I was replaced by another public defender assigned by the court."

Frank Bress became a defense witness at the competency hearing, as did Mark Mahoney. Ultimately, Christopher was deemed competent to stand trial.

In the late summer of 1983, from his cell at Riker's Island, Joe wrote a letter to his former girlfriend, Donna. Most of the strange, three-page letter seemed to be about his life at the jail and made little sense. Toward the end,

he asked Donna if she could come visit him at Rikers. If not, he wanted
her to send him a picture from a trip they had taken to the Adirondacks,
a photo of her near the Ausable River. He also asked her to send him the
book *The Boys from Brazil*, because he wanted to know "what they say I am."

———————

The Manhattan trial was delayed several times as Joseph bounced in
and out of jails and psychiatric hospitals, where authorities at Rikers
and Auburn would send him when his mental condition rendered him
unmanageable as an ordinary—or even slightly unordinary—prisoner. He
had periods of catatonia and anorexia. Other times he would pace in his
cell all night long. He often smiled bizarrely and laughed to himself in his
cell. He stuffed cotton in his ears and covered his face with a towel. And
he usually wouldn't talk, except when he was alone in his cell.

He wrote to Donna again in the spring of 1984, this time from the
Long Island Correctional Facility in West Brentwood, New York. The
first two and a half pages were neatly handwritten stanzas from Wallace
Stevens's poem "Esthétique du Mal" ("Aesthetics of Evil"), followed by a
personal observation:

> I sit and look out, today my cell is on the seventh floor. Since inter-
> viewing the reporter[3] they have been shipping me from place to
> place around the state. I think my cell count is twenty six this par-
> ticular cell has nothing in it, the mattress is on the floor cause the cot
> springs are shot They let ya in the day room fer a hour a day
> the parade of lakes continue I think they want to bite me on the neck
> I got a great neck
> Please confuse what maybe with what you know

Donna couldn't understand. The same thought rolled over and over in
her mind. *What happened to him? What* happened *to him?*

———————

3   Likely a reference to his September 1983 interview with *Buffalo News*
     reporter Gene Warner.

On July 5, 1985, Joe's Buffalo convictions were overturned by New York's highest court, the State Court of Appeals, which ruled 4-2 that Judge William Flynn had erred in rejecting the request of Christopher's defense attorneys to present new expert testimony on his fitness to stand trial. This reversed a 1984 lower court ruling that had upheld the convictions. Mark Mahoney had ultimately been proven correct when he cautioned Judge Flynn in 1982 that his decision constituted reversible error.

Joseph still had not yet stood trial in Manhattan. At the time his Buffalo convictions were overturned, he was in the Central New York Psychiatric Center at Marcy, New York, where he would remain until September 4. While at Auburn Prison, his mental state had deteriorated to the point where he was completely nonresponsive, lying on the floor of the cell wrapped tightly in a blanket. He did not eat, bathe, or come out for recreational activities he had formerly engaged in. He did not move at all. On May 16, the prison transferred him to the psychiatric center at Downstate Correctional, where he was diagnosed as schizophrenic, catatonic type. In a certification for commitment dated May 20, 1985, the examining doctor wrote, "History of suicide attempts and treatment at Mid-Hudson Psychiatric Center. He is mentally ill and dangerous to himself." He was committed by court order and delivered to Central New York Psychiatric Center on May 25.

The catatonia alternated with euphoria. He would laugh, act silly, and run high fevers. By mid-July he was protesting his commitment.

In August, the staff at Central New York Psych Center began seeing a significant change in Joseph Christopher. The constant suspicion, the "seculsive" behavior, the wild laughing and pacing, all had subsided. He stopped flushing all his food down the toilet. He became more alert, responsive, rational. He began to resemble the gentle and considerate individual his friends and family had described. He even resumed contact with his mother, whom he had refused to see for two years. For the first time ever, he was improving. For the first time ever, he was being given antipsychotic medication.

Finally, he was ready to stand trial.

On October 23, 1985, a Manhattan jury convicted Christopher of the murder of Luis Rodriguez and the stabbing of survivor Ivan Frazer. The prosecution argued that Christopher had bragged while in the army about killing blacks. Defense attorney Richard Siracusa argued that Christopher should be acquitted because "he is not a well person. His vision of reality has nothing to do with ours."

In handing down the maximum sentence of thirty-three years in prison, Judge John A. K. Bradley said, "There is no doubt that the defendant is mentally ill. It is obvious he's a menace to society."

On February 21, 1986, Joseph was transferred to the Erie County Holding Center in Buffalo to await retrial for the murders of Glenn Dunn, Harold Green, and Emanuel Thomas.

Chapter 19

CHRISTOPHER'S RETURN TO Buffalo had once again ignited the local media and factions of the community, particularly black leaders and politicians, who were less than pleased that his convictions for the three .22 caliber killings had been overturned. The demands that Christopher be tried again immediately were coupled with revived calls that the remaining murders be solved, particularly the gruesome deaths of Parler Edwards and Ernest "Shorty" Jones.

In April 1981, when Joseph Christopher had first become a suspect in the shootings and stabbings, investigators had made concerted efforts to either implicate or eliminate him as a suspect in the cabbie killings. Edward Cosgrove had personally visited the FBI lab in Washington, DC, during the evidence analysis. Christopher's fingerprints and palm prints had been checked against all of the prints lifted from both cabs (and Harold Green's car). No matches were found. The six knives seized via the search warrants had been tested for the presence of blood and fibers, with uniformly negative results. A single blue synthetic fiber had been found on one of the knives, but it did not match the clothing of the victims nor any fibers recovered at the scenes or in the cabs. In addition, the lab had conducted a meticulous microscopic tool mark analysis of all the knives against tool marks made in the cut tree branches that had covered the taxicab of Parler Edwards. The results were negative. Christopher's blood and hair samples were compared with evidence from the crime scenes, with negative results.

All of the physical evidence pointed away from Christopher, as did other facts and circumstances. Many of the key task force members, including the entire scientific investigation unit and senior police officials such as Leo Donovan who were privy to the full details of the two murders, had long ago dismissed Christopher. To those with sufficient knowledge of both police work and the specifics of the murders, Parler Edwards and Shorty Jones had not been killed by a single assailant, nor had they been random victims.

Tips received by police during the probe of the Edwards and Jones murders had led to a sting operation that in turn resulted in a sweeping arrest of more than a dozen persons involved in a numbers gambling operation on the east side. At the time of the bust, in May 1981, the operation was reported to be clearing $10,000 per week.

The cabbie murders had consistently been brought up in the press following Christopher's arrest, lumped in with recaps of the four shootings, although the negative evidentiary results between Christopher and the cabbie murders was never made public. Even before his fall of 1983 interview with *Buffalo News* reporter Gene Warner, during which Christopher had said he "wasn't denying anything" because he didn't want "sensationalism," he'd been asked on several occasions, both directly by deputies at the holding center and more indirectly by psychiatrists, if he had killed the cab drivers. His answers had ranged from perplexity at the question, to a teasing *I-won't-say*, to irritated denial. Dr. John Train had testified at Christopher's Manhattan trial and related that he'd asked Christopher if he had mutilated anyone, to which Christopher had replied, "You're asking me a question I don't want to answer. I just shot them." Dr. Train pressed and Christopher had become angry, saying, "Are you asking me if I shot a cab driver?" Dr. Train asked, "Did you?" Joseph said that he shot four men in Buffalo. "You ask if I did anything else to their bodies? I shot them."

Christopher had never spoken with police about any of the crimes. When it came to the murders of Edwards and Jones, many task force members considered it a moot point. Others on the investigating team, however, didn't want to dismiss Christopher as the killer of the cab drivers, though not necessarily because they believed he'd done it.

At the request of black leaders, the task force had been restarted at the end of January 1982 by Cosgrove's successor, District Attorney Richard Arcara. Following Christopher's first trial and conviction in April, as leaders in the black community had exerted pressure to solve the remaining crimes, a split had erupted in the task force. As one senior task force member put it, "There were basically two camps. There were those of us who said there was no way Christopher had anything to do with the cabbie murders, and those who just wanted to wrap things up."

While some were not familiar with all of the facts in the Edwards and Jones murders—information had been tightly controlled by the top-level personnel, dispensed sparingly on a need-to-know basis—there were others who were clearly more interested in solving a political problem than solving the murders. "The question became," as chief scientific investigator Tom Rowan recalled, "are we going to pursue the investigation, or are we just going to brush it all off on Joseph Christopher?"

Toward the end of 1982, the fissure had widened into a chasm. As Tom Rowan said, "Up till that time, all of us from these different agencies had worked well together on the investigation, but this fractured the team and pretty much put an end to the cooperation. Those of us who had worked the cases from the beginning were saying 'absolutely not,' as far as a link between the shootings and the cabbie murders.

"Nothing about the two sets of killings fit the picture of this being the same offender. The only reason the cabbie murders had ever been grouped in with the .22 caliber killings was because of the timing and similarity, or pseudo-similarity, of the victims. With Edwards and Jones, we had two victims who *were* connected. We also had a lot of indications that these men had not been killed by strangers."

Parler Edwards's taxicab had been loaded with various items. The cab had been combed over three separate times by both police and the FBI. Everything within, every scrap of paper and every piece of loose change pulled from between the seats, had been documented. The only items that had not been found were two of the three wallets that Edwards was known to carry. The third wallet—the one stuffed with his identification—had been placed squarely beneath his body in the trunk of the cab.

By all accounts, Parler Edwards was a very street-savvy man. He did not leave his wallets in plain sight. How would a stranger know that Edwards had two additional wallets hidden in the cab? Why would a killer who'd chosen Edwards at random have placed his identification so conspicuously beneath his body?

The placement of the body was another matter that cast serious doubt on the prospect of a lone assailant, particularly Joseph Christopher. It was virtually inconceivable that one man had lifted the body and placed it so neatly. And the evidence clearly showed that the body had been lifted. There were no bloody drag marks on the edge of the trunk (nor even any traces of blood), as there certainly would have been had the body been hauled up into the trunk. The body of Parler Edwards had been lifted into the trunk by at least two men and set right on top of a wallet that would immediately indicate to police—and anyone else—the identity of the victim. As if the killers did not want the victim's identity to be a mystery.

Edwards had cash in his pockets. His credit cards had been left. The killers had apparently only taken the wallets containing the larger sums of money—perhaps because they felt it belonged to them.

It could be deduced that there were unwritten but loud and clear messages here, both in the extreme and deliberate savagery inflicted on the victim and in what and how certain things had been left, as if the killers were saying: *We want you to know who this is. We want you to know this isn't a robbery. We want you to know what we're capable of.* A message, or perhaps a potent warning, intended not for police, but perhaps for other numbers runners who might think of running afoul of the organization.

The same could be true of the Shorty Jones murder, which had occurred the following night. There were many elements that pointed away from this being a random attack and instead toward a link with the Edwards murder. There was the fact that Shorty had inexplicably, uncharacteristically, refused all fares that night, including his regular customers (and his own daughter). He had driven his cab, keeping close to his usual hangouts, before driving off somewhere after midnight, past the time when he had told Zoe Fontaine he'd return to her, to a destination and purpose he hadn't revealed to the fellow cabbie he'd been talking to just prior. According to the fellow cabbie, Shorty had put a sum of money into a green cooler, placed the cooler in the trunk of his cab, and taken off. Shorty normally talked a lot and pretty freely about his activities, even his criminal activities, which could possibly account for why his throat had been not just cut, but purposefully, gruesomely mangled.

Those who had seen Shorty the day of his death had told police that he appeared very preoccupied and concerned, not like his happy-go-lucky self. There was also the fact that Shorty knew about the murder and identity of Parler Edwards before the news had been made public. He told Zoe about the murder. He also told her that he didn't know Parler Edwards and never had any dealings with him, which police had discerned was untrue. Edwards and Jones had at one time worked for the same cab company, one that was well known to police as complicit in the numbers racket. They'd both frequented the Chippewa area for fares (which is how they both knew Collin Cole), and Parler lived next door to the longtime girlfriend of Shorty's brother.

Beyond all of that, many seasoned investigators didn't buy Joseph Christopher as a viable suspect, regardless of the victim links and the total lack of evidence placing Christopher at any of the murder or dump scenes. "None of us in our camp really thought that Joe Christopher was physically or emotionally or psychologically capable of that," said Tom Rowan, "Not that he wasn't a stabber. But dismembering and taking a heart, that just did not fit in any way." FBI profiler John Douglas had advised early on that they had two different offenders.

A senior task force member said, "Parler Edwards and Shorty Jones were both very strong, very sharp, very streetwise guys. Frankly, the idea of a wimp like Joseph Christopher getting the jump on these two was ludicrous. Parler was older but he was a big guy and strong. Shorty Jones wasn't as physically large but he was very muscular. These two victims were confronted. They fought back. Parler had a metal pipe. Shorty's knife was found by his body. The idea that Joe Christopher brawled with these two guys, much less disarmed them and won, didn't seem likely."

There were authorities who were nevertheless content to let the public believe that all the murders were attributable to Christopher. Tom Rowan recalled, "It became an irreconcilable difference between those who wanted to tie things up and give the community 'peace of mind,' and those of us who refused to go along."

With such vehement disagreement among investigators, a resolution was needed. As Rowan explained, "Anyone who didn't march to the tune of 'we're wrapping this up' was removed from the case." This included Rowan, Leo Donovan, and all of the municipal police departments. "We were told that the state police were taking over the cab driver investigation and were ordered to turn our evidence over to them. We weren't happy about it, but there wasn't much we could do. The crime scenes crossed city and town lines. Parler Edwards was killed in Cheektowaga but dumped in Amherst, right across the town line, so the state police were the overarching authority because everything happened on New York state property."

Not all state police were on board with the theory that Christopher had killed the cab drivers. Matt Ortiz, son of state police investigator and task force member Amador Ortiz, recalled, "My dad always insisted that both of the cab killings were mob related since both [Edwards and Jones] were bookies."

Even without knowing all that pointed away from Joseph Christopher, there were people in the community who weren't content that the cabbie murders had been solved, particularly since Christopher had never been charged. In the six years that had now elapsed since the murders, the case hadn't even been presented to a grand jury.

The cabbie homicides remained a thorn in the side of the district attorney's office, festering anew with the added pain of Christopher's retrial. Prosecutors anticipated a psychiatric defense, which they regarded as no small obstacle to conviction. Failure in a high-profile case such as this, with its racial overtones and relentless media attention, was not an option.

It was in this tense atmosphere that prosecutors Al Ranni and Thomas Eoannou began preparations. The reversal of the first trial had been a public-relations nightmare. The psychiatric issues now raised a whole new dilemma. As things turned out, however, the overturn of the first convictions and mental illness would prove to be a godsend for the office of the district attorney.

Kevin Dillon and Mark Mahoney had each met separately with Joe at the holding center on the weekend following his return to Buffalo. On February 27, 1986, a day ahead of a court hearing regarding assignment of counsel for the new trial, Mark Mahoney filed a motion to withdraw as Christopher's attorney. In an eleven-page affidavit, Mahoney detailed his history with Joseph as well as their interaction, or lack thereof, during the recent visit.

"Between April of 1981 and April of 1982," Mahoney wrote, "it can be conservatively stated that Mr. Dillon and I spent more than 1800 hours on behalf of Mr. Christopher . . . our representation reflected an out-of-pocket loss in excess of $18,000. That is, far from providing any actual income, the compensation received overall fell approximately $18,000 short of covering our expenses attributable to the time we spent on this matter." Mahoney explained that for purposes of continuity of representation, he had been involved in Christopher's case and communicating with his various attorneys throughout the past five years.

"Mr. Christopher has never discussed with me any facts relevant to the actual accusations herein," Mahoney wrote. "My conclusion is that, by reason of his mental illness, he is incapable of doing so. However it also appears that I am the only attorney with whom he has ever been willing to engage in any type of colloquy, however short this may have fallen from the rational, relevant or thorough.

"When I first saw Mr. Christopher in Ft. Benning, he was forthcoming with no information. During the period of time when he was in the holding center, although he never communicated anything of substantive value concerning the charges, he did engage occasionally in superficial banter with me. I found that I am the only attorney with whom he has ever had that ability to so converse. This includes attorneys for the Legal Aid Bureau, Mr. Dillon, and four attorneys in New York City. I once asked Mr. Christopher why he only spoke to me and the only response he gave was that 'you are interesting.'"

He gave a brief recap of the history of Joseph's incompetency and reports from a multitude of psychiatrists. "I am absolutely confident that

Mr. Christopher's rigid uncommunication with counsel is not merely a question of personality, strategy, or rational choice. It is the product of deep mental illness. If Mr. Christopher were competent to assist in his defense, a wide range of strategic response was possible given various hypothetical assumptions regarding his culpability: a favorable plea arrangement in exchange for disclosure of any information Mr. Christopher may have regarding the cases; testimony by Mr. Christopher regarding his lack of involvement in offenses, and so on. His illness precluded such possibilities."

There had been only one instance throughout his entire legal process where Joseph had given information that actually assisted his defense, and that had been when he'd told his attorneys about the army stockade commander offering him sexual favors from a woman in an effort to induce Joseph to make statements to him. It had been Mahoney's impression that Joe brought the incident to their attention not because he perceived its legal significance, but because of the entertainment value.

"I testified at the competency hearing in New York City," Mahoney continued. "Though some of the expert witnesses have found that Mr. Christopher's refusal to talk to them constituted no evidence of incompetency, I believe the record is clear that his refusal to talk is the clearest evidence of his incompetency. Unfortunately, at the present time his difficulty in this regard seems worse than I've ever seen it." On his recent visit to see Joseph at the holding center, Mahoney found Joe lying on his side with a towel covering his entire face except for the area below his cheeks and nose. Mahoney knew he wasn't asleep because he'd heard Joe tell the guard, "He's not my attorney" when the guard had told him that Mark Mahoney was there to see him.

Mahoney greeted Joe and asked him to come and speak with him in a visiting room. He received no response to this or to anything else. "I attempted to be alternatively sympathetic, prodding, challenging, chiding, and amusing. He apparently does not find me interesting anymore, for he gave absolutely no verbal or physical response to my inquiries." After about ten minutes, Mahoney gave up and left.

"I conclude that Christopher is less able now than at any previous time to assist in his defense. I also believe that his genuine cooperation could greatly enhance the possibility of acquittal before a jury on these homicide charges," Mahoney wrote. "Although I would previously have acknowledged that Mr. Christopher was aware of the nature of the charges against him and so on, I would probably be less willing to do so at the present time."

The attorney felt that the issue of Christopher's competency should be seriously revisited. He wished to be relieved from representing him so that a fair determination could be made without inviting speculation that Christopher's unwillingness to communicate was the result of his relationship with Mahoney rather than mental illness. He agreed to stay on as transitional counsel and requested that the court appoint at least two attorneys to represent Joseph.

Kevin Dillon's own jailhouse visit with Joe had led him to the same conclusion. At a court appearance on February 28, Judge Joseph P. McCarthy, who would preside over the new trial, asked Joe questions about his preference for appointment of counsel. Joe sat with a fixed smile on his face and didn't answer or look at the judge.

McCarthy afterward appointed Sean Hill and David Jay, both seasoned criminal defense attorneys, to represent Christopher. David Jay was known as an ardent advocate of civil rights who had never shied from controversial or unpopular causes, which this certainly was.

Jay and Hill met their client for the first time at the holding center. Joe wouldn't speak to them.

Following his discharge from Central New York Psychiatric Center the previous fall, the antipsychotic medications had been discontinued. At the jail in Buffalo, he paced back and forth in his cell. He stared suspiciously at anyone who came by but stayed mute. He stopped eating. On March 7, he was sent to the Erie County Medical Center. The hospital gave him Prolixin Decanoate, a long-acting antipsychotic. His behavior improved. The hospital discharged him on April 10 back to the holding center.

Dr. Brian Joseph was the chief of psychiatric services for the Erie County Forensic Mental Health Service. Dr. Joseph was well acquainted with Christopher. He had examined him for the first time in 1981, prior to his first trial. He had testified at his competency hearings in

Buffalo and New York City, as well as at the 1985 trial in Manhattan. Dr. Joseph had diagnosed Christopher with paranoid schizophrenia back in November of 1981. He had never wavered on his diagnosis. On the contrary, everything he'd read, seen, and heard about Christopher or observed from the patient himself solidified his professional opinion that the man suffered from chronic and severe mental illness in the form of paranoid schizophrenia.

Dr. Joseph visited Christopher at the holding center the day after his return from the county hospital. He found him much more verbal and calm. Christopher's behavior was appropriate and he appeared to be in good contact. However, he was intent on avoiding further medication. He hated the medication. He'd been given Haldol the previous summer at the hospital and experienced dystonic side effects, such as involuntary turning of his head. Well aware of how rapidly he would degenerate without medication, Dr. Joseph wrote a letter to Judge McCarthy requesting authorization to give Christopher injectable Prolixin Decanoate over the patient's objection. The court granted the order.

Christopher had to be held down and restrained in order to make it happen, but the medication was administered.

The following week, Joe had a conversation with his new attorneys. He communicated with them fairly well. He told David Jay that he did not want an insanity defense. Jay told him that was fine; make the prosecution prove their case. Joe seemed pleased with that.

Psychiatrist S. K. Park met with Christopher for a little under an hour on April 18. Dr. Park had first met Joe in the fall of 1981, when he had conducted a competency exam and had diagnosed him as suffering from paranoid schizophrenia. In the new report he sent to Judge McCarthy, Dr. Park noted his surprise at Joe's cooperation and eagerness to start a conversation. When questioned as to what made him decide to talk so freely, Joe replied that the psychiatrist would give him medications against his will unless he talked.

Dr. Park wrote that Joe showed a mild degree of irritability and excitement during the interview. His speech was coherent and productive. Park judged that his insight was inadequate, however, as Joe told him, "I never had mental problems." Based on the exam, Dr. Park believed that

Joe's psychosis was in remission and he was currently able to assist in his defense.

Dr. Brian Joseph concurred in his own report to the court. "I have seen this man in the past and feel quite definitely that he suffers from paranoid schizophrenia," Dr. Joseph wrote, stating that the antipsychotic medication was keeping his psychosis in a state of reasonable remission.

The trial was scheduled for the fall of 1986. Christopher was maintained on daily doses of Navane, another antipsychotic medication. He experienced side effects—twitching in his right thumb and constant movement of his feet and legs—for which he was prescribed Cogentin, which helped with the side effects but did not eliminate them. Dr. Joseph monitored his condition and felt he tolerated the medication well. His mental state had stabilized. Joe cooperated with his attorneys in a rational and sustained manner for the first time. They agreed to a plea of not guilty by reason of mental disease or defect.

Dr. Brian Joseph agreed to testify for the defense. In addition to the number of times he had examined Christopher over the past six years, Dr. Joseph had looked carefully at his history. He had met with Therese Christopher. She had described Joe's behavior during the year before his arrest, the extreme withdrawal, hiding plastic spoons and forks around the house, his anxieties and suspicions and complaints that the people on TV were talking about him. To Dr. Joseph, what Therese described were the prodromal symptoms of a schizophrenic episode, the early symptoms that come before the acute onset of the illness.

Dr. Joseph had a wealth of experience in identifying and treating schizophrenia. He had practiced psychiatry at a host of medical institutes on the east coast, including Johns Hopkins and Massachusetts General Hospital. He had spent six years as an instructor in psychiatry at the Harvard University School of Medicine before returning to Buffalo in 1980. Dr. Joseph was also well versed in forensic psychiatry, a branch of psychiatry dealing with the assessment of mentally impaired offenders. He had a sophisticated understanding of the interface between mental health and the law. As he would say years later in recalling Joseph Christopher, "It's very, very hard to fake mental illness. People who are trying to fake it usually act clownish or stupid because they think that's how the mentally ill would act. I always made a point of building relationships with guards at jails so I could ask them how an inmate behaved when I wasn't around or they thought they were unobserved."

Speculation on the motive behind Christopher's criminal acts was still a frequent subject in the news. To Dr. Joseph, there was no mystery, no hidden cause or rationale to be someday unearthed. It was paranoid schizophrenia.

Just as he was certain of this, he was equally certain there would be a rejection of the explanation of mental illness, both in court and in the general public, who would continue to insist on a motive they could better understand, one that made sense to a nonpsychotic mind. As such, he was well aware of the dim prospects for Joseph Christopher. "I was convinced this was a very sick guy," said Dr. Joseph. "I was equally convinced he was going to be convicted." Decades after the trial, Brian Joseph explained, "If you do defense work as a psychiatrist for the insanity plea, the only way you can survive is if you have the attitude of Rhett Butler toward the Battle of Atlanta. Scarlett asks why he's going off to fight when the battle has already been lost. He tells her, 'I have a penchant for lost causes, once they're really and truly lost.' If you have that attitude, you'll survive in this business, because nobody ever gets the insanity defense."

Prosecutor Al Ranni informed the court that he planned to have psychiatrist Richard Weidenbacher of New York City examine the defendant on behalf of the prosecution. Two weeks before the trial was set to begin, Dr. Weidenbacher called with bad news: he was experiencing health problems that prevented his participation. He apologized profusely. He also cautioned Ranni against attempting to argue that Christopher was not mentally ill, which he stated would be "incorrect and fruitless." Weidenbacher's opinion was not that Christopher was without mental illness—he had, in fact, diagnosed him with paranoid schizophrenia in remission in January 1982—but that he knew his acts were wrong and therefore still bore responsibility under the law.

The withdrawal of Dr. Weidenbacher presented a major problem for the prosecution. They needed to find a suitable replacement as quickly as possible; a psychiatrist with credentials who would see things their way. Countering a claim of serious mental disease might not be as easy as it had been back in 1982, when Dillon and Mahoney had made their futile last attempt. This time around, the opinion of a doctor from a state hospital who kept flunking his board exams might not suffice.

Christopher now had a lengthy history of documented mental illness from a plethora of psychiatrists, hospitals, and institutions. His rambling screeds had been published in the *Buffalo News*. Overcoming a psychiatric defense, particularly with Dr. Brian Joseph testifying for the defense, would be a challenge. Dr. Joseph had spent more time with the defendant over the past five years than any other psychiatrist. The prosecution needed a countering opinion from a doctor who could come across to a jury as distinguished and authoritative.

Assistant district attorney Tom Eoannou was assisting Al Ranni with the Christopher prosecution. Eoannou was a young attorney who had joined the district attorney's office in 1982, straight from law school. Deputy DA Al Ranni had taken a liking to Eoannou and became his mentor. He admired Ranni, and was flattered when the deputy DA asked him to be co-counsel. Al Ranni was a workaholic, and in the words of Tom Eoannou, "a brilliant trial strategist." Ranni had prosecuted Christopher the first time. The retrial would be entirely different from the first. In this instance, it was not a matter of proving that Christopher had shot Dunn, Green, and Thomas, but convincing a jury to reject his defense of mental disease or defect.

Though the insanity defense had failed in the Manhattan trial, they couldn't take for granted that it would fail here, particularly since they no longer had Dr. Weidenbacher as an expert witness. As Eoannou recalled, "There was a lot of concern about finding a psychiatrist for the prosecution. We knew Brian Joseph was an excellent psychiatrist, very competent and highly regarded. We knew how talented Dr. Joseph was and we had utmost respect for him. He wasn't necessarily prone to finding a defendant mentally ill. He was a straight shooter, not predisposed one way or the other. So our concern was, from a trial standpoint, that a lot of psychiatrists might find Christopher suffering from a mental disease or defect. We had to be careful because we didn't want to generate discovery, Rosario or Brady material."

Rosario material includes statements of a witness who will testify at trial. Brady material is evidence that may be exculpatory or favorable to the defendant. Rosario and Brady material must be turned over to the defense. In other words, if the prosecution had Christopher examined by a psychiatrist who deemed him to be suffering from a mental disease or defect at the time of the commission of the crimes, that information would, by law, have to be turned over to Christopher's attorneys.

This posed a significant problem for the district attorney. They needed to find a psychiatrist who would be certain to aid their cause. As Tom Eoannou explained, "We reached out to other prosecutors' offices and learned that Dr. Barton would be the right guy."

Dr. Russell Barton was a British-born psychiatrist in his sixties who had emigrated to the United States in 1969. He was so prosecution-friendly that he was frequently called by district attorneys around the region, and was on permanent retainer with the DA's office in Monroe County in nearby Rochester, where he resided.

Barton had a long résumé as a psychiatrist and administrator at psychiatric facilities in England and the United States. His reputation was laced with controversy. He was a great proponent of the deinstitutionalization of the mentally ill, moving patients out of psychiatric hospitals and into community care, and had been accused of ethical violations such as rushing down to jails at the behest of law enforcement to examine persons arrested for violent crimes before they had been given an opportunity to speak with an attorney.

As one prosecutor described Dr. Barton, "He had a lot of far-out ideas." One of his more "far-out" ideas had sparked a great deal of outrage back in his home country. Barton had been to the Bergen-Belsen concentration camp at the time of the British liberation at the end of World War II. He had later written an article for *Purnell's History of the Second World War* in which he asserted that Bergen-Belsen had been a work camp rather than an extermination center. He concluded that there had been no deliberate intent on the part of the Germans to starve or exterminate the detainees. The massive deaths and deplorable conditions had resulted not from abuses of the German overseers, but had come about due to overcrowding and prisoner abuses of one another, as different ethnic groups had formed cliques, deprived others of their rations, and shown an indifference to their well-being that Barton attributed to "institutional neurosis." He viewed prisoner accounts of atrocities with skepticism but appeared to accept the word of Nazi commandants that Allied bombing had prevented the camp from receiving adequate food and medical supplies. The *London Times* printed a scathing response under the headline, "Belsen Not So Bad, says psychiatrist." Barton was widely excoriated for the piece, but stood by his theories. His article was later reprinted in the booklet *Did Six Million Really Die?*

Despite the baggage, Barton had a personal presentation that could score points with a jury. "He was a nice man," Tom Eoannou recalled. "He had an English accent. Very mild-mannered. He could play brilliantly to a jury." Barton had a lot of experience in court. By his own estimate, Dr. Barton testified thirty to forty times per year on average, at least 80 percent of the time for the prosecution. Eoannou continued, "He wasn't eager about taking the case at first because he had some health problems." Eoannou and Al Ranni traveled to Rochester to make a personal appeal. "Al named an exorbitant amount of money he'd be paid and said it would include everything. 'You do understand, doctor, that you'll get door-to-door service, mileage, gas . . .'

"It was the most money this man ever made in his life, no doubt about it. Ranni found out how much he made annually. We did our homework."

With the services of Dr. Barton secured, the prosecution moved forward with renewed confidence. Russell Barton could be just the man they needed. If he could find prisoners of a Nazi concentration camp culpable for their own starvation and inhuman living conditions, surely he could find Joseph Christopher sane.

Dr. Barton met with Joe in a room at the Erie County Holding Center on November 6, 1986. Al Ranni and Tom Eoannou were present. The interview was videotaped.

It was the first of two interviews Dr. Barton had with Joe Christopher over a two-day period that would span a little more than three hours in total. Dr. Brian Joseph was present for a portion of the first day's interview, though strictly as an observer.

Joe was let into the room by deputies. Unshackled and wearing green prison-issue clothing, he took a seat across the table from Barton.

Dr. Barton introduced himself and the prosecuting attorneys. "I've been asked to examine you by the district attorney," Barton said. Explaining that his relationship with Joe was not that of a doctor and patient, Barton said, "What I have to do is try to find out how your mind was doing at certain times at the end of 1980 when you're said to have killed some guys." Dr. Barton told Joe that he would appreciate his cooperation. "I try to be fair," said Barton. "Everybody thinks the DA has me in his pocket. I say it as I find it."

Barton began by asking Joe about his medications and his history in and out of psychiatric centers. Joe's manner was cordial and calm, his answers spontaneous.

For Tom Eoannou, his first meeting with Joseph Christopher was jarring, but not in the way he had anticipated. "To me, the guy just wasn't a criminal," Eoannou recalled. "From first impression, I felt sorry for him. Terribly sorry for him. He was not a monster at all. The opposite. A quiet, gentle, very nice young man. Your heart went out to him when you met him, and that's the last thing in the world you want or expect when you're a tenacious young prosecutor. You're wearing that white hat and you go in thinking, okay, I'm meeting maybe the most evil person in this community in the last century, and five minutes into it, you feel sympathy."

Prior to the Barton interview, Eoannou knew little about Christopher personally. "One thing we did know about him, that up till these events, he was very well-liked, a quiet little guy. Nobody had a bad word to say about him. He hit [age] twenty-five, and off he went."

It wasn't long into the examination before Ranni and Eoannou began to regret their decision to have it videotaped. "We knew immediately it had backfired," said Eoannou. "In my mind, the best evidence for mental disease or defect was going to be this tape." It wasn't that Christopher was behaving in a crazy or outlandish fashion. In Eoannou's view, he came across as humble and honest. He spoke of his use of street drugs, his withdrawal from people, his frequent refusals to speak to others. "I used to sit in a corner and not talk to anyone." He didn't know why. Things had first changed in the summer of 1985 when he'd been medicated, which he admitted had been done against his will. He conceded that his thinking and interactions with others had normalized with medication, but said the physical side effects bothered him a great deal.

Dr. Barton asked Joe if he'd ever heard voices when no one was talking. Joe said it began around July 1980. He remembered because it had started around the time of his birthday. "I heard voices over the TV. And they were telling me I was being drafted into the army. And I went over to the psychiatric center to try to be admitted but they wouldn't admit me. Then I joined the army. After that, after I joined the army, I thought I was in a war. I had a mission that I was supposed to kill people. And, um, I melted down a .22 and went around shooting people."

Barton had been provided with questions from the prosecutors. He asked Joe if he had killed cab drivers and removed their hearts. Joe replied that he had killed a cab driver and put a stake through his heart because he thought he was the devil.

"When he gave that answer," Tom Eoannou recalled, "Al and I were both like, 'Stop the tape.' It was so clear at that point that he had a mental disease or defect. We didn't expect him to admit it, first of all. Our trial strategy, in the words of Al Ranni, was to make him look 'bad, not mad.' This tape was demonstrating the reverse. Here was a guy on trial for murder, being interviewed on video that may be seen by the jury, and he's confessing to two others."

The videotape was stopped. It was too late to simply discontinue the taping.

Al Ranni spoke privately with Dr. Barton. When the tape resumes, Barton says to Joe, "I'm sorry. You were telling me that you killed a cab driver?"

"Mm-hm."

"And you thought he was the devil?"

"Mm-hm."

"And you put a stake through his heart?"

"A wooden stake, about this long." Joe held his hands about twelve inches apart. "I cut his heart out and pounded it in his heart. I pounded the stake in his heart."

"Do you have a knowledge of anatomy?" Barton asked.

"No special knowledge, no."

"How did you know where his heart was?"

"It's in his chest. I can feel my own heart."

"Was this cab driver black or white?"

"Black."

"Where did you do this?"

"Uh . . ." Joe thought for a moment. "Near the airport."

"In a deserted lot near a car park?" Barton asked.

"Near a building."

"How did you kill him?"

"With a hatchet."

"What did you do? Hit him on the head?"

"Mm-hm."

"Did he know you were going to kill him?"

"I don't think so."

"Did you get him to drive to this place?"

"Yes."

"Did he object at all?"

"No."

"You didn't have to threaten him?"

"No."

"Where'd you get the hatchet?"

"I was carrying it."

"And where did you hit him? On the back of the head or in the chest?"

"No, in his face."

"You hit him in his face? So he must have seen it coming," said Barton.

"Mm-hm."

"Did he yell?"

"Mm, no. He went to grab a bar. Then he started hitting me with the bar and I was hitting him with the axe."

"He was hitting you with the bar? Did you get any injuries at all?"

"No."

"Why did you kill him again?"

"I thought he was the devil. I thought I was on an Army mission."

"Had the Army given you the hatchet?"

"No. All I did was sign up for the Army. I hadn't been in anything yet."

"So you weren't in the Army at the time," said Barton, "but you signed up how long before this happened?"

"Uh, just probably not even a week."

"Do you think it was wrong to kill the cab driver?"

"Now, yes."

"At the time?"

"No."

"What did you think he was doing that merited execution?"

"I thought he was the devil. That was—it was wrong with me."

"And you tried to put a stake through his heart?"

"Mm-hm."

"But that's not the devil, is it?"

"I thought it was."

"You put the stake through the heart in vampires, don't you?"

"I thought it was the devil."

"You thought that's how you kill the devil?" Barton asked.

"Yes."

"And where did you leave the heart and the stake?"

"I threw it in a field."

"You threw it in a field? Was the field close to where . . . ?"

"Right next door."

"And then did you do that again to anyone?"

"Yes."

"Who was that?"

"Another cab driver."

"Was that the same night?"

"No."

"How long after?"

"I don't recall."

"And what did you do then?"

"I cut his heart out and pounded a stake through it."

"Where did that happen?"

"On Sheridan. End of Sheridan Drive."

"Was that in a parking lot?"

"Yes."

"And how did you kill him?"

"With a hammer."

"And where did you hit him?"

"In the head."

"Did he know you were going to do it?"

"No."

"Did you hit him once or many times?"

Joe paused. "I put two holes in his head."

"Did he shout or yell?"

"Uh . . . nah, I don't recall anything he said."

"And after you'd hit him in the head, did he slump forward?"

"He fell on the ground and I cut his throat."

"You cut his throat?"

"Mm-hm."

"Had you got a knife?"

"Mm-hm."

"And then what did you do?"

"Cut his heart out. Pounded a stake through it."

"You cut his heart out. How did you—I mean, the ribs, I've done post-mortems and the ribs are difficult to get through. How did you get at his heart?" Barton asked.

"Cut it and reached in there and grabbed it."

"Cut through the ribs?"

"Cut through the ribs. Not through the ribs, like in between them." Joe gestured to his own upper rib cage. "Opened it up and cut the heart out."

"And where'd you get the stake?"

"I brought it from home."

"What sort of stake was it? A garden stake?"

"No, about this thick," he curled his fingers in an O-shape, "inch and a half thick and maybe ten, twelve inches long. Sharpened it."

"What do you use stakes like that for?"

"I made it."

"I see. So you wanted to do this before you ever set out."

"I thought I was—I had a mission."

"How many stakes did you prepare all together?"

"Three."

"So this was the second stake you were using?"

"Mm-hm."

"When did you make these stakes?"

"The day before I did it."

"And then you killed one cab driver," said Dr. Barton, "cut his heart out, put the stake through it, threw it in the field next door, having hit him in the face with a hatchet. Second guy, you hit with a hammer twice, made holes in his head, cut his heart out and drove the stake through it."

"Mm-hm."

Barton asked what he'd done with the second heart.

"Same thing. Threw it in a field."

"You threw it in a field? And what did you do then? Drive the cab away?"

"Yes."

"Did you get a lot of blood on you?"

"No. My hands. It don't come off your hands."

"Did you get it on your clothes at all?"

"I don't recall."

"And then what did you do? Drive home, or . . . ?"

"No. I drove the cab and then walked home."

"You drove the cab. Do you know where you left the cab?"

"On the west side somewhere."

"And then you walked home?"

"Yes."

"And how were you feeling? Triumphant?" Barton asked.

"I don't recall. I was terrified that I was going to be attacked."

"By whom?"

"By other black people."

"Why should black people attack you?"

"I don't know."

"But you didn't particularly dislike black people?"

"No."

Even with Barton's leading questions, Joe was making mistakes, both in details that contradicted the physical evidence and claims that were implausible.

It is not possible to excise a human heart by slipping a knife in between two ribs. The heart is anchored in the chest by great vessels at the top, bottom, and on each side, as well as at the rear. With both victims, all the connecting vessels had been lacerated cleanly with a single precision cut, without destruction of the rib cage, chest cavity, or surrounding organs. The chest incisions were likewise precise, made with a very sharp knife. The great vessels had been cut with a very sharp instrument. This could not have been done with a weapon as clumsy as a hatchet, no matter how sharp. Three of Parler Edwards's ribs had been excised, though again, with precise cuts; not crushing blows from a hatchet.

The hearts of both victims had been removed in a manner that indicated one assailant holding the rib cage apart while another reached in and cut all of the great vessels. The jobs had been done with deliberation and exactitude.

Joe claimed that he hit Parler Edwards in the face with a hatchet and Edwards then grabbed a bar that he used to hit back as Joe continued hitting him with the axe. Skipping the question of how Parler Edwards could have picked up a bar after being hit in the face with a hatchet, how is it possible that Joe could've sustained no injury after being hit with a bar, as he claimed?

The bar, or lead pipe, found at the scene was identified as having belonged to Edwards. It was covered in blood and hair. Medical evidence showed that the blood and hair on the bar all belonged to Edwards, and further that the bludgeoning had been inflicted before the knife wounds. Why did Joe not mention taking the bar away from Edwards and beating him with it? In addition to the removal of his heart, Parler had a number of stab wounds—one in his back, one in his neck, four on the top of his head—that had been made with a sharp knife. The blade length and the depth of these wounds were not consistent with a hatchet. The only wounds on Edwards that could have come from a hatchet were the blunt-force injuries to his face and head (at least some of which had been made with the lead pipe). Why did Joe not mention the stabbings? Why did he not mention having or using a knife in addition to the hatchet?

Joe claimed he threw the staked heart in a field next to where Edwards was killed. The police had conducted a massive grid search of the area within hours of the murder. Every item on the ground within the surrounding area, every empty bottle and stray candy wrapper, was collected and catalogued as potential evidence. How likely was it that the police would not have found the staked heart? Even supposing an animal had come along and carried it off, twelve-inch stake and all, there would have been blood marks where it landed.

In the murder of Shorty Jones, Joe said he hit him twice in the head with a hammer, then cut his throat. Like Parler Edwards, Jones had also been stabbed—once in the neck, twice in his back, once behind his left ear, and once in the chest above the incision made postmortem to remove his heart. He had four blunt injuries to his head, two of them described by the medical examiner as puncture marks. Yet Joe did not mention the stabbings or the two unusual head wounds made with a separate weapon.

Joe's account of cutting Jones's throat matched only the basic information repeated time and again in the media and lacked details that the murderer would have known. The throat of Shorty Jones had in fact been sliced three separate times, once on either side and in the middle. One of the cuts was so deep it had incised the vertebra. Jones had been nearly decapitated.

Joe claimed that Jones fell on the ground and he cut his throat. Did he lift Jones up to make the two additional massive cuts?

He said he drove a stake through Jones's heart and threw it in a field. There is no field near the boat launch where Jones was killed. The murder happened steps away from the Niagara River. If he only meant to discard it anyway, why not throw the stake into the river?

Joe's claim that he only got blood on his hands defied all logic. The trail of blood at the Jones murder scene measured thirty feet long. How could he have nearly decapitated a man, cut out the heart, and only had blood on his hands?

Joe said he drove away in Jones's cab. How could he have done this without leaving any fingerprints, especially if his hands were bloody? More than twenty finger and palm prints were lifted from various areas of the cab, including the bloody palm print of the victim. Assuming Joe wiped away his prints, how did he manage to cleanly and meticulously wipe away only his own and leave so many others?

Of all the places where he could have abandoned the cab, how did he coincidentally leave it parked within a few feet of the home of Zoe Fontaine's family, particularly when this neighborhood was clear across the city from his own home?

Following the Q&A on the cab driver murders, Dr. Barton turned the interview to more general topics. He then asked Joe about crimes with which he'd actually been charged. Barton's questions on these were leading as well (On September 22 you killed Glenn Dunn? And you were sitting in front of Tops? And you had a paper bag with you?) with Joe agreeing to what Barton said rather than explaining or offering many details himself.

"How would you describe yourself?" Barton asked. "Do you think you're a good guy? A nice guy basically?"

"I don't believe this stuff happened to me," said Joe. "It's hard to believe that I would do something like this."

"It happened several times, they say," said Barton. "That you did something to these guys in New York, or Buffalo."

Dr. Barton asked Joe why he had stabbed fellow soldier, Leonard Coles. Joe replied, "I was hearing voices. I thought he was saying I was a homo. Same thing, I thought I was on a mission."

Dr. Barton pressed him on what the voices had said. Joe appeared embarrassed as he explained that he'd believed he would be sodomized had he not obeyed the order to stab Coles.

Barton asked Joe if he had ever hunted or gutted deer. Joe replied that he had and the doctor said, "Now you've answered one of my other questions—how you knew where the heart was."

"I didn't think of it," Joe said. "Besides, all you've got to do is pick them up and shake them. The guts come out, then you reach in and grab the rest of it."

"That's a deer, or a human?" Barton asked.

"Deer. I never gutted a human."

"But you took the hearts out of these guys," Barton said, returning to the subject of the cab drivers. "What did you do with the bodies?"

"Just left them there."

"On the ground?"

"Mm-hm."

"Or did you put them in the trunk?"

"One I put in the trunk."

"And the other body you left on the ground?"

"Mm-hm."

"Did you hire the cab?"

"Uh, yeah."

"Where'd you have the hatchet?"

"Inside my coat."

"And he didn't even see you?"

"Yeah, he seen me when I had the hatchet. I hit him."

"But did he talk to you before you hit him?"

"No."

"And you hit him in the face?"

"Mm-hm."

"Did he die quickly?"

There was a pause. "No. He fought," Joe said. "He was hitting me with an iron bar and I was hitting him with an axe."

"So how long did it go on for?"

"Five minutes."

"Did he hit you at all hard anywhere?"

"Didn't feel it. I was like crazy."

"And then what did you do after that?"

"Put him in the trunk and drove him someplace else and dumped the car."

"And how did you dump the car?"

"I put it along the thruway."

"Did you cover the car up? Did you disguise it? Camouflage it?"

"Yes. I cut down a tree and put it on top."

"How did you cut down the tree? With a hatchet?"

"No, with a knife."

"Couldn't have been a very big tree, could it?"

"No. Just a little . . ."

"Sapling?"

"Yeah."

"Why did you cover it up with a tree?"

"I don't know. It was an afterthought."

"How long after you'd done it was it discovered?" Barton asked. "Was it in the papers the next day?"

"I don't recall."

"What about Ernest Jones?"

"Ernest Jones?"

"He was the other cab driver. Why didn't you use the hatchet on him?"

"The hatchet broke."

"What, when you were cutting down the tree?"

"No, when I was hitting him [Edwards]. So did the hammer, matter of fact."

"What did you do with the hatchet?"

"I threw it in the field."

"Tell me about the stake in the heart," Barton said. "Why did that have to be done?"

"He was the devil."

"So when you picked him up, did you think he was the devil?"

"Yes. It was anybody. It didn't matter who," said Joe. "It was like a driving thing that I had to do. I can't explain it. Like an obsession."

"A compulsion," Barton commented. "Then the next night, the other guy, his name was Jones. You killed him with a hammer and you say the hammer broke?"

"Mm-hm. Then I cut his throat."

"And then you cut his heart out?"

"Yes. And put a stake in it."

"And then what'd you do with the body?"

"I just left it there and drove the cab away."

"Wasn't there a lot of blood in the cab?"

"No. Not that I recall. He was outside the cab, waiting for me to pay him."

"Oh, I see. It happened outside the cab?"

"Mm-hm."

"Did he fight at all?"

"No."

"He just was unconscious?"

"No. He fell down and then tried to stand up and fell down again."

"And did you hit him again?"

"Yes."

"Pretty gruesome." Barton paused. "At the time all this was happening, were you cool and relaxed about it? Emotionally sort of flat about it?"

"I was like energized, like super-charged. Like I was real strong."

"Were you taking any medication? Any street drugs?"

"No."

Even with Barton's prompting on things such as leaving one of the bodies in a trunk and camouflaging the top of Edwards's cab, Joe's answers—with the exception of details that had been in the news countless times—contradicted the evidence.

If he had thrown the hatchet into the field, why had it not been found? He claimed he'd gotten the victims to drive him willingly by hiring the cabs. How could this be, when Edwards and Jones were both off duty at the time?

Edwards was last seen at 1:45 a.m. He had to be at the train station at 2:25 to pick up his special fare. What were the chances that he would exit the Howard Johnson's, happen upon Joe Christopher, and agree to drive him to a deserted parking lot? Similarly, why would Ernest Jones suddenly decide to accept Joe Christopher as a passenger and agree to drive him to a deserted boat launch in the dead of night?

What happened to the large amounts of money Edwards and Jones were carrying? How did Joe find Parler's two hidden wallets (without leaving any trace that he'd ever touched anything in the cab) and know that there was money in the green cooler tucked in the back of Shorty's cab? Why did he not mention taking the money? For that matter, why would Joe Christopher, who didn't have a job and couldn't afford a car, have left money in the pockets of both victims?

Evidence showed conclusively that Parler had been attacked outside his cab. Assuming he drove Joe to the dark parking lot, why would Parler get out of his cab in the first place?

Evidence showed conclusively that Shorty had first been attacked *inside* his cab, by someone who had to have been sitting next to him in the passenger seat. Neither Joe Christopher nor anyone else could have struck a blow from the backseat. As typical in taxis, a partition separated the front and back seats of Shorty's cab (and Parler's as well). Crime scene photos clearly show the partition in Shorty's cab was intact and undamaged at the time police found it.

Joe claimed that Shorty was outside his cab "waiting for me to pay him." Why would Shorty have gotten out of his cab to collect a fare? If, as Joe said, he hadn't fought back, why did Shorty have defensive wounds on his hands?

Edwards and Jones were murdered following the four .22 caliber shootings, at a time when police had extra patrols out in search of a lone white man walking the streets. Ignoring the question of why Joe would have dumped the vehicles several miles away from his home, how likely is it that he could have walked back to his east-side neighborhood in the middle of the night, stained with blood or not, without drawing attention, not once, but two nights in a row?

These questions were never asked by Dr. Barton, nor by anyone else.

Tom Eoannou had never reviewed the Edwards and Jones files. He'd had no need to, since Christopher was not on trial for those murders. "He convinced me that he did it," said Eoannou. "He was anything but a braggart." The confession came across as sincere and believable to anyone unacquainted with the particulars of each case, which was nearly everyone but the core of former task force members.

The prosecutors were taken aback once again when Joe volunteered to Dr. Barton that he'd tried to strangle a hospital patient in Buffalo around the same time. He explained that he saw a looped garden hose and took it is a sign that he was meant to strangle someone. He claimed to have walked into a hospital room occupied by a black man and wrapped a bicycle chain around his neck, but a nurse had walked in and interrupted the assault and prevented him from killing the man.

This was presumably the attack on Collin Cole. Collin had identified his attacker to police months earlier. He'd nevertheless been shown a photo of Joseph Christopher at the time of his 1981 lineup and did not identify Christopher as his attacker. Nor did the nurse, who had attended the lineup.

Two hours into the examination, Dr. Barton asked Joe if he thought he'd been insane at the time he committed all of his crimes. Joe said yes.

"Do you think you have schizophrenia?" Barton asked.

"Dr. Joseph says I have schizophrenia," he answered.

Barton excused himself and spoke privately once again with Al Ranni. When he returned, he had some additional questions.

"Why would you obey voices and not your own attorney?" Barton asked. "It doesn't add up to me, Joseph."

"I thought it was real, what was happening to me," Joe answered. "I thought I was in a war. I was convinced."

"But even in a war, people will shoot themselves in the foot to get out of the front line," Barton said. "How come you were so meek? Such a wimp? So namby-pamby you had to do what the voices said?"

"I don't know."

Barton questioned him further about his actions and feelings at the time. Joe's overriding memory was feeling constant fear. He didn't know why he'd believed that black men were out to get him. "I don't like what I'm here for, killing black people. I don't feel I'm a racist and right away everybody thinks you are."

"If you had a knife or a sawn-off rifle now and there was nobody around, do you think you'd polish me off?" Barton asked.

"No, I'd throw it away. I detest that part of my life."

Going back to the time of the crimes, Barton asked, "Did you feel cold and unemotional at times?"

"I was more afraid that something was going to happen to me."

Al Ranni and Tom Eoannou agreed that the videotape had been a bad idea. Christopher did not appear to be of sound mind.

There was discussion of offering a plea. Al Ranni attended a closed-door meeting. When he came out, he told Eoannou there was not going to be any plea. There must be a prosecution and a conviction.

Tom Eoannou thought that was odd. Christopher had already been convicted in New York City. If the decision had been up to Eoannou, he would have given Christopher a mental disease or defect sentence. Al Ranni understood how Eoannou felt, and did not entirely disagree. "I can't honestly say he shared the same sympathy as I did, and that's maybe because he was such a professional," Eoannou would recall. "He had a job to do and he was very focused to get that done."

District Attorney Richard Arcara had chosen Ranni for the case. "He knew Al could get him a conviction. There was a major concern about getting a conviction, which I didn't fully understand at the time. Christopher was already serving a long prison sentence. In my opinion, it wasn't the right thing to put this young guy through this trial. I remember Al saying there was a lot of cognizant awareness in what he'd done, planning. So Al was sort of straightforward, 'he knew what he was doing, it doesn't fit the definition of mental disease or defect.' And that was the approach he took in preparation for trial."

Even with their commitment to winning a conviction, Eoannou had concerns about their chances of getting it done. "Al was very seasoned and knew how to get to a jury and I would worry about everything because I was young and he would say, 'Don't worry, we have a bunch of dead bodies. They're gonna want to hang this guy, they don't want him on the street. He killed so many people. That's a huge leg up for us.'

"Christopher, though—there was a gulf in the way he'd been portrayed to the community as a monster. He'd become a racist overnight and that was, I guess, just where his fears or delusions or whatever had led him. I mean, I don't think there was any rational connection between race and what he did. It was so not fact-based."

"[The] issue on this trial is not really what happened," defense attorney Sean Hill said to the jury in his opening statement. "The issue is going to be why did it happen."

It had taken some time to seat a jury. During the selection process, one prospective juror had asked out loud in court why they were having a trial, since everybody knew that Christopher was guilty.

Since the defense was not contesting the mechanics of the murders of Glenn Dunn, Harold Green, and Emanuel Thomas, nor the charge that Joseph Christopher had pulled the trigger, the prosecution limited their witnesses to those most pertinent to establishing the shootings had occurred as alleged, and ballistics testimony that connected evidence found at the defendant's homes to the crimes. The star witnesses in this trial would be the psychiatrists: Dr. Brian Joseph testifying for the defense, Dr. Russell Barton on behalf of the prosecution.

The courtroom was packed, mainly by members of the local media, who covered the case on a day-to-day basis, if not the hour-to-hour updates that had occurred back in 1982. Tom Eoannou was most often tasked with speaking to them. Dealing with the media circus surrounding high-profile cases had been a trial by fire for Eoannou. The Christopher case proceeded immediately after another notorious murder trial in which Eoannou had been co-counsel, the *People v John Justice*.

Justice was a seventeen-year-old honor student at a suburban high school when he murdered his mother, father, and younger brother. After stabbing his family to death, Justice had killed a man named Wayne Haun in a traffic collision. The car crash had apparently been a suicide attempt by Justice, who jumped out of the car and told police, "I killed my whole family! I killed my whole family!" Justice had pled insanity, with some success; he'd been found not guilty by reason of mental disease in the deaths of his father and brother but guilty of the intentional murder of his mother and depraved indifference in the death of Wayne Haun.

Throughout Joseph Christopher's trial, Tom Eoannou would look at the defendant sitting at the defense table and think, *this is very sad*. He was doubly haunted by the memory of John Justice, who had occupied the same chair only a month before. The thought began eating away at him: *These are two very sick people, incredibly sick human beings, and we're trying to hang them from the highest post.*

At least John Justice didn't have politics working against him. There hadn't been the same level of intense push for conviction at all costs. With Joseph Christopher, no expense had been spared. As Eoannou recalled, "We spent a ton of money. I'm sure we broke the record for that time. And I remember sitting there thinking, you know, we're probably outspending them [the defense] ten to one.

"Christopher's lawyers, David Jay and Sean Hill, had been assigned by the court. They were very high-end, top-shelf attorneys. But nevertheless, they had, I presume, limited resources, whereas ours were not. We had the unlimited taxpayer funds and we had the ability to work night and day on nothing but this case. We spent a huge amount of time with Russell Barton, preparing him to testify. He was being paid a tremendous amount of money and Al and I would go to his house, spend the day working with him, go to our hotel, then back to his house the next day. We practiced over and over."

The jury would first hear from Dr. Brian Joseph, the sole witness for the defense. As an expert witness, Dr. Joseph was also paid for his testimony. Expert witnesses typically are. In this case, Dr. Joseph could not help feeling some personal investment. He had been involved in the case far longer than any other psychiatrist, perhaps longer than any single person aside from the defendant himself. In the weeks leading up to trial, he had checked in on Christopher at the holding center on a near daily basis to monitor his medication and progress. Schizophrenia cannot be cured. A patient can only be made better with treatment. Joe Christopher had been made better, though too late, Dr. Joseph thought ruefully. It had always stayed with him that this man had tried to get help before any of these criminal acts had occurred.

"Doctor," Sean Hill asked, "may a person suffering from paranoid schizophrenia function normally in many or most aspects of his or her life?"

"Well, yes," Dr. Joseph answered. "There seems to be a popular misconception that if a person is schizophrenic, they must be so strange and so bizarre that everybody and anybody would pick them out. The fact is that that is not necessarily true. There are aspects of the person with schizophrenia who does act that way, but there are people who can certainly go through [life] and be socially superficially appropriate. For instance, if you have a delusion and you feel that the world's against you, that doesn't mean that you don't get up in the morning and have breakfast, that you can't carry on activities or drive a car or get along in the world. You don't have to be completely and absolutely in an—utterly out of touch with reality to have a mental illness, to have a form of schizophrenia.

"Some people are. That's one of the curious aspects of the illness, because it does tend to come and go, with its major symptoms. Somebody with schizophrenia, paranoid type, the major problem they have is a paranoid delusion. They don't make a lot of sense, they act odd. Some people don't move at all and are absolutely still. They can sometimes be called catatonic schizophrenia and in some people there is a blending of the symptoms. One subclass can look like another. So, depending if one doctor saw a patient in one hospital at one point in time, he might see somebody suffering from a catatonic form, but the patient may go to another hospital, the symptoms may change to some degree, the paranoia be more obvious and that doctor would say that person's suffering from paranoid type. So there is some blending in changeability in this illness. It's called variability in the medical sense that symptoms do change in one way or another.

"No two illnesses affect the same person in the exact same way. Nobody with pneumonia has the same temperature as everybody else, or has the same degree of coughing as everybody else, or responds to medication as everybody else. People respond to illnesses and treatment differently, and this is so with schizophrenia as well."

Questioning turned to specifics concerning Joseph Christopher. Reporters made occasional notes during direct and again during cross-examination by Al Ranni as the day wore on. A sudden energy filled the courtroom, at least insofar as the press, when the prosecutor asked Dr. Joseph about killings that Christopher had discussed with him, and the witness responded, "He told me about two cab drivers."

Headlines and TV broadcasts were filled with the big news: Joseph Christopher, the .22 Caliber Killer, had confessed to killing the cab drivers and cutting their hearts out.

———

Tom Eoannou would later say of Dr. Russell Barton, "He was the perfect prosecution witness. A warm, elderly man who wouldn't be rattled on the stand. He never looked like he was attacking Joe."

In his fine English accent, Dr. Barton told the jury that in his opinion, the defendant never had schizophrenia. He had borderline personality disorder. He had committed the murders, Barton said, out of a need to feel powerful. Christopher had felt like a nobody. Killing gave him a sense of strength and accomplishment.

The videotape was played for the jury. Somewhat ironically, both sides held out hope that it would bolster their case.

Christopher had murdered the cab drivers so gruesomely, Dr. Barton testified, because he wanted front-page headlines. "It's really a very sad story of a wasted life." Christopher was maladjusted, even tragic. He had a personality disorder, but he was not insane. Dr. Barton asserted that Christopher was faking insanity in the hope of getting out of a prison and into a mental hospital, and cautioned jurors that if he were to be committed to a psychiatric institution, he could be released in as little as ninety days. The average stay in a psychiatric hospital was only thirty-three months, Dr. Barton claimed.

The defense objected. Judge McCarthy instructed the jury that they were not to consider sentence in determining their verdict. They must disregard Dr. Barton's comment. But of course, the jury could not unhear it.

David Jay gave the closing argument for the defense. He focused on the psychiatric testimony, detailing his client's long history of mental disease. Jay referred to Christopher's aberrant behavior prior to the time he had even become a suspect in the killings; the self-imposed starvation, the laceration of his penis, the utter breakdown when he'd stabbed Leonard Coles in front of a dozen men in his army barracks. "Was he faking a psychiatric defense then?" Jay asked the jurors.

"The doctors agree, I believe, and have told you that the schizophrenic process, when you are in the midst of it, you can look fine one second and it's like turning on a light. Something happens; you hear a voice and back into it; you go into this crazy madness." The entirety of the evidence, David Jay argued, all pointed to a single cause for Christopher's actions. "Madness. Absolute madness."

In his closing arguments, Al Ranni argued that Christopher's past behavior had demonstrated a knowledge of right and wrong as well as premeditation. "When he was in the army, the stabbing of Leonard Coles," Ranni said, "he says it was a terrible mistake, bad mistake, I'm terribly sorry. Shows appreciation that if you put a knife in someone's stomach or chest, it's wrong.

"Taxi drivers. More evidence," said the prosecutor. "The planning. Lures those taxi drivers out there, getting in the car, preparing the stakes in advance, getting the hatchets, concealing them. Thoughtful, goal-directed behavior.

"Why did he do these crimes? Not important if you conclude that he was aware, had the capacity to be aware and had the capacity to know right from wrong. That's enough if you conclude he's legally sane. It's not important what his motive was.

"Barton gave you an explanation of why he did it," Ranni continued. "He didn't have importance. He didn't have self-esteem. He didn't have dignity. He was frustrated at his failures, which is understandable, but superimposed over this was this personality disorder, this maladjustment. The personality disorder doesn't affect your sense of reality, knowing right from wrong.

"You can conclude safely he doesn't like blacks and this was a way for him to do something. Gain self-esteem. It sounds terrible but he could gain pride and self-esteem, and that was his objective. He had to do something. Why not blacks? He didn't like them anyways since high school and he would get the thrill of it. He'd get something accomplished. Is it bad? Is it tragic? Of course it is, but did he know what he was doing? Sure."

Reminding jurors of what Dr. Barton had said about the average stay in a psych facility being only thirty-three months, Al Ranni turned his final remarks to the cab drivers—crimes for which Christopher had never been charged, for which his confessions had never been held to scrutiny, and for which he was not on trial—and told the jury, "Here is a chance to do something else before he makes his mark in the army. Things have died down and he kills two cab drivers. Maybe they would have gone unnoticed if they were just stabbed or shot, but the heart removal—here's a chance for real recognition and he got it, but at the same time, being careful to escape detection because he knew it was wrong."

The jury had three options: guilty of murder in the second degree; guilty of manslaughter in the first degree because of extreme emotional disturbance; or not guilty by reason of mental disease or defect.

On December 10, 1986, after fifteen hours of deliberation, they returned a verdict of three counts of manslaughter in the first degree because of extreme emotional disturbance.

"We're satisfied that the jury returned with a verdict of guilty," Al Ranni told reporters. "It was a complete rejection of the insanity defense."

Attorney Sean Hill said that he was not surprised. "I guess in a sense it's a verdict we can understand. The jury worked very hard to come up with a verdict, and it shows they paid attention to the psychiatric evidence."

Apparently Judge McCarthy had not. "Your acts . . . defy reason. You terminated the lives of three men solely for the color of their skin," he said at the sentencing on January 20, 1987. "You terrorized this community for months, causing great alarm." The judge went on about racism. Sean Hill pointed to the jury's verdict and said, "I hope we now know why these things happened. It serves no useful purpose to say these were racially motivated killings."

McCarthy sentenced Christopher to the maximum of eight and one-third to twenty-five years in prison to be served consecutively after he served his term of thirty-three and one-third years on the New York City convictions. Judge McCarthy told a news columnist, "Christopher's acts were so grievous that my duty was clear. This community had to be satisfied that the criminal justice system would respond in kind." McCarthy commented that the trial had established what Joseph Christopher did, "but I don't know that we found out why he did what he did."

District Attorney Richard Arcara, who had pushed for the maximum sentence, called Christopher "a racial assassin who terrorized the entire community." Al Ranni commented, "We're satisfied and happy that this man is going to be in jail for the rest of his natural life. That means he cannot further interfere with the peace and tranquility of this community."

Common Council President George Arthur expressed satisfaction with the sentence, calling it a sign that the criminal justice system was working.

The videotapes of Christopher's psychiatric interview by Dr. Barton were released to local television stations. Portions of it were played on the news. Proof for the public that Christopher killed the cab drivers.

Despite Christopher's confession to the cabbie murders, there were law enforcement officials who said publicly, and adamantly, that they didn't buy it. Buffalo Homicide Chief Leo Donovan was among the most outspoken. Officers who commented to the media were generally circumspect at the time. "We weren't happy about the coverup," Tom Rowan said years later. "I know my bosses [Cheektowaga Police Department] weren't happy about it, and I know the Amherst police weren't happy about it. To wrap all of this up with a bow for the sake of making people feel good or safer was wrong. Lying to the community is never justified, under any circumstances. Not to mention that we still had this other killer or killers out there."

Joe's confession to the cabbie killings was very convincing, insofar as his apparent sincerity. Tom Eoannou, Brian Joseph, and even Joe's own defense attorneys, David Jay and Sean Hill, were convinced by it. But of course, none of them had ever examined the case files.

It would never be known why Joe confessed to the murders of Parler Edwards and Shorty Jones and the assault on Collin Cole. It's possible that he did so to try and bolster his insanity defense. It's also possible, perhaps even likely, that he had come to believe it himself. He seemed genuinely convinced that he had committed these crimes—perhaps as he had been convinced that he had a child; as he had been convinced that he was being poisoned; as he had been convinced that someone had told him he had sexually assaulted his mother and had become distraught and hysterical in a Georgia jail cell in 1981, pleading with his mother to tell him if it was really true.

————————

The district attorney's office released a final report on the matter of Joseph Christopher. "In Erie County, Joseph G. Christopher remains under indictment for the assaults on Albert Menefee and Calvin Crippen and is the prime suspect in the murders of Parler Edwards, Ernest Jones, Roger Adams, and Wendell Barnes, as well as the attempted strangulation of Collin Cole. During psychiatric interviews conducted prior to his 1986 trial, Joseph G. Christopher spoke with psychiatrists about the crimes pending against him and those in which he was a suspect. Information from those psychiatric interviews is consistent with the hypothesis that he committed the homicides of Parler Edwards, Ernest Jones, Roger Adams, and the attempted assault upon Collin Cole . . .

"It should be noted that the psychiatric interviews are not, in and of themselves, legally admissible for purposes of Grand Jury presentments leading to further murder charges against Joseph G. Christopher. If he is tried on any of the remaining indictments and if any future jury were to find him not responsible by reason of mental disease or defect, that verdict could result in his being removed from the custody of the state commissioner of corrections and delivered to the custody of the state department of mental hygiene which would have the power to retain custody of him until he is deemed 'cured.' Thus, the possibility of complicating and/or compromising the defendant's current incarcerative [sic] status by an intervening mental health hospitalization adds a separate and distinct dimension of risk to repetitive prosecutions at this stage in the case.

"It is our conclusion that Joseph G. Christopher likely will never again menace the citizenry of New York State. It is also our conclusion that further prosecution of this defendant will not enhance the interests of justice. A horrible chapter in the history of New York State should be closed. Joseph G. Christopher should stay removed from the province of the courts and left to the province of the state correctional system."

————————

Not long after the trial, Tom Eoannou went out for lunch one day and thought about the Christopher case. When he returned to the office, he thanked the district attorney for the privilege of serving and politely handed in his resignation.

Brian Joseph went to see Joe Christopher at the holding center. In spite of his professional reserve, Dr. Joseph felt bad. He felt bad that he hadn't been able to save Joe, either from himself or from the system.

He had known Christopher through several phases of this young man's life—as a hostile and suspicious twenty-five-year-old, indicted for multiple murders; as a convicted killer, shuffled between prisons and psychiatric hospitals; as a thirty-one-year-old, on medication that helped restore him to the gentle young man he'd once been.

Doctor and patient spoke cordially for a few minutes. Of all the words they exchanged over the years, Brian Joseph would best remember the last ones Joe Christopher ever said to him. "Thank you for what you tried to do for me, doctor."

Dr. Joseph wished him well. He said good-bye to Joe Christopher for the last time and walked away. He kept walking until he was out of the holding center. For the moment, he needed to be anywhere else but here.

EPILOGUE

Do you know how to drive a dog crazy? Put him in a box and beat the box with a stick every now and then.
They tell me time is the healer of the mind. I hope that is true.
If I do not know love, I'm <u>nothing</u>.
I'm <u>nothing</u>.

—Joseph Christopher,
letter to his mother, 1981

JOSEPH CHRISTOPHER SERVED a total of twelve years in jails and New York prisons. He died on March 1, 1993, at Great Meadow Correctional Facility. Cause of death was testicular cancer that had spread to his stomach and lungs. He was thirty-seven years old.

The cancer went untreated until the late stages, when, according to family members, he was in so much pain that he couldn't lie down. Some press accounts incorrectly stated his cause of death as male breast cancer.

In the six years between his final conviction and his death, Joe spent periods of time in psychiatric facilities when his schizophrenia required more medical attention than prison staff could provide.

Commenting at the time of Christopher's death, Edward Cosgrove said, "God bless his soul, but he was an unfortunate wretch."

Kevin Dillon, Christopher's first Buffalo attorney, said of him, "There's not much doubt he was a very, very disturbed person. He could sit in a jail cell with his eyes closed and two hours after the guard came on, Christopher could tell him what time it was. He could tell by constantly tapping his foot."

"How many hundreds of thousands of dollars did Judge Marshall, Judge Flynn, and the district attorney cost taxpayers by running roughshod over him to get this to trial?" Mark Mahoney wondered, adding, "Nobody ever ruled out the possibility that Christopher had delusionally popped himself into these cases."

According to Charles Patrick Ewing, professor at the University of Buffalo School of Law, the insanity defense "is rarely raised, rarely applicable, and even more rarely successful. And when it does succeed, the defendant usually loses his or her liberty for many years, sometimes for life."

Ewing is an attorney, forensic psychologist, and author regarded as one of the leading experts on the insanity defense. "Every time a defendant pleads insanity, the case makes headlines. In those rare instances in which a defendant is actually found insane, the public is usually outraged." In his book, *Insanity: Murder, Madness, and the Law*, Ewing addresses the misconception that a successful insanity defense often leads to a shorter period of incarceration. "In most cases, a defendant acquitted by reason of insanity will spend more time locked up than a defendant who is found guilty. Being found insane almost always results in an indeterminate—sometimes lifetime—commitment to a secure mental hospital. And most of these 'hospitals' are much more like prisons than treatment facilities."

Interestingly, Professor Ewing's analysis proved to be true with the high-profile murder case that preceded Christopher's 1986 retrial. John Justice was found not guilty by reason of insanity in the deaths of his father and brother but guilty in the intentional murder of his mother and depraved indifference in the death of motorist Wayne Haun. Released from prison nearly thirty years later, having served his sentence, he was thereafter involuntarily committed to a secure psychiatric facility at the request of the state.

———

Former prosecutor Tom Eoannou became a criminal defense attorney. In 2016, the *Buffalo News* cited Eoannou as one of the ten most prominent criminal defense attorneys in Western New York. Looking back on the case of Joseph Christopher, Eoannou said, "This is a classic example of the criminal justice system handling a tragedy where there is an enormous mental health issue. The underlying thing is not criminality at all. It's not. The system failed him. He committed horrific crimes and there's no excuse, but the flip side is that our system was not equipped to handle Joe Christopher."

———

In his 1989 book, *Unnatural Death: Confessions of a Medical Examiner*, celebrity pathologist Michael Baden devoted a few pages of a chapter to the case of Joseph Christopher. Baden's only real connection to the case was a brief trip to Buffalo for the purpose of conducting second autopsies on Parler Edwards and Ernest Jones (which, according to a ranking detective present, added nothing new to what the first medical examiner had already discerned).

Baden's account of the case is so thoroughly riddled with errors of both major and minor proportion that one wonders if he didn't confuse Joseph Christopher with some other case. While it hardly seems worthwhile to address all the mistakes, there is one claim that cries out for correction. Baden writes that while Joseph Christopher was in the Fort Benning stockade, he performed fellatio on black prisoners in return for extra food. By all other accounts, including records and personal recollections of men who were actually in the stockade at the time or supervising it, this claim is false.

Baden uses this claim to assert a Freudian-esque theory that Christopher killed black men because he was physically attracted to them and wanted to "destroy the thing that was tempting him." (A psychiatrist very familiar with Christopher and the case bluntly labeled this "a crackpot theory.") While Baden is, of course, entitled to his theories, the premise on which it is based is false. By all credible accounts, and as a matter of pure logic—Christopher spent most of his stockade time in solitary, and further, his behavior was so unpredictably violent and bizarre that other prisoners didn't want to go near him—the claim that he engaged in oral sex with men in the stockade is untrue.

───────

The number of victims killed by Christopher is a question that cannot be answered with certainty. There was little physical evidence to tie him to any of the murders, and his confessions were unreliable. As reporter Gene Warner wrote following his jailhouse interview with Christopher, "He truly didn't seem to know how many people he had killed."

As far as is known, Christopher first mentioned a number in regard to his victims when speaking to army nurse Bernard Burgess, telling the nurse that he'd killed thirteen people in Buffalo and New York City. Around the same time, Joseph told his army guard, Christopher Corwin, that he had killed seven people in Buffalo and more in New York. Thirteen is also the number he gave to Gene Warner.

He also told Warner that Glenn Dunn had not been the first victim; a day or two before the shooting of Dunn, Christopher claimed to have stabbed a man in the throat. Christopher said he didn't know how badly this unknown man had been hurt, that he may not have even been hurt badly; however, it's difficult to imagine anyone being stabbed in the throat and not being badly hurt, particularly knowing the fate of Christopher's other knifing victims. He stabbed with force and deadly intent.

An educated guess on Christopher's named murder victims: Glenn Dunn, Harold Green, Emanuel Thomas, Joseph McCoy, Roger Adams (all in Buffalo); Wendell Barnes (Rochester); Luis Rodriguez, Antoine Davis, Richard Renner, Carl Ramsey (New York City).

His statement to army personnel that he killed seven people in Buffalo can add up in one of two ways: if, in addition to the five named above, the list includes Albert Menefee and the unknown male he claimed to have stabbed prior to the Dunn homicide, or by including Albert Menefee and Wendell Barnes. Though Barnes was killed in Rochester, about an hour's drive from Buffalo, Rochester is still generally within the Western New York region. Christopher may have thus considered him a "Buffalo" victim.

Though Albert Menefee survived, it's reasonable to assume that Christopher thought he had killed him at the time he made the statement. Christopher returned to Fort Benning on January 2, when Menefee was in critical condition and not expected to survive. Indeed, the Buffalo police had already opened a file titled "Albert Menefee Homicide" and had homicide detectives assigned to the case.

In a letter he sent to the *Buffalo News* in 1983, Christopher cryptically wrote of his crime spree, "So it was a baseball game. 17 hits and 13 dead if they are dead." Asked to explain the meaning of this, he told Gene Warner, "I supposedly attacked 17 people and 13 of them are dead." Again, only an educated guess can be made on his claim of "17 hits," or total gun and knife attacks. In order of occurrence: unknown male, Glenn Dunn, Harold Green, Emanuel Thomas, Joseph McCoy, John Adams, Ivan Frazer, Luis Rodriguez, Antoine Davis, Richard Renner, Carl Ramsey, Roger Adams, Wendell Barnes, Albert Menefee, Calvin Crippen, Leonard Coles. In addition, a black male reported fighting off a stabbing attempt by a white man on a Manhattan subway on Christmas Eve 1980. This would bring the total to seventeen.

Christopher later made statements about having grappled with a man on a subway. This could indicate his involvement in the Christmas Eve attack. He could also have been referring to Ivan Frazer, who followed Christopher off the train and pushed him against the door.

Christopher always denied that he attacked Calvin Crippen. Crippen, however, identified Christopher and insisted that he was the attacker. It would seem that neither man had a reason to lie. One of them must have been mistaken—or perhaps delusional.

Some have opined that the real answers were forever lost with the death of Joseph Christopher. It could be, however, that the answers were forever lost long before his death, askew and unrecoverable from the murky depths of a diseased mind.

———

In 2011, the Buffalo police cold case unit received an unsolicited tip on the Edwards and Jones murders. A detective looked at the case files and determined that the tip merited further attention. (After reading the files, the detective similarly felt that Joseph Christopher could not have been the murderer. With a rolling of the eyes, the detective commented, "He wouldn't even have needed a lawyer. Even *I* could have defended him.") The detective passed the tip along to the New York state police.

As of this writing, the murders of Parler Edwards and Ernest Jones remain unsolved.

ACKNOWLEDGMENTS

I AM PROFOUNDLY grateful to the seventy-two people I interviewed for this book, and to the dozens of others who provided assistance and otherwise contributed in a variety of ways. My thank-you list numbers well over one hundred people who showed great kindness and candor in sharing their recollections, knowledge, and insights in order to help me piece this story together.

My thanks go first and foremost to Michael Felicetta, whose help with locating records and introducing me to key figures in the case was absolutely essential. Truly, this book could not have been written without his help and generosity. The same is true for attorney Mark Mahoney, who was generous beyond measure, as well as Captain Mark Antonio and retired detective Lissa Redmond of the Buffalo Police Department, both of whom were incredibly kind (and patient) during the many days I spent at police headquarters. Likewise, I offer special thanks to former district attorney Edward C. Cosgrove, the late detective-lieutenant Thomas Rowan of the Cheektowaga Police, retired detective Mark Stambach of the Buffalo Police Department, attorneys Thomas Eoannou, Frank Bress, and Sean Hill, and reporter Gene Warner. My deep gratitude also to Daniel Jay, brother of the late attorney David Jay, for providing me with the videotapes of Joseph Christopher's 1986 interview. I likewise thank Michael Wooten of WGRZ-Channel 2, Buffalo, for allowing me to view the station's archival footage from their coverage of the case.

John Regan and Melvin Lobbett of the Buffalo Homicide Bureau played key roles in solving the .22 caliber case, as did William "Joe" Cooley of the New York state police. All three are quick to credit and praise their colleagues on the task force, and the praise is no doubt warranted. I thank John, Melvin, and Joe for their incredible kindness to me, and for their years of meritorious service in law enforcement. My thanks and compliments as well to the entire task force, under the direction of Edward Cosgrove.

Dr. Brian Joseph provided a wealth of insight and recollection, without which this book would lack essential detail. I'm deeply grateful for his contributions.

Many thanks to Leonard Coles and Kim Edmiston for sharing their stories with me. I cannot thank them enough for their courage and candor.

Daniel DiLandro and Linda Webster of the E. H. Butler Library at Buffalo State College provided enormous help in providing articles and photographs from the *Courier-Express* collection. They are my two favorite librarians in the whole world and I am indebted to them.

My thanks to the following people whose contributions brought depth and perspective to this story: Terry Belke, Christopher Belling, John Bisci, Bill Bitterman, Salvatore Castiglione, Marilyn Chamberlain, Scott Chamberlain, Anne Coleman, Claude Tim Coleman, Domenic Cortese, Christopher Corwin, Tony Costantino, Tom Diina, John E. Douglas, Patrick Dugan, Dave Dukarm, Arlene Dumke, Gene Emser, Harold Frank, Madona Gorney, Ron Gorski, Joe Gramaglia, Robert Grot, James Holley, Tina Jay, Aldrich Johnson, John Kiouses, Charlie Mecca, Marjorie Meissner, William Misztal, Mike Obenauer, Michael Olear, Matt Ortiz, James Pitts, Alvin Pustulka, George Quinlan, Dan Redmond, John Reid, Michael Rizzo, Bob Schmitt, Cheryl Schmitt, Edward Silvestrini, Darryl Smith, Ernest Smith Jr., Mark Spicer, Michael Stebick, Missy Sullivan, Dennis Vacco, Peter Vito, Charles Walker, Candice Waz, Dave Weisner, Mecislaus Wendzikowski, Al Williams, Henry Williams Jr., and Tommy Zukic.

Heartfelt thanks to several others who preferred not to have their names listed, whose contributions were indispensable.

For their support and feedback on the manuscript, I'm ever grateful to my trusted readers: Joe De May, Scotty-Miguel Sandoe, Frances Kleese, Dan Berkowitz, and Trieva Gant. Thanks also and always to my mother, Trieva Pelonero, to Joe and Tina Pelonero, and to F. Pel. for the Sunday night counsels.

Finally, very warm thanks indeed to my editor, Olga Greco, and my agent, Jennifer Carlson, both of whom have championed this project from the start and went above and beyond to help bring it to fruition.

SOURCES AND REFERENCES

THE NARRATIVE IS based on firsthand interviews, law enforcement records, audio and video recordings, personal letters, legal transcripts, news and magazine articles, and archival documents. Accounts of the police investigation come directly from the officers' reports and, in every instance possible, interviews with the officers themselves. All courtroom dialogue is taken from transcripts of the proceedings. Many of the references on the following list are quoted in the text, as noted. Books are listed alphabetically by author. Because of the great number of articles from periodicals and newspapers, I have arranged the list of publications alphabetically and then listed the articles in order of publication date.

BOOKS

Baden, Michael M., MD, and Judith Adler Hennessee. *Unnatural Death: Confessions of a Medical Examiner.* New York: Random House, 1989.

Diagnostic and Statistical Manual of Mental Disorders, Fourth Edition, Text Revision (DSM-IV-TR). Arlington, VA: American Psychiatric Association, 2000.

Douglas, John, and Mark Olshaker. *Mind Hunter: Inside the FBI's Elite Serial Crime Unit.* New York: Scribner, 1995.

Ewing, Charles Patrick. *Insanity: Murder, Madness, and the Law.* New York: Oxford University Press, 2008.

Torrey, E. Fuller, MD. *Surviving Schizophrenia, Sixth Edition: A Family Manual*. New York: HarperCollins, 2013.

MAGAZINES, NEWSPAPERS, AND PERIODICALS

Associated Press:
"Segregation Protest. Buffalo Mothers Unit Asks for a City Demonstration." September 10, 1958.
"Wilkins Cautions Whites on Riots." July 9, 1967.
"Buffalo suspect's acquaintances shocked." May 1, 1981.
"Buffalo slaying suspect was quiet churchgoer." May 1, 1981.
"Suspect Pleads Not Guilty to Three Murders in Buffalo." May 11, 1981.
"Buffalo suspect's lineups leave prosecutor pleased." May 13, 1981.
"Permission granted to take samples." May 16, 1981.
"Indictment in slashings." May 27, 1981.
"Tight Security is Set for Trial of Suspect in Slaying of Blacks." October 4, 1981.
"Soldier Who Killed Three Blacks Ordered to Serve at least 60 years." May 25, 1982.
"Murder Convictions Against '.22-Caliber Killer' Overturned." July 6, 1985.
"Christopher shuns judge's questions on lawyer issue." March 2, 1986.
"Joseph Christopher: 'paranoid schizophrenic.'" November 15, 1986.
"Retrial seeking motive for murders." December 9, 1986.
"Jury Finds Christopher Guilty of Manslaughter." December 11, 1986.
"County Judge Sentences Joseph Christopher To Maximum Term." By Stephen W. Bell. January 20, 1987.
"Killer sentence pleases blacks." January 21, 1987.
Buffalo Evening News **(Buffalo, New York):**
"The Buffalo Detectives, 1980." By Dan Herbeck. September 21, 1980.
"Two More 'Executed'; Police Look for Link." By Mike Vogel and Walter Fuszara. September 24, 1980.
"Grim Agenda." September 25, 1980.
"News, WKBW Offer Reward in Slayings." September 25, 1980.
"The Same Gun Used to Shoot 3 Victims." By Dan Herbeck and Agnes Palazzetti. September 25, 1980.

"Reward Offer Spurs Tips in Slaying Probe." September 26, 1980.

"Weapon Tied To Falls Death, 2 City Killings." By Dan Herbeck and Agnes Palazzetti. September 26, 1980.

"Witness to Be Hypnotized For Details on Slayer of 3." By Gene Warner. September 27, 1980.

".22 Gunman's Fourth Victim Dies." September 29, 1980.

"Conflicting Description Of Killer of Four Men Puzzles Police Units." By Dan Herbeck. September 29, 1980.

"Arcara Notes Violations of Civil Rights." By Margaret Hammersley. October 1, 1980.

"4 Slayings Believed Work of 1 Man." By Dan Herbeck and Gene Warner. October 2, 1980.

"Investigators Ask News Blackout On .22-Caliber Case." October 3, 1980.

"Manhunt On in Six States For Sniper Attacking Blacks." By William C. Hempel, L.A. Times-Washington Post Service. October 3, 1980.

"Psychics Fail to Boost Police Spirits in Probe." By Gene Warner. October 7, 1980.

"Black Man Found Dead in Car's Trunk." October 8, 1980.

"2 Black Murder Victims Mutilated." By Mike Vogel and James Staas. October 9, 1980.

"Bigger FBI Role Is Asked In Investigation of 6 Killings." By James Staas and Mike Vogel. October 9, 1980.

"Eve, Fisher Call for Calm Among Blacks." By Carl Allen. October 9, 1980.

"Killer in Mutilations is Bigot, Sadist, UB Prof Theorizes." By Modesto Argenio. October 9, 1980.

"State Police Join Search For Killer of 6." By Jerry Allen, News Albany Bureau. October 9, 1980.

"Black Auto Worker Escapes Bid to Kill Him in Street Attack." By Carl Allen and Ray Hill. October 10, 1980.

"Cabbies More Cautious, but Stay on Street." By Carl Allen. October 10, 1980.

"Cross-Burning Linked to Blacks." By Agnes Palazzetti. October 10, 1980.

"DA's Command Post Unites Police 'Army' Probing Killings." By Lee Coppola. October 10, 1980.

"FBI Experts to Probe Victim's Cab." By Lee Coppola and Lonny Hudkins. October 10, 1980.

"For Heaven's Sake, Give Yourself Up." By Ray Hill. October 10, 1980.

"Hotline Set Up In Murders." October 10, 1980.

"Patient Detective Work Is Key in Hunt for Killer." By Mike Vogel. October 10, 1980.

"PBA Appeals For Action to Catch Killers." October 10, 1980.

"Police See Peril Of Vigilantism On East Side." By Dan Herbeck. October 10, 1980.

"Profiles of 6 Black Murder Victims Hold Few Clues." By Lonnie Hudkins. October 10, 1980.

"Rewards Mount in Killings." October 10, 1980.

"U.S. Justice Dept. Entering Probe of 6 Area Slayings." October 10, 1980.

"Victim's Kin Claims Mutilation Hushed Up." October 10, 1980.

"Anonymous Caller Threatens Jackson." October 11, 1980.

"Attempted Strangling of Black Man Foiled by Nurse at Medical Center." By Lee Coppola and Mike Vogel. October 11, 1980.

"Black Agitators Are Suspected in Cross-Burning." October 11, 1980.

"E. Side Calm Is Broken by Shots at Cab." By Gene Warner. October 11, 1980.

"Police Scouring City for Klansmen." By Modesto Argenio. October 11, 1980.

"Rev. Jackson Wants U.S. to Lead Manhunt." By Peter Simon. October 11, 1980.

"Rev. Jackson Urges Blacks To Avoid Violence, Revenge." By Peter Simon. October 11, 1980.

"Workers Saw 4 'Fishermen' Near Where Body Was Found." By James Staas. October 11, 1980.

"Armbands Are Urged As Sign of Mourning." October 12, 1980.

"Black Men Here Wary; Some Arm Themselves." By Carl Allen. October 12, 1980.

"Comments Lead Police to Search Home." By Mike Vogel and Lee Coppola. October 12, 1980.

"Cosgrove Reassures Black Group." By Dan Herbeck. October 12, 1980.

"Few Racial Incidents Mar Uneasy Quiet on East Side." By Gene Warner and Dennis Hollins. October 12, 1980.

"Manhunt for a Killer Again Quickens the Pulse of Buffalo." By Mike Vogel. October 12, 1980.

"Nurse Is Now Star Witness in Probe." By Modesto Argenio. October 12, 1980.

"Police Force Needs Blacks, Officers Say." By Carl Allen. October 12, 1980.

"Police Try to Link Target of Choking to Cabbies." By Lonnie Hudkins. October 12, 1980.

"Police 'Rivals' Cooperating on Probe." By Ray Hill. October 12, 1980.

"'Portrait' of Murderer Shows 2 Killers, FBI Expert Says." By Lee Coppola. October 12, 1980.

"Age, Height Both Believed Inaccurate." By Lee Coppola and Mike Vogel. October 13, 1980.

"Murder Probe Beefed Up." October 13, 1980.

"Black Ribbons Distributed For Mourning Six Deaths." By Carl Allen. October 13, 1980.

"Hospitals Increase Security After Attack Against Black Patient." By Arthur Page. October 13, 1980.

"Jackson Guarded, Cunningham Insists." By Agnes Palazzetti. October 13, 1980.

"Manhunt Puts Inn on Map." By Mike Vogel. October 13, 1980.

"Racial Unrest Blamed In Shots at Whites." October 13, 1980.

"Police Task Force Finds Few New Clues In Slayings of 6 Blacks." By Mike Vogel and Matt Gryta. October 14, 1980.

"Seize Shells Found by Teen On East Side." By Agnes Palazzetti and Lee Coppola. October 15, 1980.

"No Clues Yet Tie Gun Killings, Cab Deaths, Cosgrove Says." By Matt Gryta. October 16, 1980.

"Pace of Probe Picks Up With Outpouring." By Mike Vogel and Matt Gryta. October 17, 1980.

"Blacks, Whites Joining To Support Unity Rally." October 18, 1980.

"'Insane' Label On Killer Assailed." October 18, 1980.

"FBI Official Eyes New Ways to Aid Probe of Killings." By Mike Vogel and Lee Coppola. October 18, 1980.

"Lab Tests Used to Trace Murdered Cabbie's Steps." By Lee Coppola and Matt Gryta. October 18, 1980.

"Details of Murder Probe Being Sent Across Nation." By Mike Vogel and Gene Warner. October 19, 1980.

"No Panic Gun-Buying Despite City's Fears." By Gene Warner. October 19, 1980.

"Unity Day Rally Set At Niagara Square." October 19, 1980.

"The City Proclaims Its Unity in Defying A Madman's Assault." By Ray Hill. October 20, 1980.

"Visit by Civiletti Appears Unlikely in Murder Probe." By Matt Gryta. October 20, 1980.

"Civiletti Sends Top Aide to Join Manhunt." By Mike Vogel and Matt Gryta. October 21, 1980.

"Taxi Killings May Be Linked To Betting War." By Mike Vogel and Walter Fuszara. October 22, 1980.

"3 Separate Cases Seen Emerging in Attacks on Blacks." By Agnes Palazzetti and Lee Coppola. October 25, 1980.

"Probers Rule Out Single Slayer." October 25, 1980.

"2 Tied to Killings By Tipsters Took Their Own Lives." By Dan Herbeck. October 26, 1980.

"City, County, C of C Each Add $25,000." By Lee Coppola. October 27, 1980.

"Rumor Hot Line." October 27, 1980.

"FBI Hasn't Tied Man Held In Florida to Killings Here." By Mike Vogel. October 28, 1980.

"Sheriff to Reduce Units in Slaying Probe." By Dan Herbeck. October 30, 1980.

"Knife Attack on Black Yields Clues." By Lee Coppola and Agnes Palazzetti. January 2, 1981.

"3 Want Bush To Review Slaying Probe." February 26, 1981.

"'Lineup' Fails to Tie Soldier to Probe, Ballistic Tests On Evidence Also Negative." By Lee Coppola. April 27, 1981.

"'Best News In 7 Months,' Acker Says." By Paul Carroll. April 30, 1981.

"DA's Task Force Is Back at Work On Other Cases." By Tom Buckham. April 30, 1981.

"In Big Moment, Cosgrove Is Low-Key." By Dan Herbeck. April 30, 1981.

"Suspect's Early Years Left Neighbors, Teachers With Image of 'Quiet Kid.'" By Mike Vogel. April 30, 1981.

"Tragedy of .22 Caliber Killings Stirred City, Tireless DA Emerging in Triumphant Role." By Ray Hill. April 30, 1981.

"Case Against Christopher Is Weak, Experts Assert." By Lee Coppola. May 3, 1981.

"N.Y. Police Seek Clerk to Identify Christopher." May 7, 1981.

"Christopher's Return Here Predicted Within 48 Hours." By Matt Gryta. May 8, 1981.

"Christopher Returned From Georgia." By Lee Coppola and Matt Gryta. May 9, 1981.

"Media Mull Giving Transcripts to Judge." By Matt Gryta. May 9, 1981.

"Five Identify Christopher at Police Lineup." By Agnes Palazzetti and Matt Gryta. May 13, 1981.

"DA Seeks Suspect's Blood Sample." By Matt Gryta. May 15, 1981.

".22-Caliber Probe Sparks Arrest of 13 as Gamblers." By Michael Beebe. May 20, 1981.

"Sketch 'Lineup' Confuses Christopher Case." By Dan Herbeck. June 7, 1981.

"Officials Favor Insanity Plea By Christopher." By Matt Gryta. June 9, 1981.

"Christopher's Attorneys Rule Out Insanity Plea—For the Time Being." By Matt Gryta. June 10, 1981.

"Media Bid Seen Threat to Christopher." By Matt Gryta. June 22, 1981.

"Christopher Denies Guilt In Falls Killing." By Matt Gryta. June 29, 1981.

"Christopher Prosecutors Consulting Noted Dentist About Teeth Marks." By Matt Gryta. September 10, 1981.

"Animosity for Counsel Ignited A Bombshell by Christopher." By Matt Gryta. October 21, 1981.

"Black Leaders Plan Protest To Spotlight 7 Area Slayings." By Carl Allen. December 20, 1981.

"Christopher Seeking to Get Out Of Mental Facility to Stand Trial." By Matt Gryta. January 19, 1982.

"Judge Orders Independent Test For Christopher." By Matt Gryta. January 20, 1982.

"Christopher Again Ruled Incompetent to Stand Trial." February 10, 1982.

"Christopher's Certification For Trial Is Expected Soon." By Matt Gryta. February 17, 1982.

"Ruling Imminent To Pave Way for Christopher Trial." By Matt Gryta. February 17, 1982.

"Christopher Sought Psychiatric Care Two Weeks Before Killings Started." By Lee Coppola. February 24, 1982.

"Relaxed, 'Different' Christopher Is Back In Jail Here to Await Murder Trial." By Lee Coppola. February 25, 1982.

"He Was Drugged by the Army At Ft. Benning, Christopher Says." By Lee Coppola. February 26, 1982.

"Prosecutors to Study Christopher's Words." By Matt Gryta. February 27, 1982.

"Court to Mull Trial Date for Christopher." March 3, 1982.

"Another Hearing Set On Competency of Christopher for Trial." By Matt Gryta. March 9, 1982.

"More Testing Denied for Christopher." March 13, 1982.

"Christopher Treated As a 'Courtesy' to Judge, Doctor Says." By Matt Gryta. March 16, 1982.

"Christopher Is Expected At Hearing." By Matt Gryta. March 17, 1982.

"Christopher Allowed to Leave Hearing." By Matt Gryta. March 18, 1982.

"Lawyers Vow To Fight for Christopher." By Matt Gryta. March 20, 1982.

"Judge Urging Christopher To Choose Trial by Jury." By Matt Gryta. March 24, 1982.

"Long Wait Finally Over—Christopher Goes on Trial." By Gene Warner. April 12, 1982.

"Witness Says He Saw Christopher Fire Shots That Killed Dunn but Chose to Mislead Police." By Matt Gryta. April 16, 1982.

"Christopher Defense to Open As Judge Lets Charges Stand." By Matt Gryta. April 21, 1982.

"Killer Was A Blond, Court Told." By Matt Gryta. April 22, 1982.

"Christopher Case Comes Down to Issue of Doubt." By Ray Hill. April 23, 1982.

"Christopher Defense Rests; Issue of 'Delusions' Raised." By Matt Gryta. April 23, 1982.

"For These Spectators, Justice on Trial." By Gene Warner. April 26, 1982.

"Black Leaders Happy With Verdict, Urge DA to Solve Other Slayings." By Carl Allen. April 27, 1982.

"A Justified Verdict In Christopher Trial." April 28, 1982.

"Cunningham Tips Hat to Marshall." By Dan Herbeck. April 28, 1982.

"Killed 13, Christopher Says." By Gene Warner. September 18, 1983.

"Christopher Denies Hatred of Blacks, Sees Himself as Target of Conspiracy." By Gene Warner. September 19, 1983.

"Police Regret Lost Chances in Manhunt." By Gene Warner. September 16, 1990.

"Theories Persist as Attempts to Grasp Killer's Psyche." By Gene Warner. September 16, 1990.

"'.22-Caliber Killer' Dies in Prison; Claimed to Have Murdered 13 Blacks." By Michael Beebe. March 4, 1993.

"With Christopher's Death, Much of Mystery Remains Unresolved." By Gene Warner. March 5, 1993.

"Leo J. Donovan, longest-serving Chief of Police Homicide Bureau, Dies at 78." By Barbara O'Brien. April 1, 1996.

"Legacy of Rev. Bennett Smith Evokes Wide Praise." By Tom Ernst and Dave Condren. August 9, 2001.

"The top 10 lawyers who might keep you out of prison." By Gene Warner. July 5, 2016.

"Buffalo in the '80s: Buffalo Nazis severely outnumbered by counter-rally." August 1, 2016.

Columbus Ledger (**Columbus, Georgia**):

"Atmosphere At Benning Emotional." By Nolan Waters. April 30, 1981.

Courier-Express (**Buffalo, New York**):

"Gunman's Victims Had No Reason to Expect Attacks." By Rich Scheinin. September 25, 1980.

"Police Consider 1 Gunman In 3 Killings, 4th Shooting." By Marshall J. Brown. September 25, 1980.

"Black Community Cautious." By Henry D. Locke Jr. September 26, 1980.

"Mysterious Gunman Eludes Police as Tips Are Sorted." September 26, 1980.

"Tips Flood Police In .22 Gunman Case." By Marshall J. Brown. September 27, 1980.

".22-Caliber Killer Case Frustrates Homicide Chief." By Erik Brady. September 28, 1980.

"A Tragedy for All of Us." September 28, 1980.

"Blacks to Raise Reward Fund." By Brenda Cawthon. September 28, 1980.

"Killer on Loose Stirs Black Community Fear." By Henry D. Locke Jr. September 28, 1980.

"Profile of Killer: Loner, Filled With Hatred, Will Strike Again." By Terence P. McElroy. September 30, 1980.

"Trooper-Hypnotist To Probe Witness In 22-Caliber Case." By Marshall J. Brown. September 30, 1980.

"U.S. Aide, Cunningham To Meet." By Henry D. Locke Jr. September 30, 1980.

"Decision Due on FBI Joining Probe of Killings of 4 Blacks." By Henry D. Locke Jr. and Marshall J. Brown. October 1, 1980.

"Hunting for Racist Killer." October 1, 1980.

"Area Gun Shops Quiet In Wake of .22 Killer." By Henry D. Locke Jr. October 2, 1980.

"Dogged Work by Homicide." October 2, 1980.

"Hunt for Killer of 4 Speeds Up." October 2, 1980.

"Investigators Ask News Blackout On .22-Caliber Case." October 3, 1980.

"Meeting Slated Tuesday." By Henry D. Locke Jr. October 3, 1980.

"Cops Quiz and Free Many in .22 Cal. Case." By Marshall J. Brown. October 4, 1980.

"Luck Likely to Solve Mass Murders." By Frederick Reinsch. October 5, 1980.

"No Substantial Leads In Hunt for Killer." October 5, 1980.

"Reward Upped For .22 Killer." October 6, 1980.

"Astrologist, Psychic Called in .22-Caliber Case." October 7, 1980.

"Cops Say Bus Driver May Have Been Shot." October 8, 1980.

"Donovan Mulls Occultist Data." By Marshall J. Brown. October 8, 1980.

"Local Probe of KKK, Neo-Nazis Urged." By Henry D. Locke Jr. October 8, 1980.

"Black Cabby Slain; Tie to .22-Caliber Killer Is Doubted." By Marshall J. Brown. October 9, 1980.

"Hate-Group Probe Bid Is Pushed." October 9, 1980.

"Activist Proposes Crime Task Force." October 10, 1980.

"Area Experts Tab Mutilation Murderer as Psychopathic." By Kristine Moe and Louise Leiker. October 10, 1980.

"Manhunt On For Killer After 2nd Grisly Murder." By James E. Watson and Marshall J. Brown. October 10, 1980.

"Mayor Griffin Urges City Remain Calm." October 10, 1980.

"PBA Urges All-Out Push to Solve Killings." October 10, 1980.

"Religious, Civic Leaders Decry Brutality, Dangers in Slayings." By Henry D. Locke Jr. October 10, 1980.

"800 Hear Rev. Jackson Call for Political Power." By Michelle Williams. October 11, 1980.

"Attacker Tries to Strangle Black Patient in Hospital." By Rich Scheinin and James E. Watson. October 11, 1980.

"Authorities View Killing Scenes by Air." October 11, 1980.

"Friends of Latest Victim Recall His Kindness." By Stuart Silverstein. October 11, 1980.

"Local TV Covers the Murders." By Jim Baker. October 11, 1980.

"Police Tie Two Teens to Cross-Burning." October 11, 1980.

"Rabbis, Church Board Denounce Killings As Threat to All People." October 11, 1980.

"Sheriff Assigns Crews to Patrol City." October 11, 1980.

"Acker Wants Civiletti Sent Here." October 12, 1980.

"Erie Medical Centers Beefs Up Security." October 12, 1980.

"Lockport Calls In FBI In Cross Burning Probe." By Carol Stevens. October 12, 1980.

"Man Is Questioned in 6 Killings." October 12, 1980.

"2 More Persons Grilled by Police In Killings of 6." October 13, 1980.

"Police Guard Man Who May Have Seen Attacker in Medical Center." By Henry D. Locke Jr. October 14, 1980.

"Ribbons to Mark Mourning for Six." October 14, 1980.

"A Community Mourning." October 15, 1980.

"City, County Officials Declare Mourning For Six Slain Men." By Jim Szymanski. October 15, 1980.

"Civil Rights Probe Sought." By Bob Kostoff. October 15, 1980.

"Fear Runs High in Poll Of Blacks." October 15, 1980.

"Multiple Descriptions Stymie FBI Artist." By Marshall J. Brown. October 15, 1980.

"Plea for Understanding Made At Murdered Cabby's Eulogy." By Henry D. Locke Jr. October 15, 1980.

"Unity Rally on Sunday Gains Support." October 15, 1980.

"400 Express Grief and Hope At Rites for 6th Slaying Victim." By Henry D. Locke Jr. October 16, 1980.

"Carey Urges Massive FBI Role In Probe of 6 Local Murders." By Marsha Ackermann. October 16, 1980.

"Cunningham Criticized By Black Leaders." October 16, 1980.

"DA Won't Rule Out 'One Killer.'" By Marshall J. Brown. October 16, 1980.

"Area Clergy Urge Unity Against Racism." By Marsha Ackermann. October 17, 1980.

"Hospital Force Increase OK'd." October 17, 1980.

"The Unity Day Observance." October 17, 1980.

"Top FBI Aide to Help In Probe of 6 Murders." By Marshall J. Brown and Stuart Silverstein. October 17, 1980.

"Slain Cabbies' Activities Traced in FBI Findings." By Marshall J. Brown and Greg Faherty. October 18, 1980.

"'Killer Instinct' Part of Everyone." By Louise Leiker. October 19, 1980.

"Quiz Planned for Victim." By Jim McAvey. October 19, 1980.

"Cole Interview Ruled Out As Murder Probe Stalls." October 20, 1980.

"Rally Helped Promote Unity, Members of Crowd Report." By Henry D. Locke Jr. October 20, 1980.

".22 Cal. Probers Question Victim." October 21, 1980.

"Cabbie Murder Probe Centers In Airport Area." By Marshall J. Brown. October 22, 1980.

"Griffin Quizzed Hard on Killings." By Erik Brady. October 22, 1980.

"Justice Aide Cites Push on 2 Levels Into Slayings of 6." By Greg Faherty and Marshall J. Brown. October 23, 1980.

"Newest Hot Line Will Bypass Police." October 23, 1980.

"2d 'Hot Line' In Murders Irks Mayor." October 24, 1980.

"Choking Victim Cole May Know Assailant." October 24, 1980.

"Civiletti Requests Arcara to Stay On In Murder Probe." By Greg Faherty. October 25, 1980.

"Black Community Ponders 'Whys' of Murders." By Henry D. Locke Jr. October 26, 1980.

"Griffin Disputes Racial Tensions." By Dave Condren. October 26, 1980.

"Niagara Strike Force Has Enviable Record." By G. M. Seal. October 26, 1980.

"Race Aspect of 6 Murders Has Historical Precedent." By Charles Haddad. October 26, 1980.

"Cole Doesn't Know Would-Be Killer." By Henry D. Locke Jr. October 27, 1980.

"Vigor Urged By NAACP In Murder Hunt." October 27, 1980.

"Civil Rights Prober Talks With Arcara." October 28, 1980.

"Murder Probe Spurs Rumor Control Unit." By Henry D. Locke Jr. October 28, 1980.

"State Law Blocks Boosting Reward for Killer." October 28, 1980.

"Tips Give Few Clues in Killing." By Marshall J. Brown. October 28, 1980.

"The Hot Lines." October 30, 1980.

"Sheriff's Patrols to Be Cut." By Stuart Silverstein. October 31, 1980.

"Murder Task Force Puts Stress on Computers." November 1, 1980.

"Keep Wearing Black Ribbons, Leader Asks." By Henry D. Locke Jr. November 4, 1980.

"Cosgrove Tells Blacks of Slaying Probe 'Progress.'" November 7, 1980.

"Murder Probe Targets 495 'Violents.'" By Rich Scheinin. November 8, 1980.

"New Sketch Due Of .22-Cal. Killer." November 9, 1980.

"Sketches Released of Killer Suspect." By Marshall J. Brown. November 11, 1980.

"Local Team Checking Ga. Killing Probe." By Erik Brady. November 12, 1980.

"Trio Gets Tips in Atlanta." By Margaret Doris. November 15, 1980.

"City, County To Get OK For Rewards." November 20, 1980.

"Legislators Stall DA's Money Bid." November 21, 1980.

"Two .22-Cal. Killers Possible, Say Cops." By G. M. Seal and James E. Watson. November 22, 1980.

"Sales Slump Laid To Killings Here." By Charles Haddad. December 2, 1980.

".22-Caliber Probers Find Other Crimes." By Henry D. Locke Jr. December 8, 1980.

"Black Leaders Ask Downtown Boycott." By Henry D. Locke Jr. December 17, 1980.

"Boycott Can't Help." December 18, 1980.

"DA Submits .22 Caliber Expenses." December 18, 1980.

"Murder Case Reward Stands Despite Boycott, Businessmen Say." By Nick Mason. December 18, 1980.

"Black Activist Raps Plan To Boycott Stores." December 19, 1980.

"Families of .22-Cal. Victims Given Aid." By Henry D. Locke Jr. December 24, 1980.

"Similarities Tie NYC Stabbings to .22 Cal. Killer." By Jim McAvey and Richard Schroeder. December 24, 1980.

"Police Pursue Similarities In NYC, Buffalo Slayings." By Jim McAvey. December 25, 1980.

"N.Y. Police Downplay Link Of 4 Deaths, .22-Cal. Case." December 26, 1980.

"No New Leads in .22 Probe." December 27, 1980.

".22 Caliber Team Probing Murder of Another Black Man." December 30, 1980.

"Murder of Blacks in 3 Cities Raises Hideous Specter." By Jim McAvey. December 31, 1980.

"Another Black Victim of Knifing." By Marshall J. Brown. January 1, 1981.

"Many Buffalo Blacks React to Murders By Gearing Up to Protect Themselves." By Henry D. Locke Jr. January 1, 1981.

"Police Probe Buffalo-Rochester Murder Link." By Erik Brady. January 1, 1981.

"U.S. Official Says FBI Fully Involved in Probe." By Stuart Silverstein. January 1, 1981.

"Knife Victim Gives Cops Description of Assailant." By Henry D. Locke Jr. January 2, 1981.

"Bag With Shoes Credited In Foiling Knife Attack." By Henry D. Locke Jr. January 3, 1981.

"Blacks, Whites Attend Rites for Knife Victim." By Henry D. Locke Jr. January 3, 1981.

"Intensify Murder Probe." January 3, 1981.

"Nab Killer Today, Cosgrove Is Hoping." By Marshall J. Brown. January 3, 1981.

"Violence slammed into area and eight men died." By Marshall J. Brown. January 5, 1981.

"'Bounty Men' on Prowl, Says Pitts." By Marshall J. Brown. January 8, 1981.

"Stab Victim Tabbed A 'Medical Miracle.'" By Kristine Moe. January 18, 1981.

"Weaponry Found At Soldier's Home." By Carol Stevens and Marshall J. Brown. April 25, 1981.

"FBI Due to Report Today on Evidence In .22-Caliber Case." By Carol Stevens. April 27, 1981.

".22-Caliber Case Suspect Indicted." By Marshall J. Brown and S.J. LaSpada. April 30, 1981.

"Christopher 'One Average Guy,' Say Acquaintances." By Mike Billington. April 30, 1981.

"Families of Victims Express Anger, Grief Over Losses." By Brenda Cawthon. April 30, 1981.

"Here's List of Area's 8 Black Slaying Victims." April 30, 1981.

"Weber Avenue's Peacefulness Shattered by .22-Cal. Notoriety." By Celia Viggo. April 30, 1981.

"Suspect's Friends Worried." By Richard Schroeder. May 1, 1981.

"Christopher Is Arraigned." By Marshall J. Brown and Terence P. McElroy. May 12, 1981.

"Black Leaders Blame 'Institutional Racism' for Violence in Buffalo." By Marsha Ackermann. May 12, 1981.

"Calm Christopher, Without a Mask, Pleads Innocent." By Michelle Williams. May 30, 1981.

".22 Caliber Case Going to Rochester." By Michelle Williams. August 18, 1981.

"Judge Rules Self Off Christopher Case." By Michelle Williams. August 18, 1981.

"High Court Will Not Halt '.22' Hearing." August 29, 1981.

"Jury Is Waived By Christopher." By Greg Faherty. October 21, 1981.

"Black Forum Asks Study Of Christopher Case." December 20, 1981.

"'Independent' Psychiatrist To Examine Christopher." January 21, 1982.

"Manhattan Judge Finds Christopher Unfit for Trial." February 10, 1982.

"Christopher Ruled Fit to Stand Trial." By Richard J. Roth. February 17, 1982.

"Christopher May Return Next Week." February 18, 1982.

"Christopher Return Set For Today." By G. M. Seal. February 24, 1982.

"Christopher Sought Treatment Before Killings Started." By G. M. Seal. February 25, 1982.

"An Interview With Christopher." By G. M. Seal. February 27, 1982.

"Fight Expected On Christopher Trial Competency." March 9, 1982.

"Christopher Ruling To Be Challenged." March 10, 1982.

"Christopher Leaves Competency Hearing; Doctor Calls Him Fit." By Richard J. Roth. March 17, 1982.

"Doctor Says Christopher Denied Black Bias." By Richard J. Roth. March 19, 1982.

"Ruling on Christopher Due Tuesday." By Richard J. Roth. March 20, 1982.

"Christopher Ruled Fit For Trial." By Richard J. Roth. March 24, 1982.

"Christopher Granted A Non-Jury Trial." March 25, 1982.

"Flynn Quits Christopher Case." By Richard J. Roth. April 6, 1982.

"Marshall Named Judge in Christopher Case." By Richard J. Roth. April 7, 1982.

"Christopher Prosecution Says It Has Eyewitness." By Richard J. Roth. April 13, 1982.

"Priest: Christopher Was Mocked." By Richard J. Roth. April 15, 1982.

"Christopher Put At Shooting Site." By Dave Condren. April 16, 1982.

"Christopher Trial: A Spectator's View." By Rich Scheinin. April 18, 1982.

".22-Caliber Witness Challenged." By Richard J. Roth. April 20, 1982.

"Christopher Said To Admit Killings." April 21, 1982.

"Christopher Defense Gets Slow Start." By Richard J. Roth. April 22, 1982.

"Witness Says Christopher Wasn't Killer." By Richard J. Roth. April 23, 1982.

"Drama, Levity Abound in .22-Caliber Courtroom." By Rich Scheinin. April 25, 1982.

"A Nightmare Ends." April 28, 1982.

"Christopher Guilty in 3 Slayings." By Dave Condren. By April 28, 1982.

"Christopher Team May Appeal Case On Many Fronts." By Rich Scheinin. April 28, 1982.

"Families Relieved At Verdict." By Sara Solovitch. April 28, 1982.

"Most Evidence Circumstantial In Christopher Conviction." By Rich Scheinin. May 2, 1982.

"Christopher Gets 60 Years to Life In Murders of 3." By Richard J. Roth. May 25, 1982.

"Christopher Moved to Auburn for Safety." By Richard J. Roth. May 26, 1982.

"New York Court Orders More Tests As Christopher Drama Moves There." By Richard J. Roth. June 2, 1982.

"Christopher Balks at Mental Tests." June 19, 1982.

New York Post:

"GI In Slasher Lineup Today." By Chris Oliver. May 12, 1981.

The New York Times:

"The Fugitive Slave Law a Dead Letter—A Case in Point." From the Romney (Va.) Intelligencer. September 8, 1855.

"Negro Youths Hurl Stones in Buffalo." June 28, 1967.

"14 Wounded in Buffalo As Violence Erupts Anew." By Thomas A. Johnson. June 29, 1967.

"Buffalo Violence Eases in 3D Night." By Maurice Carroll. June 30, 1967.

"Violence Called Only Language. Buffalo Rioters Say Pleas Fall on Deaf Ears." By Thomas A. Johnson. June 30, 1967.

"Buffalo Negroes Blame the Police." By Thomas A. Johnson. July 1, 1967.

"Restraint Urged in Race Riot News." By Fred P. Graham. July 8, 1967.

"Buffalo: 'Nothing's Changed' Since Riot." By Sydney H. Schanberg. September 18, 1967.

"Chattanooga Is Relatively Quiet After Violence Over Klan Verdict." July 23, 1980.

"Four Shootings in Buffalo Linked To the Same .22-Caliber Weapon." September 28, 1980.

"The Violent Rebirth Of The Klan." By Wayne King. December 7, 1980.

"Police Seeking Link in Slayings of 4 On Streets of Midtown Manhattan." By Selwyn Raab. December 24, 1980.

"Stabbing Survivor Describes His Assailant for the Police." By M. A. Farber. December 26, 1980.

"The Man in the Street." December 29, 1980.

"Black is Stabbed by a White Man in Buffalo Street." By Joseph A. Treaster. January 1, 1981.

"Buffalo Braces for a Nzai (*sic*) Rally and a Counteraction." By Sheila Rule. January 11, 1981.

"The Region; Judge Won't Enjoin Nazi Rally in Buffalo." Buffalo (AP) January 14, 1981.

"1,000 Meet in Buffalo in Tribute to Dr. King as Counter Rally Fails." By Sheila Rule. January 16, 1981.

"1980 Called Worst Year of Crime in City History." By Leonard Buder. February 25, 1981.

"Result of Inquiry on Slayings of 7 Awaited Upstate." By Robert D. McFadden. April 27, 1981.

"2 Army Nurses to Testify about Killings in Buffalo." By Sheila Rule. April 29, 1981.

"Extradition Hearing Scheduled in Georgia for Suspect in Buffalo Murders." By M. A. Farber. May 1, 1981.

"Suspect in Buffalo Slayings Tied To Manhattan Case by Remarks." By Leonard Buder. May 7, 1981.

"30 Witnesses See Slaying Suspect in Lineup at Buffalo." May 13, 1981.

"Buffalo Suspect's Friends Are Mystified." By M. A. Farber. May 16, 1981.

"Soldier, Held in 3 Buffalo Slayings, is Indicted in a Manhattan Murder." By Leonard Buder. May 27, 1981.

"Not Guilty Plea Filed by Private Held in Knifings." By E. R. Shipp. July 21, 1981.

"The Supreme Court Refuses to Bar Secret Hearings in '.22 Killer' Case." By Robert D. McFadden. August 29, 1981.

"Private Waives a Jury Trial In Slayings in Buffalo Area." By Selwyn Raab. October 21, 1981.

"Soldier, 26, is Found Competent for Trial on Murder Charges." By Robin Herman. February 18, 1982.

"Defense Rests in Case of Murdered Buffalo Blacks." UPI. April 25, 1982.

"Soldier Guilty of 3 Killings in Buffalo." April 28, 1982.

"How Release of Mental Patients Began." By Richard D. Lyons. October 30, 1984.

"Buffalo Man Guilty in '80 Killing." October 24, 1985.

"Buffalo Man Draws 33 Years In Racially Motivated Slaying." November 16, 1985.

"The F.B.I.'s New Psyche Squad." By Stephen G. Michaud. October 26, 1986.

"Numbers Game Flourishes Despite Lotteries and Raids." By Howard W. French. November 20, 1987.

Newsday:

"A Life of Guns." By Bob Keeler. December 3, 1981.

Newsweek (magazine):

"The Fears of Black America." By Dennis A. Williams with Susan Agrest in Buffalo, Vern E. Smith in Atlanta and bureau reports. October 27, 1980.

Powell Tribune (Powell, Wyoming):

"Criminal profiler; John Douglas recalls career with FBI." By Ilene Olson. April 23, 2015.

Psychology Today (magazine):

"Criminal Profiling: How It All Began." By Katherine Ramsland, Ph.D. March 23, 2014.

Purnell's History of the Second World War (magazine):

"Belsen." By Dr. Russell Barton. Volume 7, number 15. 1968.

Rolling Stone (magazine):

"How Son of Sam Changed America." By Cady Drell. July 29, 2016.

Washington Post:

"A Single Neo-Nazi Demonstrator Does Not a White-Power Rally Make." By Bill Peterson. January 16, 1981.

REPORTS

"U.S. Military Policies Concerning Homosexuals: Development, Implementation and Outcomes." Report prepared for the Center for the Study of Sexual Minorities in the Military. University of California at Santa Barbara. By Rhonda Evans. November 1, 2001.

TELEVISION

The FBI Files (television series) ".22 Caliber Killer". Season two, episode 18. Director: Dave Haycox. Written by Michael Martin & Mark Marabella. Tom Naughton, executive producer. Original airdate: May 30, 2000.

INSTITUTIONS

Archival research for this book took place at the following institutions: Erie County Public Library, downtown Buffalo; New York Public Library, Manhattan; Office of the Erie County District Attorney; Buffalo Police Headquarters, Buffalo, New York; the E. H. Butler Library, SUNY College at Buffalo; Library of the New York City Bar Association, Manhattan

ONLINE

The following were accessed at various times during 2016 and 2017:
https://www.nyheritage.org/collections/buffalo-ku-klux-klan-membership
     -list
http://uncrownedcommunitybuilders.com/person/daniel-acker-sr-2
https://profilesofmurder.com/category/the-history-of-criminal-profiling/
https://www.wunderground.com/history/airport/KBUF

INDEX